Evolution of International Aviation

The purpose of this book is twofold. First, it lays out the forces that shaped the international aviation industry and that changed all the rules in the drive for liberalization. Second, it looks at the many interesting and difficult choices ahead that the airline industry in general and the international aviation industry in particular face. These choices include many dichotomies: pulling back from the trend toward liberalization or embracing the liberalization trend, merging in search of profitability or fragmenting the industry in search of economies. These possible futures are explored, including the pros and cons of each future from a national, consumer, employer, and employee perspective. *Evolution of International Aviation* has been substantially revised to place the triple crises – 9/11, the 2008 Global Financial Crisis, and the COVID-19 pandemic – into context with the declared new Golden Age of 2018 (A4A), Brexit, renewed government aid around the globe, and the Ukraine conflict. It includes a new chapter on safety and security that will start with processes and technology introduced after 9/11 (such as the 24-hour rule, known shippers, and Global Entry programs) and end with recent biometrics and digital identity. As with the previous three editions, this fourth edition of *Evolution of International Aviation* reviews the historical development of the international aviation system. From this foundation it then provides an updated and expanded account of the current state of the aviation and aerospace industry, including profitability, consolidation, and merger activity. The book includes coverage of the industry segments – airlines, air cargo, and manufacturing – to include the emerging commercial space sector. It also emphasizes the relationship between aviation and the political process, exploring the sustainability of this mode of transportation in a world of climate change, high oil prices, and political instability. Because this book is intended for both the interested amateur and the more serious student, references are provided in the text and at the end of each chapter to allow for further in-depth study.

Dawna L. Rhoades received a Master of Public Administration with a specialization in Environmental Policy and Natural Resource Management from the University of Washington. She received her Ph.D. in Management from the University of Houston and is currently a professor of strategic management in the College of Business at Embry-Riddle Aeronautical University in Daytona Beach, Florida. She has served as the Undergraduate Program Coordinator, Associate Dean for Research and Graduate Studies, and Graduate Program Coordinator. She is currently the Chair of the Department of Management, Marketing, and Operations in the College. Her research interests include strategic alliances, regional carrier strategy, and service and safety quality at airlines and airports, intermodal transportation, sustainability, and the strategic and operational issues relating to NextGen air traffic management technology. Her work has appeared in such journals as the *Journal of Air Transport Management*, *Review of Business*, *Journal of Transportation Management*, *Journal of Managerial Issues*, *Managing Service Quality*, and the *Handbook of Airline Strategy*. She is the editor-in-chief for the *World Review of Intermodal Transportation Research*.

Jennifer L. Hinebaugh is Associate Professor of Management and Undergraduate Program Coordinator in the Department of Management, Marketing, and Operations, David B. O'Maley College of Business, Embry-Riddle Aeronautical University, USA.

Evolution of International Aviation

Seeking Profit in a Turbulent Industry

Fourth Edition

Dawna L. Rhoades and Jennifer L. Hinebaugh

Routledge
Taylor & Francis Group

LONDON AND NEW YORK

Designed cover image: murat4art / Getty Images

Fourth edition published 2025
by Routledge
4 Park Square, Milton Park, Abingdon, Oxon, OX14 4RN

and by Routledge
605 Third Avenue, New York, NY 10158

Routledge is an imprint of the Taylor & Francis Group, an informa business

© 2025 Dawna L. Rhoades and Jennifer L. Hinebaugh

The right of Dawna L. Rhoades and Jennifer L. Hinebaugh to be identified as authors of this work has been asserted in accordance with sections 77 and 78 of the Copyright, Designs and Patents Act 1988.

First edition published by Ashgate Publishing 2014
Third edition published by Routledge 2016

British Library Cataloguing-in-Publication Data
A catalogue record for this book is available from the British Library

ISBN: 978-1-032-52115-2 (hbk)
ISBN: 978-1-032-52112-1 (pbk)
ISBN: 978-1-003-40530-6 (ebk)

DOI: 10.4324/9781003405306

Typeset in Times
by SPi Technologies India Pvt Ltd (Straive)

Access the Support Material: www.routledge.com/9781032521121

Contents

PART III
CRISIS TO CRISIS (2001–2022)

PART IV
FUTURE CHALLENGES (2023–)

1 Phoenix Rising

Learning Objectives

After reading this chapter, you should have a good understanding of:

LO1: the CRAF program and its relationship to national defense
LO2: the link between aviation and economic growth
LO3: how national pride affects attitudes toward the airline industry
LO4: the cyclical nature of the aviation industry

Key Terms, Concepts & People

CRAF	EADS	"Carry the Flag"
Industry lifecycle	Punctuated Equilibrium	Discontinuous Change

Of Phoenixes and Airlines

According to legend, the phoenix was a bird of brilliant red and gold plumage whose death in a fiery blaze gave rise to a new being. Like the phoenix, the airline industry seems to have established its own cycle of destruction and renewal. From its very inception, the airline industry has been at the mercy of the business cycle, experiencing soaring profits in the upturn and rapidly falling into losses when the market dries up. The so-called new economy, which combined technological innovation, globalization, and abundant venture capital, began to transform the US and the global economy around 1995. This new economy was predicted to end the business cycle, or at least to smooth it out, so that the 'booms' were not so high and the 'busts' not so low. Under this new era of prosperity, the US economy grew at about 4.4 percent a year while unemployment dropped to around 4 percent. At the same time, productivity rose at an annual rate of 2.8 percent (Mandel, 2000). In short, growth, productivity, and employment seemed on an unstoppable path upward. The events of 9/11 and the Global Financial Crisis (GFC) of 2008 have clearly shown us that the death of the business cycle was greatly exaggerated. The Global Pandemic of 2020 showed the world that threats loomed in unseen places.

The boom times for airlines had always meant adding capacity through new aircraft acquisitions, opening new routes to unserved destinations, and negotiating bigger labor contracts (or contracts that gave back what was lost in the last downturn). The bust had always been a downward ride into declining profits, falling load factors, and destructive

DOI: 10.4324/9781003405306-1

price wars. Unfortunately, even before the events of September 11, the US airline industry was facing the return of its most dreaded foe, the business cycle, and US airlines were expected to post a $3 billion loss (Air Transport Association, 2002). While the rest of the airline world was not yet expecting losses of this magnitude, the US downturn was expected to have a substantial impact those carriers with a sizable percentage of traffic to North America (Sparaco & Wall, 2001). Post 9/11, the downturn became even steeper as many carriers struggled to avoid bankruptcy, a valiant struggle that ended in failure for many of the major carriers in the US. The US airline industry did not return to profitability until 2006, just in time to watch the 2007 rise in oil prices (Air Transport Association, 2007). This was followed by the 2008 GFC and the peak of rising fuel prices ($147 per barrel). According to the Air Transport Association (ATA), industry losses in 2008 were $18.2 billion, twice the 2006 high of $9 billion of profits. As the industry struggled back to profitability after posting a smaller $2.3 billion loss in 2009 on slumping cargo and passenger traffic, the global economy again lost altitude (Airlines for America, 2024). By comparison, US airline losses in the early 1990s were nearly $10 billion, while the losses for the industry in 2001 alone were $7 billion (Foss, 2002; Rosen, 1995). In 2021, US airline losses from the COVID pandemic topped $35 billion (Horowitz & Zaidy, 2020). In short, the industry continues to set new records for losses.

The airline industry is no stranger to bankruptcy. In the United States, the first passenger on a regularly scheduled airline flew from Tampa Bay to St. Petersburg, Florida on January 1, 1914. The airline chalked up another first when it folded four months later, after running into financial difficulties (Wells, 1994). In Europe, war and financial crisis in the 1930s and 1940s led to the nationalization of many of the continent's premier carriers as a means of insuring their survival (Graham, 1995; Sinha, 2001). Back in the US, aviation continued to expand in fits and starts aided by airmail contracts from the US Postal Service; however, since the deregulation of the US airline industry in 1978, the industry has experienced a financial crisis in the early years of each decade. In the second decade of the 21st century, the industry managed to top even its own records for losses. To those outside the industry, this brief history raises many questions: Why can't the industry make money? Why does it expect (and often get) special treatment from governments? What, if anything, can be done to stop the cycle? What is the future of the airline industry and the related aviation/aerospace firms around it? These questions are the subject of this book. The first question to tackle is why the industry is considered 'special'.

A Special Case

The aviation industry has long been treated as a special case in international business, subject to different rules and held to different standards. In fact, international aviation has been 'a serious problem in international relations, affecting the way governments view one another, the way individual citizens view their own and foreign countries, and in a variety of direct and indirect connections the security arrangements by which we live' (Lowenfeld, 1975). There are several reasons for the special status and serious problems associated with international aviation. Originally, the most compelling argument was national defense. Under programs such as the US Civil Reserve Air Fleet (CRAF) plan, civilian fleets could be used during times of military action to ferry troops and supplies. It was, therefore, vital to ensure the existence and health of this civilian reserve. In the case of CRAF, the US government got a reserve fleet for times of emergency without the cost of maintaining it and the airlines got paid a rate that during the first Middle East conflict, Desert Storm, was

1.75 times the seat mile or cargo mile rate (Kane, 1999). National defense has also been cited as the reason for insisting on home country ownership of airlines and the aerospace manufacturers that supplied their airframes, engines, and other parts. The premise of the argument is the notion that home country nationals would or could be made to cooperate in the defense of their country. As we will see, the connection between civilian and military technology at the manufacturers' level has always been close; the innovations in technology first deployed and tested on military aircraft were quickly applied to the commercial fleet. In countries such as the US, funding for research and development for these 'military' innovations came from the government and went to firms who also had sizable civilian operations, a situation that has led foreign competitors to charge 'unfair subsidy'.

The second most-cited reason for special treatment has been the economic impact of aviation. The Air Transport Action Group estimated a decade ago that air transport supported 3.5 percent of global GDP, provided 56.6 million jobs, and had a global economic impact of $2.2 trillion (Air Transport Action Group, 2012). Passenger traffic grew on average 6 percent per year during the decade of the 1980s and early 1990s driven by falling real costs of air travel, increasing economic activity, intensifying international trade, increasing disposable incomes, political stability, the relaxation of travel restrictions, expanding ethnic ties, increasing leisure time, tourism promotion, air transport liberalization, and growth in emerging regions and countries. Historically, air traffic has grown at about twice the rate of gross domestic product (GDP) and during the period 1960–1990 80 percent of traffic growth could be explained by growth in GDP. Beginning in the 1990s, falling real prices (fares) played a greater role in traffic growth. As air travel grew, so too did both the direct (value of airline and on-airport activities) and the indirect (value of off-airport activities of passengers and shippers) economic impact. In addition, there is an induced impact from the successive spending of recipients of these direct and indirect benefits. In short, the economic impact of the air transport industry makes its health a major concern of governments, businesses, and passengers around the world and prevents it from being seen as 'just another industry'. Unfortunately, this historic link between economic growth (GDP) and air transport has decoupled in the US, and it appears to be decoupling in the EU as well. It is not yet clear what this change represents. It is possible that the industry in the US and the EU has finally reached a stage of maturity that has permanently decoupled this link. It is also possible that consumers have found other ways to spend their discretionary dollars. This phenomenon may be temporary, or it may be time to acknowledge that there are limits to all economic sectors, and that nothing, including aviation, continues upward forever (Michaels, 2013). Still, there is no denying that air transport contributes in many ways to national and global economies.

The third reason for the special status of aviation is the link that exists in the minds of many between aviation and feelings of national achievement and pride. International airlines 'carry the flag' around the world. This should not be underestimated as a driver of individual and government perception. When the bankruptcy and the subsequent grounding of the Swissair fleet forced the Swiss football team to fly the Russian carrier Aeroflot to a qualifying match in Moscow, one article reported this event as a 'further humiliation for the Swiss flag carrier' (Hall, Grant, Done, & Cameron, 2001). Similar uproar occurred in Great Britain over the replacement of the Union Jack on the tail of many British Airways planes by the so-called 'ethnic tails', which were intended to show it as the airline of the world was motivated by similar nationalistic sentiment (BBC News, 1999). A similar debate in Belgium occurred over the bankruptcy of Sabena and the need for a national carrier to serve the country's interests. Again, this had more to do with nationalistic pride than airline economics (BBC News, 1999; Sparaco, 2001). The Italian efforts to save their national carrier, Alitalia, can be linked to the same national pride that has motivated so many other governments (The Economist, 2013). At the manufacturing level, nations have also mourned the loss of their aviation pioneers. One of the key arguments for the European formation of Airbus was the dominance of manufacturing by US firms. According to Aris (2004), the Airbus project was seen by the French as '*Un Grand Projet*: one of those brilliant combinations of technological and political skills that will serve to remind the French themselves – and everybody else – just what a great nation they are' (16). To the Germans, Airbus was the chance to rebuild an aerospace industry that had contributed many early innovations in aviation. In short, aviation has always been linked to national pride in their technological achievement and visionary leadership. In the US, the announcement that the US Air Force had chosen Northrop Grumman and European partner EADS, the parent of Airbus, for a refueling tanker deal worth US$35 billion was greeted with anger and calls for a political investigation. In the US House of Representatives, Todd Tiahrt, whose district includes facilities of the losing bidder Boeing, has said that the US 'should have an American tanker built by an American company with American workers' (Tessler, 2008: 2). In fact, this last example brings together the many reasons why aviation is a special case – defense, economic impact, and national pride.

Changing Times

Even without the defense, economic, and national pride arguments, aviation/aerospace is not likely to be seen as 'just another industry'. It is the stuff of dreams and has fired the imagination of much of the world's population. Alvin Toffler (1970) noted, in his bestselling book *Future Shock*, that in 6000 B.C. the fastest transportation available to mankind was the camel caravan, which averaged just 8 miles per hour. By 1600 B.C., the chariot had raised this speed to approximately 20 miles per hour. The first mail coach in England began operating in 1784 at an average of only 10 miles per hour and the first steam locomotive was capable of a mere 13 miles an hour. In fact, it was not until the invention of an improved steam engine that mankind was able to reach a speed of 100 miles per hour. In total, it took almost 8,000 years to go from the 8-mile-an-hour camel to the 100-mile-an-hour train. However, in just a further 58 years, men in aircraft were exceeding the 400-mph line. Another 20 years later, that limit doubled. By the 1960s aircraft were approaching speeds of 4000 mph, and space capsules were circling the Earth at 18,000 mph. The newest pioneers are men like Elon Musk of SpaceX and Robert Bigelow of Bigelow Aerospace, who are trying to shape the commercial space industry, giving us a private space station to visit as well as the means to get there.

The history of aviation/aerospace is filled with such larger-than-life figures. These men and women were the entrepreneurs of Joseph Schumpeter, who took on the thankless job of building and shaping an industry because

there is the dream and the will to found a private kingdom, usually, although not necessarily, also a dynasty … Then there is the will to conquer: the impulse to fight, to prove oneself superior to others, to succeed for the sake, not of the fruits of success, but of success itself … Finally, there is the joy of creating, of getting things done, or simply of exercising one's energy and imagination.

(93–94)

After all, the Wright brothers started their business career as the owners of a bicycle shop, before the dream of aviation led them in a different direction. Their innovation in heavier-than-air flight would start an industry and illustrate the promises, challenges, and pitfalls of aviation.

Whatever the challenges, there have always been individuals drawn to this field. The stories of these individuals, the planes they flew, and the companies they founded, continue to fascinate us today. While the level of innovation has slowed for the aviation industry, the manufacturers are continuing to face new challenges in design and performance. One of the greatest of these challenges will be increasing fuel efficiency and improving the emissions profile of aircraft in a world of increasing oil prices and concerns about climate change. As the demand for air travel increases in developing nations, other challenges are facing this industry. Concerns with airport and airspace capacity are leading to new systems of traffic management and optimization using satellites for navigation and new technology on the ground and in the cockpit.

Speaking at the end of the 1990s, Warren Buffet, Chairman of Berkshire Hathaway and 'world famous as the greatest stock market investor of modern times', articulated a dark vision of the airline industry (Bianco, 1999). He compared the internet industry to 'two other transforming industries, auto and aviation' (Loomis & Buffet, 1999). According to Buffet, the early aviation industry was full of promise and home to many young, vibrant companies, most of whom are a distant memory. He cited some 129 airlines that had filed for bankruptcy between 1980 and 2000. The reason for these troubles, he said, was clear; the industry had not made money overall in the long run. Buffet brutally suggested that a farsighted and public-spirited individual would have done the world's investors a favor by shooting down the Wright *Flyer* in 1903. He said all of this before the losses after 9/11 and the GFC, losses greater than all the profits made by the industry since the first flight at Kitty Hawk (Gahan, 2002). Like Joseph's 'Dream of Egypt', the aviation industry seems condemned to experience years of plenty followed by years of famine. Unlike the Egyptians, however, airlines have rarely saved in years of plenty to survive the coming famine. Instead, they have bought new planes, expanded route systems, and signed ever sweeter labor contracts. It was as though they were convinced that the airline that fattens up the most in the good times will simply outlast the others in bad times. In a truly free market, this strategy might work, but airlines do not operate in such a market and they never have, for the reasons that we have just discussed.

As Buffet has pointed out, air travel has transformed the way we live and do business. It is itself in the process of transforming; it is *becoming* something new. A debate has raged in the fields of paleontology, genetics, and evolutionary biology over whether change in living organisms takes place in a gradual, step-by-step manner or in periods of rapid, major change followed by stasis. The latter theory is known as 'punctuated equilibrium' (Gould & Eldredge, 1977). This theory has been adapted and applied to the evolution of technology (Tushman & Anderson, 1986) and to the lifecycle and evolution of organizations and their industries (Hannan & Freeman, 1984). The idea of punctuated equilibrium or discontinuous change has caught on in so many areas because it 'seems to fit' the observed evidence. In other words, investigators in all these fields have been unable to trace a slow, clear development from one form to the next. Instead, they see periods of relative stability and little change interrupted by sudden, radical alterations in form. In the evolutionary sciences, these periods of sudden change are usually connected to mass extinctions of older, existing life forms. In the areas of technology and organizations, startling innovations have arisen that make obsolete the technology and know-how that came before. Think, for example, of the impact of the telephone on the telegraph or the airplane on the long-distance train system. For organizations, these periods of rapid change have been hardest on the firms of the prior age, firms that developed, grew, and adapted to life in another time. This is seen in the traditional stock brokerage coping in the new world of the internet or the corner bookseller competing with Amazon.com. The question in the minds of organizational theorists is whether these old age firms can change quickly enough to survive in the new age. If not, they will become the dinosaurs of this new age, dying out to make room for the newer, faster, smaller mammals. The fossil records show that dinosaurs had reached their maximum size not long before the meteor that changed everything. It is possible that the airline industry has entered just such a period of discontinuous change.

More Than Airlines

In the previous section, the term aviation/aerospace was used in recognition that the 'industry' is far broader than the airlines we see landing at our local airport. There are the manufacturers that design, build, and sell aircraft to these airlines. This part of the industry is highly complex, with household names like Boeing and Airbus sitting on top of webs of suppliers that must all work together to make, assemble, ship, and deliver their 'piece of the aircraft'. There are the air carriers that specialize in cargo rather than passengers. Air cargo is often a forgotten part of the industry – that is, until the Amazon Prime packages are late. It is also one of the very first areas to feel the impact of economic downturn and one of the last to recover. The newest part of the industry, space travel, has seen an explosion in activity over the past decade. In fact, there are daily announcements of new flights, new players, and new plans. If the industry is 'bigger' than just airlines, then it also presents a bigger paradox; within the industry, it is airlines that have historically had the most difficulty making a sustainable, investment-worthy profit. For the most part, air cargo, manufacturing, and now space have succeeded in the most basic goal of companies in a free market – turning a profit. Skeptics abounded when SpaceX was originally founded, for example, yet it has become one of the most valuable private companies in history at roughly $150 billion in valuation (Ganguly, 2023). So how do we reconcile these issues of profit? Without airlines to purchase planes, where are the manufacturers? Without passenger airlines to fly additional cargo in the belly of their planes, what happens to global air cargo? Without manufacturers of all sizes to produce the materials, structures, engines, and infrastructure of flight, where is commercial space?

Where Do We Go?

The introduction began with a twisted quote from Lewis Carroll's classic *Jabberwocky*. This passage begins 'The time has come… to talk of many things. Because the aviation/aerospace industry is a special case for all the reasons stated earlier, it is important for the people of the world to be involved in the debate about the future of aviation. We are the tourists that fly to our long-awaited vacation, the businessmen that fly to important meetings, the shippers that send out goods around the world, the customers that buy grapes from Chile and wine from France, the citizens look into the sky and see a Moon ready to be conquered; finally, we are the employees in and supporting this industry.

The purpose of this book is twofold. First, the book explores the foundations of the industry – airlines, manufacturing, air cargo (1903–1950), looking at the forces that shaped the international industry. Starting with the first transborder crossing in a lighter-than-air balloon, it will trace the early technological innovations, the international conferences, and government interventions that set the early path of the industry up until World War II. Then, we will examine the opportunities that shaped the industry that entered the era of deregulation, globalization, and liberalization (1951–2000). This era changed all the rules. Next, we will explore the industry that emerged from the events of 9/11 only to face the GFC of 2008. 9/11 presented the industry with many choices: pulling back from the trend toward liberalization or embracing the liberalization trend, merging in search of profitability or fragmenting in search of economies, building a twenty-first-century airspace or muddling along with an aging World War II infrastructure, funding the next steps into space through governments or encouraging the type of entrepreneurial individuals that created the glories of the past. Finally, we will ask what impact the greatest unknown might have on the industry – climate change.

Because this book is intended for both the interested amateur and the more serious student, references are provided in the text and at the end of each chapter to allow for more in-depth study. The book is NOT intended to be a definitive work on the aviation/aerospace industry; it would require a series of books to even attempt such a feat. The book does try to include most of the major sectors of the industry in order to give the reader an overall understanding of the key sectors of this complex industry. Perhaps the only major sector left out is the airport. These buildings are obviously vital to the industry, but airports vary widely within a single country let alone across nations and regions. Still, even within sectors such as the aerospace manufacturers, the book only touches on the major players. There is a vast group of aviation suppliers that range in size from Honeywell and GE to small 'mom-and-pop' operations dealing with the maintenance and repair of select avionics. Unless otherwise stated, the views expressed in this book are those of the author and do not represent those of the airline industry, any governmental organization or private institution associated with aviation.

The book has been organized into three parts. The first part will address the early development of the aviation system. Chapter 2 will explore the inventions and innovations in aviation technology that laid the foundation for commercial success. This period saw the start of heavier-than-air flight, the first use of the airplane in military action, and the foundations of passenger travel. The implications and possibilities of this new technology would come to hold greater sway in the minds of individuals and governments in the years ahead. Chapter 3 will explore the role of airmail and freight in shaping the industry. Chapter 4 will discuss early aviation conferences and the beginning of the struggle between the proponents of free markets and those favoring tight national control. Chapter 5 will examine the most famous international aviation meeting, the 1944 Chicago Conference. This conference resulted in the Chicago Convention, which spells out the rights and obligations of states in international aviation, the creation of the international body responsible for establishing the rules and standards governing international aviation, and numerous technical drafts on recommended practices. Finally in this part, Chapter 6 will examine in more detail the structure and role of the new International Civil Aviation Organization (ICAO) in developing the standards and practices of international aviation. If the world had not already learned at the Chicago Conference that aviation could not be divorced from its economic and political consequences, it came to learn these lessons over time from the operations of the ICAO. In fact, any illusion that ICAO could deal with these technical problems on their own merit was quickly dispelled when accidental shoot downs of civil aircraft and a growing number of brutal hijackings and criminal attacks against civil aviation came to dominate the agenda of the ICAO council and that of its subordinate bodies (Sochor, 1991). This chapter will also address the development of another international organization, the International Air Transport Association (IATA), and its role in shaping the international aviation system through the setting of international fares.

Part II of the book explores the period between 1950 and 2000. Chapter 7 will examine the early efforts into outer space, beginning with Sputnik and ending with the Apollo flight. During this period the industry was growing up, maturing. Chapter 8 will return to the story of the manufacturers in an era in which air travel was becoming available to a growing number of consumers. Chapter 9 will look at another time of dramatic change for the airline industry – domestic deregulation. Domestic deregulation changed the rules of the game, allowing competition based on price as well as market-based decisions on routes served and the level of service quality provided. It also freed up the industry for greater competition through the relaxation of rules for air carrier entry. This chapter will explore the link between domestic deregulation and efforts to liberalize international aviation markets. Chapter 10 will discuss the view from Europe and Asia. In Europe, aviation would become part of a greater effort to create an integrated free market system among the nations of the European Union. While the Europeans disagreed over the pace and implementation of deregulation in the US market, they have taken the concept of aviation liberalization further than their US counterparts by opening domestic markets to foreign competition. The vast geographical diversity of the Asian region makes sweeping generalizations; however, most of this region has witnessed substantial growth in air transportation as part of its overall economic growth. Chapter 11 examines the alliance movement, whose initial impetus was to overcome the national restrictions on air transportation. In an environment of heavy international regulation, the alliance became the airline tool of choice for serving new markets and extending the global reach of your alliance. There have been – and will continue to be – obstacles to the use of the alliance. There might also be chances to trade alliance for ownership in a world where nationality is no bar to owning. Chapter 12 will outline some of the remaining legal blocks to international aviation, while Chapter 13 explores the question of airline and alliance quality in an increasingly competitive industry. Chapter 14 will look at the air cargo industry in the new era of the logistics revolution.

In the final part of the book, the future of international aviation will be examined considering changes in the environment before and after 9/11. Chapter 15 explores safety and security in an age of Artificial Intelligence (AI), cloud computing, online shopping, and continued global threats. Chapter 16 investigates the airline industry's search for profitability. Chapters 17 and 18 will examine the trend in market liberalization that began with the 1978 deregulation of US domestic markets and has continued in Europe and Asia, but now appears to be reversing before reaching all parts of the globe. In Chapter 19, we revisit the manufacturing sector to see where it is headed as we move toward the middle of the twenty-first century. Chapter 20 looks at the aviation industry in an era of concern about climate change and carbon emissions. Chapter 21 explores the air cargo industry and the weaknesses in global supply chains revealed by the COVID pandemic. Chapter 22 looks at the infrastructure that will support aviation as it moves forward, the technology, the costs, and the controversies. Chapter 23 explores the future of space exploration, particularly the efforts to foster and grow the commercial space industry. Finally, Chapter 23 will summarize where we are and where we appear to be going.

Imaging the Future

The airplane (spacecraft) and the industry that fostered them have captured the imagination of generations around the world. It is time to apply that imagination to creating a viable, stable environment for international aviation that delivers on the great promise of air travel to link the world together in peace and prosperity. It is time to regain the *Star Trek* desire to seek out new worlds. Thomas L. Friedman has said of his work that he hopes that it will evoke one of four reactions from his readers: I didn't know that; I never looked at it that way before; you said exactly what I feel, but I didn't know how to express it; or I hate you and everything you stand for (2002: xi). These reactions seem a worthy goal for any book that attempts to examine and explain complex issues. Even if the book evokes the last of these reactions, at least it should foster a debate on the ideas. It is time to begin the debate. I believe that you will find it an exciting and challenging journey.

Questions

1 Discuss the role that aviation plays in economic development and why it is described as a cyclical industry.
2 What is a mature industry? Does the airline industry qualify?
3 What was Warren Buffet's point about profits in the airline industry?
4 What new developments are likely to shape the aviation industry?
5 How has the historical connection between economic growth and air travel changed over time, particularly in the United States and the European Union? What factors may have contributed to this shift?
6 In what ways has the perception of aviation as a symbol of national achievement and pride influenced government policies and public sentiment toward airlines and aerospace manufacturers? Provide examples to support your answer.
7 The concept of punctuated equilibrium, as applied to the aviation industry, suggests periods of rapid change followed by relative stability. How has this theory manifested in the evolution of aviation technology, regulatory frameworks, and market dynamics over the past century? Provide specific examples to illustrate your points.

References

Air Transport Association (2002), *State of the airline industry: A report on recent trends for US air carriers*, Air Transport Association, Washington, DC.

Air Transport Association (2007) 'Quarterly cost index: US passenger airlines' Available at: http://www.airlines.org/economics/finance/cost

Aris, S. (2004) *Close to the sun: How Airbus challenged America's domination of the skies*, Agate Press, London.

BBC News (1999), 'BA to fly flag again'. BBC News Online Edition, June 6, www.bbc.co.uk

Bianco, A. (1999), 'The Warren Buffet you don't know: Ace stockpicker, of course – and now, an empire-builder', *Business Week*, July 5, pp. 55–66.

Foss, B. (2002), 'Airlines expect to lose $8 billion', *Associated Press Wire Service*, September 26.

Gahan, M. (2002), 'Aviation's continuing crisis,' *BBC News Online*, August 13.

Ganguly, A. (2023) Elon Musk's SpaceX rockets to $140 billion valuation following recent share sales by investors adding $61 billion to Musk's net worth. Yahoo!finance. Available at: https://finance.yahoo.com/news/elon-musks-spacex-rockets-140-173600052.html?guccounter=1&guce_referrer=aHR0cHM6Ly93d3cuZ29vZ2xlLmNvbS8&guce_referrer_sig=AQAAAKN09NZaD6WudGbgYCsoaaq8iYaQKVuLJ4GTO6D4fVAQiC-bZshvciZMr5d7rtOEFg7P-F3sgkrrqllmWI2E51_t0-YsKu6KalIAsPnqZjrDG9m8Q2sTOEGTBoK6Z9Fg17znGEigqFs7VdCks29RiR_bdLgtbKjQ7_CmBsHH8fKu

Gould, S. J. and Eldredge, N. (1977), 'Punctuated equilibria: The tempo and mode of evolution reconsidered', *Paleobiology*, vol 3, pp. 115–151.

Graham, B. (1995), *Geography and air transport*, John Wiley & Sons, New York.

Hall, W., Grant, J., Done, K., and Cameron, D. (2001), '*Swissair grounding causes travel chaos*', October 2.

Hannan, M. T. and Freeman, J. (1984), 'structural inertia and organizational change', *American Sociological Review*, vol. 49, pp. 149–164.

Horowitz, J. and Zaidy, H. (2020) Devastating and unrelenting COVID-19 crisis will cost airlines $157 billion, says IATA. CBB Business. Available at: https://www.cnn.com/2020/11/24/business/iata-airlines-coronavirus/index.html

Kane, R. M. (1999), *Air transportation*, Kendall/Hunt Publishing Company, Dubuque, Iowa.

Loomis, C. and Buffet, W. (1999), 'Mr Buffet on the stock market', *Fortune*, Special Issue, vol. 140 (10), pp. 212–220.

Lowenfeld, A. (1975), 'A new take-off for international air transport', *Foreign Affairs*, vol 54, p. 47.

Mandel, M. J. (2000), 'The next downturn', *Business Week*, October 9, pp. 173–180.

Michaels, K. (2013) The great stagnation, *Aviation Week and Space Technology*, October 14, p. 20.

Rosen, S. D. (1995), 'Corporate restructuring: A labor perspective' in Peter Cappelli (ed.), *Airline labor relations in the global era: The new frontier*, ILR Press, Ithaca, New York, pp. 31–40.

Sinha, D. (2001), *Deregulation and liberalization of the airline industry: Asia, Europe, North America, and Oceania*, Ashgate Publishing, Aldershot.

Sochor, E. (1991), *The politics of international aviation*, University of Iowa Press, Iowa City.

Sparaco, P. (2001), 'The curtain falls on sabena', *Aviation Week and Space Technology*, November 12, pp. 43–44.

Sparaco, P. and Wall, R. (2001), 'Europeans map airline survival', *Aviation Week and Space Technology*, September 24, pp. 35–36.

Tessler, J (2008) '*Northrop, EADS win $35B air force deal*', The Associated Press, Available at: http://abcnews.go.com/print?id=4367303

Toffler, A. (1970), *Future shock*, Bantam Books, New York.

Tushman, M. L. and Anderson, P. (1986), 'Technological discontinuities and organizational environments', *Administrative Science Quarterly*, vol. 31, pp. 439–465.

Wells, A. T. (1994), *Air transportation: A management perspective*, Wadsworth Publishing Company, Belmont, CA.

Websites

Air Transport Action Group (2012), '*Facts & figures*', Air Transport Action Group, Switzerland. Available at: http://www.atag.org/our-news/press-releases.html

Airlines for America (2024)Available at http://www.airlines.org

The Economist (2013) How not to rescue an airline, Available online at http://www.economist.com/news/europe/21588109-italian-government-pumping-even-more-cash-its-ailing-carrier-how-not-rescue?zid=303&ah=27090cf03414b8c5065d64ed0dad813d

PART I
IN THE BEGINNING
(1903–1970)

2 Invention to Commercial Success

Learning Objectives

After reading this chapter, you should have a good understanding of:

LO1: the difference between invention, innovation, and commercial success
LO2: why the DC-3 is considered one of the first commercially successful aircraft
LO3: the early history of aircraft design and aviation pioneers
LO4: how the airlines and the aircraft manufacturers established the close but often-contentious relationship that continues today

Key Terms, Concepts & People

Invention	Innovation	Commercialization
The Wright Brothers	Glenn Curtiss	Louis Blériot
Donald Douglas	William Boeing	DC-3

Inventions, Innovations, and Commercializations

An idea is said to have been invented when it has been proven to work. It

becomes an "innovation" only when it can be replicated reliably on a meaningful scale at practical costs. If the idea is sufficiently important, such as the telephone, the digital computer, or a commercial aircraft, it is called a "basic innovation" and it creates a new industry or transforms an existing industry.

(Senge, 1990)

Senge, author of *The Fifth Discipline: The Art and Practice of the Learning Organization*, goes on to note that ideas move from invention to innovation by combining different technologies, often from isolated developments in diverse fields. Until these diverse components come together in the right combination the product is not truly able to achieve its potential as a successful commercial product (commercialization). Until it is able to prove itself safe and reliable it may capture the imagination of the daring, those first movers who are willing to try anything new and different, but it will not capture the market, the laggards who are not interested in thrills but in performance and cost. The first fifty years of heavier-than-air

DOI: 10.4324/9781003405306-3

flight would lay the groundwork for the conquest of the laggards and a new commercial aviation industry.

First, of course, an idea needs pioneers and aviation had more than its share of larger-than-life characters. There are accounts dating back to the twelfth century B.C.E. of people in China riding in balloons. The quintessential Renaissance Man himself, Leonardo Da Vinci, sketched images in the sixteenth century of craft he believed capable of supporting a man in flight. However, it was not until 1783 that history has its first confirmable account of a manned lighter-than-air flight. Jean-Francois Pilatre de Rozier and Francois d'Arlandes flew over Paris for 25 minutes by ballon while the residents of the city watched and wondered. However, simply floating with the wind was not enough; a way needed to be found to direct these lighter-than-air craft. Thus was born the dirigible; the name forever linked in the minds of many with these dirigibles is Count Ferdinand von Zeppelin, whose airships were carrying passengers and mail on regularly scheduled trips by 1914. However, even without the tragic 1936 disaster of the *Hindenburg* in Lakehurst, New Jersey, it is doubtful that the dirigible could have held anything more than a minor place in aviation besides the new heavier-than-air craft that took to the sky in the first decade of the twentieth century (Carlson, 2002).

December 17, 1903 was the fateful day on which Orville Wright became the first person to pilot a powered heavier-than-air craft. He remained off the ground for 12 seconds and covered a distance of only 120 feet, but this single event would change the way people around the world viewed the sky; heavier-than-air flight had been invented. Over the course of the next thirty years, the new industry would struggle through a series of experiments in search of the right combination of component technologies to make it a viable, commercial product. At first, much of the focus was on the development of military aircraft, and then airmail/cargo aircraft, but more was needed for the successful establishment of viable commercial passenger travel. Finally, the Douglas DC-3 would demonstrate the right combination of features to make passenger air travel safe, comfortable, and economical to operate. The DC-3 combined five key innovations – variable-pitch propellers, retractable landing gear, lightweight molded body construction, radial air-cooled engine, and wing flaps – to produce a plane that was both aerodynamic and economical to operate (Senge, 1990). This chapter traces the beginning of this journey from invention to commercially viable product. Over the course of this period, the airplane will go from a barnstorming thrill to an essential tool of military operations to a transportation mode for the well-to-do, time-sensitive, risk-taker.

Visionaries

In the three years following their initial historic flight, the Wright brothers worked to improve the reliability, range, and maneuverability of their design, registering US patent 821,393 in 1906 (Paradowski, 2002). By 1908, the Wright brothers were working under a contract with the US War Department to build aircraft for the Army (Tischauser, 2002). In 1909, the Wright Company was incorporated in Dayton, Ohio, and over the next few years it pursued a lawsuit against another aviation pioneer, Glenn Curtiss, claiming that he had violated their patent for ailerons, which were devices to control the roll of an aircraft during flight. In fact, the Wright technology involved wing-warping rather than the use of separate attachments to the wing that would achieve the same thing; however, in the early days of aviation the importance of these distinctions was unclear to most people outside the industry.

Today, the Curtiss' White Wing is cited as the first United States plane to take off on wheels and use ailerons to control roll in turns, the point of contention with the Wrights. Another Curtiss aircraft, the June Bug, would set a new speed record in 1909 at the first great international air competition in Rheims, France and become the first flight filmed and witnessed by the press. Curtiss would go on to set a number of firsts, including the first US licensed pilot, the first person to land an aircraft on the deck of a ship in 1910, and the designer of the first aircraft to cross the Atlantic. He founded the Curtiss Aeroplane and Motor Company before World War I and engaged both in aircraft design and flight training for the US Army and Navy. In addition to the legal battles over the invention of ailerons, Curtiss would side with Albert Zahn, Director of the Smithsonian Institute in Washington, D.C., suggesting that Samuel Langley, rather than the Wright Brothers, actually invented the airplane. Even though the courts would eventually side with the Wrights on the question of ailerons, granting some money to Orville, the surviving brother, and the Smithsonian would recognize the Wrights as the first to achieve powered flight, Orville would sell out all of their patents by 1915 and the company that they founded in 1909 would be bought by Glenn Curtiss in 1929 and become known as the Curtiss-Wright Corporation (Niemann, 2007; Tischauser, 2002).

Two other aviation pioneers would also get their start before World War I: William Boeing and Donald W. Douglas. On July 15, 1916, Bill Boeing incorporated the company founded the previous year, Pacific Aero Products. This company would begin by producing a seaplane copied from a Martin aircraft. They would also work on an aircraft, later called the Model C, that they hoped to sell to the US Navy (50 would be ordered with the start of World War I). This, along with the one to manufacture the Curtiss HS-2L, would occupy the company through the war (Serling, 1992). Meanwhile, Donald Douglas would go on to work for the Glen L. Martin Co as a chief engineer where he would design the Martin MB-1 bomber, the first US-designed bomber to enter production (Boeing History, 2014).

On the other side of the Atlantic, other visionaries were hard at work. In 1909, Louis Blériot became the first pilot to cross the English Channel in a craft he designed himself called the Blériot XI. Two years later, this plane would go into war with the Italian forces in North Africa (Allaz, 2004). Around the same tine another pioneer, Anthony Fokker, started his first aviation company at the age of 21 and built his first aircraft, called the Spin, in 1910. Both the Spin I and Spin II would crash. Spin III, however, would be sold to the German army. Fokker would go on to design the triplane made famous by Manfred von Richthofen, the so-called 'Red Baron', in World War I.

The Airplane in War

The US government intervened in the lawsuit between the Wright brothers and Curtiss as the US entered World War I. The Curtiss Company would go on to become the largest US aircraft manufacturer in World War I, supplying over 10,000 aircraft to the war effort. The US Navy, for whom Curtiss began building planes in 1911, would also use the Curtiss NC-4 to make the first trans-Atlantic flight in 1919 (Marchman, 2002; Roseberry, 1991). The French and the English entered World War I with the English Channel crossing Blériot XI. Prior to the war, the English had also deployed the BE.2, designed by Geoffrey de Havilland. These aircraft started the war classified as scouts and many would end the war with the same designation; however, Fokker would introduce his Eindecker series of monoplanes equipped with fixed, synchronized, forward-firing machine guns during this war and they would become known on the Western Front as the 'Fokker Scourge' (McDermott,

2002; Milstein, 2002). In addition to the famous Red Baron triplane, the British took to the skies in an aircraft designed by Royal Aircraft called the Sopwith Camel, later to become the favorite aircraft of Snoopy from the *Charlie Brown* cartoons. Other aircraft, such as the DH-4, were used in battle as bombers or in support of advancing ground forces. Another important force in the world of aviation would find the wartime experience invaluable in staking its claim to the future – Rolls-Royce. Rolls-Royce came out of WWI ready to take its place as one of the foremost manufacturers of aircraft engines.

In short, the aircraft that emerged from World War I would be sleeker, faster, more powerful, and better-armed. World War I saw the introduction of the low-wing aircraft, the all-metal body, and the thickened cantilever wing; however, most of the aircraft that entered the war would not survive the conflict; the attrition rate on all sides would be very high. The mass production of aircraft needed to supply the war effort had supported many of the newly emerging aviation companies. With the end of the war, most of these companies had to find other means of support. However, the military was still the best game in town and the lucky few would continue to research and produce the newest weapons in the military arsenal (Allaz, 2004).

Back to Business

In the years immediately after World War I, the fledgling US aircraft manufacturers continued to focus on the military side of the market, albeit with some initial forays into aircraft designed for the growing airmail market. Both Boeing and Douglas introduced an airmail plane during 1925, the Model 40 and M-1, respectively. When Boeing replaced the old Liberty engines with the new Pratt & Whitney 425-horsepower air-cooled Wasp engine, the Model 40 not only became a reliable cargo craft but the addition of two passenger seats also made it Boeing's first commercial passenger aircraft. This new engine made it superior to its main competitors – the Douglas M-2 and the Curtiss Carrier Pigeon – which continued to use the Liberty. Boeing bid for and won one of the early airmail routes and established its first subsidiary, Boeing Air Transport, to handle the growing airmail business (Serling, 1992).

In 1927, Boeing purchased Pacific Air Transport (PAT) and introduced the Model 80 and 80A trimotors equipped with Pratt & Whitney Hornet engines and capable of carrying 18 passengers attended by a registered nurse who also acted as a flight attendant. It should be noted that the engines of the 80A were enclosed in streamlined cowlings that improved their performance. In 1929, the Boeing/Pratt & Whitney relationship grew even closer when the two companies merged to form United Aircraft & Transport Corporation. The new company acquired several other aircraft companies, including Stearman Aircraft, Northrop Aircraft, and Sikorsky. The new holding company purchased several airlines, including Varney, Stout, and National Air Transport, which it combined with BAT to form United Air Lines, Inc. While the company was consolidating, it was also working on its next major entry into the market – the B-247. This aircraft started the familiar Boeing numbering scheme. Given the company structure, it is unsurprising that United Air Lines took delivery of the first 60 B-247s, leaving the other carriers to look for their own answer to the fleet question (Johansen, 2002; Serling, 1992). The airmail scandal, which resulted in the passage of the Air Mail Act of 1934, hit Boeing very hard. Airline executives who had participated in the illegal 'division' of mail contracts with the US Post Office were prohibited from holding office in an airline; additionally, no airline that had participated could bid on an air mail contract. Further, aircraft and engine companies were prohibited from owning airlines. This scandal led to the break up the holding company of United Aircraft and Transport and destroyed one of William Boeing's great dreams (Serling, 1992).

For the Boeing Company, the exclusive deal with United also proved to be a very bad move; for the Douglas Aircraft Company, however, it started a wonderful thing (Serling, 1992). Transcontinental & Western Air (TWA), anxious to replace its Fokker-10 trimotors after the fatal 1931 crash involving Knute Rockne, was looking for a plane. The first plane they considered was the B-247, but the UAL order pushed the TWA delivery date well into the future. After the TWA Technical Committee examined several other proposed aircraft, it chose the Douglas Aircraft Company and the DC-1. The DC-1, which was introduced in 1933, would be the first of a series of aircraft destined to dominate the industry for many years (Rummel, 1991). The DC-2, released the following year, was capable of carrying 14 passengers over a distance of 1,000 miles. With the introduction of the DC-2 even United would race to sell its 247s for less than half their original price (Serling, 1992). In 1935, the best-known plane in the series, the DC-3, was released. With 14 seats capable of folding into sleeping berths, the DC-3, first sold to American Airlines, would set a new standard in passenger travel. By the 1940s, approximately 90 percent of the passenger aircraft flying in the US would be either DC-2 or DC-3s (Clouatre, 2002).

Another legendary US manufacturer would also be incorporated in the years between the wars – Lockheed Aircraft. Lockheed, founded by Allan Loughead and Jack Northrop, began work on a Northrop-designed aircraft later called the Vega. Wiley Post used the Vega to set his around-the-world record of 8 days, 16 hours in 1931. Lockheed was purchased in 1929 by Detroit Aircraft Company. Subsequently Jack Northrop left to found Avion Corporation, which was later renamed the Northrop Corporation. Detroit Aircraft went into bankruptcy during the Great Depression and emerged after a buyout in 1932 as the Lockheed Aircraft Company. Lockheed went on to build the Electra in which Amelia Earhart would make her last flight (McCoy, 2002).

In Europe, Anthony Fokker incorporated his aircraft company in the Netherlands in 1919 and released the F.II, one of the first passenger transport aircraft, in 1920. Although he became the main supplier of KLM, the Dutch airline, his passenger aircraft would fall out of favor when Douglas introduced his all-metal aircraft with retractable undercarriages (Milstein, 2002). In England, Geoffrey de Havilland continued to focus on his single and two-seat biplane powered by the Gipsy engine. First came the Gipsy Moth, the Tiger Moth, the Hornet Moth, and then the Moth Minor, a low-wing, wooden monoplane. De Havilland, like Fokker, would continue to produce cutting-edge aircraft for military and civil use through both wars and beyond.

A Strange, Yet Beautiful, Relationship

The aviation industry has always been imperfect by economic standards. First and foremost, it is characterized in both the manufacturing and the airline sides of the industry by small numbers. Perfect competition, according to Adam Smith, is possible when there are many buyers and many sellers. It is assumed that such a market will drive prices down toward costs. Even in the early days before crisis would fuel consolidation and market power would come to rival innovation, there were a limited number of buyers and suppliers. This has not meant that there has been no competition between manufacturers or within the airline and manufacturing sectors, but at times it has led to some very strange relationships, sometimes too close for comfort and at other times as antagonistic as a divorcing couple. Airlines would come to play one manufacturer off against another while at the same time cooperating closely on design and specifications. They would threaten to 'go to the competitors' and then seek out special first delivery rights. For their side, the manufacturers would come to the airlines with concepts seeking orders for yet-to-be-built planes, promising first delivery for key orders, and, eventually, using political clout of all forms to make the sell. These patterns started early.

The story of the DC-1 illustrates this close but imperfect relationship. Frustrated by the rate of progress of his Technical Committee, Jack Frye, the TWA CEO, would write directly to the manufacturers, saying the airline was interested in purchasing 10 or more aircraft meeting attached specifications and performance standards. He requested the manufacturers' to give notice of interest and approximate date of first delivery. His requirements: capacity for 12 or more passengers, 1,080 mile range at 150 miles per hour and a one-engine-out ceiling of 10,000 feet. Three companies would respond – Sikorsky, General Aviation (a subsidiary of General Motors who had purchased the troubled Fokker), and Douglas Aircraft. TWA would now proceed with a series of visits, reviews, and expert analyses that would pit each aircraft maker against the other to improve performance, reduce costs, and speed up delivery dates (Rummel, 1991).

The Next War

The decade of the 1930s saw the beginning of a race in military aviation between the Great Powers of Europe. In Germany, Junkers, Dornier, Messerschmitt, Focke-Wulf, and Heinkel emerged as leading aircraft manufacturers turning out a series of aircraft that would lead the Germany Luftwaffe into World War II. The Heinkel He-178 became the first turbojet aircraft to fly successfully in 1939 and began a new era of aerial warfare. Other notable achievements of these manufacturers include the Me-262 Komet, which utilized a thrust rocket motor to travel at almost 600 miles an hour, and the Ju-287, which sported forward-swept wings over back-swept wings, the Messerschmitt P-1011, with a swept-wing design later used in the USA on the F-14, and the Blitz, a twin-engine Arado 234B bomber capable of speeds of up to 461 miles per hour (Graetzer, 2002).

In Great Britain, the defense industry tripled its employment between 1930 and 1936, even as the industry struggled to adapt its manufacturing methods to mass production. Still, the Hawker Hurricane and Spitfire fighters, as well as the Lancaster bomber, would prove their value in the coming war (McCoy, 2002). The Spitfire gained a huge reputation during the crucial Battle of Britain in 1940. By the end of the war, the Spitfire version, equipped with the Rolls-Royce Griffin engine, would reach speeds of 460 miles per hour (Wheeler, 2002).

In the US, Boeing had continued work despite the airmail controversy on two aircraft designs that would be critical to the war effort – the B-17 Flying Fortress and the B-29 Superfortress. Although these two aircraft represented only 17 percent of all US bombers, they were responsible for 46 percent of the ordinance dropped on Germany during the war. Further, the B-17 has been credited with shooting down 67 percent of enemy fighters in the European theatre of operations. At the height of production, Boeing was producing 363 B-17s a month for the Army Air Corp (Johansen, 2002; Serling, 1992).

Seeing the Enemy

The airplane had grown far more deadly in the decade leading up to World War II, but another invention was to be the salvation of Britain during the early years of the war.

Radar, an outgrowth of the radio experiments of the 1930s, sent radio waves out into the atmosphere and measured the time that elapsed before the signal bounced off a solid object and returned to the receiver. Great Britain had begun deploying this new technology along their coast before the start of the war and its use during the early years of the war would help Britain beat back the waves of German bombers that were streaming across the Channel. In addition to detecting incoming aircraft, the system could be used to direct intercepting aircraft to their target, help aircraft determine their height from the ground, and identify friendly and enemy aircraft with the use of small broadcasting beacons. The 'enemy' would also eventually deploy radar, but the invention of the microwave-cavity magnetron which generated a high-power radio wave and required a smaller antenna would continue to give the British the advantage during the war. Of course, this new technology also had significant civilian applications and would become the backbone of the civil aviation systems that developed after the end of World War II. In fact, the system used through the end of the twentieth century to track, identify, and direct aircraft was not very different from this early system, a fact that we will discuss in Chapter 20 as the industry implemented a twenty-first-century solution to air traffic congestion.

Conquering the Civilian Market

During its first fifty years of life, the aviation industry witnessed a number of high-profile firsts (Table 2.1) and captured the imagination of a whole generation, but it had not yet conquered the traveling public, those ordinary citizens who would pay to ride on a flight from point A to point B. The airplane had proven its value in war and was being mass-produced on a large scale by the end of World War II. The basic elements of a successful and viable product had been invented and tested in the heat of war. Still, the airplane probably still looked in 1950 like the playground of the rich and the daring; it was not yet the transportation mode of choice for visiting grandma in Iowa or Ontario. The task of creating a commercial aviation industry that would attract this kind of a market would be left to the pioneers of the next fifty years who would make flying a commonplace occurrence, even a necessity (Chapter 7). First, the industry would conquer the cargo market, specifically airmail. Chapter 3 will discuss the development of this industry and how it came to shape the future of the US airline industry. The tale of how a few daring individuals would be thrown on top of the mail will have to wait, but it would come.

Table 2.1 Aviation Firsts

Date	Event
1903	First heavier-than-air flight
	Wilbur and Orville Wright
1906	First European flight
	Alberto Santos-Dumont
1908	First airplane fatality
	Lt. Thomas E. Selfridge
1909	First cross-channel flight
	Louis Blériot
	First international aviation competition
	Rheims, France

(Continued)

Table 2.1 (Continued)

Date	Event
1910	First licensed woman pilot
	Baroness de la Roche
	First aviation conference
	Paris, France
1913	First multi-engine aircraft
	Igor Sikorsky
1914	First aerial combat
1917	First black combat pilot
	Eugene J. Bullard
1918	First regular US airmail
1919	First transatlantic flight
	Lt Cmdr Albert Read
1921	First naval vessel sunk by aircraft
1924	First round-the-world flight
	Maj. Frederick Marin
1927	First solo non-stop trans-Atlantic flight
	Charles A. Lindbergh
1931	First nonstop trans-Pacific flight
	Hugh Herndon and Clyde Pangborn
1932	First woman trans-Atlantic flight
	Amelia Earhart
1933	First round-the-world solo
	Wiley Post
1937	First successful helicopter flight
	Hanna Reitsch
1939	First turbojet flight
	He-178
1947	First piloted supersonic flight
	Capt Charles E. Yeagar

Source: Information gathered from Infoplease. www. infoplease/ipa/A0004537.html

Questions

1 What is the difference between invention and innovation?
2 How is war 'good' for the aviation industry?
3 What combination of innovations made the DC-3 a commercial success?
4 What legal battle divided the Wright Brothers and Glen Curtiss?
5 Discuss the early history of the Boeing Company.

References

Allaz, C. (2004) *The history of air cargo and airmail from the 18th Century*, Christopher Foyle Publishing, Paris.

Carlson, R. V. (2002) 'Dirigibles' in Tracy Irons-Georges (Ed.) *Encyclopedia of flight*, pp 211–215, Salem Press, Pasadena, CA.

Clouatre, D. (2002) 'DC plane family' in Tracy Irons-Georges (Ed.) *Encyclopedia of flight*, pp 205–207, Salem Press, Pasadena, CA.

Graetzer, D. G. (2002) 'World War II"' in Tracy Irons-Georges (Ed.) *Encyclopedia of flight*, pp 779–785, Salem Press, Pasadena, CA.

Johansen, B. E. (2002) 'Boeing' in Tracy Irons-Georges (Ed.) *Encyclopedia of flight*, pp 154–156, Salem Press, Pasadena, CA.

Marchman, J. F. 2002) 'Glenn H. Curtiss', in Tracy Irons-Georges (Ed.) *Encyclopedia of flight*, pp 203–204, Salem Press, Pasadena, CA.

McCoy, M. G. (2002) 'Lockheed Martin' in Tracy Irons-Georges (Ed.) *Encyclopedia of flight*, pp 420–423, Salem Press, Pasadena, CA.

McDermott, D. P. (2002) 'World War I', in Tracy Irons-Georges (Ed.) *Encyclopedia of flight*, pp 774–779, Salem Press, Pasadena, CA.

Milstein, R. L. (2002) 'Fokker Aircraft' in Tracy Irons-Georges (Ed.) *Encyclopedia of flight*, pp 275–278, Salem Press, Pasadena, CA.

Niemann, G. (2007) *Big Brown: The untold story of UPS*, John Wiley & Sons, San Francisco, CA.

Paradowski, R. J. (2002) 'Wright Flyer', in Tracy Irons-Georges (Ed.) *Encyclopedia of flight*, pp 786–788, Salem Press, Pasadena, CA.

Roseberry, C. R. (1991) *Glenn Curtiss: Pioneer of flight*, Syracuse University Press, Syracuse, NY.

Rummel, R. W. (1991) *Howard Hughes and TWA*. Smithsonian Institution Press, Washington.

Senge, P. M. (1990) *The fifth discipline: The art & practice of the learning organization*, Doubleday, New York.

Serling, R. J. (1992) *Legend and legacy: The story of Boeing and its people*, St. Martin Press, New York.

Tischauser, L. V. (2002) 'Wright Brothers', in Tracy Irons-Georges (Ed.) *Encyclopedia of flight*, pp 785–786, Salem Press, Pasadena, CA

Wheeler, H (2002) 'Spitfire' in Tracy Irons-Georges (Ed.) *Encyclopedia of flight*, pp 625–626, Salem Press, Pasadena, CA

Websites

Boeing History,(2014) http://www.boeing.com/boeing/history/narrative/n002boe.page

3 The Other Source of Revenue

Learning Objectives

After reading this chapter, you should have a good understanding of:

LO1:   the beginnings of the air cargo industry
LO2:   the role that aviation prizes had in fostering the development of aviation
LO3:   the role of the Post Office in the US in shaping the aviation industry, including the scandal over airmail contract
LO4:   the background that shaped UPS

Key Terms, Concepts & People

US Post Office	Kelly Act of 1925	CAM
William Folger Brown	Trunk route	Airmail Act of 1934
Deutsche Lufthansa	UPS	Charles Lindbergh

Following the Money

The first non-mail cargo flight took place on November 7, 1910 from Dayton to Columbus, Ohio. Commissioned by Max Morehouse to celebrate the annual autumn sale of his Home Dry Goods Store, the Wright Model B carried 200 pounds of silk and ribbon 70 miles to successfully deliver its goods. While this delivery is a noteworthy first, it should probably be considered an even more successful marketing and publicity event (Allaz, 2004). In the beginning, airmail and air cargo were more novelty and show than serious business. In fact, 1911 marked the first airmail exhibition in which souvenir cards and stamps were flown around a local area in India and then sold to collectors. Other such events followed in Great Britain, France, Germany, and the United States. In 1911, the Grahame-White Aviation Company carried 130,000 cards and letters between London and Windsor Castle as part of the celebration for the coronation of George V (Glines, 1990).

While, the idea of airmail and air cargo fired the imagination of aviators and some businessmen around the world, it was the William Randolph Hearst announcement of the creation of a $50,000 prize to the first pilot who could fly coast to coast in the US within 30 days that sparked efforts to prove this new technology. Calbraith P. Rodgers was one of the pilots determined to collect the prize. He eventually completed the coast-to-coast flight,

DOI: 10.4324/9781003405306-4

crashing 16 times. Unfortunately, it took him 55 days and he was unable to collect the Hearst prize (Glines, 1990). Others would follow, but it was not until the US government got involved that regularly scheduled, transcontinental airmail became a reality in the US. In Europe, sporadic efforts would be interrupted by World War I.

Officially Speaking

India holds the honor of having not only the first airmail exhibition but also the first official airmail flight on February 18, 1911; however, like so many other efforts this first flight did not translate into a regular service (Allaz, 2004). In the US, the Post Office Department had asked for $50,000 in 1911 to explore airmail delivery, but it was not until 1916 that funds were made available. By 1918, Congress was prepared to authorize $100,000 for an experimental airmail route between Washington and New York. It was left up to Major Reuben H. Fleet of the Army Air Service to make this air service work despite the fact that there was: 1) a shortage of pilots, 2) almost no pilots with cross-country flying experience, 3) no adequate maps, 4) few experienced mechanics, and 5) no planes modified to carry airmail. Still, with President Wilson set to attend the official take-off, Glen Curtiss was contacted and asked to modify his Curtis JN6H to leave out the front seat and front controls and add a second gas tank. While this experiment had its share of mishaps and lost pilots, it was deemed a success and the US Post Office Department officially took over the service in August of 1918, buying their own planes and hiring their own pilots. According to official records, the Army Air Service delivered 193,021 pounds of mail, completing 92 percent of their scheduled flights. They flew 128,255 route miles without a fatality. Ben Lipsner, who had officially organized the experiment for the Army Air Service, became the first Superintendent of the United States Aerial Mail Service. One of his first tasks upon assuming his position was to commission the design of the first aircraft specifically for airmail delivery. This plane, the Standard Aero-mail, was designed by the Standard Aircraft Company of Elizabeth, New Jersey. It was powered by a 150 horsepower engine and had a load specification of 180 pounds. It could travel at speeds of 100 miles per hour and was able to climb to a height of 6,000 feet in 10 minutes. The next task was to begin a transcontinental service with the first leg from New York to Cleveland followed over the next two years by New York–Chicago, Chicago–Omaha, Chicago–St. Louis, Chicago–Minneapolis, and Omaha–San Francisco. On July 1, 1924, regular transcontinental service was inaugurated. In 1923 and 1924, the Airmail Service received the Collier Trophy for 'the greatest achievement in aviation in America' (Glines, 1990).

The US Post Office would gradually close down its Airmail Service with the passage of the Kelly Act of 1925 entitled 'An Act to Encourage Commercial Aviation and to authorize the Postmaster General to Contract for the Mail Service'. US Representative Clyde Kelly, who sponsored the act, believed that private operators rather than the government should assume the risks and reap the rewards of the airmail business. With this act, advertisements were placed in newspapers asking for bids on eight feeder airmail routes to be awarded by the Postmaster General. By 1926, 12 airmail contracts had been awarded. The last flight of the Post Office was conducted in 1927 (Kane, 1998). In order to qualify for these routes, individuals had to be US citizens backed by at least 75 percent US controlled capital stock. Aircraft had to qualify for airworthiness certificates and pilots had to produce certificates of fitness (Glines, 1990).

Table 3.1 lists the route number and the company receiving the award. There are several items of note in this list. The first route to be put into operation was Ford Air Transport.

Table 3.1 The First Contract Airmail Routes

Route Number	Company
CAM 1	Colonial Air Lines
CAM 2	Robertson Aircraft Corp
CAM 3	National Air Transport
CAM 4	Western Air Express
CAM 5	Varney Speed Lines
CAM 6 & 7	Ford Air Transport
CAM 8	Pacific Air Transport
CAM 9	Charles Dickenson
CAM 10	Florida Airways Corp
CAM 11	Clifford Ball
CAM 12	Western Air Express

Source: Kane, R.M. *Air Transportation.*

This company was another venture by a man more associated with the automobile sector – Henry Ford. Ford Air Transport manufactured a plane which had been designed by William B. Stout. This aircraft was an all-metal monoplane with internally stressed wings and a Liberty engine. A later version, the Ford Trimotor, would go on to become one of the great classic airplanes of the period. Western Air Express, which had the airmail route from Los Angeles to Salt Lake City, would become one of the first carriers to try to boost revenues by carrying passengers. In 1927, Western received a grant from the Daniel Guggenheim Fund to purchase passenger aircraft. A slightly later effort to combine cargo and passengers was Transcontinental Air Transport (TAT). TAT planned to use trains by night and air by day to offer luxury passenger service. The venture lost almost $3 million in the first year-and-a-half. TAT would later merge with several other carriers to become Transcontinental & Western Air (TWA). Eventually, this name would change to Trans World Airlines (Glines, 1990). It should be noted that the original list of CAM awards includes carriers that would go on to form the nucleus of familiar US major and national carriers. National Air Transport and Pacific Air Transport, for example, would go on to combine with a later CAM awardee, Boeing Air Transport, to form United Airlines (Davies, 1998). Similarly, Varney Speed Lines would go on to become Continental Airlines (Davies, 1984), Robertson Aircraft Corporation would become one of eighty carriers merged to form American Airlines (Bedwell & Wegg, 2000), and All American Aviation, who would receive a CAM in 1939, would go on to become US Airways (Jones & Jones, 1999). This consolidation would not occur by accident. As the TAT and Western experiments proved, passengers could provide good additional revenue, but airmail revenue was essential. In fact, these CAM routes would establish a basic pattern of air transportation in the US that continues to this day. Creating this pattern of trunk routes, large coast-to-coast operations flowing east-to-west, would be the 'mission' of Walter Brown.

In 1929, Walter Folger Brown was appointed as the US postmaster general. Brown would work diligently for the passage of the Air Mail Act of 1930, also known as the McNary–Watres Airmail Act, which gave the postmaster total control over the airmail bidding process. He believed that the airline business model should be based on passenger revenue, rather than excess airmail payments (Glines, 1990). According to Brown, the aviation industry suffered from four problems: '1) being unwilling to invest in new equipment, 2) operating obsolete aircraft, 3) demonstrating questionable safety performance from cost cutting, and 4) maintaining marginal operations with no growth' (Kane, 1998, p. 107). To remedy this situation, Brown eliminated the competitive bidding process for contract air mail routes in favor of a system that granted awards to large, well-financed operators. Only these large operators were invited to attend the so-called 'spoils conferences' that were held in Washington, D.C. to award contracts. In essence, the US government, through the office of the postmaster, forced small carriers to merge in order to obtain the lucrative airmail contracts (Glines, 1968). Brown envisioned an air map of the US with three transcontinental routes – a northern, a central, and a southern one. These routes would be connected by shorter, regional north–south routes (Glines, 1990). A look at a map of the early air mail routes and stops will show that he succeeded to some extent, creating a long east–west trunk route with shorter north–south legs. This general structure would be the backbone for the airline networks that followed. Unfortunately, this heavy-handed 'indirect' intervention did not sit well with many stakeholders. Certainly, the carriers left out of the spoils conferences had ample reason to complain, and they did so strongly (Airmail Pioneers, 2012).

By 1932, charges of graft and collision led US President Franklin Roosevelt to cancel all contracts and return responsibility for the airmail to the US Army. It was decided that the Army Air Corps would operate only 12 of the 26 civilian routes. Unfortunately, even this reduction was not enough for the Corps, which had a limited number of pilots and even fewer with night flying or instrument experience. Their aircraft often did not have landing, navigation or cockpit lights, and nor were they equipped with the new gyro instruments or radios. Given these deficiencies, it is unsurprising that the Corps quickly ran into trouble. After a series of accidents, the airmail service was returned to private operators by June 1, 1934 (Glines, 1990). The Airmail Act of 1934, also known as the Black–McKellar Act, provided for a return to the competitive bidding process of the past and prohibited awards to carriers involved in the supposed collusion. Three of these carriers – American Airways, Eastern Air Transport and Transcontinental & Western Air – changed their names respectively to American Airlines, Eastern Airlines, and Transcontinental & Western Air Inc. to avoid this restriction and continue in the airmail business. The administration of contracts would be divided between the Post Office, Interstate Commerce Commission, and the Department of Commerce. Beginning in 1938, rates would be set by the newly created Civil Aviation Bureau (Kane, 1998).

Mail, Morale, and War

In Europe, the years just before World War I saw a number of efforts to begin airmail services. In 1911, Henri Pequet transported 6,500 letters and postcards from Allahabad to Naini Junction in France, while in Italy a similar shipment was made between Bologna and Venice. In 1912, both Germany and Japan celebrated their first official airmail flight; however, as World War I approached,, the balloons of Paris which had operated during the Prussian siege of the city between 1980–71, remained the only example of a regularly scheduled airmail service (Allaz, 2004). Europe would have to wait until the end of the war to achieve this milestone; however, military airmail was established between several areas of the continent during the war. For the most part, these services utilized military aircraft, but allowed some civilian correspondence.

As World War I came to an end, aircraft had new cargo and a new mission – humanitarian relief. In 1919, an airlift was established between Folkestone and Ghent to provide bedding, medicine, and food. In France, similar efforts were organized along a number of routes: Paris–Lille, Paris–Maubeuge–Valenciennes, Paris–Longwy, Paris–Mulhouse,

Paris–Strasbourg, and Paris–Brussels. Most of these efforts were short-lived, but they did give a number of individuals and firms experience in airmail and air cargo. This experience, combined with the flying experience of former soldiers, would prove useful after the war when nations moved to re-establish their commercial aviation systems. As we will discuss in Chapter 4, Europe would move quickly in association with the Universal Postal Union (UPU) to integrate airmail into Europe's postal system.

As in the case of the US, airmail would continue to receive priority in the air cargo business of Europe until after World War II; however, several airlines did attempt to expand into other forms of cargo. By 1938, Deutsche Lufthansa was already the world's leading scheduled carrier for freight, a position that it continued to hold in 2008 according to that year's Air Cargo World survey. It would introduce the first long-haul transoceanic freight charter in 1939. According to Allaz (2004), a total of 57,000 tons of cargo were shipped by air in 1938. As is still the case today, the most common items of shipment were highly perishable, urgent, and high value. These included newspapers, bank notes, perfumes, spare parts, and the occasional live animal. With the introduction of new aircraft designed with cargo operations in mind, such as the Junkers W33 and the Ju52, the volume and size of cargo improved, thereby lowering the cost. By 1940, Transportes Aereos Centro-Americanos (TACA) was the world's leading air-freight company, shipping 12,640 tons of goods throughout Central America. In other regions with poor or challenging surface transportation features, the idea of offering bulk, low rates for air shipment was considered and tried; however, the volumes of air freight would continue to be relatively low in the period between World Wars I and II.

A Brown Beginning

In 1899, 11-year-old Jim Casey went to work to help support his family. His first job was with the delivery department at Bon Marche, a Seattle department store. From here, he would go on to start several of his own businesses in the area, including a messenger and telephone service. The American Messenger Company was founded in 1907. It would later merge with the Motorcycle Delivery Company to become Merchants Parcel Delivery. This new company would handle outsource department store delivery with a small fleet of brown trucks. After World War I, the company would begin the process of expanding down the US West Coast. They would purchase the Motor Parcel Company in Oakland, California and change the name again to United Parcel Service (UPS).

These early years would lay the foundation for many of the features that would later 'define' UPS. The first, of course, was the color of their delivery vans, selected so that the original department store customers would not see them as a threat. Second, the early years established the pattern of learning the intimate details of an area and utilizing this knowledge to provide better, faster time-definite services. Third, each new merger, acquisition, or key hire would bring more people into the family that would become UPS. These employees would be seen as the backbone of their success. When the company expanded to Los Angeles, it would advertise their delivery men as the type 'you yourself would hire' and they would become known for their neat appearance and prompt, courteous service.

Evert 'Mac' McDabe, one of the UPS partners, was an early enthusiast of the airplane. Eventually, in 1929 he would convince the others to form United Air Express. This company contracted with three air companies to fly packages delivered by UPS to selected airports. At the same time, UPS was looking to expand its delivery business into the

New York City area. The Curtiss Aeroplane Motor Company, which had recently merged with Wright Aeronautical to form the Curtiss-Wright Corporation, made an offer to UPS to buy the company for $2 million and 600,000 shares in Curtiss Aeroplane. The UPS partners would remain with the company and were guaranteed management control for a period of five years. This deal seemed a perfect way to expand the business to the East Coast, but the financial collapse that followed the 1929 stock market crash ended the deal and UPS' first foray into the air service business (Niemann, 2007).

Conclusion

It has been noted that the first decade of aviation in the US was synonymous with airmail. In part, this was due to the drive of Otto Praeger, who became the second Assistant Postmaster General in 1915, and Walter Folger Brown, Postmaster General from 1929, who was determined to 'create' the airline industry in the US. Even after the Post Office officially left the airmail delivery business to the private sector, its indirect influence was substantial and far-reaching. While the accomplishments of the early airmail pilots were significant steps in establishing airmail and air cargo as viable modes of transportation, it was probably the 1927 flight by Charles A. Lindbergh, himself an airmail pilot, that truly captured the imagination of the world and the attention of serious business investors. One month after the historic New York to Paris flight, there was a 20 percent increase in mail on contract mail routes (Glines, 1990).

Thirty-five years after the first air cargo flight, the world had not yet fully accepted the concept, but it had perhaps seen enough evidence of potential in air cargo to set the stage for the post-World War II industry that was to come. As with all aspects of aviation, World War II would be a turning point. The technical innovations and individual and collective achievements that occurred during this war would change the nature and shape the popular perception of the industry as it moves into the second half of the twentieth century. However, it would be the logistics revolution and the globalization movement of the latter part of the twentieth century that would make air cargo a force to be reckoned with in the aviation industry (Chapter 13). For now, the fantasy of the balloon would give way to the cold, hard calculation of governments and businessmen. These calculations are the subject of the next three chapters.

Questions

1 What role did the US Post Office play in air cargo?
2 Discuss the first airmail routes and trace these early companies through history
3 What were the spoils conferences and how did this scandal affect the industry?
4 What role did air cargo play during and after World War II?
5 Discuss how the beginnings of UPS helped to shape its culture and future.
6 How did the Airmail Act of 1934 reshape the landscape of airmail contracting and the competitive bidding process?
7 Discuss the significance of the logistical challenges faced by the US Army during its brief period of operating airmail services in the early 1930s.
8 How did the experience gained from humanitarian relief efforts and military logistics during World War I contribute to the development of commercial aviation systems in Europe?

References

Airmail Pioneers (2012) Map. Available at http://www.airmailpioneers.org/

Allaz, C. (2004) *The history of air cargo and airmail from the 18th century*, Christopher Foyle Publishing, Paris.

Bedwell, D. and Wegg, J. (2000), *Silverbird: The American Airlines story*, Plymouth Press, Boston.

Davies, R. E. G. (1998), *Airlines of the United States since 1914*, Smithsonian Institution Press, Washington, DC.

Davies, R. E. G. (1984), *Continental Airlines: The first fifty years*, Pioneer Publications, The Woodlands, TX.

Glines, C. V. (1990) *Airmail: How it all began*, TAB Aero, Blue Ridge Summit, PA.

Glines, C. V. (1968), *The Saga of the airmail*, D. Van Nostrand, Princeton, NJ.

Jones, G. and Jones, G. P. (1999), *US Airways*, Ian Allan, Shepperton, England.

Kane, R. M. (1998), *Air transportation*, 13th ed., Kendall/Hunt Publishing, Dubuque, IA.

Niemann, G. (2007) *Big Brown: The untold story of UPS*, John Wiley & Sons, San Francisco, CA.

4 A Dangerous Idea?

Learning Objectives

After reading this chapter, you should have a good understanding of:

LO1:   the early developments in manned flight
LO2:   the issues that divided the 1910 Aviation Conference
LO3:   the regulations proposed in the 1919 Convention
LO4:   the domestic development of the aviation industry on both sides of the Atlantic between the world wars.

Key Terms, Concepts & People

1910 Conference	Paris Convention	Freedom of the skies
UPU	Par Avion	British Airways
Air France	Rolls-Royce	Messerschmitt

Imagined Possibilities

On January 7, 1785, less than two years after the first recorded balloon flight, Jean-Pierre Blanchard and John Jeffries became the first individuals to cross above a national border when they flew their balloon across the English Channel to France. This event was not viewed at the time as an 'invasion' but a triumph of mankind. While experimentation with lighter-than-air flight continued, the balloon inspired thoughts of fancy not fear. Even the development of the dirigible, an elongated balloon with a system of propulsion and guidance did not change the general view of lighter-than-air flight. Still at the mercy of the winds, the balloon did not seem to pose the threat or hold the promise of heavier-than-air travel. It is true that the French used balloons in a military setting as early as 1793, when they provided reconnaissance during conflicts following the French Revolution. It is also true that the first recorded air-to-air combat occurred in 1870 between a French and a Prussian balloonist during the siege of Paris, but the balloons of war still did not raise the international concerns that their heavier-than-air cousins would provoke (Glines, 1968; Wirth & Young, 1980). The world's governments, however, would not wait for the aircraft to enter battle before acting. By 1910, they had already seen enough to know that the airplane was no passing fancy, but rather a new technology with great promise and dangerous

DOI: 10.4324/9781003405306-5

potential. New regulations were needed to insure the development of international aviation and to protect the interests of nations. This was the goal of the Paris Conference. It would not achieve the goals that its organizers had hoped, but it did make one thing abundantly clear; international aviation would not be divorced from politics and national interests (Sochor, 1991).

Let the Conferences Begin

The French government convened the first ever conference on aviation in 1910 to draft a convention on air navigation. The conference was attended by the representatives of 19 European countries. It quickly became apparent that there were conflicting opinions among the delegates present with regard to the rights and privileges of flying. The French and German delegations favored a system of extensive freedom based on the Freedom of the Seas model of Hugo Grotius. The British, by contrast, insisted on complete state sovereignty and control over the airspace above a country's land borders. This fundamental disagreement prevented the conference from achieving its principal goal of establishing a broad framework for international aviation; however, the convention did identify many of the key terms, concepts, and technical provisions that would become standard in later conferences. In the absence of agreement over an international framework, the British became the first nation to declare its sovereignty over the airspace above their country in 1911. The British Aerial Navigation Act gave the Home Secretary full power to regulate the entry and activities of aircraft into its airspace. The other European nations quickly followed suit in the years prior to World War I (Sochor, 1991). The debate over freedom of the skies would resume at the 1913 Madrid Conference, which would also fail to reach consensus (Allaz, 2004).

The Peace Conference at the end of World War I faced two key aviation issues. The first was the disposition of the military and civilian fleets of the defeated countries. The second issue was to complete the work begun in 1910. This meeting, known as the Convention Relating to the Regulation of Aerial Navigation, accepted the US position which permitted German civil aviation development within their national borders while eliminating all of the military aspects of aviation. The conference also produced the so-called Paris Convention of 1919. The first article of the Convention declared the complete and exclusive sovereignty of each nation over its airspace. It went on to call for: 1) prescribed national registration of aircraft, 2) restrictions on the movement of military aircraft, 3) prescribed rules of airworthiness i.e. certification that an aircraft is safe to fly through a range of operations, 4) the regulation of pilots, and 5) the establishment of police measures. A permanent commission was established in Paris to continue the study of international aviation legal issues, the International Commission on Air Navigation (ICAN) (Kane, 1998; Sochor, 1991). The Paris Convention was eventually ratified by 26 countries, the most notable exceptions being the US and Russia, who both chose to distance themselves from international affairs after the end of World War I. The US did later sign the Commercial Aviation Convention, also known as the Havana Convention, in 1928. This convention resulted from the Sixth International Conference of the American States and differed from the Paris Convention in several key respects. The Havana Convention did not seek to establish a uniform international standard on aviation for aircraft or pilot regulation, nor did it contain any provision for influencing future aviation development such as ICAN (Groenewedge, 1996).

Postal Agenda

The Universal Postal Union (UPU) was established in 1874 on the initiative of Heinrich von Stephan, the Director General of Post for Prussia (later Germany). The primary concern of the UPU was the free transit of international mail, and Article I of the Universal Postal Convention considered all the countries under the treaty a single territory over which the UPU imposed fixed transit fees for sea and rail. In 1920, the UPU met in Madrid and began the process of incorporating air services into the Convention. This proceeded in three phases: recognition (1920–1927); integration (1927–1938); and full incorporation (1938–). Article 4b – Aerial Services – was inserted into the Convention. It stated that:

> Aerial services established for the conveyance of correspondence between two or more countries are considered as analogous to the extraordinary services to which Article 4, section 6 refers. The conditions of conveyance are settled by mutual consent between the Administrations concerned. The transit charges applicable to each aerial service are, however, uniform for all Administrations which use the service…

As an extraordinary service, however, there was no uniform regulation common to all companies or air routes. A special conference called by the UPU at The Hague in 1927 would change this status, including aerial conveyance under all the articles covering other modes of conveyance and establishing a basic and surcharge rate based on weight. It would also require that the classic blue label 'Par Avion' be applied to the outside of the correspondence. Three further conferences were held prior to the outbreak of World War II – Brussels in 1929 and 1931 and Cairo in 1934. The unstated goal was to eliminate the surcharge. No official action was taken, but from the 1930s a number of European postal administrators began to unofficially remove it. The surcharge was officially removed in the Brussels Conference of 1938 (Allaz, 2004).

Domestic Developments

While the international aviation community remained divided on the general question of freedom versus sovereignty, the course of domestic aviation development also diverged in the years leading up to World War II. Direct governmental intervention became the most frequent method of promoting the growth and development of domestic aviation. Governments provided direct subsidies and/or assumed full or partial ownership of domestic air transport companies. British Airways and Air France are two classic examples of this strategy. A privately owned British Airways was formed in 1935 from the merger of several smaller British carriers. British Airways and Imperial Airways were merged and nationalized to form British Overseas Airways Corporation (BOAC) in 1939. BOAC and British European Airways (BEA) would be merged under the name British Airways in 1974 and remain under government ownership until 1987 (Marriott, 1998). Air France was founded in 1933 through the merger of five smaller French carriers and negotiated with the French government to become the country's national carrier. In 1948, the government assumed a 70 percent ownership stake in the newly reincorporated Air France. All four of the government-owned airlines of France were merged in 1990 into the Air France Group (Gross, 2002). By the mid-1950s, most of the carriers of Europe were wholly or partly owned by their respective governments (Graham, 1995). Although many of Asia's national carriers were formed after their European counterparts, the pattern of government ownership was also widespread there (Sinha, 2001).

This direct intervention did not suit the philosophical and political tastes of US lawmakers and officials. This did not mean the US government did not feel that it had a stake and a role to play in the development of domestic aviation. As noted in Chapter 3, the early development of US aviation was closely tied to airmail and it was largely at the urging of the US Post Office that experimentation with airmail delivery and route creation was begun. After the transition from government to private airmail delivery prompted by the Kelly Act of 1925, the Postmaster General would unofficially continue to intervene in the private airlines that emerged to shape the aviation industry. While this intervention was later deemed illegal, it provided the financial support and strategic vision that shaped the industry that went to war in World War II.

By the beginning of World War II, the domestic aviation environment of the Americas and Europe was in place, although the strain of the Great Depression was putting pressure on these systems. Government ownership was the preferred method of domestic support and development in most of the world's nations while the US government intervened in equally significant, though indirect ways to create a large, stable aviation system. A question occasionally arises from aviation interested individuals from outside the US as to what factors account for the different indirect path taken toward the development of domestic aviation by the US government. There are probably a number of concrete economic and geographical explanations, but the more intuitive and less obvious answer may lie in the basic, shared attitude of many of the individuals that originally colonized and later immigrated to the US – namely a general distrust of organized government. This distrust grows in direct proportion to the distance that the government is from the individual or individuals in question. It has often been noted that in a number of slightly varying ways citizens in the United States tend to believe that their government was invented by geniuses to be run by idiots (Friedman, 2000). These sentiments are clearly and forcefully expressed by such economists as Hayek, Milton Friedman, and other individuals associated with the so-called Chicago School. Simply put, government intervention distorts the functioning of free market forces preventing the efficient allocation of resources and the establishment of natural prices (Friedman, 1980, 1982; Hayek, 1960, 1980, 1994; Yergin & Stanislaw, 2002). Clearly, such an attitude does not predispose the average US citizen to favoring greater government involvement in their daily lives. The federalization of airport screening in the wake of 9/11 probably reflects the confusion, shock, fear, and uncertainty created by those events far more than it represents a true belief that the government can perform this function better than private enterprise. It is likely that within a few years there will be increasing pressure to 'privatize' that which was once 'federalized' for just these reasons. Likewise, the US reluctance to privatize airports and air traffic control service, like so much of the rest of the world would do so in the latter part of the twentieth century, has more to do with entrenched political forces and powerful labor groups than it does with a belief in the efficiency and effectiveness of governments, although airports in the US do actually tend to be run by local (city, county) governments who do meet the 'closer-to-me' test of the US citizen and thus get a slightly higher level of trust.

Lessons of War

During the first half of the twentieth century, the world would experience two great wars and the airplane would play a role in each of these conflicts. Although the airplane first went to war in 1911 with the Italian forces in North Africa, its initial role was only to provide reconnaissance. In World War I, it would assume an offensive role first as a bomber and later in aerial combat with mounted machine guns. The airplane that saw service in World War I was propelled by an engine capable of generating about 90 horsepower and traveling at 75 miles per hour. By the end of the war, Rolls-Royce and American Liberty engines were producing 360 and 400 horsepower, respectively, speed had doubled, and innovations such as cantilever wings and all metal fuselages were in place (Allaz, 2004). While World War I evokes images of flying aces such as Manfred von Richthofen, commonly called the Red Baron, twisting and turning in an aerial ballet with his opponents, the war also saw the first large-scale bombing of such cities as London. On June 13, 1917 alone, the Germans dropped 118 high-explosive bombs on the city of London. By this time the airplane had clearly arrived as a weapon of war.

If World War I saw the airplane become more than an observer of the action, then World War II saw it become an integral, vital part of the grand strategy of nations and allies. The war itself began with the Blitzkrieg carried out against Poland – a tactic which was later extended across much of Europe. The aircraft made these lightning strikes both possible and devastating. The desperate Battle of Britain demonstrated the important role of aircraft for both offensive and defensive purposes. The aircraft in fact took several major leaps forward in design and performance during the war years. One of the most significant developments was the development of the turbojet aircraft. Germany followed this innovation with the launch of the Messerschmitt (Me-262), which was capable of carrying 550-pound bombs installed on the aircraft's wing racks as well as 12 R4M rockets fitted under the wings. The Me-163 Komet was fitted with a rocket motor that could propel it at almost 600 miles per hour and climb vertically at 11,810 feet per minute. Other advances during the war included the use of rocket boosters for short take-offs, pressurized cabins, four-engine aircraft, forward-swept wings mounted over swept-back wings to establish stability at low speeds, and drag-resistant body designs (Badsey, 1990; Cooksley & Robertson, 1998).

Aircraft were not the only beneficiaries of the wartime push to innovation. The British development of radar (discussed in Chapter 2) was critical to the defense of Britain and also to the Allies' ability to avoid detection during bombing raids over Germany. This innovation led to early efforts at reducing aircraft detectability, and stealth technology, through the use of deflected radar beams and radar-absorbing materials. Work was also begun on the use of thinner, flatter, heat-resistant materials for aircraft construction. Finally, unmanned, armed aircraft, and guided missiles would make their appearance toward the end of the war (Cooksley & Robertson, 1998).

In short, the aircraft came out of these two conflicts as a more powerful and deadlier device. As has always been the case with aviation, however, the innovations initially developed for military application can also have important impacts on the civilian sector. By 1946, just one year after the end of World War II, aircraft such as the Douglas DC-6 would be carrying 102 passengers at 20,000 feet in a pressurized cabin (Badrocke & Sunston, 1999). Commercial aviation was coming of age and prepared to launch the world on the path toward a globalized, interconnected world.

Coming Out with Different Agendas

As World War II was coming to an end, the Allied powers would turn at least some of their attention back to the issue of creating an international aviation system. This interest would result in the Chicago Conference (Chapter 5), but the countries attending that conference had been changed by the years of war in ways that would echo through the halls in Chicago. It has been said that the United States was the only country to emerge from World War II richer. In fact, the US gold reserves at the end of the war amounted to $20 billion, two-thirds of the world's total (Matloff, 1959). The US would be responsible for more than half of the world's manufacturing production and also account for one-third of the production of all types of goods (Ashworth, 1975). In the aviation area, the United States production of aircraft had risen by 1945 to 49,761 per year, up from 5,856 in 1939. It would account for more aircraft per year than the combined manufacturing of Britain and the USSR (Overy, 1980).

For its part, the USSR had not only lost 20–25 million citizens between 1941 and 1945; it had also lost a substantial portion of its infrastructure (Hosking, 1985). It is estimated that in the transportation sector alone the USSR 'was hit by the destruction of 65,000 kilometers of railway track, loss of or damage to 15,800 locomotives, 428,000 goods wagons, 4,280 river boats, and half of all the railway bridges in the occupied territory' (Nove, 1969, p. 285). The losses to infrastructure were devastating in the nations of other Allied and Great Powers as well. In 1946, German national income and output was one-third of its 1938 level (Landes, 1969). Japanese real income had fallen to only 57 percent of its 1934–1936 levels and exports were only 8 percent of the 1934–1936 figures (Allen, 1981). Similarly, Italy's gross national product had declined by 40 percent to its 1911 level (Ricossa, 1972). The Allied Powers, with the exception of the US, had not fared any better. By 1944, years of war and occupation had left France with a situation in which 'most of the waterways and harbors were blocked, most of the bridges destroyed, much of the railway system temporarily unusable' (Wright, 1968, p. 264). The French national income in 1945 was half of its 1938 level. In Great Britain, years of bombing had severely weakened the industrial base and damaged the overall civilian infrastructure. Exports had fallen to 31 percent of their 1938 figures with a resulting surge in the British trade deficit (Kennedy, 1981).

It is against this backdrop that the Allied and Neutral powers would meet in Chicago to decide the shape of the post-war international aviation system. The fact that the meeting would take place even before the conclusion of the war was an indication of the importance this young industry had gained in the eyes of world governments and their citizens. While the industry itself was young, the arguments heard in Chicago were old. The aviation community had heard them before Chicago and would hear them again over the subsequent years. The successes and failures of Chicago live on in today's international aviation system.

Questions

1 Why was the sky not treated in the same way as the seas when it came to freedoms?
2 Why do you believe the UK favored strict regulation of international aviation?
3 How did the US and European approaches to the aviation industry differ in the 1930s?
4 Justify the US approach to domestic development between the wars.
5 How did the end of World War II affect the agendas going into the Chicago Conference?
6 What role did the development of aircraft technology play in shaping the outcomes of World War I and World War II, particularly in terms of offensive and defensive strategies?
7 Discuss the impact of government intervention and ownership on the development of domestic aviation in Europe, using examples such as British Airways and Air France.
8 How did the economic and infrastructural devastation experienced by countries during and after World War II influence their priorities and agendas in the negotiations leading up to the Chicago Conference?

References

Allaz, C. (2004), *The history of air cargo and airmail from the 18th century*, Christopher Foyle Publishing, Paris.

Allen, G. S. (1981), *A short economic history of Japan*, McMillan, New York.

Ashworth, W. A. (1975), *A short history of the international economy since 1850*, Prentice Hall, London.

Badrocke, M. and Sunston, B. (1999), *The illustrated history of McDonnell Douglas Aircraft from Cloudster to Boeing*, Osprey, Oxford.

Badsey, S. (1990), *Modern air power: Fighters*, Gallery Books, New York.

Cooksley, M. K. and Robertson, B. (1998), *Air Warfare: The encyclopedia of twentieth century conflict*, Frank Cass, London.

Friedman, M. (1980), *Free to choose*, Harcourt Brace Jovanovich, New York.

Friedman, M. (1982), *Capitalism and freedom*, University of Chicago Press, Chicago.

Friedman, T. L. (2000), *The lexus and the olive tree*, 2nd ed., Farrar, Straus & Giroux, New York.

Glines, C. V. (1968), *The Saga of the airmail*, Van Nostrand, Princeton, NJ.

Graham, B. (1995), *Geography and air transport*, John Wiley and Sons, New York.

Groenewedge, A. D. (1996), *Compendium of international civil aviation*, International Aviation Development Corporation, Quebec.

Gross, P. M. (2002). 'Air France' in Tracy Irons-Georges (Ed.) *Encyclopedia of flight*, pp 52–54, Salem Press, Pasadena, CA

Hayek, F. A. (1960), *The constitution of liberty*, University of Chicago Press, Chicago.

Hayek, F. A. (1980), *Individualism and economic order*, University of Chicago Press, Chicago.

Hayek, F. A. (1994), *Hayek on Hayek: An autobiographical dialogue*, University of Chicago Press, Chicago.

Hosking, G. A. (1985), *A history of the Soviet Union*, London.

Kane, R. M. (1998), *Air transportation*, 13th ed., Kendall/Hunt Publishing, Allen & Unwin, Dubuque, IA.

Kennedy, P. M. (1981), *The realities behind diplomacy*, Cambridge University Press, London.

Landes, D. (1969), *The unbound prometheus: Technological change and industrial development in Western Europe from 1970 to the present*, Cambridge.

Marriott, L. (1998), *British airways book*, 2nd ed., Plymouth Publishing, Plymouth, MI.

Matloff, M. (1959), *Strategic planning for coalition warfare, 1943-1944*, US Government Printing Office, Washington, DC.

Nove, A. (1969), *An economic history of the USSR*, Penguin Group, Harmondsworth.

Overy, R. J. (1980), *The air war, 1939-1945*, Potomac Books Inc, New York.

Ricossa, A. (1972), 'Italy 1920-1970' in C. Cipolla (Ed.) *The fortuna economic history of Europe*, Barnes & Noble, London.

Sinha, D. (2001), *Deregulation and liberalization of the airline industry: Asia, Europe, North America, and Oceania*, Ashgate, Aldershot.

Sochor, E. (1991), *The politics of international aviation*, University of Iowa Press, Iowa City.

Wirth, D. and Young, J. (1980), *Ballooning: The compelte guide to riding the winds*, Random Hourse: New York.

Wright, G. (1968), *The ordeal of total war, 1939-1945*, Harper & Row, New York.

Yergin, D. and Stanislaw, J. (2002), *The commanding heights: The battle for the world economy*, Simon & Schuster, New York.

5 Chicago, The Windy City

Learning Objectives

After reading this chapter, you should have a good understanding of:

LO1: the four proposals considered at the Chicago Conference
LO2: the meaning of open skies as used by President Roosevelt and its implication for international aviation
LO3: the freedoms of the air – their application and limits
LO4: how the British All-Red Line ploy helped to bolster their position on international regulation
LO5: the economic and political interests that played out in Chicago among nations and airlines

Key Terms, Concepts & People

Dominion & Empire Conference	Chicago Conference	Technical Freedoms
ICAO	All-Red Line	IATA
Committee I	Bilateral	Bermuda Agreement

Crosswinds

The wind can be either a friend or a foe to the air traveler. A strong headwind can add time to your journey. A strong tailwind can help speed you along your way. Crosswinds, however, are unpredictable, and often dangerous. At the very least they can make it very difficult to maintain your planned course and reach your planned destination. Chicago has long been called the Windy City and anyone who has ever looked out over the lakefront on a fall day can understand the nickname. It is perhaps fitting that Chicago was the chosen site for the most famous aviation conference in history. The events that happened and didn't happen in Chicago still resonate. To understand the forces that created the international aviation landscape of today, you must understand Chicago.

Even as US President Franklin D. Roosevelt and British Prime Minister Winston Churchill were meeting in Quebec to plan the cross-channel invasion of Normandy and turn the tide of the war in Europe, the topic of a general meeting to discuss the future of air transportation was raised as an issue. US politicians had already begun to explore the

DOI: 10.4324/9781003405306-6

nature of a post-war aviation system. Henry Wallace, the US Vice-President, proposed a global network of air routes and international airports under the envisioned United Nations while Clare Boothe Luce, the American writer and politician, denounced this notion as 'globaloney' in her maiden address to the US Congress. Edward Warner, the vice-chairman of the US Civil Aviation Bureau, envisioned air navigation agreements that would prevent the 'return to the evil days when air transportation was regarded with caution and suspicion' (Sochor, 1990, p. 4).

The British had also been considering the issue of aviation. At the 1943 Dominion and Empire Conference, and then again at a May 1944 meeting of the Dominion ministers there were discussions about creating some system of reciprocal rights between the nations of the British Empire. Given the pre-war size of this empire, the British were well positioned by geography to establish a post-war global airline. In a White Paper published shortly after the 1944 meeting, the British proposed an international regulatory body with the power to make decisions about routes, frequencies, and fares. Yet, despite all this maneuvering about aviation, these two allies still had a war to win and the need to keep some level of internal peace and cooperation. Clearly, the crosswinds would be blowing in Chicago.

Setting the Table

When the delegates arrived in Chicago on November 1, 1944, they found four proposals awaiting them on the future shaping of the international environment. The opening message of President Roosevelt called on the delegates 'not to dally with the thought of creating great blocs of closed air, thereby tracing in the sky the conditions of future war' (Sochor, 1990, p. 8). His call was for an 'open sky' that could be exploited for the good of all mankind. Unsurprisingly, the US proposal called for a system of complete market access without any restrictions on routes, frequency, and fares. The British, who rightly feared that the large, undamaged aviation infrastructure, commercial fleet, and manufacturing capacity of the US would come to dominate the war-ravaged systems of Europe, saw the US proposal as self-interest masquerading as philosophical principle. The British plan reiterated their earlier White Paper, calling for a tightly regulated system governed by an independent international regulatory body. The Canadian proposal attempted to steer a middle course between the US and British positions by creating a multilateral regulatory body that would allow for limited competition within the overall system. The last proposal, jointly sponsored by the Australians and New Zealanders, called for the international ownership and management of all international air service. Committee I of the Chicago Conference, which was tasked with finding a clear way forward, would clearly have its work cut out.

Meanwhile, the other three committees worked on the technical issues of the conference, eventually completing work on the Interim Agreement on International Aviation, the Chicago Convention on International Civil Aviation, and the International Air Transport Agreement. The first treaty or convention established a temporary organization called the Provisional International Civil Aviation Organization to operate until the permanent organization created in the second document came into effect, the International Civil Aviation Organization (ICAO). The third convention is also known as the Five Freedoms Agreement (Table 5.1 the freedoms of the air including the subsequently added sixth, seventh, and eighth freedoms). The first two freedoms are known as technical freedoms. The remaining freedoms deal with the commercial rights of aviation to pick up and discharge passengers and cargo to, from, and through foreign nations.

Table 5.1 The Freedoms of the Air

Freedom	Description
First	The right to fly over the territory of a contracting State without landing
Second	The right to land on the territory of a contracting State for non-commercial purposes
Third	The right to transport passengers, cargo and mail from the State of registration of the aircraft to another State and set them down there
Fourth	The right to take on board passengers, cargo and mail in another contracting State and to transport them to the State of registration of the aircraft
Fifth	The right to transport passengers, cargo and mail between two other States as a continuation of, or as a preliminary to, the operation of the third or fourth freedoms
Sixth	The right to take on board passengers, cargo and mail in one State and to transport them to a third State after a stopover in the aircraft's State of registration and vice versa
Seventh	The right to transport passengers, cargo, and mail between two other States on a service which does not touch the aircraft's country of registration
Eighth	The right to transport passengers, cargo, and mail within the territory of a State which is not the aircraft's State of registration (full cabotage)
Ninth	The right to interrupt a service

While the technical committees were concluding their work, Committee I was dead-locked. Despite several exchanges between Roosevelt and Churchill on the issues facing the Committee and a series of private meetings between the key players, there would be no compromise on the basic positions of either the US or Great Britain. The US might have the planes to fly, but without landing rights they had only half the resources needed for a viable international system of carriers. They needed landing rights and Great Britain had potential landing sites galore. In fact, as the conference was opening the British publicized a 'plan' for creating an all-Commonwealth airline, which was called the All-Red Line after the cartographic practice of depicting Commonwealth nations in red. This All-Red line would be given exclusive rights to land on Commonwealth territory. In a world in which the Sun never set on the British flag, the All-Red Line was a reminder that the British did not come to the table empty-handed and nor would they allow a system of international aviation to be put in place that created serious disadvantages for Britain and other, smaller aviation nations.

Just as it began to seem that nothing would be achieved in Committee I, the Netherlands broke the deadlock by suggesting that the British might join in an agreement on the first two freedoms of overflight and technical landing or stopover. The Netherlands then moved immediately to guarantee these rights as part of a multilateral agreement. The British agreed to this proposal which became the fourth treaty or convention to come out of the Chicago Conference. The International Air Services Transit Agreement would eventually be signed by all of the participants and come into effect on June 30, 1945. It is now recognized by over 100 nations. The International Air Transport Agreement, which contained the remaining commercial freedoms, would be signed by 19 of the participants, but 9, including the US, would subsequently denounce it. The remaining nations would not endorse it, primarily for its fifth freedom condition. One final document would come out of the Convention. This form, the Bilateral Agreement for the Exchange of Routes and Services, would be adopted as part of the Final Act and serve to move the international aviation community forward in the absence of a broader, multilateral agreement on commercial aviation rights. The gavel fell on December 7, 1944, ending the Chicago Conference and the governmental delegates went home with their treaties and the bilateral form to decide on the next steps in the process of creating an international aviation system.

Not all of the individuals present in Chicago, however, went home immediately. Airline executives who had attended the conference as delegates or advisors to their national governments had quickly realized the implications of a failure by the conference to reach a broad multilateral agreement on commercial rights and fares. Showing admirable restraint, they waited until December 6 to begin discussions on the formation of a trade association for international carriers. This new association would be their voice in the international system and they hoped to be able to fill the void left in the commercial aviation system by the events in Chicago. The newly formed International Air Transport Association (IATA) called its first meeting in Havana in April 1945.

A Bilateral World

Without a multilateral agreement, it was left to the national governments of the world to begin the process of negotiating bilateral air service agreements. In fact, the United States had opened bilateral talks with the Dominions, China, and Russia even before the conference began and quickly returned to this process after the conference, signing a bilateral agreement with Spain on December 2, 1944, Denmark and Sweden on December 16, 1944, Iceland on January 27, 1945, Canada on February 7, 1945, and Switzerland and Norway on July 13, 1945 (Kane, 1999). However, it was not until 1946 that the United States and Great Britain were ready to sit down again and discuss those issues that had not been resolved at Chicago. The agreement that emerged from these talks would be called the Bermuda Agreement and would, by the agreement of both governments, become the model for all of the future agreements either side would negotiate. This form would henceforth replace the Chicago form as the world's standard Air Service Agreement.

The United States agreed to accept the British position on fares and rates which allowed the airlines to mutually set these matters subject to prior approval by both governments. The United Kingdom agreed to allow airlines to unilaterally set their own capacity, i.e. aircraft size and service frequency subject to subsequent review for unfair practices. Other key features of the agreement included designated (or named) routes and multiple carrier designation. In total, 'the Agreement clearly favored the United States which then accounted for about 60 percent of the world's passenger airline traffic and which had the largest and most efficient international airlines' (Toh, 1998, p. 61). This might reflect the fact that the British were also in negotiations with the US over a US$3.75 billion loan to rebuild its economy and thus had to negotiate from a position of relative weakness (Sochor, 1990). As a concession to the British, the United States did agree to allow the International Air Transport Association (IATA) to set international fares and cargo rates. They also decided to limit their pursuit of fifth freedom rights, which are seen in aviation circles as placing a foreign carrier in too close a competition for domestic traffic with a state's national carriers (Toh, 1998). By 1947, over 100 bilaterals had been signed around the world and the fare-setting power of IATA accepted in subsequent aviation accords (Sochor, 1990).

The last bilateral between the US and UK also illustrates the key points of bilaterals and the specific and restrictive nature of such air service agreements (Air Transport Association of America, 2001). Under the portion of the air service agreement (Table 5.2) entitled United Kingdom Routes: Atlantic combination air service is the following list:

Table 5.2 US–UK Bilateral Agreement

(A)	(B)	(C)
UK gateway points	Intermediate points	Points in US territory
London, Manchester, Prestwick/Glasgow, Belfast. Any UK point, excluding London.	Points in Luxembourg, The Netherlands, and the Republic of Ireland.	Atlanta, Boston, Charlotte, Chicago, Dallas/Fort Worth, Denver, Detroit, Houston, Las Vegas, Los Angeles, Miami, New Orleans, New York, Orlando, Phoenix
Up to two points to be selected and notified to the United States.	Points in Belgium, France, and Germany	Philadelphia, San Diego, San Francisco, Seattle, Tampa, Washington/ Baltimore.

In addition to the Atlantic combination air service, lists are provided of named routes for the Atlantic regional combination air service, Atlantic combination air service via Canada, Atlantic combination air service beyond Mexico City, Atlantic combination air service beyond to South America, Atlantic combination service beyond to Japan, Atlantic combination service beyond to the Pacific, Atlantic combination service beyond to Australia, Pacific combination service, Pacific combination service via Tarawa, Bermuda combination service, Caribbean combination service, Caribbean combination air service, Atlantic all-cargo service, Atlantic all-cargo service beyond to South America, Atlantic all cargo service beyond to Mexico, Pacific all-cargo services, Pacific all-cargo service via Tarawa, Bermuda all-cargo service, Caribbean all-cargo service, and Caribbean all-cargo air service.

Conversely, the principle of reciprocity demands that similar lists of named routes be included for US passenger and all-cargo service (Table 5.3). The following is the list of United States Routes: Atlantic combination service.

These excerpts demonstrate the reciprocal exchange of named routes as well as the application of fifth freedom (beyond) rights between the US and the UK. By the old

Table 5.3 US–UK Bilateral Agreement

(A)	(B)	(C)	(D)
US gateway points	Intermediate points	Points in UK territory	Points beyond
Anchorage, Atlanta Boston, Charlotte, Chicago, Cincinnati, Dallas/Fort Worth Detroit, Houston, Los Angeles, Miami, Minneapolis/St. Paul, Newark, New York, Philadelphia, Pittsburgh, Raleigh-Durham, San Francisco, Seattle, St. Louis, Washington/Baltimore	Shannon	London, Prestwick/ Glascow.	Berlin, Frankfurt, Hamburg, Munich,
Up to three points to be selected and notified to the United Kingdom.		Any UK point exc.	Oslo, one point in Western Europe to be selected

bilateral standards, the US–UK agreement was considered liberal in that it did not include capacity (aircraft size and route frequency) restrictions.

As an example of further restrictions, the US–Japanese bilateral distinguished between incumbent carriers which were provided for by the 1952 agreement (Northwest and United Airlines for the US and Japan Airlines and All Nippon Airways for the Japanese) and non-incumbent carriers (Delta Air Lines, American Airlines, and Continental Airlines) in naming routes. It also included sections on restricted frequency routes. In this case, non-incumbent airlines are permitted to operate up to 42 additional aggregate weekly round-trip frequencies on the following city-pair markets: Tokyo–New York, Tokyo–Chicago, Tokyo–San Francisco, Tokyo–Los Angeles, Tokyo–Honolulu, Tokyo–Guam/Saipan, Osaka–Los Angeles, Osaka–Los Angeles, Osaka–Honolulu, Nagoya–Honolulu, and Fukuoka–Honolulu (Air Transport Association of America, 2001).

Thus, a system for international aviation was established that pleased neither the US nor the UK, but it did create a framework that allowed the post-war world to take to the air again. By the standards of the twenty-first century, there was no 'shopping for the best airfare'; the airlines serving the same route charged the IATA agreed fare and this fare was set by those airlines so that it covered all the necessary costs and provided a profit to the participating airlines. There was no possibility of flying from a city or to a city not listed on the bilateral agreement; a country or an airline who wanted to provide such a service had to ask that the bilateral agreement be r-negotiated. If the response from either party was no, then there was little recourse.

Looking Back

Looking back on the Chicago Conference, it is clear that no compromise could have bridged the gap between the basic US and British positions. In the tug-of-war between free markets and political reality, political reality was the victor. Ironically, the lever that had allowed the British to hold off the US push for open skies would not long survive the end of World War II. At this point the British Empire would be replaced by a much looser Commonwealth of independent nations, all of whom had the right to determine the disposition of their own landing rights. Unfortunately, the system created by the major aeronautical players to meet their needs would not give these newly emerging nations a great deal of clout in the international system even if it did recognize their sovereign rights to control their own airspace.

The United States, for all of its philosophical preaching on open skies, was unwilling to grant more open access to the US market as it proved later when it renounced the International Air Transport Agreement rather than grant foreign carriers greater fifth freedom rights through the US (Sochor, 1990). This was seen as an admission by the US that there could be no stable commercial aviation system without reciprocity between countries (De la Rochere, 1971). While the United States was able to use its power and prestige following the war to sign a number of bilaterals advantageous to the US carriers, it did so by giving up the right to allow the markets to determine price. The US would again be accused of abandoning philosophical principle in favor of commercial and political reality when it began to take up the cause of open skies again after airline deregulation (Chapter 9). Frederik Sorensen of the European Commission Air Transport Policy Unit has said that "[o]pen skies is an American term which, as we see it, is synonymous with a free for all system depending on the good behavior of air carriers and only partial opening of the market" (1998, p. 125).

Looking Ahead

Out of the ashes of the post-World War II world, the phoenix of international aviation took off. If it did not fly as high as some would have liked or take the paths its creators envisioned, it did at least fly. The winds blowing out of Chicago did not make its flight either smooth or steady, but it has remained aloft. The next decades would see less dramatic but no less significant progress in the world of international aviation. The two international organizations born in Chicago, ICAO and IATA, would build on the framework laid out there (Chapter 6) only to have many of the structures set in place challenged by deregulation of the US airline industry (Chapter 9) and liberalization in European and Asian markets (Chapter 10). The events of the past would come back to challenge the future and demand that the world community grapple with them again.

The preamble to the Convention on International Civil Aviation laid out the goals of the Chicago Convention as follows:

WHEREAS the future development of international civil aviation can greatly help to create and preserve friendship and understanding among nations and peoples of the world, yet its abuse can become a threat to the general security; and

WHEREAS it is desirable to avoid friction and to promote that cooperation between nations and peoples upon which peace of the world depends;

THEREFORE, the undersigned governments having agreed on certain principles and arrangements in order that international civil aviation may be developed in a safe and orderly manner and that international air transport services may be established on the basis of equality of opportunity and operated soundly and economically; (Reprinted in Sochor, 1990)

This vision of international aviation as a global force for peace was perhaps utopian, but air travel has certainly brought the world closer together in time and space. Unfortunately, the events of 9/11 temporarily replaced this unifying vision with a grimmer reality of the role of aviation. The Russian–Ukrainian conflict has witnessed aviation as a tool of punishment rather than freedom. The fact remains that an airplane was merely the tool used to perpetrate the destruction of 9/11 and, like any tool, it served the wishes of its user. The US might continue to champion open skies while punishing the Russians for their invasion of Ukraine by denying Russian carriers the right of overflight. While the vision of ICAO has proven elusive, the goals have also presented their own challenges. As we will see in the next chapter ICAO would work hard to create a safe, orderly, and economical air transportation system and, by-and-large, they will achieve this goal.

The difficulty lies in the basis for this system – equality of opportunity. Free markets guarantee all the right to participate. They do not guarantee that the opportunities are equal or that the outcomes are equitable. In fact, free markets are about access rather than success and neither of these commodities is equally distributed. In a free market the opportunities of large, wealthy nations are greater than those of small, poor nations. The chances of success are also greater for the large and wealthy. Equity is about fairness, impartiality, and justice. Free markets are about competition and 'winner-takes-all'. Governments intervene in the market to provide opportunity and equity. All governments intervene to some extent. The level of intervention or regulation has been a subject for debate in economic and policy circles since Adam Smith. The push for liberalization in the airline industry would raise these issues once again for policy makers and the people they represent.

Questions

1 Analyze and assess the interests of the US and the UK in Chicago.
2 What were the four proposals for international regulation discussed in Chicago?
3 Imagine a world in which the Australian–New Zealand proposal had come to pass. How would it look?
4 Outline the freedoms of the air, including origin, destination and any intermediate points.
5 Discuss the achievements of the Chicago Convention.
6 Identify the defining features of a bilateral air service agreement.
7 How did bilateral air agreements, like the Bermuda Agreement between the US and UK, shape post-World War II aviation regarding routes, capacity, and fares?
8 What challenges and limitations did bilateral agreements pose in terms of promoting fair competition and accommodating emerging aviation markets?
9 How did outcomes from the Chicago Conference, including the creation of ICAO and IATA, influence the evolution of international aviation governance amid challenges like deregulation and liberalization?

References

Air Transport Association of America (2001), '*Air service rights in US international air transport agreements: A compilation of scheduled and charter service rights contained in US bilateral aviation agreements*', Washington, DC.
De la Rochere, J. D. (1971), *La Politique des Etats-Unis en matiere d'aviation civile*, Libraire de Droit et de Jurisprudence, Paris, pp. 30–36.
Kane, R. M. (1999), *Air transportation*, 13th ed., Kendall/Hunt Publishing, Dubuque, Iowa.
Sochor, E. (1990), *The politics of international aviation*, University of Iowa Press, Iowa City.
Sorensen, F. (1998), 'Open skies in Europe', in U.S. Department of Transportation (Ed.), *FAA commercial aviation forecast conference proceedings: Overcoming barriers to world competition and growth*, pp. 125–132, Office of Aviation Policy and Plans, Washington, DC.
Toh, R. S. (1998), 'Toward an international open skies regime: Advances, impediments, and impacts', *Journal of Air Transportation World Wide*, 3, pp. 61–70.

6 Shaping the World

Learning Objectives

After reading this chapter, you should have a good understanding of:

LO1: the founding of ICAO and IATA
LO2: the structure and policy-making process at ICAO
LO3: how IATA contributed to the early success of international aviation
LO4: the issues and outcomes of IATA Traffic Conferences
LO5: the economic and political interests that drive these two international organizations

Key Terms, Concepts & People

ICAO	IATA	ICAO Council
Warsaw Convention	SARPs & PANS	Traffic Conferences
Bermuda Agreement	Annexes	

First Chicago Then the World

The interim Agreement on International Civil Aviation established the framework for a Provisional International Civil Aviation Organization (PICAO), which functioned until 1947, when the required number of countries ratified the agreement to create a permanent organization. Over the coming years the International Civil Aviation Organization (ICAO) would work to develop the standards and practices followed by much of the world's aviation community. They would do so amidst the push and pull of the Cold War, the rapid development of aviation technology, and the limited funding often available to organizations associated with the United Nations. Like the United Nations, their actions could not be enforced on the world community; their recommendations could only be considered advisory. ICAO would thus struggle like the UN to achieve a consensus that would allow it to foster and develop the aviation system while balancing the needs of a diverse and fractious constituency.

The other organization born in Chicago, the International Air Transport Association (IATA), would receive recognition of its role at the 1946 bilateral talks between the US and the UK. It would not suffer from the kind of tension that divided ICAO. Its members, international airlines, would set about the task of setting the fares, dividing the world's

DOI: 10.4324/9781003405306-7

international routes, establishing the standards for interlining (transfer between carriers), and devising the methods of revenue sharing that would govern the international aviation system until these powers were slowly eroded by domestic air transport deregulation and international liberalization (Chapter 9). ICAO and IATA would work together on many issues related to safe air transport operation, the standardization of documentation and procedures, and the development of legal agreements such as the Warsaw Convention on airline liability. Together, these two organizations would shape the post-World War II international aviation system.

Setting the Standards

ICAO is composed of appointed representatives of all nations interested in international civil aviation (now totaling 193 contracting states as of January 2023). It is governed by a sovereign body, the Assembly, which meets at least once every three years. Each nation represented has one vote on key matters and the majority rules. The governing body of ICAO is the Council. The Council is elected from the Assembly for a three-year term and is composed of 36 members, who are elected from three categories of ICAO general members. The first category is states of chief importance to air transport. The second is states that make the largest contribution to the provision of air navigation facilities. The final category is composed of states designated to insure that all of the regions of the globe are represented. Table 6.1 provides a list of the nation's currently serving on the Council.

These nations maintain a permanent presence at ICAO's headquarters in Montreal, Canada, where they are responsible for the day-to-day operations of the organization. The Council adopts the Standards and Recommended Practices (SARPs) and approves the Procedures of Air Navigation Services (PANS) that are at the heart of the work of ICAO. Assisting the Council are the Air Navigation Commission (consisting of 19 members with "suitable qualifications and experience") which is responsible for technical matters, the Air Transport Bureau responsible for matters relating to sustainable development (economic, environmental, and security), the Air Navigation Bureau, the Legal

Table 6.1 ICAO Council Membership – 2022–25

Argentina	Jamaica
Australia	Japan
Austria	Malaysia
Bolivia	Mauritania
Brazil	Mexico
Canada	Nigeria
Chile	Qatar
China	Republic of Korea
Egypt	Romania
El Salvador	Saudi Arabia
Equatorial Guinea	Singapore
Ethiopia	South Africa
France	Spain
Germany	United Arab Emirates
Ghana	United Kingdom
Iceland	United States
India	Venezuela
Italy	United Arab Emirates

Affairs and External Relations Bureau, the Administration Bureau, and the Technical Cooperation Bureau.

Proposals to amend or add new SARPs come from ICAO-sponsored international meetings, deliberative bodies within the organization itself, the Secretariat, the United Nations or other interested international organizations. ICAO works closely with such organizations as the World Meteorological Organization, the International Telecommunications Union, the Universal Postal Union, the World Health Organization, the International Maritime Organization (all U.N.-affiliated), the International Air Transport Association, the Airports Council International, the International Federation of Air Line Pilots, and the International Council of Aircraft Owner and Pilots Association (all non-governmental organizations).

Once an issue is brought to ICAO for consideration, it is referred on to the Air Navigation Commission. These individuals are nominated by Contracting States and appointed by the Council. Other persons may participate as observers. The Commission is assisted by the Air Navigation Bureau as well as panels and working groups nominated by Contracting States and appointed by the Commission. These individuals serve based on their personal expertise rather than as representatives of any Contracting State. Once the Commission submits a SARP to the Council, a two-thirds vote of its members is required for adoption. If a majority of the Contracting States do not disapprove it, the SARP becomes effective on the established date. SARPs are considered binding, although States that cannot comply can file a 'difference' that is published by ICAO in Supplements to the Annexes. This process takes roughly 5–7 years to reach completion, which means that the work of ICAO progresses slowly. PANS are developed in a similar way; however, they are not binding and no differences need to be filed. Table 6.2 lists the annexes and areas, which are covered by ICAO.

Other activities of ICAO include the joint financing of navigation services on the high seas or in areas where no nation can be charged with the responsibility. Iceland and

Table 6.2 Annexes to the ICAO Convention

Annex	Subject
1	Personnel Licensing
2	Rules of the Air
3	Meteorological Service
4	Aeronautical Charts
5	Units of Measurement
6	Operation of Aircraft
7	Aircraft Nationality and Registration Marks
8	Airworthiness of Aircraft
9	Facilitation
10	Aeronautical Telecommunications
11	Air Traffic Service
12	Search and Rescue
13	Aircraft Accident and Incident Investigation
14	Aerodromes
15	Aeronautical Information Service
16	Environmental Protection
17	Security
18	Safe Transport of Dangerous Goods
19	Safety Management

Greenland are examples of the latter. Considering that their own aircraft represent less than 3 percent of the trans-Atlantic traffic, the burden for navigational services is shared by other nations. The Legal Affairs Committee prepares drafts for key international conferences related to aviation such as the conventions held in Geneva (1948) and Rome (1952). ICAO's Technical Co-operation Programme works with the United Nations Development Programme (UNDP) on projects aimed at developing the aviation system of developing nations. The Trainair programme provides assistance to national and regional civil aviation training institutes. Finally, ICAO provides expert services such as site selection and the design of airstrips and air traffic control systems. The magnitude of work of ICAO seems overwhelming, particularly in light of their limited funding. Much of their efforts depend on the support, both technical and monetary, that comes from the Contracting States (ICAO, 2002).

The key to understanding ICAO is in realizing that like the United Nations in general it has *no* independent enforcement power; it cannot make its members implement any of its standards. In fact, its website clearly points out that it is not a global regulator and its standards never supersede national regulatory requirements. Countries that transgress ICAO standards are offered support to achieve compliance and might be condemned for certain actions by ICAO members, but this is an exercise in public relations and free expression. When or if a vote is taken on the issue of SARPs or PANS, it is the perfunctory end to months or years of consensus building at ICAO. If consensus is not initially achieved on certain issues, then all parties revise, rework, or reframe the issue until it is secured. It is a painstaking process, but it has (and is) producing some very positive results.

After years of debate, ICAO established in January 1999, the Universal Safety Oversight Program. The program was expanded in 2005 to include provisions in all the safety-related annexes of the Chicago Convention. In 2010, ICAO adopted a resolution to transition the program to a Continuous Monitoring Approach. The objectives of this program include 1) monitoring State oversight systems through an online platform, 2) validating State progress through on- and off-site activities, and 3) assessing the effectiveness and sustainability of oversight systems (ICAO, 2023).

Setting the Fares

Under the 1945 Articles of Association, the aims of IATA are:

To promote safe, regular, and economical air transportation for the benefit of the peoples of the world, to foster air commerce, and to study the problems connected therewith;

To provide means for collaboration among the air transport enterprise engaged directly or indirectly in international air transport service;

To cooperate with the newly created International Civil Aviation Organization and other international organizations (IATA, 2002).

In the early years, IATA worked on such issues as the Multilateral Interline Traffic Agreements, Passenger and Cargo Services Conference Resolutions, and Passenger and Cargo Agency Agreements & Sales Agency Rules. The Interline Agreements involved ensuring the acceptance of other carriers' tickets and waybills. The Conference Resolutions prescribed standard formats and specifications for tickets and waybills. The Agency Agreements governed the relationships between IATA airlines and their accredited agents. A Clearing House was also established in 1947 to handle debt settlements between carriers largely arising from interlining (flights involving multiple carriers with each flying a different leg of the total trip). In the twenty-first century, we tend to take the modern banking system for granted, but in the years following World War II, international aviation was hampered by the fact when a ticket was sold in Country A involving airlines from Country A and Country B, there was no certainty in the mind of the airline from Country B that they would receive their share of the proceeds from that sold ticket. IATA stepped in to become the trusted intermediary, holding the money from the sold tickets and dispersing them accordingly to each prospective airline. There is no doubt that this system, and the many other actions to standardize and facilitate international air travel, allowed for the market to grow and improve in safety and efficiency. However, it was a system designed by airlines to benefit airlines. Like tightly regulated systems everywhere, it was a comfortable, low-stress/low-competition environment where higher costs could be passed on to consumers.

It was the role of IATA's Traffic Conferences that would eventually come under intense scrutiny from a liberalizing world air transportation system. Under the Bermuda Agreement of 1946, IATA was delegated the role of establishing fares and rates subject to government approval. According to IATA, the goal of the system was to establish 'coherent fares and rates patterns'. Such a system would avoid 'inconsistencies between tariffs affecting neighboring countries – and thereby avoiding traffic diversion' (IATA, 1996). In effect, there was a set fare for any given international route that any IATA member was expected to charge. If there continued to be an imbalance in the revenues earned by the designated carriers on such a route, then a revenue-sharing or pooling agreement could be worked out to equalize the revenues of both sides (Taneja, 1988). There were intermittent efforts in ICAO to question the tariff (fare) setting role of IATA, but during the last such effort ICAO concluded that 'at present, there is no justification for ICAO to undertake specific studies and other economic work on the subject of airline tariffs' (Sochor, 1990, p. 17).

Following the events discussed in Chapter 9, IATA would be forced to reconsider its role in fare setting. It did so first by establishing a 'two-tier' system. Under this system, the IATA Trade Association became responsible for technical, legal, financial, and traffic services. The Tariff Coordination became responsible for fares and rates. An airline could participate in the Trade Association without participating in the Tariff Coordination activities. Over time, IATA has placed increasing emphasis on the trade association activities and come to derive much of its funding from the educational and product marketing activities of the Association. To all intents and purposes, the new IATA does not engage in fare or rate setting but allows these activities to be the domain of the airlines themselves.

A New Day Dawning

IATA and ICAO would emerge from the Chicago Convention to shape the aviation system that would develop after World War II. This system would preside over an aviation era in which air travel would come to be seen as a safe and reliable mode of transportation, but it would not yet be seen as a transportation mode for the masses; achieving this goal would require fares to fall to levels that the 'common man' could afford. This vision of air travel was the goal of deregulation. Markets and competition, rather than governments, would determine fares, destinations, and service levels (Chapter 9). First, the manufacturers and the airlines that they supplied would have to get back to the business of civil aviation and establish the industry that would be turned on its head in the late 1970s. Few people in the international aviation system would realize that the 'end of an era' was coming, but the passage in the United States of the Airline Deregulation Act of 1978 would be just such a watershed. For the cozy system of routes and fares set up by IATA, it would mean radical change. For ICAO, this new era would mean more issues of safety and security would be added to their already full plate of issues.

Questions

1 How is ICAO structured and funded?
2 How are SARPs developed?
3 What role does ICAO play in developed and developing nations?
4 Has ICAO fulfilled the vision of its founders? Why or why not?
5 Who controls the bulk of the work and agenda at ICAO?
6 What was the effect of IATA's Traffic Conferences on fares and competition?
7 Assess the role of IATA in aviation. Whose interests does it serve?
8 How has ICAO adapted to the changing dynamics of the aviation industry since its establishment, particularly in addressing emerging challenges such as cybersecurity and climate change?
9 In what ways has IATA's role shifted over time from fare setting to focusing more on technical, legal, and financial aspects of air transportation? What factors influenced this transition?
10 How did the Airline Deregulation Act of 1978 in the United States reshape the international aviation landscape, particularly in terms of challenging the traditional roles of ICAO and IATA?

References

International Air Transport Association (1996), 'Early days', electronic edition, www.iata.org
International Air Transport Association (2002), electronic edition, www.iata.org
International Civil Aviation Organization (2002), 'Meeting caps most productive triennium in recent ICAO history', News Release, October 9, pp. 1–4.
International Civil Aviation Organization (2023), electronic edition, www.icao.int
Sochor, E. (1990), *The politics of international aviation*, University of Iowa Press, Iowa City.
Taneja, N. K. (1988), *The international airline industry*, Lexington Books, Lexington.

7   The View from Space

Learning Objectives

After reading this chapter, you should have a good understanding of:

LO1:   the early history of the US and USSR space programs
LO2:   the history and extent of satellite activity, including early commercial launches
LO3:   the unmanned exploration activity of various countries
LO4:   the current space station activity
LO5:   the five United Nations space treaties

Key Terms, Concepts & People

V2 rockets	Robert Goddard	Werner von Braun
Yuri Gagarin	Neil Armstrong	Soyuz
Mercury	Apollo	Sputnik
Outer Space Treaty	ISS	Tiangong

Science Fiction

It is amazing to remember that Jules Verne published *From the Earth to the Moon* in 1865 at a time when the US was still struggling to overcome the Civil War, but he was only the first of many authors in what would become known as the field of science fiction to imagine trips to the Moon, Mars, or other distant places in the dark of space. Even as aviators like as Jorge Chavez were striving to set new altitude records by flying over the Alps – a feat he accomplished on September 8, 1910, reaching a height of 1,647 meters – space was still the stuff of fiction for much of the rest of the world (Gagliardi, 2009). This did not, however, stop a young man, Robert H. Goddard, from experimenting with rockets and the fuel to propel them. On March 26, 1926, these experiments paid off and Goddard is now credited with the first launch of a liquid-fuel rocket. This event was not widely reported at the time and did not fire the imagination or the fears of the world as much as happened with the USSR's 1957 launch of Sputnik. Weighing 183 lb, and being only the size of a basketball, this little satellite 'fired the shot' that started the Great Space Race (Bellis, 2013).

DOI: 10.4324/9781003405306-8

Racing for Space

In his introduction to the 1994 book *Moon Shot: The Inside Story of America's Race to the Moon* by fellow astronauts Alan Sheppard and Deke Slayton, Neil Armstrong would sum up the space race as an effort to demonstrate ideological superiority through technological leadership. The effort, he noted, would consume enormous resources, enjoy great successes, suffer tragic failures, and end with the Cold War enemies joining forces to continue exploring space. While Armstrong saw the race ending with the Cold War, the truth is that Americans claimed victory in the space race in 1969 when he set foot on the Moon and the human spaceflight program in the US has been largely adrift since achieving this goal (Coppinger, 2010). However, this is a question that we will explore later in the chapter. For now, it is enough to relive the excitement of the first steps into space.

If Sputnik is seen as the public event that started the race, then the hidden beginning was in Germany at the end of World War II when the wartime allies, the United States and the Union of Soviet Socialist Republics, were quietly appropriating scientists from the German V2 project (Boyne, 2007). The US was fortunate to accept the surrender of Dr. Werner von Braun along with 117 of his key V2 team near the Bavarian ski resort of Oberjoch in May of 1945; however, they were to languish in Fort Bliss, Texas until 1950 when the US Army confirmed the existence of a Soviet rocket program. At this point von Brain and his team were moved to Huntsville, Alabama to begin work on the Redstone rocket, which was named after the arsenal there. Meanwhile in Central Asia, at a site that would become the world's first spaceport (Baikonur Cosmodrome), the Russians were working hard on the R-7 (Sheppard & Slayton, 1994). Their initial goal was the development of Inter-Continental Ballistic Missiles (ICBM), a race the Russians won in 1957 with the launch of the R-7, a rocket four times more powerful than the Redstone. This vehicle certainly proved powerful enough to launch Sputnik I and Sputnik 2 just 31 days later. The US response was the Atlas rocket, which would then launch America's first satellite, Explorer I, in 1958 (Godwin, 2006).

For the sake of simplifying our journey, we will divide the discussion of space into the following broad sections: manned spaceflight, space stations, orbital satellites, and exploration. Each of these areas would witness great progress over the decades, but nothing would evoke the excitement of humanity as much as the thought of manned exploration.

Manned Spaceflight

Table 7.1 outlines the key events in the race for space, listing both its accomplishments and its tragedies, but the men who would be part of the race were already breaking speed and altitude records as military test pilots for the US and USSR. The manned space effort of the US would officially begin with the April 9, 1959 announcement of the selection of the first seven astronauts for the Mercury program – Malcolm Scott Carpenter, Leroy Gordon Cooper, John Herschel Glenn, Virgil Grissom, Walter M Schirra, Alan Shepard, and Deke Slayton. Their story was later chronicled in the book (and movie) *The Right Stuff*. The book first appeared in 1979 with the movie appearing in 1983 (Wolfe, 2001). Of the seven, Alan Sheppard would be selected to become the first American in space (May 1961). He would be followed in July 1961 by Virgil Grissom. Of course, neither could claim to be the first man in space. That honor had already been taken by the Russian cosmonaut, Yuri Gagarin, who would launch in April 1961. The Russians had scored another first in the Great Race. Two days after Gagarin's flight, US President John F. Kennedy would call together a group to discuss the US response. This would become clear just 20 days after

Table 7.1 Key Events in the Race for Space

Date	Event
March 26, 1926	Robert H. Goddard launches the first liquid-fuel rocket
June 13, 1940	The first V-2 rocket launched from Peenemunde, Germany
October 4, 1957	The USSR launches the first manmade satellite named Sputnik
January 31, 1958	The US successfully launches its first satellite, Explorer I
August 27, 1958	The USSR launches Sputnik 3 with two dogs aboard
October 1, 1958	NASA is established to take over from NACA
May 28, 1959	The US launches monkeys Able & Baker into space
April 12, 1961	Russian Yuri Gagarin becomes the first man in space
May 5, 1961	Alan Sheppard Jr becomes the first American in space
May 25, 1961	President John F. Kennedy calls for the US to put a man on the Moon by the end of the decade
February 20, 1962	John Glenn becomes the first American to orbit the Earth
June 16, 1963	Russian Valentina Tereshkova becomes the first woman in space
March 18, 1965	Russian Aleksei Leonov performs the first spacewalk.
February 3, 1966	Russian probe Luna 9 becomes the first manmade object to land on the Moon
January 27, 1967	US-USSR sign a treaty banning nuclear weapons in space Apollo I cabin fire kills astronauts Grissom, White, and Chaffee
April 23, 1967	Cosmonaut Vladimir Komarov killed in Soyuz 1after failure during orbit led to crash landing
July 20, 1969	Neil Armstrong and Buzz Aldrin make the first successful manned landing on the Moon
November 1969	Apollo 12 lands on the Moon
April 1970	Apollo 13 launches for the Moon but a liquid oxygen tank prevents a landing
February 1971	Apollo 14 lands on the Moon
July 1971	Apollo 15 lands on the Moon
April 1972	Apollo 16 lands on the Moon
December 1972	Apollo 17 is the last manned spacecraft to land on the Moon

Shepard's first flight when President Kennedy would tell Congress that the US was committed to landing a man on the Moon before the end of the decade (Sheppard & Slayton, 1994). The finish line had now been set and the racers now had their sights set on a clear goal.

Of course, there was a long way to go from becoming the first man in space to a landing on the Moon. For the US, the single-man Mercury program would give way to the Gemini program, which launched its first two Americans, Virgil Grissom and John Young, into space in March 1965 in Gemini 3. While the Mercury program involved a largely automated craft, the Gemini was designed to maneuver in space and would be the testing ground for both the spacewalk (Gemini 4 & 9) and a docking between two orbital craft (Geminis 6 and 8).

For the US, the next step would now be the Apollo manned lunar landing program. This began tragically as the crew of Apollo I, Virgil Grissom, Edward H. White, and Roger B. Chaffee, were all killed in a command module fire on January 27, 1967. On the very same day the US and USSR had signed a treaty banning nuclear weapons in space. In a 3,300-page report into the Apollo fire, the investigating committee cited deficiencies in the areas of design, engineering, manufacturing, and quality with examples of flaws in the installation, wiring, welding, and soldering of joints that led to the presence of flammable coolant in the module. This coolant combined with a spark to kill the astronauts in just 8.5 seconds, destroying the module and dealing the US space effort its first major setback. It also prompted a massive effort of redesign and construction that would result in the development of a new Apollo. In 1968, the backup crew for Apollo I would launch in Apollo 7, marking a point at which the US space effort was firmly back on track (Sheppard & Slayton, 1994).

The Russians had been busy during the Mercury and Gemini program, making more history with the 1963 launch of the first woman in space (Valentina Tereshkova) and the first man to walk in space in 1965 (Aleksei Leonov). They had also landed the first spacecraft on the Moon. Sadly, eighty-six days after the Apollo I fire, they too experienced tragedy as Cosmonaut Vladimir Komarov crashed in Soyuz 1 following technical problems in orbit which caused the spacecraft to lose stability. The Russians would experience further problems with their N-1 superbooster. In early 1969, the N-1 had a catastrophic failure on launch that would clear the way for the US to achieve its goal of landing a man on the Moon by the end of the decade. While there would be six more Apollo flights after Apollo 11 made the first manned landing, it was the Apollo 11 flight that captured the world's imagination. With the exception of Apollo 13, whose malfunctions threatened the safety of its crew, none of the other Apollo missions is remembered, although five more did land at various locations. Apollos 18 to 20 was canceled in the aftermath of the failed Apollo 13 mission amid growing complaints about the costs and risks of manned exploration. There have been no new footprints on the Moon or any other heavenly body since the Apollo 17 landing in December 1972. Human exploration in space would now move on to a focus on a series of space stations. The unmanned activity in satellites and exploration would continue, but without the same fanfare that had accompanied the Great (Manned) Race to Space.

Space Stations

While President Kennedy made the Moon the ultimate goal of the Great Space Race, it was certainly not the ultimate goal for many of those involved in the space effort in either the US or Soviet Union; many involved in these countries' space programs had even more far-reaching ambitions for mankind's efforts, but, as Neil Armstrong noted above, political ideology and military ambitions drove many of the supporters of such exploration. These backers would decide on the short- and long-term goals and also the budget to achieve them. As far back as the 1940s, Werner von Braun and his German collaborators had envisioned a path into space that started with a space station, followed by bases on the Moon and Mars. For the engineers and early visionaries in the space movement, there were a range of goals. For them, the station was not a goal in itself but rather a means to reach many grander objectives; this was to be where great interplanetary spaceships were constructed and launched to avoid the technical problems of launch through the atmosphere. Not everyone would agree with the stepping stone approach to interplanetary exploration and colonization, but it would become the default, notional vision against which others would argue (Zubrin & Wagner, 1994). In the US, NASA had been considering and planning for an orbiting station since the early 1960s; however, the Apollo program, with its goal of landing a man on the Moon, had pushed the idea off of the radar until NASA engineers proposed launching the third stage of the Saturn rocket (which had been used for the Apollo program) as a first-step space station. The idea had obvious appeal because of the relatively low cost, since it involved existing technology. The program was named Skylab and was to consist of an orbital workshop, airlock, multiple docking adapter and telescope mount (Belew & Stuhlinger, 1973). All components were launched over a period in 1973 and housed nine astronauts for 171 days in 1973–74. For NASA, Skylab was already a race against government funders. With the space race to the Moon won and the failure of Apollo 13 (1970), many critics of the cost of the space program were questioning what they saw as a waste of taxpayer money (Sheppard & Slayton, 1994). Skylab would keep the US manned space effort alive until a new goal (and budget) could be agreed upon in Washington. While its mission officially ended in 1973, Skylab stayed in orbit until 1979, when it disintegrated in the Earth's atmosphere.

While the US was developing Skylab, the Soviet Union launched Salyut-1 in 1971. Several versions of the first-generation station were launched before a second generation of Soviet stations replaced them, beginning in 1977. The third-generation Soviet station was the Mir, which first launched in 1986. Cosmonauts Titov and Maranov set a record for the longest stay in space when they returned to Earth after spending a year on the station. The Mir space station continued in operation until January 2001 (Launius, 2003). Over this period, the Soviets would amass a great deal of experience in space from their space station platforms.

The International Space Station (ISS) is a cooperative program between various national space agencies with each country contributing and operating different modules on the ISS. The current members of the ISS program are the United States (NASA), Europe (ESA), Russia (Russian Federal Space Agency), Canada (CSA), and Japan (JAXA). The ISS presented several challenges. The first was integrating hardware produced through different engineering approaches and built by different manufacturing processes (Stockman, Boyle, & Bacon, 2009). The second challenge was a legal one which was resolved with the Intergovernmental Agreement signed in January 1998. The agreement established each partner's rights and responsibilities in addition to guaranteeing that new inventions would be registered in the country of their discoverer. Module launches were conducted with the Space Shuttle and Soyuz rocket, then assembly occurred in space over the course of 125 flights (Stockman, Boyle, & Bacon, 2009). Table 7.2 outlines the contribution of each partner to the ISS. In addition to the many science experiments conducted on the ISS, the station has hosted the first space tourists who have traveled courtesy of the Russian Space Agency, Roscosmos.

Table 7.2 ISS Equipment and Components

Component	Country
Centrifuge	USA
Columbus Laboratory	Europe
Cupola Observational Module	Europe
Destiny Lab Module	USA
Hab Module	USA
Integrated Truss Assembly	USA
Joint Airlock	USA
Kibo Laboratory	Japan
Multi-purpose Logistics Module	Europe
Port Solar Panels	USA
Progress Resupply Vehicle	Russia
Science Power Platform Solar Panels	Russia
Space Robotics System	Canada
Soyuz Russian Capsule	Russia
Starboard Solar Panels	USA
Thermal Control System Radiators	USA
Zarya Control Module	Russia
Zvezda Service Module	Russia

Source: http://old.mfb-geo/lev0/News_old_e/news_old_e4.html

The Chinese have announced plans for their own space station, Tiangong (Palace of the Heavens), to be fully operational in the 2020–22 timeframe. The first module, which was launched in September 2011, is composed of a laboratory, a resource module and a docking mechanism and will be powered by two solar arrays. In June 2012, three Chinese astronauts became the first to visit the station (David, 2011).

Space Shuttle. For the US, the era of the space station was also the era of the Space Shuttle. Born in a time of declining NASA budgets and questions on the direction of the US space program, the Space Shuttle was the first reusable spacecraft, designed to launch like a rocket and land like an aircraft (a glider actually). It was also designed to carry large payloads, such as satellites and equipment needed for the ISS. In essence, the Shuttle would be the bus that flew people and material to the space station to prepare for the long-range exploration of space envisioned by the early pioneers. In an effort to gain funding for the project, NASA would design a shuttle to meet both military and civilian needs. Originally estimated to cost $10 billion to develop and with an annual operating cost of $2 billion, NASA envisioned a launch rate of 30 flights per year, but military requirements raised both the payload weight and design costs. Ultimately, compromises to get military support and congressional budget approval meant 'getting' a shuttle that was not what NASA wanted. Conflicting goals and constant budget wars would take its toll on the future life of the Shuttle. The true launch costs would prove to be 20 times more than the original estimates, which was too high to attract a large number of commercial customers. Further, the engines were not powerful enough to support the original projected payload weight. Turnaround times for this reusable space vehicle would be longer than anticipated. In short, the Shuttle would never even achieve 12 launches a year. It would never break even and there would be no profit with this bus line to the space station (Vaughan, 1996). The Shuttle would fly 135 missions between April 2, 1981 and July 21, 2011 from its home base at Kennedy Space Center in Florida before its retirement (NASA, 2013). It would give the world many thrilling take-offs and landings as well as a number of major accomplishments, but it is perhaps the tragedies associated with it that will linger the longest in the memory of a generation. These tragedies would come to tarnish the image of NASA as Congressional investigations, mountains of official reports, and a series of books would explore how the agency and industry that 'put a man on the Moon' had failed so badly. The official verdicts would argue that both the *Challenger* and *Columbia* accidents were not simply the result of individual mistakes, although these did occur. Officially, it would be concluded that the accidents were 'socially organized and systematically produced' by a dysfunctional organization (NASA) that had allowed the shifting winds of government funding and goal setting to distort their decision-making, risk estimating, and organizational culture in ways that created the climate for these technological failures (Vaughan, 1996). Perhaps Robert Zubrin summed up the post-Moon landing US space effort best when he noted that "[t]here can be no progress without a goal. The American space program, which began so brilliantly with Apollo…has spent most of the subsequent…years floundering without direction" (Zubrin & Wagner, 1994). He might have also added without adequate and stable budget as a further reason for floundering, but this is a topic that we will pick up again in Chapter 22.

Satellites

In 1945, a genuine science fiction writer, Arthur C. Clarke, proposed the concept of geostationary satellite communications. These involve three types of orbits: geostationary (or geosynchronous), asynchronous, and polar. A geosynchronous satellite is always positioned over the same area of land, asynchronous orbits pass overhead multiple times in a day, and polar orbits are designed for low altitude and are commonly used for mapping and photography. In order to place a satellite in a given orbit, a precise launch window must be calculated to consider escape velocity and the Earth's rotation around its own axis (Brown, 2000). Such issues will also affect the 'ideal' location of a spaceport (Chapter 22).

The first commercial satellite launch in the US occurred in 1962 after President John F. Kennedy signed the Communications Satellite Act (1962). This satellite, Telstar 1, was privately funded by AT&T and Bell Telephone Laboratories (Findley, 1962). One of the missions for the Space Shuttle was satellite launching; however, following the *Challenger* accident, President Reagan stopped this activity, opening the way for private launch providers (Fought, 1989).

According to LaFleur (2010), there were 6,854 satellites launched by 30 countries as of December 31, 2009 for a yearly average of 132. Of this total, Russia has launched 60.5 percent, the US 30 percent, and the rest of the world less than 10 percent. The most common type of satellite is used for forecasting and tracking weather. Communication satellites are another common type of satellite that makes possible satellite TV and radio as well as global phone coverage. Navigation systems, such as the US Global Positioning System (GPS), the European Galileo, Russian GLONASS, Chinese Compass, and India Regional Navigational Satellite System, also rely on satellites. The US system includes 31 Navstar satellites in 6 orbital planes to provide global coverage. A number of other satellites provide either search and rescue services (Emergency Locator Transmitters or ELTs) or they provide information of a military nature.

Finally, there is a large class of satellites used for scientific research. One of the most famous is the Hubble Space Telescope, which was launched in 1990 from the US Space Shuttle. Other science satellites include the Compton Gamma Ray Observatory, the Chandra X-Ray Observatory, the Spitzer Space Telescope, and the James Webb Space Telescope (JWST). This last satellite is the planned replacement for the Hubble and is set to launch in 2018. Since it is estimated that over 9,000 scientific papers have been published based on the data from Hubble alone, this class of satellite has been invaluable to the pursuit of scientific discovery (The Space Telescope Science Institute, 2013).

Building and launching satellites is an expensive proposition and was once the sole domain of large governments. It is estimated that the James Webb Space Telescope (JWST) will have a total cost of $6.5 billion (JWST Independent Comprehensive Review Panel, 2010). Of course, not all satellites are this complex or expensive. Brown (2000) has estimated that launching a satellite costs between $50 and $400 million. Thus, a growing number of private companies are launching their own satellites, such as DirecTV and Dish Network. In addition, private companies such as SpaceX and Virgin Galactic are planning to enter the launch business.

Exploration

The list of unmanned space exploration would stretch for several pages and include many failures. Excluding satellites intended solely for Earth orbit, the first mission outside Earth orbit was Luna 1 launched by the USSR in 1959 and intended for impact with the lunar surface; it missed and ended up in solar orbit. On September 12, 1959, Luna 2 became the first object to reach the lunar surface. Table 7.3 lists some of the successful highlights of unmanned exploration. Sadly, there have often been more misses than successes because the craft missed the target, failed to launch, or failed to land successfully. In fact, *Universe Today* noted in 2008 that nearly two-thirds of the mission to Mars failed in some way.

Table 7.3 Highlights of Unmanned Space Exploration

Mission (Country)	Launch date	Purpose
Luna 1 (USSR)	January 2, 1959	Impact the Moon; Now orbiting the Sun
Luna 2 (USSR)	September 12, 1959	Impacted the Moon
Pioneer 5 (US)	March 11, 1960	Solar monitor
Mariner 2	August 27, 1962	Venus flyby
Venera 7 (USSR)	August 17, 1970	Successfully landed on Venus
Mar 3 (USSR)	May 28, 1971	First successful landing on Mars
Pioneer 10	March 3, 1972	Jupiter flyby
Mariner 10	November 3, 1973	First aircraft to visit Mercury
Voyager 1 (US)	September 5, 1977	Flyby outer planets
Voyager 2 (US)	August 20, 1977	Flyby Jupiter & Saturn
Sakiqake (Japan)	January 7, 1985	Flyby Halley's Comet
Giotto (EU)	July 2, 1985	Flyby comets
Hubble Space Telescope	April 25, 1990	Exploration of deep space
Cassini & Huygen Probe	October 15, 1997	Saturn Orbiter
New Horizon	January 19, 2006	Keiper Belt object
Mars Rover	November 26, 2011	Exploring Mars

Source: Windows to the Universe http://www.windows2universe.org/space_missions/unmanned_table.html

While this is a very high failure rate, even for space exploration, it does serve to illustrate the risks involved in space exploration, manned and unmanned. Perhaps one of the most successful robotic missions to Mars has been the rover *Opportunity*, which was launched in 2003 and continues to operate. It recently made one of its most amazing discoveries – a rock rich in clay materials with a water content that might have favored early life (and was less acidic than observed in earlier discoveries). The more recently launched *Curiosity* rover has found similar formations (Morris, 2013). These types of missions have yielded data that scientists around the world consider groundbreaking, but while the volume of information sent back to Earth would fill many library bookshelves, some have questioned the cost of such endeavors (Foust, 2012). It is certainly true that unmanned exploration has never captured the attention or imagination like the manned accomplishments of space. To a generation raised on *Star Trek*, the marvels of new special effects space adventures are poor compensation for the real thing – bases on the Moon and Mars, journeys beyond the solar system.

For All Mankind

Before ending this chapter, it is important to note the five international treaties adopted regarding space activities. Commonly referred to as the 'five United Nations treaties on outer space', these treaties were adopted between 1967 and 1984. Below is a brief description of each of these treaties:

Treaty on Principles Governing the Activities of States in the Exploration and Use of Outer Space, including the Moon and Other Celestial Bodies (commonly called the Outer Space Treaty)

This treaty was adopted by the General Assembly on January 27, 1967 and entered into force on October 10, 1967. The key principles of the treaty are: 1) free exploration by all nations, 2) no national appropriation, claims of sovereignty or occupation by nation-states, 3) no nuclear weapons or weapons of mass destruction in orbit or on celestial bodies, 4) use of the Moon and celestial bodies for peaceful purposes only, 5) states responsible for national space efforts and liable for damages caused, 6) states to avoid harmful contamination, and 7) astronauts to be regarded as envoys of mankind.

Agreement on the Rescue of Astronauts, the Return of Astronauts and the Return of Objects Launched into Outer Space (commonly called the Rescue Agreement)

The treaty was adopted and signed on April 22, 1968 and entered into force in December of that year. This treaty elaborates on Articles 5 and 8 of the Outer Space Treaty to emphasize that States should take all possible steps to rescue and assist astronauts in distress, including launching assistance in recovering objects that return to Earth outside the territory of the launching state.

Convention on International Liability for damage caused by Space Objects (commonly called the Liability Convention)

This treaty was adopted and opened for signature on March 29, 1972 and entered into force in September of that year. It elaborates on Article 7 of the Outer Space Treaty to confirm that the launching state is absolutely liable to pay compensation for damages caused by space objects on the surface of the Earth or aircraft in the skies and provides a procedure for settlement.

Convention on registration of Objects Launched into Outer Space (commonly called the Registration Convention)

This treaty was adopted and opened for signature on January 14, 1975 and entered into force on September 15, 1976. This treaty expanded the scope of the United Nations register of Objects Launched into Outer Space which had been stabilized in December 1961.

Agreement Governing the Activities of States on the Moon and Other Celestial Bodies (commonly called the Moon Agreement).

This treaty was adopted and opened for signature on December 18, 1979 and entered into force on July 11, 1984. This treaty elaborated on the original Outer Space Treaty, specifically emphasizing the exclusive use for peaceful purposes and the common heritage of mankind as it applied to the potential exploitation of natural resources in outer space.

While these five treaties provide the broad framework around which all other issues hang, there is also a body of nonbinding resolutions that have been adopted over the years by the United Nations and a host of bilateral and multilateral agreements between various nations. The United Nations Office for Outer Space Affairs (UNOOSA) website is an excellent starting point for understanding the legal frameworks of space, but at this point it is important to note that treaties 'only apply' to nations who have agreed to adopt them and that nations are 'free' to withdraw from a previously signed treaty with notification to the other parties. As such, many of the provisions of the treaties cited above have never been tested. For example, to date no nation has attempted to exploit the natural resources of a celestial body for its own benefit rather than that of all mankind so it is unclear what the rest of the nations would do to force compliance. It is also not clear what rules apply to commercial interests rather than nation-states. If a Chinese mining company attempted to exploit resources on the Moon, then what would be the response from other nations regarding these actions. The world may be on the verge of finding out answers to these questions as we are entering the era of commercial space.

Conclusion

If Neil Armstrong took 'one small step for man and one giant leap for mankind' when he stepped onto the Moon, then the space industry and the many supporters of space exploration have been waiting over three decades for the next great leap. Like Arthur C. Clarke, many space supporters were optimistic enough after the 1969 Moon landing to envision men on Mars by the 1990s (Clarke, 1993). Increasingly, many have begun to ask: 'If not now, when?' At the height of the Great Space Race (1966), the budget for NASA represented 4.41 percent of the US Federal budget. This is US$49 billion in 2021 dollars (Wikipedia, 2023). Given the War in Vietnam, the War on Poverty, and the social unrest of the Civil Rights movement, critics found it easy to argue that the money was better spent at home. The NASA budget for 2020 would be less than one half of one percent of the US budget (Wikipedia, 2023). For 2023, NASA is expected to receive $25.4 billion, an increase over 2022, but a very small part of an overall $1.7 trillion US budget (The Planetary Society, 2023).

As the US space program floundered and other countries stepped into space, the Soviet program would have its own identity crisis as the breakup of the Soviet Union would see the greatest of their spaceport, Baikonur, become the property of a foreign government, Kazahstan. Baikonur was the site of some of the Soviet's greatest accomplishments in space – the first man and first women in space, all the manned Soviet missions, the first piece of the ISS, etc. While Russia would continue to use the cosmodrome under an agreement with the government of the newly independent Kazakhstan, they would go on to build a new Russian spaceport – Vostochny. This new cosmodrome is located near the Pacific Coast of Russia and is intended as the new home for Russian manned missions. As the price tag for this new home rises, some in Russia are calling this project a 'dolgostroi' (or Russian white elephant) (Zak, 2013). Further, the announced plan to launch a manned mission to orbit the Moon was derided in the Russian media as "a 60 year old achievement" (Kramnik, 2013). In an announcement on the 52nd anniversary of the Gagarin flight, Russian President Vladmir Putin called for an increase in the Roscosmos budget in order to catch up with NASA, preserve their achievements in manned space flight, and spur scientific discovery (Steadman, 2013). However, the Russian space program was struggling even before the war in Ukraine, with low levels of funding and a series of high-profile failures. While China has a rover on the dark side of the Moon and orbiters around Mars which joined orbiters from India and the UAE, the Russian effort seems to be lagging behind (Koren, 2022). Meanwhile, the US effort is increasingly focused on commercial efforts, leaving NASA to try to define its role. In Chapter 22, we will look at the future of space for the old Space Race competitors and the rest of the world. Will mankind be reaching for the stars or simply staring at them from the back porch?

Questions

1 What role did German scientists play in the space programs of the US and USSR?
2 Discuss the milestones in the Race for the Moon.

References

Belew, L. F. & Stuhlinger, E (1973) *Skylab: A guidebook EP-107*. US Government Printing Office, Washington, DC.

Bellis, M (2013) First United States Satellite and Space Launch Vehicles, retrieved online June 4, 2013 at: http://inventors.about.com

Boyne, W. J. (2007), 'Project Paperclip', retrieved online May 18, 2013 at: http://www.airforcemag.com/MagazineArchive/Pages/2007/June%202007/0607paperclip.aspx, Air Force Magazine (Vol. 90, No.6), Arlington, VA.

Brown, G. (2000) How satellites work, retrieved online May 19, 2013 from How Stuff Works, http://science.howstuffworks.com/satellite.htm

Clarke, A. C. (1993) *Forward* in *the case for Mars: The plan to settle the red planet and why we must* by Robert Zubrin and Richard Wagner, Simon & Schuster, New York.

Coppinger, R. (2010) Will congress keep US space programme adrift, Hyperbola. Available at http://www.flightglobal.com/blogs/hyperbola/2010/02/will_congress_keep_us_space_pr/

David, L. (2011) China's first space station: A new foothold in earth orbit, Space.com, May 6. Available at: http://www.space.com/11592-china-space-station-tiangong-details.html

Findley, R. (1962, May). Telephone a star. *National Geographic*, 638–651. Retrieved from http://www.beatriceco.com/bti/porticus/bell/pdf/nat_geo_telstar_ocr.pdf

Fought, B. E. (1989). *Legal aspects of the commercialization of space transportation systems.* (Master's thesis, University of Berkley) Retrieved from http://www.law.berkeley.edu/journals/btlj/articles/vol3/fought.html

Foust, J. (2012) House panel agrees on lack of NASA strategic direction, but disagrees on what it should be, retrieved at http://www.spacepolitics.com/2012/12/13/house-panel-agrees-on-lack-of-nasa-strategic-direction-but-disagrees-on-what-it-should-be/

Gagliardi, O. (2009). *The feat of Jorge Chavez*. Emmitsburg, FAP

Godwin, M. (2006), 'The Cold War and the Early Space Race', retrieved online May 20, 2013 at: http://www.history.ac.uk/ihr/Focus/cold/articles/godwin.html, Department of Science and Technology Studies, University College London, London.

JWST Independent Comprehensive Review Panel (2010). *James webb space telescope final report*, NASA JPL.

Koren, M. (2022) The Russian space program is falling back to earth. The Atlantic. Available at: https://www.theatlantic.com/science/archive/2022/10/us-russia-space-programs-spacex-collaboration-ukraine/671740/

Kramnik, I (2013) *Opinion: Roskosmos at a crossroads*, retrieved June 14, 2013 at http://rbth.ru/articles/2012/03/16/roscosmos_takes_on_nasa_15096.html retrieved 6/18/13

LaFleur, C. (2010). Spacecraft Stats and Insights, retrieved from The Space Review, http://www.thespacereview,com/article/1598/1

Launius, R. D. (2003) *Space stations – base camps to the stars*, Smithsonian Institution, Washington, DC.

Morris, J. (2013) Opportunity lives, *Aviation Week & Space Technology*, June 17, p. 34.

NASA (2013) Space Shuttle, retrieved on June 13, 2013 at http://www.nasa.gov/mission_pages/shuttle/launch/index.html

Sheppard, A. & Slayton, D. (1994) *Moon shot: The inside story of America's race to the Moon*. Turner Publishing: Atlanta.

Steadman, I (2013). Vladimir Putin announces big new budget for Russian space agency, retrieved June 16, 2013 at http://www.wired.co.uk/news/archive/2013-04/12/russian-space-budget

Stockman, B., Boyle, J. S., & Bacon, J. (2009) International Space Station Systems Engineering Case Study. Available at: http://www.green-ebookshop.com/get_book.php?file=International-Space-Station-Systems-Engineering-Case-Study-d48141176

The Planetary Society (2023) NASA's FY 2023 Budget. Available at: https://www.planetary.org/space-policy/nasas-fy-2023-budget#:~:text=NASA%20will%20receive%20%2425.4%20billion,purchasing%20power%20of%20this%20increase

The Space Telescope Science Institute (2013). *HST Publications Statistics*, retrieved from the The Space telescope Science Institute: http://archives.stsci.edu/hst/bibliography/pubstat.html

Vaughan, D. (1996) *The challenger launch decision: Risky technology, culture, and deviance at NASA*, The University of Chicago Press, Chicago.

Wikipedia (2023) ANSA Annual Budget, retrieved March 22, 2023 from https://en.wikipedia.org/wiki/Budget_of_NASA

Wolfe, T (2001) *The right stuff*, Bantam Books, New York.

Zak, A. (2013). Vostochny (formerly Svobodny) Cosmodrome, retrieved April 10, 2013 from http://www.russianspaceweb.com/svobodny.html

Zubrin, R. & Wagner, R. (1994) *The case for Mars: The plan to settle the red planet and why we must*, Simon & Schuster, New York.

8   Taking Off

Learning Objectives

After reading this chapter, you should have a good understanding of:

LO1:   the beginnings of the 'jet age'
LO2:   the factors driving aircraft size and speed
LO3:   the early history of supersonic transport
LO4:   the background for mergers, acquisition, and bankruptcy among the aircraft manufacturers

Key Terms, Concepts & People

Constellation	De Havilland Comet	Eddie Rickenbacker
Pan Am	B-747	Embraer & Bombardier
SST & Concorde	Henri Ziegler	Boeing-McDonnell Merger
Airbus	Fly-by-wire	

Back to Business

For obvious reasons, civil aviation in Europe was placed on hold during World War II. In the US, civil aviation continued a somewhat limited basis, while the manufacturers thrived under government orders for military equipment. As the war approached a recognizable end, several manufacturers began to shift more focus back to the civilian market and anxiously waited to be released from government obligation. Within days of the events at Hiroshima and Nagasaki, others found their government contract cancelled and quickly had to shift gears back to a more civilian manufacturing position (Rummel, 1991). Most companies had prospered during the war, racing to keep up with demand. Many would struggle with the end of the war, converting aircraft either built or partially built at contract cancellation to civilian use. However, the end of lucrative government contracts was only part of the concern; the volume of war surplus aircraft also threatened to depress possible civilian orders (Rummel, 1991; Serling, 1992). Still, civil aviation was about to reap the benefits of all that wartime innovation, including the amazing feats of aerial combat and the list of aviation achievements had captured the imagination of the population. Now the industry needed to convince the general public that aviation was a safe, affordable,

DOI: 10.4324/9781003405306-9

comfortable travel experience. The rise in passenger traffic during the post-war period suggests that they were successful; people around the world were getting ready to take to the skies. Airlines and their manufacturers would work closely together to create the planes that would attract new flyers, the kind that were not looking to push the envelope as first movers in a new and untried field but the more cautious followers. During the last half of the twentieth century, aviation would grow up.

First Out of the Gate

Lockheed and Douglas were two of the first manufacturers to be released by the US government. Both would begin working on projects to bring the pressurized cabin to civil aviation. The DC series for Douglas and the Lockheed Constellations (popularly known as Connies) would compete with Convair (General Dynamics) to offer bigger and faster aircraft to the airlines. Two goals fuelled the competition – the 'fastest coast-to-coast' service in the US and a trans-Atlantic nonstop range (Rummel, 1991). Both of these companies would compete aggressively to sell their aircraft to the major carriers – United, American, TWA, and Pan Am. In such a competitive field, a few more feet in length (L1049) or the provision of more efficient engines and propellers (DC-7) were the selling points, although in some cases the delivery schedule also became a 'make-or-break' issue. The DC-6, first released in 1946, would feature a pressurized cabin and a 102-passenger seating configuration. It would regularly be used in around-the-world flights by the major international airlines and also become the first official US presidential aircraft (used by President Harry Truman). The next Douglas aircraft, the DC-7, became the first aircraft to fly non-stop from New York to Los Angeles (Clouatre, 2002). Despite some early problems with the Constellation series, TWA and a number of other international airlines would make the aircraft a fondly remembered part of aviation history (McCoy, 2002; Rummel, 1991).

In 1950, the Farnborough Air Show in the UK acted as the showcase for the plane seen as the 'wave of the future', the de Havilland Comet. The Comet, which had made its maiden flight the previous year, was set to enter commercial airline service in 1952, when it became the first operational commercial jet transport. One of the people attending the air show was Ron Allen, then CEO of Boeing. Allen was convinced that Boeing could develop a better aircraft and would return to Seattle to set his engineers to work. At the April 22, 1952, meeting of the Boeing Board, tentative approval was given to the project to design and construct a jet plane which would become the B-707. The aircraft would feature sweptback wings and engine pods. Seating for 100 passengers would compete well with the Comet's more limited 36 seat capacity. Development of the 707 would prove far more costly than the original Boeing estimate, making the breakeven point far higher, but Pam Am agreed to be the launch customer. Meanwhile, the rest of the industry appeared to be opting for the DC-8, the planned Douglas entry into the world of commercial jet transport. The DC-8 was only a 'paper aircraft' at this stage; that is, it was still in the very preliminary stages of design. The Douglas company, however, did have a family of aircraft and a proven record of success. These factors gave them an edge and guaranteed that airlines would listen when they suggested that their aircraft would have greater range, power, and size than the Boeing aircraft, and also that it would be cheaper (Serling, 1992).

On January 10, 1954, the industry was shaken when a BOAC Comet exploded in mid-air over the Mediterranean. A second Comet would disappear soon afterwards on a flight from Rome to Cairo. The cause of both crashes was the explosive decompression of the fuselage caused by metal fatigue cracks, which occurred as a result of the pressurization and depressurization of the cabin. This phenomenon was familiar from the experience of military jet aircraft. Fortunately, both Boeing and Douglas were aware of the problem and were busy working on solutions. In fact, at the rollout of the B-707 prospective customers were shown a film entitled *Operation Guillotine*. This illustrated the results of explosive decompression and the solutions that Boeing had implemented. These solutions included triple-strength windows rounded at the corners, thicker-gauged skin braced with metal stripping, and small stopper straps running the length of the fuselage. The result was that the cabin remained intact after being deliberately pierced by several blades. The Comet also convinced Boeing that more pilot training would be needed to fly the faster, more unforgiving jet aircraft (Serling, 1992).

With the 1959 release of the DC-8 jet, the future of air transportation appeared clear to almost all. The DC-8 was equipped with four engines and capable of over 600 miles per hour. An extended fuselage allowed for the seating of 260 passengers (Clouatre, 2002). Of course, not all airlines were convinced. Despite being impressed by the barrel roll of the Dash-80 (demonstration model for the B-707), Eddie Rickenbacker, the former World War I flying ace and then CEO of Eastern Air Line, preferred propeller-driven craft, which he viewed as safer and more reliable. This kept Eastern out of the jet era until the early 1960s, when Rickenbacker's successors began a buying spree to catch up that left the airline heavily in debt at the time it was going into deregulation (Bernstein, 1999). While the new jets did prove to be fuel hogs, guzzling more fuel on takeoff than the *Spirit of St. Louis* consumed during it crossing of the Atlantic, the new jet engines proved far safer and more reliable (Serling, 1992). In fact, the introduction of the jet engine would dramatically lower accident rates. These rates would experience a sharp decline in the 1950s and 1960s, which primarily attributable to the widespread introduction of the jet engine and improvements in jet engine reliability (Barnett & Higgins, 1989). In their study, Oster and Zorn (1989) found an overall decline in accidents of 54 percent, with a 71 percent reduction in accidents attributed to equipment failure.

Too Big to fly?

Pan Am wanted a bigger plane and the B-707 could not be stretched any further. The answer, therefore, was the B-747. In their letter of intent, Pan Am called for a 400-passenger aircraft with a range of 5,000 and a cruising altitude of 35,000 feet. The plane had to be able to take off in no more than 8,000 feet fully loaded and be capable of cargo nose loading. It seemed a very tall order for a company that did not even possess a building large enough to construct such a plane. Nevertheless, just three years after this letter, the first B-747 would be rolled out. Building the aircraft would strain Boeing to breaking point, and the company laid off 5,000 people in just a single week in 1970. By the end of that year, the number of office staff had dropped from 24,000 to 9,000, and the hourly workers declined from 45,000 to 15,000. This crisis inspired the famous billboard in Seattle, asking, 'Will the last person leaving SEATTLE – Turn out the light' (Serling, 1992). The first flight of the B-747 from New York to London would take place on January 22, 1970. Of course, almost everyone who flew internationally in the five decades following its release would likely have sat aboard a B-747, which became the symbol of international aviation during this period. The B-747 would go through a number of variants over the years that would reflect extended range and capacity as well as a special purpose, freighter. The latest is the – 800 series. The B-747 would eventually prove to be one of the best-selling planes in history and the only plane in its 'class' until the launch of the A-380.

Down But Not Out

The idea of supersonic commercial flight became part of the dream list of aeronautical engineers and their companies within a decade after the 1947 flight of the Bell X-1. Reaching a speed of 700 miles per hour, Captain Charles 'Chuck' Yeager officially achieved Mach 1.06, breaking the sound barrier. By 1953, the Douglas Skyrocket would break Mach 2, but Douglas would drop out of the US race for a commercial aircraft fairly early in the design competition in the US (Marchman, 2002). Boeing established its own small supersonic transport (SST) design team in 1957 and started building a supersonic wind tunnel three years later. In 1963, the Federal Aviation Administration announced plans to invite US aerospace companies to submit plans for an SST (Lynn, 1998). Boeing's US competitors in this enterprise were Lockheed and North American, although the latter, with its Curtiss Wright engine, would eventually drop out of the race. In 1966, Boeing unveiled its $11 million mockup to the media. Later that year, the FAA proclaimed the Boeing-GE design the SST winner, but years of work would not result in an American SST; the US Senate would refuse to fund further development in 1971. Still, the dream would live on and be revived at Boeing briefly as the Sonic Cruiser before the decision was made to proceed with the plane that would become the B-777 (Serling, 1992).

Over in Europe, Sud Aviation unveiled a scale model of a medium-range SST named the Super Caravelle at the 1960 Paris Air Show. By 1962, the French and British had signed the Anglo-French Supersonic Aircraft Agreement to jointly develop an SST, following a decision by the FAA and US companies not to consider a partnership with the British to design an aluminum SST. The Anglo-French alliance (later joined by the Germans) would eventually result in the Concorde, but the project was not without significant challenges. In addition to numerous technical challenges, the cost of the project continued to rise to well over 10 times the original estimate, threatening to create a political backlash in each of the key countries. The French would ask Henri Ziegler, war hero, resistance fighter, head of Air France, and proponent of a very different concept in aerospace design, later called Airbus, to rescue the supersonic effort. The Concorde would make its maiden flight in March 1969, two months after the Soviet SST became the first SST into the air. The Soviet aircraft, the TU-144, would crash in 1973 at the Paris Air Show. Meanwhile, the Concorde would not make it into commercial service until 1976 with its maiden voyage from London to Bahrain. While TWA and Pan Am in the US had taken options to pursue the Concorde, both would eventually back out, leaving British Airways and Air France as the only commercial operators. Despite safety concerns during its development stages, the Concorde would fly accident-free until the 2000 crash of AF 4590 on take-off from Paris. Unfortunately, the premium pricing for the very narrow-bodied Concorde, along with its high operating costs, meant that the aircraft could never be a money-winning proposition, sadly confirming the predictions of Henri Ziegler that the plane would not sell and amounted to little more than a remarkable technical achievement in aviation (Aris, 2002; Serling, 1992; Shuman, 2002).

Ziegler was particularly concerned that the Concorde would draw European focus away from the one project that he did believe had the potential to re-establish Europe in the commercial aviation industry – Airbus. Airbus was to be headquartered in France, but the final product of its labor would come from the assembly of parts designed and manufactured all over Europe. Establishing common rules and standards would prove simple compared to the logistics involved in moving large aircraft parts from one end of Europe to the other. Although many thought that the concept of a wide-body, 200 passenger, twin-engine airplane was madness, the Airbus A-300 would launch in 1972 and begin commercial service

Table 8.1 Airbus Family of Aircraft

Aircraft	Seating	First FLT	Delivered	Orders
A-220	108–130	Sept. 2016	200	740
A-300[a]	228–254	Oct. 1972	816	0
A-310[a]	190–230	May 1982	255	0
A-320	107–185	Feb. 1987	10,230	16,022
A-330	246–300	Nov. 1992	1,529	1,822
A-340[a]	239–377	Oct. 1991	377	0
A-350	270–350	Jun. 2013	471	917
A-380[a]	525–853	Apr. 2005	251	0

[a] No longer in production.

in 1974. By 1978, the A310, a shortened version of the A300 seating 218 passengers, had been launched. The Airbus family continued to grow with the A320, a single-aisle 130–170-passenger aircraft, the A321, a lengthened version of the A320 seating 180–200 passengers, the A330, a twin-engine 235-passenger aircraft, and the A340, an ultra-long four-engine aircraft seating 295 passengers. Table 8.1 shows clearly the members of the Airbus family, along with other details such as the basic seating number, the release date of first aircraft, and the total number of aircraft delivered. Several features distinguished the Airbus family from the start. First, the flight deck was standardized across models, making training and operation simpler and less costly. Second, there was a two-person cockpit design, also a cost-saver. Finally, the aircraft utilized the latest technology, including the fly-by-wire controls which replaced the old mechanical systems with their cables attached to pulleys and later aided by hydraulics as the size of the rudder and the flaps increased with computer systems that would send electrical impulses to the moveable surfaces. Fly-by-wire had been used before in military aircraft and on the Concorde, but there was resistance to the new technology, particularly from pilot groups. Boeing would not take the plunge into fly-by-wire for another decade.

Breaking the Mold

The book *Twenty-first Century Jet: The Making and Marketing of the Boeing 777*, Chapter 1 begins with a quote from Alan Mulally, who eventually took over as general manager of the 777 team when Phil Condit was promoted to President of the Boeing Company. His answer to the question (Why a new place?) was that airlines wanted an airplane that was bigger than the B-767 but smaller than the B-747. Boeing first tried several scenarios for stretching the 767, but the aerodynamics did not work well. In fact, the design was dubbed a Chipolata Sausage – very long and skinny – by unnamed representatives of a British airline. Design issues were not the only driver of a new plane; the 767 project was launched in 1978 and first delivered in 1982, and the technological advances since then seemed to argue for a new redesign rather than a retrofit of an older one. The 777 would represent a number of firsts for Boeing, including the first paperless design, the first fly-by-wire, the first experiments in design-build teams and a new employee relationship, and the first efforts to involve customers early in the process. In the early days of manufacturing, a plane was designed on paper and then a full-scale mock-up was used to catch any 'conflicts' in the design, that is, such as a call button placed being placed where an air duct was also planned. Computer-aided design (CAD) allowed the process to take place virtually. The 777 would use fly-by-wire like the Airbus aircraft on the market but would rely on a back-up system written separately to avoid the possibility of a 'computer glitch' in the first software being re-created in the back-up, a possible safety problem. Two new concepts would emerge with the 777 – Working Together and design-build teams (DBTs). Working Together embodies the idea that the 777 team create an environment where everyone came together in "a shared thought, a shared vision, a shared appreciation, a shared understanding of what it is we're really going to try to accomplish together" (Sabbagh, 1996, p. 66). For a company with a history of tense labor relations, layoffs, and union strife, the concept was a departure. Equally novel for Boeing was the Japanese concept of design-build teams linked vertically and horizontally to each other by a common team member. The DBTs were to ensure that communications did occur between the design teams so that 'interferences' were reduced. The program eventually had 250 DBTs coordinating design. The final new element was the Boeing effort to involve customers early and often. In the past, 'Boeing policy had been to dream up a new plane, design it, make it, and then sit around and hope that enough people would buy it' (Sabbagh, 1996, p. 27). The costs and uncertainties made this old approach too risky even for Boeing who had 'bet the farm' on projects such as the 707 and the 747 (Table 8.2). The 777 would become everything that the designers hoped that it would be after some early issues with its twin-engine design. Since the aircraft range was intended to allow extended over water operations, there was some concern that the failure of one engine would create a safety hazard over water. This issue was resolved, and the aircraft has proved to be remarkably successful, and safe (Sabbagh, 1996).

Let the Mergers Begin

By the middle of the 1960s, the company had amassed huge losses and was ripe for a take-over by McDonnell of St. Louis, until then primarily a weapons manufacturer. Although the new McDonnell-Douglas would re-enter the commercial market with the DC-10, it would never regain its former glories (Lynn, 1998). The main competitor for the DC-10 was the Lockheed L-1011 Tristar, Lockheed's first jetliner. Lockheed would sell 250 L-1011s, but the cost of developing the aircraft at the same time as the C-5, which was a form of military cargo transport, would drive the company to the brink of bankruptcy, an event

Table 8.2 Boeing Family of Aircraft

Aircraft	Seating	First FLT	Delivered	Orders
B-707[a]	141	Dec. 1957	865	0
B-717[a]	106	Sept. 1998	155	0
B-727[a]	106–125	Feb. 1963	1,832	0
B-737[a]	110–215	Apr. 1967	3,102	0
B-737 NG	110–220	Feb. 1997	7,088	7,124
B-737 MAX	138–153	Jan. 2016	686	4,821
B-747[a]	416–500	Sep. 1968	1,424	0
B-747-8	375–467	Feb. 2010	155	0
B-757[a]	200	Feb. 1982	1,050	0
B-767	180–375	Sept. 1981	1,240	1,346
B-777	300–550	Jun. 1994	1,679	2,100
B-777X	384–450	2025?	0	334
B-787	210–330	Dec. 2009	1,006	1,490

[a] No longer in production.

averted by a US government credit guarantee to lenders. The L-1011 would lose some $2.5 billion by the time it was retired in 1981 (Newhouse, 2007). At McDonnell-Douglas, things were not much better. By the 1990s, employees of the Douglas unit would complain that the company pencils were designed so that when they were sharpened the Douglas disappeared. The DC-10 was in fact inferior to the L-1011 in a number of ways and would prove to be the last commercial aircraft produced by the company. It would increasingly rely on its military aircraft and weapons development for the company's profits (McCoy, 2002; Newhouse, 2007).

It became clear to even those outside the industry that McDonnell-Douglas was struggling in 1992 when the company posted a 51 percent drop in overall earnings with a 62 percent drop for the Douglas unit. By 1996, Douglas Aircraft had only 40 new aircraft orders. Without a viable commercial business, the company had to commit to an all-out effort to win the Joint Strike Force (JSF) fighter project for the US combined forces aircraft of the future, which was estimated to be worth approximately $300 billion in future sales. When McDonnell-Douglas was 'deselected' by the Pentagon in 1996, there appeared to be little future for the company. The following year Boeing would pay $13.3 billion for this former competitor. This move was not widely popular within Boeing's Commercial Division, who felt that the Douglas unit was even weaker than projected and that the two cultures would clash. Strategic reasons that favored the merger, however, were that the combined company better balanced the commercial and military sides of the industry (Newhouse, 2007). The McDonnell-Douglas merger failed to forge a common culture and identity for the company. It would be a different story for the merger with Boeing. Surprisingly, Boeing employees would complain that the financial focus of McDonnell-Douglas would come to dominate the engineering focus of Boeing, leading to the disaster that was the B-737 MAX (Useem, 2019).

Another commercial aviation pioneer was to disappear during this era – Fokker. This company began to struggle in the 1970s and briefly explored a collaboration with McDonnell-Douglas in 1981. The company received a financial bailout from the Dutch government in 1987 as development costs for their new line of aircraft soared. One condition of the government was that they seek out new partners for the company. DASA, the parent company of Daimler-Benz, was that partner. Their decision to focus on core operations in 1996 forced Fokker into bankruptcy. Stork Aerospace took over the repair and maintenance business while various interests have continued to raise the prospects of a re-entry into the civil aviation market. Thus, a decade after Airbus entered the commercial airline industry, there were only four major players in the market, with Boeing in top spot. Lockheed and McDonnell-Douglas, as noted above, would continue to decline, weighed down by their own mistakes. This would set the stage for the new kid-on-the-block, Airbus, to emerge as the dominant threat in the large commercial aircraft (LCA) market, but the major players would ignore a segment of the market that other companies would target – the small regional jet market.

Small Is Beautiful?

In 1986, a Canadian company founded in 1942 to manufacturer tracked vehicles for transport over snow bought Canadair, a leading Canadian aircraft manufacturer. This company, Bombardier, purchased Short Brothers in 1989, de Havilland in 1992 (51 percent stake and remaining 49 percent in 1997), and LearJet in 1995. Aviation was part of a broader diversification into transportation that included bus, rail, and water vehicles, as well as services such as FlexJet and SkyJet. Bombardier would develop a line of commercial vehicles, ranging from the 30-seat Dash to the 100–150-seat C-series. In the 2000s, they would end production on a number of their aircraft, including the CRJ 111/200/440 in 2006, the Learjet 60 in 2012, the Learjet 40 in 2013, the Learjet 85 in 2014, the Challenger 850 in 2015, the Learjet 70/75 in 2021, and the CRJ 550/700/900/1000 in 2020. Sadly, the cost of moving into the 100-plus market would put great stress on the company, which would sell 50.01 percent of the aviation unit to Airbus in 2017, getting out of the market for large commercial aircraft. Rebranded as the A220-100 and A220-200, the sales of these aircraft would rise by 50 percent in the first year (Hayward, 2022).

A second entrant into this segment of the commercial industry was Embraer, a Brazilian company that began in the 1960s with general aviation and military aircraft. They too would go on to offer a line of commercial aircraft, ranging from 30 to 122 seats (Table 8.3). These aircraft are referred to in the industry as regional jets and they flourished on a wave of the strategic changes at the major carriers to move toward point-to-point service and/or a hubbing structure where these smaller aircraft were used to serve less dense routes that were then channeled into the major carrier hubs where traffic could be concentrated and placed on larger aircraft into the final destination. From a major carrier perspective, they could fill smaller aircraft and serve these markets more frequently. From an airport perspective, this often resulted in more flights but little increase in overall passengers or revenue. This would become a bigger problem at heavily congested airports in the Northeast US. From a passenger perspective, it often meant more cramped seating and less overhead space. From the perspective of the LCA manufacturers, it represented a potential, but unrealized source of future competition.

Powering the Planes

Pratt & Whitney, the company that had been founded in 1925 and formed one leg of William Boeing's vision of a fully integrated air transport company, would continue to produce engines for both military and civilian use as part of the United Aircraft Corporation (a name which was changed to the United Technologies Corporation (UTC) in 1975), which merged with Raytheon Technologies in 2020. UTC would a very become a diversified company with business units, including Otis Elevator, Hamilton Sundstrand, Carrier Heating and Air Conditioning, and Sikorsky Helicopter as well as Pratt & Whitney. In

Table 8.3 Embraer Jet Family

Aircraft	Seating	Delivered	Orders
ERJ135	30–37	108	0
ERJ140	44	74	0
ERJ145	50	708	0
ERJ145XR	50		
Embraer 170	66–78	191	191
Embraer 175	76–88	705	848
Embraer 190	96–114	565	568
Embraer 195	100–124	172	172
E-175 E2	80–90		
E-190 E2	97–114	15	20
E-195 E2	120–146	38	201

Source: Embraer website, https://www.embraercommercialaviation.com/commercial-jets/e175-e2-commercial-jet/

Table 8.4 Large Commercial Aircraft Engines

Manufacturer	Engine	In-service date	Aircraft example
Pratt & Whitney	JT8D	1964	B-737 MD-80
	PW2000	1984	B-757
	PW4000	1987	B-747
	PW6000	2000	A-318/320
	V2500	2008	A-320
	GP7200	2008	A-380
	GTF	TBD	
General Electric	CF34	1983	CRJ-100
	CF6	1971	A-300
	CFM56 (LEAP)	2016	A-320neo
	CT7	1984	Saab 340
	GE90	1995	B-777
	GE9X	2020	B-777X
	GENx	2012	B747-800
Rolls-Royce	Trent 500	2002	A-340-500
	Trent 700	1995	A-330
	Trent 800	1996	B-777
	Trent 900	2012	A-380
	Trent 1000	2011	B-787
	Trent 7000	2017	A330NEO
	Trent XWB	2014	A-350

Source: Various company websites.

1996, Pratt & Whitney would form an alliance with another engine manufacturer, GE, to begin work on an engine that would power the world's largest commercial aircraft, the A-380. Table 8.4 provides an overview of the Pratt & Whitney commercial engine family (Pratt & Whitney website, 2023).

The company that first entered the 'aviation business' in 1917 in response to the US government's search for a way to boost engine power at high altitude would go on, in 1942, to produce the nation's first jet engine, the I-A. Further development would result two years later in the J33 which would power the US Air Corps' first operational jet fighter. Building on years of expertise in the military market, GE would move into the civilian market in 1971 with the CF6, a high bypass turbofan engine which was first installed on the DC-10. The same year GE began its partnership with Snecma, a French engine firm. This partnership was formalized in 1974 with the formation of CFM International, a 50/50 joint venture. CFM International would become one of the most successful aviation partnerships in history. Over the years, CFM engines would grab an increasing share of the short- to medium-range commercial aviation market and become the exclusive power plant for the long-range A-340 (General Electric website, 2023).

In the early 1950s Rolls-Royce, at the time a company better known for its cars, had entered the aviation industry with a number of engines: the Dart for the Vickers Viscount, the Avon for the Comet, and the Conway for the B-707. By 1966, the main British engine makers – de Havilland, Bristol Siddeley, Blackburn, Napier Aero Engines – had merged into Rolls-Royce. Unfortunately, this was the same year in which Lockheed began work on its first jetliner, the L-1011 Tristar, which would feature the Rolls-Royce RB211. The high cost of these developments would drive Lockheed to the brink of bankruptcy while costs and early problems with the engine would lead Rolls-Royce into state ownership in 1971. The car divisions would be separated in 1973 and Rolls-Royce would return to the private sector in 1987. In 1990, Rolls-Royce would form an aero engine joint venture with BMW, a venture of which they assumed full control of in 2000. They would continue to design engines for commercial and private aviation, announcing new initiatives for net zero carbon in 2021 (Rolls-Royce website, 2023).

Conclusion

As the twentieth century came to an end, there were only two manufacturers left standing in the LCA market – Airbus and Boeing. Embraer and Bombardier would begin to work their way into the sector in the twenty-first century, but only Embraer would survive this jump from regional to large commercial as a separate company with its E-190 and E-195 series. However, competition would continue to be high in this sector of the industry. In fact, it would intensify in the twenty-first century. The events of September 11 would naturally impact the manufacturing firms, but this time there would be a difference; the US domestic market no longer dominated the industry or the thinking of the aerospace manufacturers. The global airline industry would recover much more quickly than their US counterparts who would struggle to stay out, or get out, of bankruptcy. Meanwhile, the phenomenal growth in Asia would also be reflected in their aviation industry. China and India would lead the region while airlines in the Middle East, notably Emirates and Qatar Air, would expand to position themselves as the link between Europe and Asia.

Even more noteworthy is that the twenty-first century became the stage for a new battle between Airbus and Boeing, a battle of visions. These two companies would begin to diverge sharply in their strategic vision of the future of the aviation industry. Boeing would plan for a future where point-to-point traffic would become the growing and driving force behind air travel. Airbus would envision a future in which aircraft even larger than the B-747 would carry air travelers to the major international hubs. These visions would have a definite effect on the products each planned to release in the first decade of the new century, and their fortunes would be measured by how the 'market' appeared to be validating their vision. Still, as we will see in Chapter 19, it is never wise to declare victory too soon. While the Boeing vision did appear to win the day, other factors will cause a new shift in the very important battle for aircraft orders.

Questions

1 What was the cause of the de Havilland Comet crashes and what was the solution to this problem?
2 Discuss the advantages and disadvantages of the jet engine and aircraft.
3 Discuss the founding of Airbus.
4 What events led to the merger of McDonnell-Douglas and Boeing?
5 Why did supersonic transport fail and what is its future in the airline industry?
6 What were some of the key challenges faced by aircraft manufacturers as they transitioned from wartime production to civilian aircraft manufacturing in the aftermath of World War II?
7 Discuss the significance of the de Havilland Comet and the Boeing B-707 in the evolution of commercial aviation. How did these aircraft influence the direction of the industry?
8 Explain the factors that led to the rise and eventual decline of supersonic commercial flight, with a focus on the Concorde and its impact on the aviation industry.

References

Aris, S. (2002), *Close to the Sun: How Airbus challenged America's domination of the skies*, Arum Press, London.

Barnett, A. & Higgins, M. K. (1989), 'Airline safety: The last decade'. *The Institute of Management Sciences* 35 (1), pp. 1–21.

Bernstein, A. (1999), *Grounded: Frank Lorenzo and the destruction of Eastern Airlines*, Beard Books, Washington, DC.

Clouatre, D. (2002), 'DC plane family' in Tracy Irons-Georges (Ed.) *Encyclopedia of flight*, pp. 205–207, Salem Press, Pasadena, CA.

General Electric (2023), https://www.geaerospace.com/propulsion/commercial

Hayward, J. (2022), Why did Airbus buy the Bombardier CSeries, Simple Flying. Retrieved at https://simpleflying.com/airbus-c-series-purchase/#:~:text=The%20Bombardier%20CSeries%20was%20a,rebranding%20to%20the%20Airbus%20A220%3F

Lynn, M. (1998), *Birds of prey: Boeing Vs Airbus – A battle for the skies*, Four Walls Eight Windows, New York.

Marchman, J. F. (2002), 'Supersonic aircraft' in Tracy Irons-Georges (Ed.) *Encyclopedia of flight*, pp. 205–207, Salem Press, Pasadena, CA.

McCoy, M. G. (2002), 'Lockheed-Martin', in Tracy Irons-Georges (Ed.) *Encyclopedia of flight*, pp. 420–423, Salem Press, Pasadena, CA.

Newhouse, J. (2007), *Boeing versus Airbus: The inside story of the greatest international competition in business*, Alfred A. Knopf, New York.

Oster, C. V. & Zorn, C. K. (1989), 'Is it still safe to fly?' in Moses, L. N. & Savage, I. (eds), *Transportation safety in an age of deregulation*. Oxford University Press, New York.

Pratt & Whitney (2023), https://prattwhitney.com/products-and-services/products/commercial-engines

Royce (2023), https://www.rolls-royce.com/products-and-services/civil-aerospace.aspx

Rummel, R. W. (1991), *Howard Hughes and TWA*, Smithsonian Institution Press, Washington, DC.

Sabbagh, K. (1996), *Twenty-first century jet: The making and marketing of the Boeing 777*, Scribner, New York.

Serling, R. J. (1992), *Legend and legacy: The story of Boeing and its people*, St. Martin's Press, New York.

Shuman, R. B. (2002), 'Concorde' in Tracy Irons-Georges (Ed.) *Encyclopedia of flight*, pp. 420–423, Salem Press, Pasadena, CA

Useem, J. (2019), *The long-forgotten flight that sent Boeing off course*. The Atlantic.

PART II
THE INDUSTRY GROWS UP (1970–2000)

9 A Brave New World

Learning Objectives

After reading this chapter, you should have a good understanding of:

LO1: the US decision to pursue liberalization and the actions that were taken
LO2: the arguments for and against deregulation and liberalization
LO3: the history and progress of open skies
LO4: the basic elements of bilateral air service agreements

Key Terms, Concepts & People

Airline Deregulation Act	Bermuda II	Show cause
Encirclement	Open skies	Anti-trust
Fifth freedom	Netherlands	

New Deal

In 1976, the British gave notice to the US government that it was terminating Bermuda I. According to the British, Bermuda I gave American carriers a disproportionate share of traffic in large measure due to the liberal fifth freedom rights granted to US carriers. It had been thirty years since the events at Chicago and the signing of Bermuda I. The world was now a very different place. The Asian miracle saw, first Japan, then other Asian nations achieve double digit-levels of economic growth. Between 1950 and 1973, the Japanese gross domestic product grew at a rate of 10.5 percent a year. By the 1970s, the Japanese were producing over half the world's tonnage of shipping and as much steel as their US counter-parts (Kennedy, 1987). In Europe, most of the nations were back to their pre-war levels of output by 1950. Between 1950 and 1970, European gross domestic product grew on average 5.5 percent a year while industrial product rose 7.1 percent (Landes, 1969). By contrast, the US economy was losing the relative advantages it possessed coming out of World War II. At the Bretton Woods conference in 1944, the world monetary system had been established, pegging all major currencies to the US dollar. Unfortunately, US policies to finance both the war in Vietnam and domestic, social spending without increasing taxes had led the government to print more money, i.e. increase the money supply. This in turn led to inflation and put pressure on the international monetary system. This system was abandoned in

DOI: 10.4324/9781003405306-11

1973 (Solomon, 1982). Rising inflation, declining shares of exports, and new foreign competition at home were taking their toll on the US economy.

For the British, the time appeared right to make a change. For their part, the US government, fearing a complete breakdown of the commercial air traffic with Great Britain, agreed to sign what became known as Bermuda II in 1977. This bilateral agreement virtually eliminated multiple carrier designations, established capacity limitations, and redressed the imbalance in fifth freedom rights. Bermuda II was seen as a major policy setback by the US government and a direct challenge to competitive markets.

Not Taking It Laying Down

In 1978, in an attempt to demonstrate its commitment to air transport liberalization, the US initiated three actions. The first of these was to issue a statement entitled 'Policy for the Conduct of International Air Transportation'. This statement declared the US intention to 'trade competitive opportunities, rather than restrictions' in order to expand competition and reduce prices (95th Congress, 1978). This policy was a denunciation of Bermuda II and a clear challenge to the rest of the aviation community. Shortly afterwards, the US Civil Aeronautics Board (CAB) issued an order to IATA to 'show cause' why they should not be considered an illegal cartel as prohibited by US anti-trust law. Since IATA membership was restricted to international carriers whose major tasks included setting fares and capacity, there was little argument that a violation was taking place. This was also a warning to US carriers that their participation in the tariff- and capacity-setting activities of IATA would not be acceptable. Finally, in late 1978, the US became the first nation in the world to deregulate its air transport industry, with the passage of the Airline Deregulation Act (Toh, 1998).

The purpose of the Airline Deregulation Act was "to encourage, develop, and attain an air transportation system which relies on competitive market forces to determine the quality, variety, and price of air services, and of other purposes". The Act phased out the CAB with its market control of entry/exit, pricing, and service levels. The proponents of deregulation argued that regulation forced competition based solely on service quality and thus created fares that in many cases were 50 percent higher than comparable intrastate (unregulated) fares. Studies had concluded that regulation also forced carriers to accept low, uneconomical load factors, raised labor costs, protected inefficient carriers, and prevented them from establishing economies of scale that would allow them to lower unit prices (Caves, 1962; Douglas & Miller, 1974; Jordan, 1970; Kahn, 1971). It should be noted that several studies found that the average cost per passenger did not fall as firm size increased which tended to indicate that airlines were not natural monopolies that should be subject to regulation (Eads, Nerlove, & Raduchel, 1969; Straszheim, 1969; White, 1979). On the other hand, larger aircraft and increasing density (increased frequency of flights, additional seats in existing flights) did appear to lower unit costs (Caves, Christensen, & Tretheway, 1984; Graham & Kaplan, 1982). Overall, deregulation was expected to improve service to the public, lower fares, allow carriers to achieve higher profits, and create a more competitive airline industry through the entry of new carriers as well as the freer regulatory environment afforded to existing competitors (Kane, 1998). These proponents noted that almost twenty years after deregulation there were more carriers flying and that prices had fallen. Morrison and Winston (1997) have estimated that airfares fell 33 percent in real terms between 1976 and 1993. They attributed at least 20 percent of the decline in fares to deregulation itself, which increased competition and reduced costs at large and medium-sized airports. A 1998 study of international carriers found that the major US carriers as a whole were more cost-competitive than all but some of the lower-wage Asian carriers (Oum & Yu, 1998).

While the impact of deregulation is still under debate after all these years, it is clear that following deregulation many US carriers were forced to undergo a painful process of restructuring that not all of them completed successfully. The financial crisis in the early 1980s hit all the US carriers hard and led to industry consolidation and the creation of the hub-and-spoke system. In addition to the disappearance of such pre-deregulation carriers as Eastern Air Lines and Pan Am, more than two hundred new-entrant carriers have started and failed in the two decades following deregulation. By the early 1990s, financial crisis led the industry to develop complex holding structures, expand non-airline and/or discrete services, and race to create a seamless global network of strategic alliances (Rosen, 1995). Studies showed that although there were more carriers flying two decades later, the top six carriers accounted for an increasingly large proportion of the total traffic. In 1985, the top six accounted for 62 percent of the domestic US traffic. By the early 1990s, these same six controlled 86 percent of the market (Kim & Singal, 1993). Several studies have even suggested that real prices fell faster under regulation than they did in the post-deregulation period (Dempsey & Goetz, 1992; Dempsey & Gesell, 1997). In addition, it has been suggested that deregulation did not benefit all consumers in terms of the level of service or price. Small, outlying communities in fact lost some portion of the service they enjoyed prior to deregulation and the fact that they were often linked to a single dominant hub may have increased their fares (Goetz & Dempsey, 1989; Jones, 1998). While there are no quantitative studies examining the pre- and post-deregulation levels of service quality among US carriers, there is a general consensus that it declined significantly following deregulation and US carriers are conspicuously absent from surveys ranking the service quality of international carriers (Kahn, 1990; Dempsey & Goetz, 1992; Towers & Perrin, 1991; Zagat, 1992).

The benefits and costs of domestic regulation can and have been the subject of an entire book (or series of books) and are mentioned here only because freeing domestic markets added philosophical and economic pressure to the liberalization of international markets. The arguments briefly presented here are also intended to suggest some of the effects that might occur in a truly deregulated international market. Deregulation in the US market did appear to result in overall declines in fare prices and the appearance, at least temporarily, of new entrant carriers. These pressures forced the industry to restructure to lower costs, as noted above by Oum and Yu (1998). Whatever the successes or failures of deregulation in the long run, the US was now ready to push forward on the international scene with new initiatives designed to open international markets to greater competition and more market-based controls.

Encircling the World

In 1979, the US passed the International Air Transportation Competition Act, which set out three goals for future US aviation policy. First, the US would push for multiple carrier designations, permissive route authority, and no operational restrictions on capacity and frequency. Second, air fares would be freed to respond to consumer demand. Finally, the US would work to eliminate discriminatory practices preventing US carriers from effectively competing in international markets. Among the practices targeted for change were foreign computer reservation systems that favored other national carriers, government user fees at international airports that were excessive compared to solely domestic airports (the contention being that national governments were using these fees to subsidize smaller, local airports), and policies that required exclusive contracts for ground handling and other services (Toh, 1998).

The US would now pursue its new open skies policy through the application of two levers. The first of these was laid out by the Director of the Bureau of Pricing and Domestic Aviation, and the CAB. The so-called Encirclement Strategy called for the US to bring pressure on smaller market countries to sign open skies agreements by diverting traffic with lower open skies fares. This was based on the assumption that open skies would lower fares between those countries involved in the bilateral agreement and cause passengers to change their traveling patterns in pursuit of lower fares. Two nations were primarily targeted for encirclement – Japan and Great Britain – because they represented the key entry ports for US travelers to Asia and Europe, respectively (Levine, 1979). The US first targeted smaller market countries that generated very little third and fourth freedom traffic (to and from the US) since these countries stood to gain by simply getting greater access to US destinations. There could also be no question of exchanging domestic opportunities (cabotage) with these nations since they had little or no domestic markets to exchange for the sizable US domestic market (think of countries like Singapore or The Netherlands).

The second lever to open skies came through the application of the US Department of Transportation's (DOT) policy on the approval of airline alliances. This policy based approval on either the coverage of the rights under existing bilateral or proven benefits to the US (Gellman Research Associates, 1994). In addition, the US DOT granted immunity from anti-trust enforcement to alliances between carriers from open skies countries (see Chapter 11 for a further discussion). The arguments being that there were proven benefits to the US deriving from these agreements. Anti-trust immunity allows competitors to coordinate on issues of pricing, capacity, and scheduling. Thus, they can achieve greater levels of operational integration, cut costing, and improved quality through coordination (Oum & Park, 1997).

Opening Up

Table 9.1a lists the open skies agreements signed by the US prior to 2001 and the dates of their signing. Table 9.1b lists the open skies agreements since 2001. It is interesting to note the momentum that was building in the US efforts prior to September 11th. In part, this momentum represented the liberalization focus of the Clinton presidency as well as the growing international movement toward liberalization. Following September 11th, security issues dominated the aviation agenda. When aviation liberalization returned to the agenda, the issue that took center stage was the proposed multilateral agreement with the European Union. This very complex and contentious agreement would take precedence over single country open skies.

Tables 9.1a & 9.1b also illustrate the advance of the Encirclement Strategy, which dictated that the countries approached first were small market nations surrounding the target markets of Japan and the UK Assuming that open skies did indeed divert traffic to open skies markets by lowering fares, then these nations would seek their own open skies to prevent traffic loss. To understand the difference open skies has made in the bilateral process, it is interesting to note that the length of the bilateral agreement discussed in Chapter 5 between the US and Great Britain and the US and Japan were sixteen pages in length. The US–Netherlands agreement was on just one page (Table 9.2).

Table 9.1a Open Skies Agreements 1992–2001

Year	Month	Country	Year	Month	Country
2001	10	France	1997	7	Aruba
	9	Oman		2	Brunei
	5	Poland		10	Chile
	11	Sri Lanka		4	Costa Rica
				4	El Salvador
2000	11	Benin		4	Guatemala
	2	Burkina Faso		4	Honduras
	5	Gambia		6	Malaysia
	3	Ghana		12	Nether. Antilles
	10	Malta		5	New Zealand
	10	Morocco		5	Nicaragua
	2	Namibia		3	Panama
	8	Nigeria		12	Romania
	10	Rwanda		1	Singapore
	12	Senegal		3	Taiwan
	1	Slovak Republic			
	3	Turkey	1996	11	Jordan
				2	Germany
1999	8	Argentina			
	5	Bahrain	1995	6	Austria
	12	Dom Republic		3	Belgium
	4	Pakistan		12	Czech Republic
	12	Portugal		4	Denmark
	10	Qatar		3	Finland
	11	Tanzania		6	Iceland
	4	UAE		6	Luxembourg
				4	Norway
1998	11	Italy		4	Sweden
	4	S. Korea			
	5	Peru			
	2	Uzbekistan	1992	10	Netherlands

There is no mention of pricing, capacity, or frequency restrictions in these agreements. Clearly, open skies agreements have been helpful in saving the world's trees. One might ask whether they have achieved the goals set forth by US policy and whether the consumers of the world have benefited from these new bilateral.

Conspicuously absent from the open skies list in Tables 9.1a, 9.1b are two countries – Japan and Great Britain. Understanding the reasons for their absence illustrates several key issues in international aviation. To those outside the industry it may be surprising to discover that not all the disagreement during the bilateral negotiations between these countries took place between national governments; airlines on both sides of the debate disagreed among themselves and thus, did not present a unified voice to their respective governments. The 1952 agreement between the US and Japan had given broad rights to three carriers – United, Northwest, and Japan Airlines. The remaining US carriers and All Nippon Airways (ANA) received limited access in the 1980s due to a series of Memoranda of Understanding between Washington and Tokyo. Although Northwest, an incumbent carrier, supported open skies, United Airlines did not favor such an agreement, which would have allowed more US competition into the Japanese market. From a policy perspective, the non-incumbent US carriers would have received more access under a

Table 9.1b Open Skies Agreements 2002 to Present

Year	Month	Country	Year	Month	Country
2012	6	Suriname[c]	2007	4	Latvia[a]
	6	Sierra		4	Lithuania[a]
	12	Seychelles		4	Slovenia[a]
	12	Yemen		4	Spain[a]
				4	United Kingdom[a]
2011	3	Brazil[b]		12	Georgia
	4	Saudi			
	7	Macedonia	2006	2	Cameroon
	11	St. Kitts		2	Cook Islands
	12	Montenegro		5	Chad
				8	Kuwait
2010	3	Zambia			
	4	Israel	2005	1	India
	5	Trinidad & Tobago		5	Paraguay
	6	Switzerland		5	Maldives
	7	Barbados[c]		5	Ethiopia
	10	Japan		9	Thailand
	11	Colombia		10	Mali
				11	Bosnia And Herzegovina
2008	2	Australia			
	3	Croatia[b]	2004	3	Madagascar
	5	Kenya		5	Gabon
	10	Laos		7	Indonesia
	11	Armenia		10	Uruguay
2007	2	Liberia	2003	9	Tonga
	3	Canada		9	Albania
	4	Bulgaria[a]			
	4	Cyprus[a]	2002	6	Uganda
	4	Estonia[a]		6	Cape Verde
	4	Greece[a]		7	Samoa
	4	Hungary[a]		10	Jamaica
	4	Ireland[a]			

[a] The US–EU Air Transport Agreement, signed April 30, 2007, was provisionally applied March 30, 2008, for all 27 European Union Member States, and Amended by a Protocol, signed and provisionally applied June 24, 2010.
[b] Agreement signed but not applied.
[c] Date agreement reached, but not yet signed or applied.

Table 9.2 US–Netherlands Open Skies Agreement

Netherlands

A.   The Netherlands via intermediate points to a point or points in the United States and beyond.
B.   The Netherlands Antilles via the intermediate points Santo Domingo, Port au Prince, Kingston, Montego Bay, Camaguey, and Havana, to Miami.
C.   The Netherlands Antilles to New York.
D.   The Netherlands Antilles to San Juan.

United States

A.   The United States via intermediate points to a point or points in the Netherlands and beyond.
B.   The United States via intermediate points to Aruba, Curacao, St. Maarten and beyond (Air Transport Association of America).

'not-quite-open-skies' agreement and felt that the US should not push for open skies if that push jeopardized an overall agreement (Goldman, 1997). Similar issues surfaced in the open skies negotiations between the US and the UK. As part of their One World alliance, American Airlines and British Airways had asked the US government for anti-trust immunity which would only be granted in the presence of an open skies agreement. As Richard Branson, Chairman of Virgin Atlantic Airways, has often noted,

> they thought they had the British Department of Transport in their pocket, which unfortunately at the time was probably true. They also thought that the US Department of Transportation would be so eager to get rid of the Bermuda II disagreement, that it would be blind to the dire consequences such an alliance would hold for competition on the North Atlantic.
>
> (100)

As this quote indicates, the competitors in both countries were generally more interested in simply gaining more access to US–UK markets than pursuing a broad open skies agreement. Carriers such as British Airways and American saw open skies initially as the only way to gain even more from the system. However, even these two carriers began to have doubts when they realized the price that the European Union intended to extract for its approval. Access to Heathrow Airport in London, the number one destination airport for North Atlantic passengers, was tightly constrained. In order to free up landing slots for new entrant carriers, European officials had sought ways to encourage incumbent carriers to give up slots. It should be noted that, unlike in the US, slots could be sold as an asset. In Europe, a carrier either used a slot or lost it. The price of European approval was the surrender of 300 landing slots by British Airways and American Airlines (Phillips, 1999). British Airways 'apparently decided the price for opening up Heathrow to new competition might not be offset by revenues gained from a full alliance with American' (Morrocco, 1998, p. 45).

If opening Japan and the United Kingdom were the key goals of open skies, then the policy was not a complete success. Although both markets are now part of open skies, the journey was far longer than anticipated and many other factors came to play bigger roles; however, the example of US–Japan and US–UK internal divisions illustrates the interplay that occurs in free market systems where competitors look to individual profit and advantage over mutual, assured benefits. According to Adam Smith, the father of market economics, individuals each acting in their own self-interest were supposed to result in a more perfect distribution of goods and determination of price. In the case of airlines, market operation was never separated from government intervention. In a broader sense, open skies helped to spread a more liberal environment for international pricing and capacity. In 1984, the US signed a multilateral agreement with the European Civil Aviation Conference that created zones of reasonableness for each fare class allowing individual carriers latitude in setting prices. The US also pushed for the inclusion of language within bilateral agreements that disallowed fares only with the mutual disapproval of the two parties to the agreement. This new pricing freedom placed tremendous pressure on IATA members to find ways around the set fares. Many IATA members resorted to illegal discounting of fares through extra commissions to travel agents (Toh, 1998). These 'bucket shops' sold blocks of tickets at prices more competitive with US carriers, but without sales receipt documentation that would be evidence of violation. Over time, the zones of reasonableness became so broad that, to all intents and purposes, the market ruled in matters of pricing and IATA abandoned its role in fare setting.

Several studies by the US Department of Transportation have concluded that open skies bilateral have been effective in lowering fares. In the 1999 report *International Aviation Developments: Global Deregulation Takes Off*, the DOT reported that fares in open skies markets dropped 17.5 percent between 1996 and 1998 compared to only a 3.5 percent drop in no-open skies markets. Fares increased slightly in non-open skies gateway-to-gateway markets, but dropped 11.1 percent in open skies markets. In the 2000 report *International Aviation Developments: Transatlantic Deregulation – The Alliance Network Effect*, the DOT concluded that average fares to open skies countries declined by 20 percent overall compared to 1996 and approached 25 percent in connecting markets beyond European gateways. Significantly, double-digit fare reductions have occurred even in gate-to-gate markets in open skies countries (3). This report goes on to suggest that the link between open skies and strategic alliances have created an 'alliance network effect' that has further lowered prices. In fact, it concludes that 'alliance-based networks are the principle driving force behind transatlantic price reductions and traffic gains' (5). In Chapter 16, we will discuss the benefits of the long-awaited EU–US Open Skies agreement.

The Next Step

The US deregulation of air transportation and the concomitant push for open skies would slowly erode the old system of international aviation set up in the post-World War II era. The liberalization and economic integration of Europe and Asia (Chapter 10) would further press the cause of liberalization. However, the fact remains that the system remained far from open. Branson (1998) has observed that the Virgin retail division in the US

> has a rapidly growing chain of Megastores in this country (U.S.), selling CDs, books, computer games, etc. We employ several thousand U.S. staff and the increased competition our stores have brought clearly benefits the consumer. No one stands in our way when we want to invest…What a difference from aviation, where if Virgin wanted to establish a U.S. airline, we would be restricted to a mere 25% of the voting shares, and thus prevented from exercising any form of control.

(101)

The events of 9/11 propelled the already slumping international airline industry to the brink of one of its greatest disasters; in every crisis, however, there is also the possibility of creating new futures. Some of these possible new futures will be the subject of later chapters. First, we will look at the progress of deregulation and liberalization in Europe and Asia (Chapter 10). Then, we will look at the way airlines attempted to create global seamless networks that extend their reach throughout the world before liberalization took hold (Chapter 11).

Questions

1 Discuss the 'show cause' order the US filed against IATA.
2 Analyze the impact of domestic deregulation in the US
3 What is encirclement and what were its goals?
4 How did the US define open skies? What is not included?
5 Did US policy succeed in opening markets?

6 Evaluate the effectiveness of the Airline Deregulation Act in achieving its stated goals of promoting competitive market forces and lowering air service prices.

7 Compare and contrast the approaches taken by the US in pursuing open skies agreements with smaller market countries versus larger market countries like Japan and Great Britain.

8 Assess the role of airline alliances in the context of open skies agreements and international air transportation competition.

References

Branson, R. (1998), 'Luncheon address', *FAA commercial aviation forecast conference proceedings: Overcoming barriers to world competition and growth, March 12–13*, pp. 99–102.

Caves, R. (1962), *Air transport and its regulators: An industry study*, Harvard University Press, Cambridge, MA.

Caves, R. E., Christensen, L. R., & Tretheway, M. W. (1984), 'Economies of density versus economies of scale: Why trunk and local service airline costs differ,' *RAND Journal of Economics*, 15, pp. 471–489.

Dempsey, P. & Gesell, L. (1997), '*Airline management: Strategies for the 21st century*', Coast Aire Publications, Chandler, AZ.

Dempsey, P. & Goetz, A. (1992), '*Airline deregulation and Laissez Faire mythology*', Praeger, Santa Barbara, CA.

Douglas, G. W. & Miller, J. C. (1974), *Economic regulation of domestic air transport: Theory and policy*, The Brookings Institution, Washington, DC.

Eads, G., Nerlov, M. & Raduchel, W. (1969), 'A long-run cost function for the local service airline industry: An experiment in non-linear estimation,' *Review of Economics and Statistics*, 51, pp. 258–270.

Gellman Research Associates (1994), '*A study of international airline codesharing*', report submitted to *Office of Aviation and International Economics*, Office of the Secretary of Transportation, U.S. Department of Transportation, Washington, DC.

Goetz, A. R. & Dempsey, P. S. (1989), 'Airline deregulation ten years after: Something foul in the air,' *Journal of Air Law and Commerce*, 54, pp. 927–963.

Goldman, M. (1997), 'Negotiating not-quite-open-skies', *The Journal of Commerce*, November 1, p. 4.

Graham, D. R. & Kaplan, D. P. (1982), 'Airlines deregulation is working,' *Regulation*, 6, pp. 26–32.

Jones, J. R. (1998), 'Twenty years of airline deregulation: The impact on outlying and small communities,' *Journal of Transportation Management*, 10, pp. 33–43.

Jordan, W. A. (1970), *Airline regulation in America: Effects and imperfections*, Johns Hopkins University Press, Baltimore, MD.

Kahn, A. E. (1971), *The economics of regulation*, Wiley, NY.

Kahn, A. E. (1990), 'Deregulation: Looking backward and looking forward,' *Yale Journal of Regulation*, 7, pp. 325–354.

Kane, R. M. (1998), *Air transportation*, 13th ed., Kendall/Hunt Publishing Company, Dubuque, IA.

Kennedy, P. (1987), *The rise and fall of the great powers*, Random House, NY.

Kim, E. H. & Singal, V. (1993), 'Mergers and market power: Evidence from the airline industry', *American Economic Review*, 83, pp. 549–569.

Landes, D. (1969), *The unbound prometheus: Technological change and industrial development in Western Europe from 1970 to the present*, Cambridge University Press, Cambridge.

Levine, M. E. (1979), 'Civil aeronautics memo by Michael E. Levine', *Aviation Daily*, March 8, pp. 1–7.

Morrison, S. A. & Winston, C. (1997), 'The fare skies: Air transportation and Middle America,' *The Brookings Review*, 15, pp. 42–45.

Morrocco, J. D. (1998), 'Open skies impasse shifts alliance plans', *Aviation Week and Space Technology*, November 9, pp. 45–46.

Oum, T. H. & Park, J. (1997), 'Airline alliances: Current status, policy issues, and future directions', *Journal of Air Transport Management*, 3, pp. 133–144.

Oum, T. H. & Yu, C. (1998), *Winning airlines: Productivity and cost competitiveness of the world's major airlines*, Kluwer Academic Press, Boston, MA.

Phillips, E. H. (1999), 'Oneworld late, but powerful', *Aviation Week and Space Technology*, August 23, pp. 63–64.

Rosen, S. D. (1995), 'Corporate restructuring: A labor perspective', in P. Cappelli (Ed.), *Airline labor relations in the global era: The new frontier*, pp. 31–40, ILR Press, Ithaca, NY.

Solomon, R. (1982), *The international monetary system*, Harper & Row, NY.

Straszheim, M. R. (1969), *The international airline industry*, The Brookings Institution, Washington, DC.

Toh, R. S. (1998), 'Towards an international open skies regime: Advances, impediments, and impacts', *Journal of Air Transportation World Wide*, 3, pp. 61–70.

Towers and Perrin (1991), *Competing in a new market: Is airline management prepared?*, Towers and Perrin, San Francisco, CA.

U.S. Congress (1978), *Hearings before the Subcommittee on Aviation of the Committee on Commerce, Science and Transportation, United States Senate, 95th Congress Second Session on S.3363*, pp. 19–20.

White, L. J. (1979), 'Economies of scale and the question of 'natural monopoly' in the airline industry,' *Journal of Air Law and Commerce*, 46, pp. 545–573.

Zagat, W. (1992), *Zagat United States travel survey*, Zagat, NY.

10   A Different View?

Learning Objectives

After reading this chapter, you should have a good understanding of:

LO1:   the differences in the European and Asian markets that influenced their approaches
         to deregulation and liberalization
LO2:   the EU approach to deregulation
LO3:   the early results of deregulation
LO4:   the remaining barriers to open markets

Key Terms, Concepts & People

Big Bang	Common Transport Policy	Three packages
Charter Operator	Two airline policy	LCC

Different Markets, Different Views

As the US struggled with its Big Bang deregulation and pressured the rest of the world to open
its markets, Europe and Asia proceeded to follow their own path to opening up their markets.
In Europe, the process of aviation liberalization would be a part of a much bigger effort to
integrate the countries in the European Community into the European Union and then deal
with enlargement; aviation would be just one of the industries that would have to adjust to the
changing times. In Asia, the story of liberalization and deregulation would be a more mixed
one. There would be no overarching efforts at true political and economic union. The
Association of Southeast Asian Nations (ASEAN), for example, would focus on accelerating
growth through loosening trade restrictions. In other words, they would begin the first stages
of integration and be largely content to remain at this stage rather than pursue a path to union.

In any event, international politics probably guaranteed that the rest of the world would
not fall in line with the US position on deregulation. After all, the Cold War was still in
effect in 1978 and independence needed to be demonstrated whatever side you took in that
war. Still, some of the variations in attitudes and approaches had their roots in the fact that
different regions and nations were faced with very different historic, geographic, and economic realities that inevitably shaped their approach to these issues. The conditions and
needs of a small island nation in the Caribbean or the South Pacific, for example, were very
different from those of a large, rapidly developing country or a wealthy developed nation.
Still, the pressure remained.

DOI: 10.4324/9781003405306-12

The View from Europe

From a historical and geographic standpoint, Europe can be said to include all the nations west of the Russian Ural Mountains; however, this chapter will focus primarily on the nations of the European Union (EU) (Table 10.1) with a brief look at the other nations that have asked to be considered for membership of that association (Table 10.2). These

Table 10.1 Information on European Union Nations

Country	Area*	Population**	Airports (paved)
Austria	83,871	8,221,646	52 (24)
Belgium	30,528	10,444,268	41 (26)
Bulgaria	110,879	6,981,642	68 (57)
Croatia	56,594	4,475,611	69 (24)
Cyprus	9,251	1,155,403	15 (13)
Czech Rep.	78,867	10,609,762	128 (41)
Denmark	43,094	5,556,452	80 (28)
Estonia	45,228	1,266,375	18 (13)
Finland	338,145	5,266,114	148 (74)
France	551,500	65,951,611	464 (294)
Germany	357,022	81,147,265	539 (318)
Greece	131,957	10,772,967	77 (68)
Hungary	93,028	9,939,470	41 (20)
Ireland	70,273	4,775,982	40 (16)
Italy	301,340	61,482,297	129 (98)
Latvia	64,589	2,178,443	42 (18)
Lithuania	65,300	3,515,858	61 (22)
Luxembourg	2,586	514,862	2 (1)
Malta	316	411,277	1 (1)
The Netherlands	41,543	16,805,037	29 (23)
Poland	312,685	38,383,809	126 (87)
Portugal	92,090	10,799,270	64 (43)
Romania	238,391	21,790,479	45 (26)
Slovakia	49,035	5,488,339	35 (21)
Slovenia	20,273	1,992,690	16 (7)
Spain	505,370	47,370,542	150 (99)
Sweden	450,295	9,647,386	231 (149)
UK	243,610	63,395,574	460 (271)

Source: CIA Factbook.
* Square km. ** Estimated July 2013 figures. Data on airports from 2013.

Table 10.2 Information on Selected EU Enlargement Countries

Country	Area*	Population**	Airports (paved)
Iceland	103,000	315,281	96 (7)
Macedonia	25,713	2,087,171	10 (8)
Montenegro	13,812	653,474	5 (5)
Serbia	77,474	7,243,007	26 (10)
Turkey	783,562	80,694,485	98 (91)

Source: CIA Factbook.
* Square km. ** Estimated July 2013 figures. Data on airports from 2013.

nations represent a very diverse set of languages, cultures, histories, and geographies. As Table 10.1 shows, the landmass of the various EU countries ranges from 316 square kilometers for Malta to 551,500 square kilometers for France. Similarly, the population of EU countries ranges from 411,277 for Malta to 81,147,265 for Germany. This diversity in size and population is reflected in the level of aviation infrastructure within these countries as well as the importance of aviation to domestic travel and commerce. The geographic location of nations also influences the ability of potential hub city airports to attract traffic. Those countries requesting consideration for admission to the EU under enlargement plans also show considerable diversity in size and population, ranging from Macedonia with an area of 25,713 square kilometers and 2,087,171 people to Turkey with an area of 783,562 square kilometers and 80,694,485 people.

There are several key differences between the air transport market in Europe and the US that have influenced the development of, and approach to, domestic deregulation and international liberalization. The Chicago Convention of 1944 led to the adoption of a one-airline policy in most of the nations of Europe. This airline, the de jure flag carrier, was seen as more of an instrument of state policy than a moneymaking enterprise (Graham, 1995). The typical European carrier was to be completely or partially owned by the state, which would provide direct financial assistance to carriers: (1) to compensate airlines for the imposition of a public service obligation; (2) to develop and operate domestic service; (3) to provide service to economically underdeveloped regions.

(4) to encourage the acquisition and operation of specific airplanes; or (5) simply to cover an airline's operating losses' (Taneja, 1988, p. 59). This flag carrier would develop its national hub, usually at the nation's capital, and dominate that hub accounting for over 50 percent of the departures (Borestein, 1992). The network of airline routes would reflect national requirements and former colonial ties. As a whole, the old European air transport market was characterized by low productivity, high unit costs, and high fares. In contrast, the US domestic market was substantially larger than that of any single EU nation and benefited from several privately owned carriers throughout its history, although it too received government assistance in its early development from airmail rates (Graham, 1995; Sinha, 2001). In fact, the US industry would receive significant assistance through the years, but in indirect ways.

Another feature that distinguishes the European market from the US is the higher level of inter-modal competition from automobiles and high-speed trains. The average length of a haul in Europe is 750 kilometers, half the US average length of a haul. This increases the competition from other modes of transportation and has limited the ability of airlines to develop hub-and-spoke systems like their US counterparts. This, in turn, has limited consumer ability to achieve reduced fares by accepting indirect routing over direct flights to destination. With the exception of the northeastern corridor of the US, train services do not offer a viable substitute to air travel for US consumers (Graham, 1995; Sinha, 2001). With a cruising speed of 185 miles per hour, the Trains à Grande Vitesse (TGV) in France became a serious, viable competitor for Air France. A market analysis by the French civil aviation authority found that only domestic routes not served by the TGV remain healthy for the air carrier. Similar concerns arose in other European countries with high-speed train options (Sparaco, 2012a). European carriers have also faced competition from a well-developed air charter market. In the early 1990s, charter service in the US accounted for less than 2 percent of all passenger miles, but more than 25 percent of the passenger miles in Europe. These European charter passengers were predominantly leisure travelers, leaving scheduled carriers to serve business travel needs (Sinha, 2001). The rise of the low-cost carriers (LCCs) has also created new pressure on the legacy carriers. According to the European Low-Fare Airlines Association, their members carried over 200 million passengers in 2012 (Sparaco, 2012b). The ELFAA was disbanded in 2016 as members joined the new trade group Airlines for Europe (A4E). Finally, there was a significant difference in the product mix between US and European carriers as they deregulated. For US carriers, only 15.4 percent of the departures were international as late as 1990. In 1990, international departures represented 52.9 percent of the departures of European carriers (Sinha, 2001). In short, it was neither feasible nor probably possible to institute US-style deregulation in Europe.

The European Way

When the European Economic Community, a predecessor of the current European Union, was formed in 1957, it established a Common Transport Policy, but failed to include aviation in the original draft (Button, 1997). This oversight was corrected in a 1986 ruling by the European Court of Justice, which declared that air transport would henceforth be subject to the competition rules of the Treaty of Rome. The following year, the Council of Ministers adopted the so-called First Package, which allowed multiple designation of carriers on country-to-country routes and high-volume city-to-city routes, 5th freedom rights on city-to-city routes up to 30 percent of capacity, automatic approval of discount fares up to 55 percent, and double approval of full fares. The Second Package, adopted in 1990, included a double-disapproval provision for full fares and an extension of 5th freedom rights on city-to-city routes up to 50 percent of capacity. Protection was also granted for routes designated as public service obligations. The Third, and final, Package was implemented in 1993 and ended on April 1, 1997. This package granted full access to all routes, including cabotage, which went into effect on April 1. It removed all restrictions on fares subject to the right of the European Commission to intervene in matters of predatory pricing and seat (capacity) dumping. All distinctions were removed between charter and scheduled carriers and freedom was granted to start an airline provided it was: 1) EU-owned, 2) financially sound, and 3) in compliance with all safety requirements (Graham, 1995, 1997; Sinha, 2001).

Overall Results

The early packages, combined with the more liberal bilateral agreements signed during the 1980s, did increase the frequency on some routes and reduce leisure fares, particularly where multiple carrier designation allowed new market entry (Button & Swann, 1989; Graham, 1995). A study of the air transport market between the UK and Ireland reported a 50 percent reduction in fares and a doubling in passenger numbers following deregulation (Barrett, 1999). Ironically, financial troubles at the Irish flag carrier Aer Lingus saw 'the other Irish carrier', Ryanair, attempt to buy it, a situation that would lead back to the near-monopoly of yesteryear (Convery, 2012). Other early study results were more mixed. Morrell (1998) found that the number of cross-border routes served increased by 11 percent between 1989 and 1992. This number rose to 25 percent between 1992 and 1995. The number of flights operated also increased during these periods, by 14 and 18 percent respectively. The average frequency on all intra-EU routes increased from 13.9 departures per week in 1989 to 15.5 in 1992. Seat capacity did not increase, but it did go up after 1992 on routes that were served by three or more carriers. A 1995 study by the Civil Aviation

Authority of Great Britain also found that consumers only gained from lower fares, better service, and better connecting flights when there were at least three competitors on a given route. In effect, actual, rather than threatened, entry was essential to realizing benefits from liberalization (Abbott & Thompson, 1989; Humphries, 1996). A study by the European Commission (1996) concluded that competition had little effect on routes run as a monopoly or duopoly. Unfortunately, approximately 94 percent of the intra-EU routes fell into this category.

By the late 1990s, there were five low-cost carriers operating in Europe – Go, Buzz, EasyJet, Ryanair, and Virgin Express. Three of these had been founded as subsidiaries of legacy carriers – BA (Go), KLM (Buzz), and Virgin Atlantic (Virgin Group). It would, however, be the other two, particularly Ryanair, that would have the most dramatic impact on mobility and airfares. LCCs would truly take advantage of the new single market. By 2022, Ryanair would have used its LCC model to become the 5th-largest airline in the world in terms of capacity (Rowland, 2022).

The effect of liberalization on established EU legacy carriers had been relatively limited until the rise of the LCCs. Carriers such as British Airways and KLM worked to improve their long-haul market and hub system more than their intra-EU system (CAA, 1995). While one of the key features of the first two packages was the extension of 5th freedom rights, evidence indicates that few carriers exploited these rights (Graham, 1995). Some of the peripheral EU countries did initially attempt to exploit the intra-EU opportunities of cabotage, but many of these services were discontinued due to limited profitability (Morrell, 1998). Thus, there was generally little third carrier entry in many markets, certainly not by the traditional flag carriers; this would be the area in which the LCCs would excel, and Ryanair alone has been credited with doing more to reduce fares and increase passenger numbers than any other single factor associated with deregulation (Convery, 2012). Between 1992 and 1995, there was an EU net gain of six carriers (Morrell, 1998). The most successful of these carriers were Ireland's Ryanair and the UK's EasyJet. In 2001, these carriers continued to post significant profits compared to their traditional counterparts in the EU. In fact, 2001 was a turning point for the low-cost European entrants. Industry experts had expected LCCs to increase their share of intra-European passenger traffic from 7 percent in 2001 to over 14 percent by 2006 (Binggeli & Pompeo, 2002; R2A, 2002). In fact, the number of seats offered by LCCs in Europe grew an average of 14% per year, compared to 1% for legacy carriers over the same period. In some countries such as Spain, LCCs accounted for over 50 percent of the market by the second decade of the twenty-first century (Turner, 2013). As with US LCCs, the events of September 11th created new opportunities in Europe for this model of aviation business. The Global Financial Crisis (GFC) of 2008, with its economy-weakening effects, hit Europe particularly hard and continued the trend toward LCCs.

With liberalization, particularly the implementation of the Third package, charter operators in the EU were presented with several options. They could now: (1) enter scheduled service in a head-to-head competition with EU flag carriers; (2) enter scheduled service on leisure routes; or (3) stay in the core charter market and develop their long-haul operations. Those operators that chose option 1 were not particularly successful (Air Europe, Dan Air, Trans European). Some carriers did have limited success on certain routes (Maersk Air, Transwede, Transavia), but generally charter operators did not present a serious challenge to the established carriers (Morrell, 1998). Wallace et al. (2008) found that despite a good deal of consolidation in the charter industry most of the chapter companies had lost passengers since 2001 while the LCCs appear to be major winners.

Remaining Obstacles

One of the most significant obstacles to progress in the EU was the issue of airline subsidies. In 1993, six EU carriers – Air France, Olympic, Iberia, TAP-Air Portugal, Alitalia, and Aer Lingus – required government subsidies to remain in business (Graham, 1995). Then, the Belgium government stepped in to salvage something of its flag carrier, Sabena. These early subsidies were approved by the European Commission, although vigorously opposed by some members of the EU. Later, the eastern European carriers – LOT (Poland), Malev (Hungary) and AirBaltic (Latvia) – were the focus of subsidy debate. In early 2012, the European Commission ruled that Malev had to repay subsidies received from 2007 to 2010, forcing the carrier into bankruptcy (Clark & Jolly, 2012). The preference of governments for national carriers flies in the face of the objective to remove such barriers to free trade in the EU as a whole. It also keeps excess capacity in the European market in a way similar to the liberal bankruptcy laws of the US. In both cases, artificial barriers prevent the market from adjusting quickly in market demand downturns and spread the problem to other carriers. This issue would continue to be a subject of debate with ITA, the new Italian airline launched to replace Alitalia (former flag carrier), receiving illegal state air prior to the pandemic. The EC would rule that ITA would not be liable for the aid given to Alitalia, although it would inherit much of the aircraft, landing slots, etc. of the former carrier (Leali & Eccles, 2021).

A somewhat related problem is the question of hubs. LLCs tend more often to fly point-to-point, so this is another legacy carrier problem. London Heathrow is a case in point. While it remains a major airport (and destination) in Europe, it does not truly operate under the traditional hub-and-spoke model since capacity constraints keep it from building the type of spoke traffic flows that are supposed to be the hallmark of 'successful' hubs. Since hubs are an expensive operational feature, an unsuccessful hub becomes doubly disastrous. Restructuring at some hubs is attempting to reduce or eliminate the short-haul to short-haul operations in favor of the short-haul to long-haul connections that are a part of the traditional hub model. High fuel cost is the main issue as they make smaller aircraft less economical to fly and these have typically been the aircraft assigned to small feed markets (Flottau, 2013a & b).

The View from Asia

According to the ICAO regional classification, the Asia-Pacific is composed of 34 nations covering 16,000 kilometers. It extends from Afghanistan in the west to Tahiti in the east and from Mongolia in the north to New Zealand in the south. Asia-Pacific accounted for roughly 50 percent of the total world population and was responsible for 25 percent of the world's scheduled passenger traffic in 2001 (ICAO, 2012). ICAO has projected that the region could increase its share of traffic to 42 percent by 2020 (Sinha, 2001). This growth is obviously tied to the rapid economic development of the region and the rising level of income, both of which are closely linked to aviation activity.

Taneja (1988) attributed the early growth in Asian-Pacific aviation to several factors, including high-growth export-oriented economies, productive and lower-cost airlines, and coordination and cooperation between airlines and their respective governments, all of which remain true today. According to ICAO (2012), the average annual growth in Asia from 2001 to 2011 was 6.4 percent with continued growth through 2014. While there is a great deal of variation in the general approaches of the countries in the Asia-Pacific region, they too have been on a path toward greater deregulation and liberalization, even if the pace has been somewhat slower and more uneven than the North American and European markets.

Variations on a Theme

The Centre for Aviation (CAPA) divides Asia into three regions: (1) North Asia including China, Japan, and Korea, (2) South Asia including India, and (3) South Pacific, including Australia, New Zealand, and Singapore. These divisions will be used to explore the aviation environment in Asia (CAPA, 2013a, 2013b, 2013c).

North Asia – China. With a population of more than 1.3 billion and an area of 9,596,961 square kilometers (Table 10.3), China cannot be excluded from any discussion on aviation. In 1988, China had only one state airline, CAAC, which was a division of the Civil Aviation Administration of China. In 1998, the CAAC created six regional airlines – Air China, China Eastern, China Southern, China Northern, China Northwest, and China Southwest – which were expected to run as more or less independent carriers by 1995. In April 2001, the CAAC announced plans to merge nine airlines under its control into three larger group-ings – China Southern Airlines Group, China Eastern Airlines Group, and Air China Group (Centre for Asian Business Cases, 2002). Air China, originally designated as the international division, took over China Southwest in 2002. In the same year, China Eastern also took over China Northwest. In 2003, China Southern absorbed China Northern. The CAAC also announced plans to overhaul the domestic air route network, permit ticket discounting, encourage airport alliances, and raise air transport service fees (Centre for Asian Business Cases, 2002; Aerospace Daily, 2001). The CAAC is now attempting to rationalize the hub system for the three main carriers so that each would have only a single hub – Air China (Beijing), China Eastern (Shanghai), and China Southern (Guangzhou).

Table 10.3 Information of Selected Asia-Pacific Countries

Country	Area[a]	Population[b]	Airports (paved)
Australia	7,741,220	22,262,501	480 (349)
China	9,596,961	1,349,585,838	507 (463)
Cook Islands	236	10,447	11 (1)
Fiji	18,274	896,758	28 (4)
India	3,287,263	1,220,800,359	346 (253)
Indonesia	1,904,569	251,160,124	673 (186)
Japan	377,915	127,253,075	175 (142)
Malaysia	329,847	29,628,392	114 (39)
New Zealand	267,710	4,365,113	123 (39)
Pakistan	796,095	193,238,868	151 (108)
Philippines	300,000	105,720,644	247 (89)
Singapore	697	5,460,302	9 (9)
Taiwan	35,980	23,299,716	37 (35)
Thailand	513,120	67,497,151	101 (63)
Timor-Leste	14,874	1,172,390	6 (2)
Vietnam	331,210	92,477,857	45 (38)

Source: CIA Factbook.
[a] Square Km.
[b] Estimated July 2013 figures.
Data for airports from 2013.

All these hubs are coastal, with no clear central Chinese hub (Perrett, 2013). According to CAPA, Chinese carriers were not taking advantage of many sixth freedom rights and were limited by their long-haul fleet. Chinese policy at this time was to limit long-haul routes to a single carrier. Of the three carriers, China Southern was having the most difficulty in the long-haul market (CAPA, 2013a).

China continues to be the source of global growth in air travel. The fleet of aircraft there is expected to triple by 2040 and to surpass the US as the largest aviation market shortly before this date. One key question for the manufacturers of Large Commercial Aircraft (and their engines) is whether this growth will include their aircraft or rely on the home-grown Commercial Aircraft Corporation of China (COMAC) who launched their first product, C919, in 2022 (Li, 2022).

North Asia – Japan. As you will remember from Chapter 8, the United States policy of encirclement in Asia was aimed at opening the Japanese market, at that time the key Asian market from North America. The policy was less than successful. Historically, Japanese policy was marked by a strict regulation of the aviation system after the so-called 'aviation constitution' was adopted in 1972, dividing the market among the three Japanese carriers – Japan Air Lines (JAL), All Nippon Airways (ANA), and Japan Air Systems (JAS). JAL was to serve the main domestic trunk routes and the international market, ANA was assigned short-haul international charter flights and other domestic trunk routes, and JAS was to serve primarily on local routes. Little or no competition was allowed between these carriers. In 1986, the Council for Transport Policy recommended the privatization of JAL, the introduction of greater domestic competition, including new entrant carriers, and the end of JAL's international monopoly. In 1996, a zone fare system was introduced which allowed carriers to offer a discount up to 50 percent of the minimum fare; however, fares for all carriers operating on the same routes were to be the same. Although new entrants were allowed in the market, restrictive regulations and limited airport capacity hindered the development of more carriers for several years (Graham, 1995). In 2001, Sinha concluded that Japanese consumers have not yet fully benefited from the more liberal policies of the government, although there was some evidence that airlines had been able to lower their own costs.

Internationally, JAL and ANA suffered from higher input costs and lower efficiency than most of their US and European competitors and all but Thai Airways in Asia during much of the late 1990s. According to Oum and Yu (1998), these carriers were 52.7 and 63.5 percent less cost-competitive in 1993 than the benchmark US carrier American Airlines. Unfortunately, the airlines, like the rest of the Japanese economy, have continued to experience sustained, weak economic growth. The international traffic for Japanese carriers in 2012 was only slightly better than 1999 levels. During the COVID pandemic in 2020, the Japanese government suggested a merger between ANA and Japan Airlines as both carriers faced growing losses (Pande, 2020). While both carriers remain independent, they are struggling to recover after a very slow re-opening of the country post-Pandemic.

North Asia – Korea. South Korea had two major international carriers – Korean Airlines and Asiana – but a merger was proposed and approved by Korean authorities pending the transfer of slots to other airlines. If approved by international authorities, this would have make the new airline the seventh largest in the world (Sun, 2023). Both Korean Airlines and Asiana were privately owned. In 1992, the South Korean government stopped setting fares, although Korean domestic air travel did not see significant drops in fares. The entry of Asiana in 1988 did begin to increase passenger enplanements, but again with little or no effect on fares. In effect, the Korean government allowed a collusive duopoly to form following changes introduced in 1994 (Sinha, 2001).

Korean Airlines and Asiana were both hit hard by the Asian crisis; however, these problems were overshadowed in many ways by the decision of the US Federal Aviation Administration to downgrade them from a Category 1 to a Category 2, meaning that they failed to meet the minimum international safety standards set by ICAO. As a result of this action, Asiana, the second-largest carrier in South Korea, lost its code-sharing pact with American Airlines, costing it an estimated US$16 million. Korean Airlines had earlier lost its international alliance with the US carrier Delta Air Lines following a series of accidents in 1999. The Korean government temporarily banned it from making international flights in 1999. Following joint efforts by the Korean government and the FAA, Category 1 status was renewed. Korean Airlines made a series of changes that allowed it to rejoin the SkyTeam alliance with Delta and Air France. Since the 1990s, both carriers have appeared to make progress on the safety issues that had plagued them. In addition, Asiana was named the 2012 Best Overall Airline in the World by Business Traveler magazine (Aratani, 2013).

In terms of size, Korean Air served 90 destinations in 38 countries in 2022, compared with 61 destinations in 38 countries for Asiana; however, Asiana was a member of the larger Star alliance, with connections to over 1,300 destinations (Loh, 2022). In addition to EU concerns over the competition impacts of the proposed merger, US regulators are expected to return to issues of safety as it ponders approval.

South Asia. The South Asian region includes India, Pakistan, Bangladesh, Sri Lanka, and the small Himalayan states of Nepal and Bhutan. India has had by far some of the most dynamic growth in the region. India was second only to China in population and since the 1991 crisis triggered by the collapse of the Soviet Union, a major trading partner of India, it has been on a path toward economic liberalization. Until the early 1990s, the Indian government maintained a virtual monopoly over the airline industry with the market divided between Indian Airlines, which served the domestic market, and Air India, which provided international service and limited connecting flights. Under the Air Corporation Act of 1953, these two government-owned carriers were the only ones permitted to offer air service in India. The open skies policy introduced in 1990 allowed air taxi operations, charters, and new entrants to begin serving the domestic market. In 1993, Indian Airlines was allowed to begin international operations to the Gulf countries where many expatriate Indians worked. Indian Airlines continued to serve the bulk of the domestic markets; however, their share declined to only about 46 percent as of 2000 due to new carrier competition. During the mid-1990s, India witnessed the establishment of six private carriers intent on competing against state-controlled Air India and Indian Airlines. It seemed that Indian aviation was set to take off. Unfortunately, only one of these early private airlines, Jet Airways, survived the decade. Most of these carriers were classified as LCCs. In 2004, LCCs represented just 1.3 percent of the market in India, but this sector had grown to represent 67.5 percent in 2012 (CAPA, 2013b). The primary international destination for Indian carriers continued to be the Middle East with South Asia second. Despite showing great promise, the Indian commercial aviation market remained only one-fifth of the Chinese market (The Times of India, 2012). In the wake of continuing financial troubles for its two historic carriers, the Indian government announced in 2007 that it had approved the merger of Air India and Indian Airlines under the label of Air India (Air Transport Intelligence, 2008). This step has solved neither the financial nor the quality problems that plagued both carriers prior to the decision.

Many factors have been cited for the failure of early new entrants in India, including overexpansion, high debt, and continued government control over routes served, aircraft imported, and feeder service requirements. In addition to these burdens, carriers were prohibited from exiting loss-making routes and required to purchase state-controlled aviation fuel at almost twice the world price. One of the most high-profile recent failures has been Kingfisher Airlines. This company was founded on May 7, 2005, by Vijay Mallya, an Indian tycoon best known for his beer, to celebrate the 18th birthday of his son. Mallya promised an 'unparalleled in-flight experience' – personal flight entertainment systems, fine dining, and model-like attendants, but the growth of the LCC prompted Kingfisher to acquire troubled no-frills carrier Air Deccan several years later. This acquisition saddled the carrier with substantial debt that became unbearable as the global financial crisis continued (Datta, 2012). Weighed down with debt, rising fuel costs and price wars with its rivals, Kingfisher was unable to pay suppliers and pilots (50 of whom subsequently left for a rival carrier) and was forced to cancel flights and ground planes (Singhal, 2012; Sinha & Sinha, 2012). The carrier was grounded in October following unrest from a labor force who were seeking back wages (Menon, 2012). Supporters of Kingfisher and the airline industry have argued that government policies bear much of the blame for airline crises, citing continued restriction on bilateral traffic rights, above-global average taxes on aviation fuel, restrictions on foreign investment in domestic Indian airlines, infrastructure problems, and continued support for Air India (The Times of India, 2012). Those on the other side of the debate asked, 'Will the heavens fall if Kingfisher Airlines shuts down?' and concluded that the failure was part of the creative destruction that is part of capitalism; there might be some structural unemployment as laid-off workers find jobs in other airlines or sectors, but Kingfisher's death would make way for a trimmer, more efficient carrier (Malik, 2012). The government change to allow greater foreign direct investment has yet to save Kingfisher, although it might benefit Jet Airways, the last of the early private carriers. Unfortunately, many of the same problems that plagued early start-up carriers continue to persist – high fuel costs, poor infrastructure, etc. (Menon, 2012).

Creative destruction aside, India became the third-largest domestic aviation market in 2023. There was a 33 percent growth in passenger numbers between 2020 and 2021 and India's domestic traffic now makes up 69 percent of the total air traffic in South Asia. Growing household income, investment in airport infrastructure, and increased tourism have combined with a 2016 government policy to offer half of Indian flights at subsidized fares (IBEF, 2023). Set to pass China in total population in 2023, Indian aviation will look to continue to grow as the 10-year subsidy of fare ends in 2026.

South Pacific – Australia and New Zealand. The first act regulating aviation in Australia was the Navigation Act of 1920, but confusion over the role of state and Commonwealth governments in air transport regulation led to an amended Air Navigation Act in 1936. According to this act, the Commonwealth was authorized to control air transportation with other countries and also within the two territories of Australia. It was left to the states to control intra-state air transportation, although this did not keep the Commonwealth government from attempting to regulate intra-state aviation.

One of the most significant aviation policies of the Australian government occurred in the 1950s when then Prime Minister Robert Menzies decided that it was essential to prevent a monopoly from developing in Australian domestic airline service. The Two Airline Policy became official in 1952 with the passage of the Civil Aviation Agreement Act. Henceforth, there would be two carriers in Australia. Trans-Australian Airlines (later Australian Airlines), the state-owned carrier, would operate alongside the privately owned Australian

National Airways (later Ansett). The government guaranteed the loans of Australian National up to a specified limit and later loosened the requirement that all government employees fly Trans-Australian. International service would be the province of Qantas. In 1957, the government further declared that two and only two trunk carriers would exist in Australia and established a Rationalization Committee composed of a member of each airline and a coordinator nominated by the Transport Minister. The Airlines Equipment Act of 1958 authorized the government to restrict the size of each carrier's fleet. In 1961, two additional acts authorized the Rationalization Committee to establish timetables, frequencies, aircraft types, capacity, fares, freight levels, and overall load factors on groups of routes.

By 1981, criticism of the Two Airline Policy led to the Holcroft Inquiry, which recommended a pricing policy based on cost that would be nationally consistent and allow discounted fares to be determined by the airlines. This same year, Trans-Australia Airlines was made a public company, although the government continued to maintain effective ownership. Other actions in 1981 created an Independent Air Fares Committee to review fares, approve discounts, and change fare formulas to consider cost and efficiency and strengthened the government's ability to control the capacity of regional and cargo carriers through licensing of aircraft imports (Sinha, 2001).

Overall, limited information has suggested that while the Two Airline Policy did create a stable aviation system of high yield and profitable carriers with an excellent safety record, it was characterized by higher costs and lower productivity (Kirby, 1979; Sinha, 2001). The perception of Australian consumers was that it also resulted in higher fares than the deregulated market of the US. Under pressure, the Australian government decided in 1990 to deregulate its domestic market. In the first year of deregulation, the Australian market experienced a growth of 66 percent and average airfares dropped 41.3 percent; however, both numbers have fluctuated in the years since then in part due to the entry and failure of new carriers. Forsyth (1991) has argued that entry into the Australian market was destined to be difficult because of the advantages incumbent carriers possessed, particularly in terms of airport and terminal access. In a further effort to foster competition, the Australian government proposed a single trans-Tasman aviation market with New Zealand, granted Air New Zealand greater fifth freedom rights, and opened the international market to other carriers (after allowing Qantas to purchase Australian). Two new carriers entered the Australian domestic market, Impulse Airlines and Virgin Blue (owned by Richard Branson of Virgin Airlines), which led to price wars on the main routes and temporarily lowered fares to Australian consumers. In 2001, the Australian Competition and Consumer Commission approved the acquisition of Impulse Airlines by Qantas, which had also signaled its intent to improve fleet allocation, and costs to more effectively compete against the lower cost Virgin Blue (Cahners Publishing Company, 2000; M2 Communications Ltd., 2001a; M2 Communications Ltd., 2001b).

The year 2002 also marked the end of Ansett Airways, one of the 'two-policy' airlines, following its acquisition by Air New Zealand. Of course, 2001 was a difficult year for many global carriers, but the entry of other carriers into the market did not help. Virgin Australia, as it is now called, became the second-largest carrier in Australia behind flag carrier Qantas Airways during this period, but they posted losses for the 2012–2013 year citing carbon tax, a booking system upgrade, and recent acquisitions (60 percent share in Tiger Australia and Skywest) as the cause. Given that Singapore Airlines, Air New Zealand, and Etihad Airways had recently invested in the carrier, this news was surprising to some (Kelly, 2013). Qantas, which was also facing financial troubles, further shook the global industry by announcing a partnership with Emirates Airlines that shifted its European hub to Dubai (Fickling, 2013). Both airlines are seeking a North Asia alliance partner to gain greater reach in this region. The battles between Qantas and Virgin Australia (which included the acquisition of LCCs) left Regional Express (Rex) the largest independent regional carrier in Australia (CAPA, 2013c). By the second decade of the twenty-first century, Qantas continued to hold on to its top position in the country, operating JetStar as its low-cost arm; however, it is unclear if their proposed acquisition of Alliance, a private charter company with about 30 percent of this segment of the market, will be allowed to go forward because of competition concerns. Qantas and Virgin each control 23 and 23 percent of this market (Yun & Muroi, 2023).

Airline deregulation in New Zealand predates that of Australia, having begun in 1983 with the abolishment of domestic fare and entry controls. The flag carrier, Air New Zealand, was privatized in 1989 and Australian-based Ansett was invited to set up a subsidiary to serve the New Zealand domestic market. However, internationally the market continued to be restricted, particularly between New Zealand and its neighbor, Australia. Beginning in 1992, there was some movement to provide greater flexibility in pricing, fares, and capacity in international service between the two countries. Like the Australian market, New Zealand has found it difficult to retain new entrant carriers. Kiwi Airlines started service in 1995 between Australia and New Zealand, but halted its operations in 1996. After Ansett New Zealand and its parent company began to experience financial difficulty, Qantas considered making a financial investment in the New Zealand carrier. When this deal fell through, Qantas New Zealand was allowed to begin domestic service (Sinha, 2001). In an interesting twist on Australian–New Zealand aviation relations, Air New Zealand went on to purchase Ansett Australia in 2000 only to cut it loose on September 12 when it was placed in voluntary administration (bankruptcy). Following allegations that they had stripped Ansett of assets before its collapse, Air New Zealand agreed to pay the administrators of Ansett NZD180 million (M2 Communications, 2001a, 2002). Singapore Airlines had purchased 25 percent of Air New Zealand, but this share was reduced to 4.3 percent after the New Zealand government renationalized the carrier in October 2001 (BBC News, 2001). During 2002–2004, there were talks about a major alliance between Qantas and Air New Zealand that would have seen Qantas invest $550 million in Air New Zealand, assuming a 15 percent stake in the company. These were eventually abandoned, and Qantas sold its remaining stake in ANZ in 2007 (Air Transport Intelligence, 2008). In 2010, Air New Zealand purchased 19 percent of the shareholding of Virgin Australia as part of their trans-Tasman alliance. They have recently asked the Australian competition regulator to renew the alliance to help them compete against the Qantas–Emirates alliance (Freed, 2013). They increased it to 26 percent before selling their stake in 2016 and end their joint venture in 2018. The next few years would be ones featuring new alliances and expanded international routes, but like most carriers the Pandemic would mark an era of losses, government assistance, and rebuilding.

For its part, Qantas' New Zealand subsidiary, Jetconnect, struggled, particularly on the Tasman route. The main domestic rival for ANZ was Jetstar, which captured about a 30 percent share of the main trunk routes in New Zealand, that is, the routes between Auckland, Wellington, Christchurch, Dunedin, and Queenstown. JetStar's domestic market share in New Zealand had dropped to about 17 percent by 2018 as it continued to face an aggressively expanding ANZ (CTC, 2023). Coming out of the Pandemic, ANZ would have 75 percent of the market with JetStar and four other competitors (Corridore, 2023).

Looking Backward and Forward

Although both Asia and Europe were slower to liberalize and deregulate their aviation markets following the US, they both made great strides in developing their aviation systems and reducing fares while increasing services once they began. While both areas were affected by the many crises that have plagued the world's airlines, they have continued their efforts with Asia still set to make major advances in their share of world travel and Europe promising to redouble efforts to address climate change that include aviation. Heading deeper into the new century, the problems of infrastructure, competition, climate, and costs will represent a major challenge to these regions.

Questions

1 Discuss the European approach to deregulation.
2 What role did charter airlines play in Europe?
3 What influenced the EU approach? Has it been more successful than the US 'Big Bang'?
4 Has deregulation led to more competition? Has it led to the creation of more carriers or more carrier entry at the route level? Have fares dropped?
5 Discuss the progress of deregulation in Asian countries.
6 Explore the impact of deregulation on consumer choice and market dynamics in the European airline industry.
7 How have budget airlines reshaped travel patterns and tourism trends within Europe?
8 Compare and contrast the regulatory frameworks governing aviation in the European Union and the United States, assessing their respective impacts on industry growth and innovation.

References

Abbott, K. & Thompson, D. (1989), *Deregulating European aviation: The impact of bilateral liberalization*, Center for Business Strategy Working Paper Series no 73, London.

Aerospace Daily (2001), '*CAAC readies for airport, carrier alliance*,' October 30, Aviation Week Group.

Air Transport Intelligence (2008) Available at: www.rati.com

Aratani, L. (2013) Korean airlines have had a troubled past, The Washington Post, retrieved at http://articles.washingtonpost.com/2013-07-06/local/40408386_1_asiana-pilot-south-korea-asiana-airlines-boeing August 6, 2013.

Barrett, S. D. (1999), 'Peripheral market entry, product differentiation, supplier rents, and sustainability in the deregulated European airline market – A case study,' *Journal of Air Transport Management*, 5, pp. 21–30.

BBC News (2001), 'Air New Zealand renationalized,' *BBC News Wireservice*, October 4.

Binggeli, U. & Pompeo, L. (2002), 'Hyped hopes for Europe's low-cost airlines,' *The McKinsey Quarterly*, 4.

Borestein, S. (1992), 'Prospects for competitive air travel in Europe,' in W. J. Adams (Ed.), *Singular Europe: Economy and policy of the european community after 1992*, University of Michigan Press, Ann Arbor.

Button, K. J. (1997), 'Developments in the European Union: Lessons for the Pacific Asia Region,' in C. Findley, C. I. Sien, and K. Singh (Eds.), *Asia Pacific air transport: Challenges and policy reform*, Institute of Southeast Asian Studies, Singapore.

Button, K. J. & Swann, D. (1989), 'European community airlines-deregulation and its problems,' *Journal of Common Market Studies*, 37, 259–282.

Cahners Publishing Company (2000), 'Virgin Blue Launches Service; Second Route to Debut Sept. 7,' Gale Group wireservice, September 4, www.findarticles.com

Centre for Asian Business Cases (2002), *Preparing for China's entry to the WTO: China's airline industry*, The University of Hong Kong School of Business, Hong Kong.

Centre for Aviation (2013a) *World aviation yearbook 2013-North Asia Pacific*, CAPA, available at centreforaviation.com

Centre for Aviation (2013b) *World aviation yearbook 2013-South Asia*, CAPA, available at centre-foraviation.com

Centre for Aviation (2013c) *World aviation yearbook 2013-South Pacific*, CAPA, available at centre-foraviation.com

Civil Aviation Authority (1995), *CAP 654 The single aviation market: Progress so far*, Civil Aviation Authority, London.

Clark, N. & Jolly, D. (2012) Hungarian national airline halts flights, The New York Times, retrieved at http://www.nytimes.com/2012/02/04/business/global/hungarian-national-airline-halts-flights.html?_r=0 August 1, 2013.

Convery, F. (2012) Airline competition in Ireland – back to monopoly retrieved at http://www.publicpolicy.ie/airline-competition-in-ireland-back-to-monopoly/ August 1, 2013.

Corridore, J. (2023) Air New Zealand web traffic is 5X next largest competitor. Retrieved at https://www.similarweb.com/blog/insights/airlines-news/similarweb-data-on-air-travel-in-new-zealand/

CTC (2023) JetStar's domestic market share in New Zealand slips as Air New Zealand expands faster. Retrieved at https://corporatetravelcommunity.com/analysis/jetstars-domestic-market-share-in-new-zealand-slips-as-air-new-zealand-expands-faster-583330

Datta, K. (2012) He predicted KF turbulence before takeoff. *The Economic Times*, February 20, pp. 1 & 6.

European Commission (1996), *Impact of the third package of air transport liberalization measures COM 96*, European Commission, Brussels.

Fickling, D. (2013) Outsider CEO remakes Qantas allying with ex-nemesis Emirates, Bloomberg, retrieved at http://www.bloomberg.com/news/2013-07-14/outsider-ceo-remakes-qantas-tying-up-with-ex-nemesis-emirates.html, August 5, 2013.

Flottau, J. (2013a), Evolving paradigm, *Aviation Week & Space Technology*, July 8, pp. 36–39.

Flottau, J. (2013b), Stabilizing at best, *Aviation Week & Space Technology*, July 8, pp. 38–39.

Forsyth, P. (1991), 'The regulation and deregulation of Australia's domestic airline industry,' in K. J. Button (Ed.) *Airline deregulation: International experiences*, David Fulton, London, pp. 48–84.

Freed, J. (2013) Air NZ and Virgin want more time, Business Day, retrieved at http://www.stuff.co.nz/business/industries/8994563/Air-NZ-and-Virgin-want-more-time, August 5, 2013.

Graham, B. (1995), *Geography and air transport*, John Wiley and Sons, New York.

Graham, B. (1997), 'Air transport liberalization in the European Union: An assessment,' *Regional Studies*, 31, pp. 87–104.

Humphries, B. (1996), 'The UK Civil Aviation Authority and European air services liberalization,' *Journal of Transport Economics and Policy*, 3, pp. 213–220.

IBEF (2023) The rise of the Indian aviation market. Retrieved at https://www.ibef.org/research/case-study/rise-of-the-indian-aviation-market

ICAO (2012), *Robust traffic growth expected until 2014*, International Civil Aviation Authority, July 5, retrieved at http://www.icao.int/Newsroom/Pages/robust-traffic-growth-expected-until-2014.aspx August 1.

Kelly, R. (2013) Virgin Australia warns of steep net loss, *The Wall Street Journal*, retrieved at http://online.wsj.com/article/SB10001424127887323514404578649032614620240.html August 5, 2013.

Kirby (1979), 'An economic assessment of Australia's two airline policy,' *Australian Journal of Management*, 5, pp. 105–111

Leali, G. & Eccles, M. (2021) *Italy's new airline cleared for takeoff without Alitalia's baggage*, Politico. Retrieved at https://www.politico.eu/article/alitalia-ita-airline-italy-eu-mario-draghi-margrethe-vestager-subsidies-state-aid/

Li, C. (2022) Chin's growing prominence in the aviation market and the 'space club', China/US focus. Retrieved at https://www.chinausfocus.com/2022-CPC-congress/chinas-growing-prominence-in-the-aviation-market-and-the-space-club

Loh, C. (2022) Korean Air vs Asiana – What airline is better? Simple Flying. Retrieved at https://simpleflying.com/korean-air-vs-asiana/?newsletter_popup=1

M2 Communications Ltd. (2001a), 'Air New Zealand Denies Stripping Ansett Assets,' Gale Group wireservice, November 13, www.findarticles.com

M2 Communications Ltd. (2001b), 'Virgin Blue may be able to Open Review into Qantas' Takeover of Impulse Airline,' Gale Group wireservice, September 7, www.findarticles.com

M2 Communications Ltd. (2002), '*Air New Zealand increases flights in Asia after Ansett Collapse*,' Gale Group wireservice, www.findarticles.com

Malik, A. (2012) "Not at taxpayer's expense: By hinting at a bailout for Kingfisher, the government is making a mockery of market forces" *The Times of India*, February 29, p 16.8.

Menon, J. (2012) Last Gasps? India's Kingfisher Airlines looks to Etihad Airways for salvation, *Aviation Week & Space Technology*, December 17, p. 38.

Morrell, P. (1998), 'Air transport liberalization in Europe: The progress so far,' *Journal of Air Transportation World Wide*, 3, pp. 42–60.

Oum, T. H. & Yu, C. (1998), *Winning airlines: Productivity and cost competitiveness of the world's major airlines*, Kluwer Academic Publishers, Boston.

Pande, P. (2020) Japanese government suggests merging ANA & Japan Airlines. Simple Flying. Retrieved at https://simpleflying.com/ana-japan-airlines-merger/

Perrett, B. (2013). Hub envy, *Aviation Week & Space Technology*, July 8, p. 42.

R2A (2002), *Unisys R2A scorecard: Airline industry cost measurement*, Unisys Corporation, Blue Bell, Pennsylvania.

Rowland, B. (2022) Ryanair leads the way among Europe's top three low-cost carriers. OAG Aviation Market Analysis. Retrieved at https://www.oag.com/blog/ryanair-leads-the-way-among-europes-top-three-low-cost-carriers

Singhal, M. (2012) Kingfisher likely to lose prime slots to rivals, *The Economic Times*, February 23, p. 5.

Sinha, D. (2001), *Deregulation and liberalization of the airline industry: Asia, Europe, North America, and Oceania*, Ashgate, Aldershot.

Sinha, M. V. & Sinha, S. (2012) Kingfisher left high & dry as 50 pilots quit in a week, *The Times of India*, February 23, p. 26.

Sparaco, P. (2012a), Trains reign supreme, *Aviation Week & Space Technology*, September 3, p. 22.

Sparaco, P. (2012b) Worst-case scenario, *Aviation Week & Space Technology*, November 26, p. 16.

Sun, S. (2023) Korean Air-Asiana merger faces further delays from European regulators. Airline Weekly. Retrieved at https://airlineweekly.com/2023/03/korean-air-asiana-merger-faces-further-delays-from-european-regulators/

Taneja, N. K. (1988), *The international airline industry: Trends, issues and challenges*, Lexington Books, Lexington, MA.

The Times of India (2012) "Turbulent Flight: Improving viability of airlines should be top priority for government". *The Times of India*, February 22. p. 12

Turner, A. (2013) Europe low cost carrier growth outstrips legacy airline rivals, retrieved at http://www.airtrafficmanagement.net/2013/05/europe-lcc-growth-outstrips-legacy-rivals/ August 2, 2013.

Wallace, M., Tiernan, S., Rhoades, D. L., and Linck, T (2008), 'European tour operators and low-cost carriers: Strategic options in a changing marketplace', *Journal of Air Transportation*, 12 (3).

Yun, J & Muroi, M. (2023) 'Ball in their court': ACCC makes Qantas wait after blocking Alliance acquisition. The Sydney Morning Herald. Retrieved at https://www.smh.com.au/business/companies/competition-watchdog-rejects-qantas-acquisition-of-alliance-20230420-p5d1wq.html

11   The Defining Deal of the Next Century?

Learning Objectives

After reading this chapter, you should have a good understanding of:

LO1:   the definition of strategic alliance
LO2:   the reasons for and growth of alliances in the international airline industry
LO3:   the alliance types commonly found in airlines and their definition
LO4:   the reasons for alliance failure
LO5:   the meaning of mega-alliance, its shape and challenges

Key Terms, Concepts & People

Alliance	GM Model	Joint venture
Mega-alliances	Airline alliance types	Instability
Resource commitment	Complexity	Multipoint Competition

A New Model?

While the United States circled key markets trying to open the skies (Chapter 9) and the Europeans attempted to integrate the economies of 15 different countries, the airlines looked for ways to provide global service in a bilateral world. Part of the push for global networks was based on studies that indicate that consumers chose an airline based on schedule first rather than price and preferred to fly with an airline serving a large number of cities (Tretheway & Oum, 1992). Consumers also preferred a nonstop or single carrier connecting service to a non-interline connecting service. Interlining, which refers to the situation whereby a consumer changes from one carrier to another, carries certain penalties for the consumer such as aircraft and terminal changes, baggage transfers (and added risk of baggage loss), etc. Carriers with interlining agreement are expected to provide for more seamless service with joint ticketing and baggage transfers (Dempsey, 2001). If bilateral agreements prevented carriers from achieving nonstop or single carrier connecting service, then carriers needed to find ways to imitate this service to attract consumers. The strategic alliance seemed to offer an answer to this problem.

Conventional wisdom from the years after World War II once suggested that the primary business decision corporations had to deal with was to 'make or buy'. In other words:

DOI: 10.4324/9781003405306-13

do we engage in arm's-length contractual relationships to obtain important resources or do we internally develop and/or purchase the resources to carry out our strategic plan? The arm's-length contractual choice created so-called transaction costs, costs of buying and selling. These costs include the time and financial resources involved in selecting partners, negotiating the deal, and monitoring the relationship to insure contract compliance. These costs could be substantial depending on the number of suppliers to be considered, the reputation of the individual suppliers, and the information available on actual supplier costs. These costs multiplied exponentially for corporations with many suppliers. Unsurprisingly, firms also felt at the mercy of suppliers when it came to guaranteeing deliveries and quality. These costs, and the lack of control, led many to adopt the 'GM model'. The 'GM model' was a vertically integrated company that sought to do it all – making its own spark plugs, radiators, lights, ball bearings, etc. Ownership eliminated transaction cost uncertainty and provided greater control of the operational aspects of the relationship. This obsession with 'owning' in the United States led to the merger mania of the 1980s and the takeover mania of the 1990s. During the three busiest years of the 1990s (1998–2000), merger deals totaled almost US$44 trillion, which was more than the preceding 30 years combined (Henry, 2002). Greater economic integration in Europe has also led to an increase in owning, often fueled by economic crises that created deals out of stressed companies in many industries. However, evidence has indicated that this obsession may not have benefited buyers and shareholders. A *Business Week* study indicates one reason why the trend is declining. According to their study, 61 percent of the 'buyers' actually destroyed shareholder wealth by picking bad acquisitions and paying too much for them (Henry, 2002).

In 1999, *Business Week* declared that 'the defining deal for the next decade and beyond may well be the alliance, the joint venture, the partnership' (Sparks, 1999, p. 106). This article argued that alliances provided greater flexibility, speed, informality, and economy than traditional business arrangements. These qualities appeared to make them ideal in rapidly changing business environments. Industries cited as embracing the alliance movement included media, entertainment, financial services, pharmaceuticals, biotech, high tech, and airlines. However, a large body of evidence has accumulated on the instability in alliances across industries. As we will see, this instability can be attributed to a number of factors, including poor selection, governance (control) and failure to meet expectations, largely in the area of financial return. There are signs that the alliance landscape merely shifted competition to a higher level of abstraction as alliance groups compete in terms of price, choice and brand. Within the airline industry, the primary focus of alliances has become the mega-alliance and even this form has come under pressure as merger, acquisition and unaligned carriers have challenged their trajectories. Still, they have come to dominate 55 percent of the seats flown around the world by the second decade of the twenty-first century. Even so, it is still possible that the liberalization of markets and ownership rules could cause some to rethink the 'make-or-buy' decision once again in light of the instability and complexity in alliances as well as the failure of the alliance model to provide the kind of economic and legal incentives that lead to deeper cooperation between members (Flottau & Buyck, 2013).

Defining the Terms and Conditions

A strategic alliance can be defined as a 'relatively enduring interfirm cooperative arrangement, involving flows and linkages that utilize resources and/or governance structures from autonomous organizations, for the joint accomplishment of individual goals' (Parkhe,

1991, p. 581). In other words, a strategic alliance is an agreement between two independent firms to share resources in a jointly governed project that helps each individual firm achieve specific, but not necessarily shared, goals. While the old business model equated control with ownership, control in alliance arrangements is gained through one of three means. The first means of control is through active participation in the management of the enterprise or operation. The second means of exercising control is through withholding or threatening to withhold some resource or capability vital to the success of the overall operation and/or desired by the other partner. The final means of control is through legal or de facto prohibitions on the actions of alliance partners. Areas where firms might seek control include daily operations, quality of products or services, physical assets, brand name, tacit knowledge of procedures and processes, and codified knowledge such as computer reservation systems (Contractor & Kundu, 1998).

The international joint venture (IJV) used to be the preferred mode of conducting international business, but a joint venture is a legally separate entity with a mission and administration separate from that of its parents. The alliance, by contrast, can be formed and dissolved quickly, and 'entail(s) little if any paperwork – maybe only a handshake' (Sparks, 1999, p. 134). According to Jurgen Weber, CEO of Lufthansa Airlines, the Star Alliance started with a 2½-page contract and its members 'will cooperate forever as long as we like it' (Feldman, 1998, p. 27). This sounds very similar to a comment made by Leo Mullin, CEO of Delta Air Lines, who declared that Delta was 'extraordinarily committed to the Atlantic Excellence Alliance' (Flint, 1999, p. 33). Delta was so committed in fact that less than a year later they announced the termination of its involvement and a new partnership with Air France (Hill, 1999).

One issue that appears repeatedly in the popular accounts of airline alliances is the level of time and coordination required by many such arrangements. There are several issues involved. First, alliances often involve information sharing and/or the 'outsourcing' of some activities to alliance partners. This requires trust. As Jurgen Weber, CEO of Lufthansa, has noted, a key issue in many alliances is trust and the willingness to sell the other's seats as forcefully as your own (Feldman, 1998). According to past research, trust is a function of three factors: Ability, benevolence and integrity. Trust develops when the trustor believes that the trustee has the ability to do what they promise, the desire to do good for the trustor, and the value set that is consistent with that of the trustor (Cook & Wall, 1980; McFall, 1987; Sitkin & Roth, 1993). Mayer, Davis, and Schoorman (1995) have suggested that the perceived integrity of a partner is more important early on in the relationship when other information is unavailable. Benevolence develops in a relationship over time. In fact, the outcome of prior trusting behavior will influence a partner's perception of the ability, benevolence, and integrity of other parties in a relationship. A second key factor is differences in corporate culture and philosophy. Atlantic Excellence members found that different philosophies in terms of service quality, pricing and other important operational issues created problems. Strong personalities and size differences between members also contributed to the perception and resolution of problems (Feldman, 1998). A third factor affecting coordination is the number of partners involved. As noted above, the more parties involved in a negotiating situation, the more potential there is for disagreement and gamesmanship. A fourth factor is the compatibility of partner systems. The final factor relates to the very real limitations placed on international airlines by laws restricting foreign ownership and limiting the scope of allowed activities. Initial results from the earlier mentioned survey of international airlines confirm these problems in alliance governance. The most frequently cited problem with alliance partners was incompatible systems, policies, or procedures.

The result of these limitations is that airline alliances are most often coordinated or managed by a committee; agreement is achieved by arriving at the lowest common denominator or minimally acceptable standard to all members (Feldman, 1998). Star Alliance struggled with governance arrangements, reducing the number of coordinating committees several years ago from 25 to 15, and established a policy group to oversee the activities of these committees (Feldman, 1998; Nelms, 1999). Star was the first mega-alliance to take steps to create a more formal structure of governance for its alliance.

Alliances in the Airline Industry

According to Oum and Yu (1998), the first international alliance of the modern era was between Air Florida and British Island in 1986. It was not until the mid-1990s, however, that the number of alliances in the airline industry began to accelerate. Table 11.1 summarizes the alliance activity documented by *Airline Business* over the seven years prior to 2001. September 11 was a watershed for the industry in many ways, certainly it temporarily halted new alliance activity in the industry and we have not seen a return to the levels of the 1990s. There are several striking trends in the 1990s numbers. First, the total number of alliances rose almost 45 percent between 1994 and 1999 (see Figure 11.1). Second, the majority of

Table 11.1 Alliance Summary 1994–2000

	1994	1995	1996	1997	1998	1999	2000
Number of alliances	280	324	389	363	502	513	579
With equity stakes	58	58	62	54	56	53	–
Without equity	222	266	327	309	446	460	–
New alliances	21	34	26	56	84	79	72
Number of airlines	136	153	159	177	196	204	220

Source: Airline Business June 1994–June 2000. Reporting of equity change in 2000.

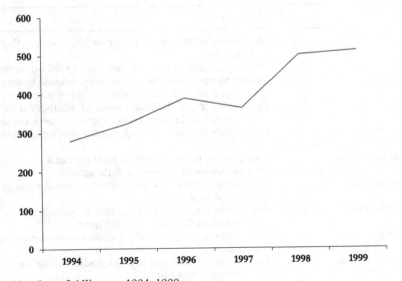

Figure 11.1 Number of Alliances, 1994–1999.

alliances did not involve equity stakes and those that did declined. Third, between one-fourth and one-sixth of the reported total yearly alliances were newly created. Finally, the number of airlines participating in some form of alliance was steadily increasing.

The term 'strategic alliance' covers a multitude of different forms or types of arrangements in the airline industry, possibly more than in any other industry. To understand the airline alliance, it is necessary to understand that alliance activities can range from a simple, single route codeshare or bundle of codeshares all the way to the so-called 'mega-alliances' created by international groups of competing airlines such as Star, Oneworld and SkyTeam. Table 11.2 lists the most common types of alliance activities and a basic definition of each.

Not only is there a wide range of alliance activities or types of arrangements possible; there are also a large number of type combinations that can be created between any two or more carriers. The mega-alliance (discussed later) combine many of these types; however, not all types are equally likely to occur. Several studies have reported that the most common types of alliances involve codesharing, blockspace/franchising/feeding agreements, joint marketing, and joint service agreements (Table 11.3). Least common are alliances involving the sharing and/or adoption of information technology systems, including computer reservation systems. This is probably unsurprising given the proprietary nature of such information in the airline industry (Rhoades & Waguespack Jr., 2000; Zwart, 1999).

An airline's choice of alliance partner and alliance type is a function of its objectives, which are believed to center around four strategic drivers. The first and traditionally most popular driver has been the need to gain entry into international markets restricted by bilateral agreements. Alliances allow foreign carriers to serve international destinations without obtaining the right through country-negotiated bilateral agreements, a political process that many carriers have found difficult to influence. The second driver is the desire to build a global, seamless network that allows consumers to reduce travel costs, take advantage of expanded frequent flyer programs, and obtain better services. The third driver of alliance formation is cost reduction. Cost reduction can be achieved in several ways.

Table 11.2 Definition of Airline Alliances

Alliance type	Definition
Codeshare	One carrier offers service under another carrier's flight designator
Blockspace	One carrier allocates to another seats to sell on its flight
Revenue sharing	Two or more carrier share revenues generated by joint activity
Wet lease	One carrier rents the aircraft/personnel of another
Franchising	One carrier 'rents' the brand name of another for the purpose of offering flight service but supplies its own aircraft/staff
Computer reservation system	One carrier shares and/or adopts the reservation system of another
Insurance/parts pooling	Two or more carriers agree to joint purchase
Joint service	Two carriers offer combined flight service
Management contract	One carrier contracts with another carrier to manage some aspect of its operation
Baggage handling/maintenance	One carrier contracts with another to provide services/personnel/facilities at specified sites
Joint marketing	Two or more carriers combine efforts to market joint services/activities
Equity swap/governance	Two or more carriers swap stock and/or create joint governance structures

Table 11.3 Alliances by Type

Alliance type	Description	Percentage of total
Type I	Codeshare	29
Type II	Block-space	15
Type III	CRS/Accting/IT	2
Type IV	Pooling	6
Type V	Joint service	13
Type VI	Commercial agreements	3
Type VII	Facilities/ground handling	9
Type VIII	Marketing	16
Type IX	Equity	7

Source: Zwart, M.L. (1999), 'Duration and Stability of Strategic Alliances in the Airline Industry'.

Alliances can be used to enter and develop a new market without an actual presence in that market. In this case, the entering carrier may rely on its alliance partner to provide the aircraft, ground handling, maintenance, customer service personnel, and other services in the new market. Carriers may also seek to reduce costs through arrangements creating joint activities such as marketing, maintenance, insurance, parts pooling, etc. These joint activities not only reduce redundancy but may also create cost savings through economy of scale effects. A fourth driver can be the desire to maintain market presence in an area whose traffic pattern and growth make it unprofitable to serve alone (Merrill Lynch, Pierce, Fenner & Smith, Inc., 1998; Oum & Yu, 1998). For many airlines, their alliance activity is driven by more than one objective and, clearly, carriers may have a different set of objectives for each market or region that they serve. This diversity of objectives can make the scope and depth of interaction important issues in negotiating and governing an alliance.

Unstable Creations

Unfortunately, strategic alliances have also been defined as arrangements 'characterized by inherent instability arising from uncertainty regarding a partner's future behavior and the absence of a higher authority to ensure compliance' (Parkhe, 1993, p. 794). Doorley III (1993) found that 60 percent of the alliances he examined had a survival rate of only four years. Less than 20 percent survived for ten years. An Anderson Consulting survey found that 61 percent of corporate partnerships were either outright failures or performing below expectations (Sparks, 1999). Michael Porter of Harvard University believes that we should not be surprised by these numbers since he sees alliances as transitional rather than stable arrangements that rarely result in sustainable competitive advantage (Porter, 1990). Hamel (1991) has even suggested that many alliances are simply a race to learn in which the winner will eventually establish dominance in the partnership or dissolve it before its partner can catch up.

Whichever means of control partners select, the fact remains that most interfirm alliances involve attempts by competitors to cooperate in some aspect of their operation. It has been suggested that such firms have an 'inalienable de facto right to pursue their own interests' (Buckley & Casson, 1988, p. 34). This perception, however, may make it inevitable that problems will arise as partners seek to control the alliance to their benefit. Another reason for instability in alliance arrangements may be the failure of partners to clearly define objectives and establish means of measuring performance. A surprising 49 percent of alliances in the *Business Week* survey did not have formal performance guidelines (Sparks, 1999).

The first step in understanding the issue of stability is achieving a consensus on the meaning of our terms. From an alliance point of view, failure occurs when one or all parties fail to achieve their objectives. Obviously, it is possible for one member to achieve their goals when other parties do not. This type of failure can occur either because of a problem in the objective-setting process or because of deliberate action on the part of one member. A more ominous reason for failure is the possibility that one or more partners enter an alliance seeking to gain competitive advantage (Buckley & Casson, 1988; Hamel, 1991). Given this definition, a terminating alliance is only unsuccessful if it is 'unplanned and premature from the perspective of either or both partners' (Inkpen & Beamish, 1997, p. 182). Duration simply refers to the length of time between the initiation of an alliance and its termination.

Researchers have defined instability in terms of changes in equity and/or governance control, termination, and duration (Franko, 1971; Killing, 1983; Kogut, 1988). From a theoretical perspective, instability should be separated from duration and termination. If a stable relationship is defined as one in which there have been no major changes in the relationship design to either increase or decrease the linkages between firms, then an alliance could terminate without experiencing instability. Actions which would indicate instability include changes in strategic direction, renegotiation of contracts or agreements, and reconfiguration of ownership and/or management structure (Yan, 1998). It would not include alliance termination. A stable alliance may terminate when the strategic goals of partners have been met, or when the strategic needs of partners change. By the same token, an unstable alliance will not necessarily end in termination. Instability may arise because partners are adjusting their expectations or objectives. It may indicate that partners have decided to commit themselves to even higher levels of interaction or to a longer-term strategy to disengage from or de-emphasize the relationship.

Lasting Relationships

Given the high failure rates already cited, it is reasonable to ask what factors contribute to longevity. Bleeke and Ernst (1995) have categorized alliances based on three factors – market strength of partners, motivation of alliance partners, and alliance outcome – to create six classes or types of alliances. These six types are 1) collisions between competitors, 2) alliances of the weak, 3) disguised sales, 4) bootstrap alliances, 5) evolutions to a sale, and 6) complementary equals. According to their typology, an alliance between a weak firm and a strong firm can be either a disguised sale, that is, it will result in the weaker firm failing to gain strength and being acquired (and, hence, the alliance terminated) by the stronger firm, or a bootstrap alliance in which the weaker firm increases its strength and dissolves the alliance. In their typology, only one type of alliance will survive longer than the median age of seven, complementary equals. This alliance involves two firms with truly complementary skills, assets, and/or resources. Unfortunately, many alliances are entered in the belief that partner complementarity exists. It is usually only in the process of implementing the alliance that partners discover incompatibility. The other weakness of the Bleeke and Ernst (1995) typology is that it is post hoc; it classifies alliances after the outcome of the alliance is known. It does not predict which alliances will succeed nor does it lay out conditions for success.

Park and Cho (1997) examined the market strength of codesharing partners and its effect on market share performance, presumably a goal of such alliances. They found that the most successful alliances occurred between partners of equal size. They also reported that the performance effects were greater in growing markets with few competitors and flexible market share changes. Here, at least, we have two factors that might be useful in selecting partners and/or predicting alliance outcome.

Khanna, Gulati, and Nohria (1998) offer us another way. They focus not on the strengths of alliance partners but on the nature of the benefits arising from alliance activity. They suggest that alliances create two types of benefits – common and private. Common benefits 'accrue to each partner in an alliance from the collective application of the learning both firms go through as a consequence of being part of the alliance' (195). By contrast, private benefits can accrue to a firm that can pick up partner skills and apply them to areas unrelated to alliance activity. In the case of an alliance with purely common benefits, 'all firms must finish learning in order for any of them to derive the common benefits' (197). Thus, such an alliance may be expected to last longer and result, even if terminated, in a successful alliance from the viewpoint of all parties. The alliance with purely private benefits is indeed a race to see which partner can finish learning first. That partner will then have no further incentive to incur alliance costs and will terminate the relationship. In reality, most alliances are a combination of both types of benefits. It is the ratio of private to common benefits that will affect a firm's decision to stay in or quit an alliance. All things being equal, the greater the scope of the alliance relative to the total market scope of the partners, the greater the common benefits and the lower the private benefits. In this regard, the mega-alliances with their increased alliance scope relative to firm scope should create more common benefits and last longer than their narrow alliance scope competitors. In connection with learning in alliance arrangements, Simonin (1999) has suggested that the more ambiguous and tacit the information to be transferred, the longer the process will take. In other words, it should be more difficult for Singapore Airlines to transfer the rich, experience-laden knowledge that has made it an industry leader in service quality than to train alliance partners in line maintenance procedures.

A number of studies have examined the role of resource commitment to alliance duration. Resource commitment involves dedicating assets to a particular use in such a way that their redeployment to other uses would result in some level of cost to the firm. By limiting strategic flexibility and acting as a barrier to exit, the willingness to commit resources lessens the perception of opportunistic behavior on the part of other alliance members (Parkhe, 1993). The more non-recoverable and alliance-specific the investment, the greater the potential effect on alliance duration.

Resource commitment can also have a positive effect on alliance stability and performance (Freeman, 1987; Heide & Johns, 1988; Smith & Aldrich, 1991). Resource commitment affects stability for much the same reason as it increases duration, namely that it creates incentives to stay in the relationship rather than quit. Its effect on performance is due to the link between resource commitment, firm control, and involvement in operations. The higher the level of commitment by the firm, the more likely it is to exercise control in the alliance and seek involvement in decision-making (Anderson & Gatignon, 1986; Root, 1987). On the other hand, high levels of commitment are often associated with more alliance complexity. The more complex the relationship, the greater the 'fundamental problem of cooperation' (Ouchi, 1980, p. 130). Alliances that involve greater coordination and integration of resources require a level of trust and interaction that is generally foreign to competitive firms. The more highly concentrated the industry, the more unstable the relationship may be, particularly when the scope of the venture involved marketing and after-sales service (Kogut, 1988). The need for higher levels of coordination and integration is also likely to increase problems relating to incompatible systems, procedures, training, and organizational/national cultures.

According to Yan (1998), four forces act to destabilize alliance arrangements: unexpected changes in the environment, undesirable alliance performance, obsolescing bargain effects, and inter-partner competitive learning. Clearly, changing environmental conditions and poor performance can cause partners to reevaluate/restructure their relationship. The obsolescing bargain occurs when the foreign partners' relative bargaining power erodes over time as it invests increasing, unrecoverable resources in a local economy. Finally, the race to learn can lead to various strategic maneuvering in an alliance. Yan (1998) also cites four factors that can increase alliance stability: the political and legal environment at founding, the initial resource mix, the initial balance of bargaining power, and the inter-partner, pre-venture relationship. As we have discussed earlier in this book, the airline industry is currently facing a series of challenges to the existing political and legal structure that has governed the industry since the end of World War II. When this challenge is added to alliance-specific differences in resource mix, balance of power, and pre-venture relationships, the results can be volatile.

Scott (1992) has noted that the forms organizations establish at founding are likely to persist over their lifespan. This is called structural inertia. The initial form may reflect the task environment (Stinchcombe, 1965), the characteristics of executives (Mintzberg & Waters, 1982) or top management team (Eisenhardt & Schoonhoven, 1990), or institutional factors such as laws, organizational or national culture (Meyer & Scott, 1983). The initial resources and bargaining power partners bring into an alliance can also create stability, as can a pre-alliance relationship of trust and respect. The stability of the alliance depends on the delicate balance between these eight forces.

A Balancing Act

In a 1997 article in the *Journal of Air Transportation Management*, Rhoades and Lush proposed an alliance typology that involved another delicate balancing act. Their typology was based on the premise that airline alliances could be classified according to two dimensions: commitment of resources and complexity of arrangement. In general, the typology predicted that the level of resource commitment should increase both the duration and stability of alliances while the complexity of the alliance arrangement should decrease both duration and stability. These predictions are consistent with theory and research in other industries. The difficulty lies in assessing the interaction effects of these two dimensions on duration and stability. For example, what is likely to happen to an alliance that involves a low level of resource commitment to a complex task requiring partners to integrate different systems, cultures, or tasks. Rhoades and Lush (1997) attempted to address this difficulty by assigning each of the activities defined above in Table 10.2 based on the level of resource commitment and complexity. Figure 11.2 outlines a refined version of the typology used in a test of the model. Type I alliances involve low levels of resource commitment and complexity. The relatively simple nature of the activity should make them more stable and lasting. However, these types of codesharing arrangements are normally driven by the desire for market access and/or market presence in a restricted or undeveloped market. The lasting nature of Type I alliances could change if liberalization continues and carriers can enter markets freely in their own right. On the other hand, financial crisis in the wake of 9/11 has seen cost-cutting carriers withdraw from increasingly marginal routes in favor of alliance partners.

Diagonally across from Type I alliances is Type IX. These alliances involve multiple activities, complex integration efforts, extensive resource commitment, shared decision-making, and, often, equity investment. High resource commitment makes the exit cost of

COMPLEXITY

	Type III (IT)	Type VI (Management)	Type IX (Equity)	
	Accounting services CRS links Data processing Freight IT IT development	Commercial agreements Commercial support management Management contract MOU Spares management cooperation Strategic Partnership	Equity	
	Type II (Block-Space) Block seat agreements Block space agreements Feeding agreement Franchise agreement Revenue sharing Wet lease	Type V (Joint-Service) Cargo cooperation Freight handling Joint cargo terminal Joint flight Joint freighter flight Joint route development Joint venture Schedule coordination Shared routes	Type VIII (Marketing) Coop on Sales Gen sales agency Joint mkt Joint FFP Joint advertising Marketing agreement Marketing alliance Reservations	
	Type I (Code-Share) Cargo code-share Code sharing	Type IV (Pooling) Fuel purchasing Financial access arrangements Joint insurance purchase Freight return pool Joint purchase Pool agreement Revenue Pooling Space swap	Type VII (Ground Facilities) Slot-sharing Maintenance Catering JV Joint check-in Ground handling Shared terminal Shared lounge Through check-in	

(left axis: RESOURCES) (right axis: DURATION)

DURATION

Figure 11.2 Alliance Activity by Type.

these alliance types high. On the other hand, the complex nature of the tasks to be coordinated and integrated will make these alliances unstable as well. On balance, resource commitment should provide Type IX partners with greater incentives to work through complexity. Type III alliances involve low complexity, and high resource commitment should make these alliances some of the most durable. On the diagonal from Type III are Type VIII alliances, which tend to involve low levels of resource commitment and high complexity. These types of arrangements should experience some of the highest failure rates. An increasing focus on quality may make the potentially undesirable outcomes of some of these complex and important activities too great to bear. Of course, it is possible that the cost savings benefits of these arrangements and/or airport-specific restrictions on facilities or eligible grand handling firms will override the destabilizing effects of complexity.

This typology was tested for its duration predictions using data from the *Airline Business* surveys. Gudmunssson and Rhoades (2001) found that alliances in general were at greater risk of termination in year 2. The rate of termination decreased from years 3–6. Four types of alliance arrangements demonstrated a lower risk of termination, Type IV-pooling, Type VIII-marketing, Type II-block space, and Type I-codesharing. Type V (joint service) and Type VII (ground/facilities) showed a significant relationship with higher risk of early termination. Type IX (equity) alliances were also associated with high risk of termination. The remaining two types of alliances, Type III (CRS/IT) and Type VI (commercial agreements), contained too few cases to test. While this study did not provide unqualified support for the typology, it does demonstrate that different alliance activities are at greater risk for termination.

The Gudmunssson and Rhoades (2001) study also found that the more extensive the alliance, i.e. the more types of activities involved, the lower the risk of termination. Since each additional alliance activity adds incrementally to the level of resource commitment, this finding is supportive of the general proposition that resource commitment increases duration. The attempt by mega-alliances to increase the breadth and scope of partner activity also supports the contention of Khanna, Gulati, and Nohria (1998) that the higher the level of common benefits to private, the more likely the alliance is to survive. In the case of the mega-alliances, resource commitment appears to outweigh complexity as a factor in alliance duration. In the case of Type IX equity alliances, the troubles of shared governance and organizational control created instability in a number of alliances, notably KLM–Northwest, and Northwest and Continental. However, the control benefits of ownership might create the incentive to remain in a relationship and work through instability.

To date, there has been no test of the stability predictions of the typology. As Rhoades and Lush (1997) noted in their original article, 'instability in and of itself is not necessarily a "bad thing." It can be an indication that the parties in the alliance are committed to establishing a successful partnership' (113). On the other hand, too much instability should have a negative effect on an alliance's ability to function and produce profitable returns. Testing the stability predictions would require a careful year-by-year survey of changes (major and minor) within alliances. A related area of study would be to examine the possibility of sequencing as it relates to alliance stability and duration. For example, are alliances that begin their relationship with relatively simple, low-resource activities and then move to more complex arrangements more successful than those who jump right into equity and/or other complex activities?

Strategic Actions

As noted earlier, airlines that serve a large number of destinations tend to be preferred by consumers because such an airline can minimize their travel time and offer a higher quality of service (Tretheway & Oum, 1992). Responding to this preference, carriers sought to develop extensive domestic, continental, and international service networks. In the US, following deregulation, carriers consolidated and created hub-and-spoke networks to achieve continental coverage. Achieving international coverage, however, proved more difficult. American Airlines initially attempted to apply the domestic model of network coverage to foreign markets by creating foreign spokes to their US hubs. They encountered two problems: legal barriers created by the bilateral system and high financial costs. We have already discussed many of the legal barriers to establishing an efficient foreign network (Chapter 9). In regard to the financial costs, Oum, Taylor, and Zhang (1993) have estimated that the potential revenues of a 'successful' global network would be more than $30 billion. This is at least twice the revenue level of the largest existing mega-carriers. They argued that a single carrier simply could not marshal the financial resources to establish such a network. Whether a single carrier could administer such a network is a matter we will address later.

Given these problems and the legal restrictions on international mergers and acquisitions, strategic alliances became the method of choice in global network construction.

They allowed individual carriers to compensate for strategic weaknesses in their operations or route structure. The savings in cost and time over internal development could be substantial. In fact, outsourcing to alliance partners was the easiest way to control costs, but there were additional problems with this approach. First, it was difficult to restart an activity once it is discontinued. So, if the alliance fell apart or the quality of the work did not meet standards, bringing that activity back in-house would be expensive. Second, such cost savings required more airline integration than many carriers were currently willing to accept (Feldman, 1999).

Research on competitive behavior suggests that it is driven by both the ability to compete and the motivation to engage in competition (Chen, 1996). Global networks give alliances the ability to compete in numerous markets. The motivation to compete (or not to compete) is based on other considerations, including expected retaliation by competitors. Research at the firm level indicates that multi-market contact 'gives a firm the option to respond to an attack by a rival not only in the challenged market, but also in other markets in which both compete' (Gimeno, 1999, p. 102). In the United States, major airlines seek to maintain some presence in all their competitors' markets. Those that are successful 'are able to simultaneously: (a) enjoy lower intensity of price competition from their rivals, (b) display less intense competitive behavior of their own, and (c) maintain a higher equilibrium market share' (Gimeno, 1999, p. 122). Retaliation in an attacker's hub has been shown to be a powerful and effective response to attacks on one's own hub (Nomani, 1990). Assuming that competition eventually moves from the airline to the alliance level, then multipoint alliance contact will gain increasing importance. This also assumes that a liberalizing global aviation system allows for the development of such a framework. Merrill Lynch (1999) has examined the market presence of the mega-alliances in thirty world markets. Of these thirty markets, fifteen have an alliance with 50 percent or more market share. This indicates the basic framework of a multipoint system that, given regulatory freedom, would allow one alliance group to respond to an attack in their dominant market by acting in the attacker's market.

The Mega-Alliance

The frenzy of alliance activity was largely extinguished by 9/11 as individual airlines struggled for survival. The action shifted to the mega-alliance, although mergers and acquisitions of airlines from different groups have created some turmoil. Table 11.4 shows the current mega-alliance structure. Oneworld continues to lag behind the other two alliances in size as well as the integration of alliance members. What this table does not indicate is the level of within-group joint venture activity in the alliances fostered in part by the fact that some carriers have been legally freer to integrate their cooperation (Flottau & Buyck, 2013).

Oum and Park (1997) envisioned the following future for airline alliances. First, global alliances would consist of a two-tier system of super-hub anchor carriers on each continent and junior spoke carriers feeding the continental super-hubs. Star Alliance has even created third-tier members and all the mega-alliances have worked in the last decade to fill gaps in their network. Many of the smaller carriers have had to work very hard to get benefits from the mega-alliances and balance this with the sometimes-substantial costs (Buyck, 2013). Second, the number of major global alliances, constrained by the limited number of major continental carriers, would be no more than five or so. Finally, carriers left out of the 'system' would be forced to become niche players. Some of these predictions have come to pass

Table 11.4 Mega-Alliance Size and Coverage by 2018

Global alliance members	Oneworld	SkyTeam	Star Alliance
Members	13	20	28
Revenue	123	148	164
Destinations	1,012	1,074	1,300
Daily flights	12,738	17,343	18,400
Yearly passengers	527.9	730	725
Lounges	650+	600+	1,000+
Countries served	158	177	191
Fleet	3,447	4,467	4,700

Source: SIA Partners (2018) https://www.sia-partners.com/en/insights/publications/partnerships-between-airlines-strategy-win-asian-market

with the formation of three major mega-alliances (Star, Oneworld and SkyTeam) and the announcement of secondary and tertiary carriers (Merrill Lynch, 1999). Consolidation in the North American and European airline industry has shifted some alliance partnerships, and some alliance members have remained on the periphery of their mega-alliance either unable or unwilling to deepen ties, but it remains to be seen whether non-alliance status will consign carriers to niche status. This has certainly not been true of the Middle Eastern carriers to date. Since many of the niche players are low-cost carriers (LCCs), a growing segment of the airline industry, it is not clear what happens if the alliance and LCC model begin to collide more directly in international markets.

Internationally, competition has tended to shift to the alliance level. Research also points to other behavioral possibilities in alliance strategic action. At the firm level, organizational size has been positively associated with economies of scale, experience, brand name recognition, and market power (Hambrick, MacMillan, & Day, 1982; Kelly & Amburgey, 1991). Small firms tend to be more flexible, faster, innovative and risk-seeking. Such firms initiate more competitive moves and implement them quicker than their larger rivals (Chen & Hambrick, 1995; Fiegenbaum & Karnani, 1991; Hitt, Hoskisson, & Harrison, 1991; Katz, 1970). Large firms initiate fewer actions, tend to be slower to implement agreed-upon actions, and are less likely to change core features (Chen & Hambrick, 1995; Kelly & Amburgey, 1991). However, as Chen and Hambrick (1995) found, they respond quickly to perceived attack. This rapid response to attack may indicate a greater need to protect their reputation (Fombrun & Shanley, 1990), to signal stakeholders (Pfeffer, 1982) and competitors (Axelrod, 1984) that they are not passive, and to deter further attack (Chen and MacMillan, 1992).

As we have noted earlier, the size of an organization or alliance necessary to establish a successful global network is tremendous (Oum, Taylor, & Zhang, 1993). There are signs that administering these networks are time-consuming, frustrating and cumbersome. Further, it is not always clear that alliances truly deliver the seamless service that was supposed to be one of their benefits, a challenge that alliances are trying to address to insure the survival of the model (Buyck & Flottau, 2013). However, by the end of the second decade of the twenty-first century, the three mega-alliances accounted for 61 percent of global sales. As Table 11.4 noted, the Star Alliance continues to lead in overall size. Within each of the alliances, there has been some equity investment between key members as well as some more formalized joint-venture arrangement (SIAPartners, 2018).

Strange Bedfellows

While international airlines appear committed to the idea of an alliance world, there are many problems facing alliances as they try to provide the seamless service that their founders promised, and the profits that they hoped to achieve. If the negotiating and governance process looks complex, then imagine the complexity of day-to-day activity. Michael E. Levine, the Executive VP-Marketing for Northwest Airlines, has said that

> the hardest thing in working on an alliance is to coordinate the activities of people who have different instincts and a different language, and maybe worship slightly different travel gods, to get them to work together in a culture that allows them to respect each other's habits and convictions, and yet work productively together in an environment in which you can't specify everything in advance.
>
> (1993, p. 69)

Resolving these human issues, as well as the legal issues surrounding alliances, is one of the chief challenges of the alliance movement and one of the causes of instability in alliance arrangements.

Questions

1 Discuss the reasons for the use of strategic alliances in international aviation.
2 Discuss the alliance types common in airlines and how they are combined in the complex mega-alliances.
3 Discuss stability and failure in strategic alliances.
4 How can firms foster greater stability in alliances?
5 Would airlines choose ownership or alliance if regulations permitted them?
6 Analyze the role of strategic partnerships in the pharmaceutical industry and how they facilitate global market penetration and innovation.
7 Explore the dynamics of strategic collaborations in the technology sector, focusing on the evolution from traditional partnerships to ecosystem-based alliances and their impact on industry competitiveness.
8 Evaluate the challenges and benefits of forming strategic alliances in the renewable energy sector, considering factors such as resource sharing, technology transfer, and market expansion strategies.

References

Anderson, E. (1990), 'Two firms, one frontier: On assessing joint venture performance', *Sloan Management Review*, 31, pp. 19–30.

Anderson, E. & Gatignon, H. (1986), 'Modes of entry: A transaction cost analysis and propositions', *Journal of International Business Studies*, 17, pp. 1–26.

Axelrod, R. (1984), *The evolution of cooperation*, Basic Books, New York.

Bleeke, J. & Ernst, D. (1995), 'Is your strategic alliance a sale?' *Harvard Business Review*, 73, pp. 97–105.

Buckley, P. & Casson, M. (1988), 'A theory of cooperation in international business', in F. J. Contractor & Peter Lorange (Eds.) *Cooperative strategies in international business*, D.C. Heath & Company, Lexington.

Buyck, C. (2013) Filling in the blanks, *Aviation Week & Space Technology*, April 29, pp. 41–43.

Buyck, C. & Flottau, J (2013) From scale to service, *Aviation Week & Space Technology*, April 29, pp. 42–43.

Chen, M. J. (1996), 'Competitor analysis and inter-firm rivalry: Toward a theoretical integration,' *Academy of Management Review*, 21, pp. 100–134.

Chen, M. J. & Hambrick, D. C. (1995), 'Speed, stealth, and selective attack: How small firms differ from large firms in competitive behavior', *Academy of Management Journal*, 38, pp. 453–482.

Chen, M. J., & MacMillan, I. C. (1992), 'Nonresponse and delayed response to competitive moves: The role competitor dependence and action irreversibility,' *Academy of Management Journal*, 35, pp. 359–370.

Contractor, F. J. & Kundu, S. K. (1998), 'Modal choice in a world of alliances: Analyzing organizational forms in the international hotel sector', *Journal of International Business Studies*, 29, pp. 325–358.

Contractor & P. Lorange (Eds.), *Cooperative strategies in international business*, Lexington Books, Lexington, pp. 31–54.

Cook, J. & Wall, T. (1980), 'New work attitude measures trust, organizational commitment and personal need fulfillment,' *Journal of Occupational Psychology*, 53, pp. 39–52.

Dempsey, P. S. (2001), 'Carving the world into fiefdoms: The anticompetitive future of international aviation' Working Paper.

Doorley III, T. L. (1993), 'Teaming up for success', *Business Quarterly*, 57, pp. 99–103.

Eisenhardt, K. & Schoonhoven, C. B. (1990), 'Organizational growth: Linking founding team strategy, environment, and growth among semiconductor ventures, 1978–1988', *Administrative Science Quarterly*, 35, pp. 504–529.

Feldman, J (1998), 'Making alliances work', *Air Transport World*, June, pp. 27–35.

Feldman, J. M. (1999), 'Disappearing act', *Air Transport World*, February, pp. 25–30.

Fiegenbaum, A. & Karnani, A. (1991), 'Output flexibility – A competitive advantage for small firms,' *Strategic Management Journal*, 12, pp. 101–124.

Flint, P. (1999), 'Alliance paradox', *Air Transport World*, April, pp. 33–36.

Flottau, J. & Buyck, C (2013) Group dynamics', *Aviation Week & Space Technology*, April 29, pp. 39–41.

Fombrun, C. & Shanley, M. (1990), 'What's in a name? Reputation building and corporate strategy,' *Academy of Management Journal*, 33, pp. 233–258.

Franko, L. (1971), *Joint venture survival in multinational companies*, Praeger, New York.

Freeman, R. E. (1987), 'Review of the economic institutions of capitalism, by O. W. Williamson', *Academy of Management Review*, 12, pp. 385–387.

Gallacher, J. (1994), 'Airline alliance survey', *Airline Business*, June, pp. 25–53.

Gallacher, J. (1995), 'Airline alliance survey', *Airline Business*, June, pp. 26–53.

Gallacher, J. (1996), 'A clearer direction', *Airline Business*, June, pp. 23–51.

Gallacher, J. (1997), 'Partners for now', *Airline Business*, June, pp. 26–67.

Gallacher, J. (1998), 'Hold your horses', *Airline Business*, June, pp. 42–81.

Gimeno, J. (1999), 'Reciprocal threats in multimarket rivalry: Staking out spheres of influence in the US airline industry,' *Strategic Management Journal*, 20, 101–128.

Gudmunssson, S. V. & Rhoades, D. L. (2001). Airline alliance survival: Analysis, strategy, and duration. *Transport Policy*, 8(3).

Hambrick, D. C., MacMillan, I. C., & Day, D. L. (1982), 'Strategic attributes and performance in the BCG matrix-A PIMS-based analysis of industrial product businesses," *Academy of Management Journal*, 25, pp. 510–531

Hamel, G. (1991), 'Competition for competence and inter-partner learning within international strategic alliances', *Strategic Management Journal*, 12, pp. 83–104.

Heide, J. B. & Johns, G. (1988), 'The role of dependence balancing in safeguarding transaction-specific assets in conventional channels', *Journal of Marketing*, 52, pp. 20–35.

Henry, D. (2002), 'Mergers: Why most big deals don't pay off', *Business Week*, October 14, pp. 60–70.

Hitt, M. A., Hoskisson, R. E., & Harrison, J. S. (1991), 'Strategic competitiveness in the 1990s challenges and opportunities for US executives,' *Academy of Management Executive*, 5, pp. 7–22.

Inkpen, A. C. & Beamish, P. W. (1997), 'Knowledge, bargaining power, and the instability of international joint ventures', *Academy of Management Review*, 22, pp. 177–202.

Katz, R. L. (1970), *Cases and concepts in corporate strategy*, Prentice-Hall, Englewood Cliffs.

Kelly, D. & Amburgey, T. L. (1991), 'Organizational inertia and momentum: A dynamic model of strategic change,' *Academy of Management Journal*, 34, pp. 591–612.

Khanna, T., Gulati, R, & Nohria, N. (1998), 'The dynamics of learning alliances: Competition, cooperation, and relative scope', *Strategic Management Journal*, 9, pp. 193–210.

Killing, J. P. (1983), *Strategies for joint venture success*, Praeger, New York.

Kogut, B. (1988), 'Joint ventures: Theoretical and empirical perspectives,' *Strategic Management Journal*, 9, pp. 319–332.

Levine, M. E. (1993), 'Interview', *Air Transport World*, January, pp. 69–70.

Mayer, R. C., Davis, J. H., & Schoorman, F. D. (1995), 'An integrative model of organizational trust,' *Academy of Management Review*, 20, pp. 709–734.

McFall, L. (1987), 'Integrity,' *Ethics*, 98, pp. 5–20.

Merrill Lynch, Pierce, Fenner & Smith (1999), *Global airline alliances: Global alliance brands create value*, Merrill Lynch, New York.

Merrill Lynch, Pierce, Fenner & Smith Inc. (1998), *Global airline alliances: Why alliances really matter from an investment perspective*, Merrill Lynch, Pierce, Fenner & Smith Inc., New York.

Meyer, J. W. & Scott, W. R. (1983), *Organizational environments: Ritual and rationality*, Sage, Beverly Hills.

Mintzberg, H. & Waters, J. A. (1982), 'Tracking strategy in an entrepreneurial firm', *Academy of Management Journal*, 25, pp. 465–499.

Nelms, D. W. (1999), 'Getting their acts together,' *Air Transport World*, April, pp. 27–36.

Nomani, A. Q. (1990), 'Fare warning: How airlines trade price plans,' *Wall Street Journal*, October 9, pp. B1–B10.

Ouchi, W. G. (1980), 'Markets, bureaucracies, and clans', *Administrative Science Quarterly*, 25, pp. 129–142.

Oum, T. H. & Park, J. H. (1997), 'Airline alliances: Current status, policy issues, and future directions,' *Journal of Air Transport Management*, 3, pp. 133–144.

Oum, T. H. & Yu, C. (1998), *Winning airlines: Productivity and cost competitiveness of the world's major airlines*, Kluwer Academic Publishers, Boston.

Oum, T. H., Taylor, A. J., & Zhang, A. (1993), 'Strategic airline policy in the globalizing airline network,' *Transportation Journal*, 32, pp. 14–30.

Park, N. K. & Cho, D. (1997), 'The effect of strategic alliance on performance,' *Journal of Air Transport Management*, 3, pp. 155–164.

Parkhe, A. (1991), 'Interfirm diversity, organizational learning, and longevity in global strategic alliances', *Journal of International Business Studies*, 22, pp. 579–601.

Parkhe, A. (1993), 'Strategic alliance structuring: A game theoretic and transaction cost examination of interfirm cooperation', *The Academy of Management Journal*, 36, pp. 794–829.

Pfeffer, J. (1982), *Organizations and organizational theory*, Pitman, Boston.

Porter, M. E. (1990), *The competitive advantage of nations*, Free Press, New York.

Reuters (2000), 'KLM, MAS in quite intensive Wings Talks, March 15.

Rhoades, D. L. & Lush, H. (1997), 'A typology of strategic alliances in the airline industry: Propositions for stability and duration', *Journal of Air Transport Management*, 3, pp. 109–114.

Rhoades, D. L. & Waguespack, B., Jr. (2000), 'Divorce airline style', Working paper, Embry-Riddle Aeronautical University.

Root, F. R. (1987), *Entry strategies for international markets*. Lexington Books, Lexington.

Scott, W. R. (1992), *Organizations: Rational, natural, and open systems'* 3rd ed. Prentice-Hall: Englewood Cliffs.

SIAPartners (2018) Partnerships between airlines: The strategy to win the Asian market. Retrieved at https://www.sia-partners.com/en/insights/publications/partnerships-between-airlines-strategy-win-asian-market

Simonin, B.L. (1999), 'Ambiguity and the process of knowledge transfer in strategic alliances', *Strategic Management Journal*, 20, pp. 595–624.

Sitkin, S. B. & Roth, N. L. (1993), 'Explaining the limited effectiveness of legalistic "remedies" for trust/distrust,' *Organization Science*, 4, pp. 367–392.

Smith, A. & Aldrich, H. E. (1991), 'The role of trust in the transaction cost economics framework', Paper presented at *the annual meeting of the Academy of Management, Miami*.

Sparks, D. (1999), 'Partners', *Business Week*, October 25, pp. 106–112.

Stinchcombe, A. L. (1965), 'Organizations and social structures'. In James G. March (ed) *Handbook of organizations*, Rand McNally, Chicago.

Tretheway, M. W. & Oum, T. H. (1992), *Airline economics: Foundation for strategy and policy*, The Centre for Transportation Studies, University of British Columbia.

US General Accounting Office (US GAO) (1995), 'Airline alliances product benefits, but effect on competition is uncertain,' *GAO/RCED-95*, April.

Yan, A. (1998), 'Structural stability and reconfiguration of international joint ventures', *Journal of International Business Studies*, 29, pp. 773–796.

Zwart, M. L. (1999), 'Duration and stability of strategic alliances in the airline industry,' Dissertation at Maastricht University.

12 The Slippery Legal Slope

Learning Objectives

After reading this chapter, you should have a good understanding of:

LO1: the early developments in aviation liability
LO2: the background of anti-trust and competitive policy
LO3: the different approaches to anti-trust/competitive policy around the world
LO4: the issues involving competition between airlines and between the large aircraft manufacturers

Key Terms, Concepts & People

FCPA	Warsaw Convention	Montreal Convention
Anti-trust	Sherman Act	Fair competition
EU Court of Justice	JETRO	predatory behavior

Legally Speaking

One of the first issues that any student of international relations must deal with is the fact that there is no nice body of 'law' for most things international. In this sense, the student of international aviation is better positioned to accept this reality because that student has already grappled with the bilateral system of treaties that governed (and still governs) airline affairs between nations. In international law, treaties (bilateral and multilateral) are negotiated and signed (or not signed) by the parties involved in the negotiation and they set out how the system in question works, what the rules are, and who (or how) disputes are resolved. As discussed in Chapters 5 and 6, aviation law still rests firmly on the Chicago Convention and ICAO. Just as a reminder of what this means, let's go back to Chapter 6 for the following quote;

> The key to understanding ICAO is in realizing that like the United Nations in general it has *no* independent enforcement power; it can not make it members implement any of its standards. Its main bodies may act to support or condemn certain actions by members that relate to aviation, but this is an exercise in public relations and free expression. When or if a vote is taken on the issue of SARPs or PANS, it is the perfunctory end to

DOI: 10.4324/9781003405306-14

months or years of consensus building at ICAO. If consensus is not initially achieved on certain issues, then all parties revise, rework, or reframe the issue until consensus is obtained. It is a painstaking process, but it has and is producing some very positive results.

(XX)

In short, if a nation or a firm from a given nation violates the international rules set down by treaty, there may be little recourse for the aggrieved party except international mediation and dispute resolution by a body that both parties recognize (Abeyratne, 2002).

Within any given country's boundaries, the rules and laws of that nation, however they came into existence, are in force. In only rare occasions can a firm from one country operating in another country avoid complying with the latter country's laws. While one country may attempt to extend its laws beyond its borders (in what is termed extraterritoriality), such attempts are widely frowned upon by the rest of the world. A case in point is the 1977 Foreign Corrupt Practices Act (FCPA), which prohibited US companies from making illegal payments to foreign government officials for the purposes of influencing their decisions in matters of business. Many saw this act as an attempt by the US to impose their standards on the rest of the world and thus they lodged objections. This example also illustrates the problem with 'international law.' In 1997 the Organization for Economic Co-operation and Development Convention on Bribery was signed by 36 of the nations that had addressed these issues. Any nation not signing the treaty is not obligated to abide by it and even those nations that did sign it can renounce it, should they choose to do so. Aviation has recently experienced its own version of the FCPA as the European Union (EU) sought to apply the Emission Trading System (ETS) to international carriers outside their territorial boundaries (Labrousse, DeVore & Hayes, 2013). So, while it is possible to discuss the question of aviation or aerospace law in an international context, we will either be talking about 'domestic laws' relating to (or applied to) aviation or international treaties relating to aviation/aerospace. Whole texts have been written and courses have been taught on these subjects. The goal of this chapter is simply to introduce some of the broad legal areas affecting aviation, aerospace, and strategic alliances – liability issues, noise and non-carbon pollution issues, and economic issues, particularly anti-trust, or competition policy.

A Bumpy Ride

It is unsurprising that one of the first issues to concern the aviation industry was liability in event of a crash. The Warsaw Convention of 1929 was the first to address this matter to protect the newly forming airlines from the possibility that a single crash would put them out of business. Article 17 of the Warsaw Convention states that a carrier is liable for

damage sustained in the event of the death or wounding of a passenger, if the accident which caused the damage so sustained took place on board the aircraft or in the course of any of the operations of embarking or disembarking.

Over the years, legal experts have debated the meaning of 'accident' and wounding, whether passengers are duly notified of the opportunity to pursue liability insurance (and/or have the opportunity to do so), the meaning of willful misconduct and negligence, and the limits to liability. More recent issues are the liability in case of pulmonary embolism, the lack of medical equipment on board aircraft, and contaminated cabins and the spread of disease such as SARS (see Abeyratne, 2002 for more discussion). The Warsaw Convention set a damage limit of US$8,300 per person. The Chicago Convention avoided this issue, deferring to the agreement in Warsaw. This did not settle the matter, however. Developing countries complained that the limit was too high and, over time, developed countries have considered the limit to be too low. The Hague Protocol of 1955 sought to re-examine the issue. This was followed by a series of subsequent proclamations: the Montreal Agreement (1966), the Montreal Convention (1971), and a second Montreal Convention (1999). The limit for liability was progressively raised, but the latest limit under the treaty is the equivalent of US$168,372 unless the carrier can prove that neither it nor its agents had been negligent or committed a wrongful act or omission. This does not preclude victims from filing a lawsuit against any and all defendants. It also does not preclude airlines from carrying liability insurance for more than the amount in the Convention (Abeyratne, 2002; Pender, 2013). The events of September 11, 2001 obviously raised the issue of airline liability (and insurance) again, as we will discuss in Chapter 15.

Environmental Impacts

Like any other industry, aviation is subject to the rules and regulations in place to 'protect' the environment and the health and wellbeing of the citizens. The set of rules that applies depends on the location, rather than the nationality of the firm involved. For example, when American Airlines is conducting its operations in London, it is the rules of the UK and the broader European Commission that apply. The International Civil Aviation Organization (ICAO)'s inventory of aviation environmental problems range from site-specific issues of noise and flora and fauna impacts in airport construction to acid rain and carbon pollution. The latter has taken on new meaning with the concern about climate change, and will be discussed separately in Chapter 18. This issue is another example of the differences in aviation as ICAO was called on to address the issues of carbon emissions after individual nations reached an impasse. Given the nature of ICAO, nations could be confident that any resolution would represent the lowest common denominator and be notional in terms of enforcement.

For now, we will examine the question of aircraft noise. This issue took on new meaning with the advent of the jet age. ICAO created the Committee on Aircraft Noise (CAN) to deal with this issue and the national regulatory bodies governing aviation in respective countries have established extensive rules and procedures for addressing noise that attempt to establish acceptable decibel levels, hours of operation, distances involved, remediation efforts, etc. (Aris, 2002; Michaels, 2008a). A good deal of effort has been expended to determine what level of noise is harmful, both physically, and mentally. Daley (2010) provides an extensive discussion of aircraft noise in his book *Air Transport and the Environment*, including discussion of noise measurement, impacts, and methods of reducing it.

The Politics of Anti-trust

Perhaps no area of the 'law' has bedeviled the aviation industry more than anti-trust legislation (or competitive policy as it is commonly called in Europe and Asia). Once you understand the concepts involved, it is not hard to see why. Anti-trust is that body of principles and statutes whereby governments seek to promote forms of competition that benefit society and consumers. In many cases, this means restraining the use of market power (the ability to control prices, supplies, distribution channels, etc.) by firms within an industry or preventing mergers or acquisitions that would create excessive market power. In an industry in which many segments (airline, manufacturing, engines, avionics, air cargo, alliances) may have only a few players or a few players with most of the market share, anti-trust questions arise frequently. While all countries have some statutes addressing the behavior of firms within their domestic markets, the background and philosophy of countries regarding business itself, the role of government, and the limits of free enterprise differ. We will examine the background and philosophy of anti-trust law and its application to aviation in the United States, Europe, and Asia. We will attempt to chart the future direction of anti-trust enforcement and discuss critical issues impacting airline alliances.

In the years following the American Civil War (1861–1865), the United States witnessed a renewed westward expansion fueled by the growth of the US railroad industry. As the economy became more integrated, there was an effort by several smaller companies to combine their businesses to increase market power. The most notorious examples of this involved Standard Oil, led by John D. Rockefeller. The Standard Oil 'trust' was a device to gain market power by requiring participants to transfer stock from their company to a trustee in exchange for trust certificates. This trustee was then empowered to fix prices, control output, and allocate markets to other trust members. A series of scandals fueled the public perception that 'trusts' were designed to drive smaller competitors out of business through the use of predatory tactics. Public outcry led the US Congress to pass a series of acts which were designed to curb activities that sought to restrain trade or establish excessive market power. Accordingly, 'anti-trust' legislation was born.

United States

The first US legislation dealing with anti-trust was the Sherman Act (1890) which was concerned with 'horizontal restraints', i.e. agreements between rival firms in the same market or industry that sought to fix prices, restrain output, divide markets, exclude other competitors, or erect barriers that impeded free markets. In 1914, the Clayton Act (amended by the Robinson–Patman Act of 1936 and the Cellar–Kefauver Act of 1950) attempted to correct publicly perceived flaws in the Sherman Act by clearly prescribing actions that were deemed 'anti-competitive'. These actions include price discrimination, exclusionary practices such as exclusive dealing contracts and tying arrangements (tie-in sales agreements), and mergers that may have the effect of reducing competition.[1] The Civil Aviation Act of 1938 applied anti-trust specifically to airlines. Section 408 of the Civil Aviation Act, later recreated in virtually unchanged form in the Federal Aviation Act of 1958 and amended by the Airline Deregulation Act of 1978, made it unlawful for 1) two or more carriers to merge, 2) any carrier to control a substantial portion of the properties of another, or 3) any carrier to acquire control of another carrier. Section 414 provided the Civil Aviation Bureau (CAB) with the authority to grant limited immunity (exemption) from anti-trust enforcement if it deemed the action to be 'in the public interest'. With the termination of the CAB in 1985, the Assistant Secretary for Policy and International Affairs in the Department of Transportation was given anti-trust responsibility. Anti-trust issues for other segments of the industry tend to fall under the auspices of the Department of Justice and the Federal Trade Commission, although other departments may be consulted.

Domestic airline issues. Table 12.1 lists the merger/acquisition and bankruptcy activity in the US among national and major carriers since deregulation. The rationale for some of the mergers was the *failing company doctrine*, a legal principle that allows a company to take certain actions that would normally be prohibited under antitrust laws. However,

Table 12.1 Sample of US Airline History Since Deregulation

Carrier name	Status
AirTran	Merged with Southwest in 2010
Aloha	Ceased Operations 2008
Alaska	Continuing; Merged with Virgin America 2016
America West	Merged with US Airways in 2005
American	Bankruptcy in 2011; Merged with US Airways
Braniff	Bankruptcy 1994
Continental	Merged with United in 2010
Delta	Continuing
Eastern	Bankruptcy 1991; Ceased Operations
Flying Tigers	Acquired by FedEx 1988
Hawaiian Airlines	Continuing
Northwest	Merged with Delta
Pan American	Bankruptcy 1991; Ceased operations
Piedmont	Acquired by USAir
Republic	Acquired by Northwest 1986
Southwest Air Lines	Continuing
Trans World Airways	Assets acquired by American 2001
United Airlines	Continuing
US Airways	Merged with American 2013
Western	Acquired Delta 1986

Robert Pitofsky, formerly with the Federal Trade Commission, told the Commerce, Science, and Transportation Committee of the US Senate that some of these mergers were clearly 'anti-competitive' in nature. He specifically cited the example of the TWA–Ozark merger in his testimony (The impact, 1999). Alfred Kahn, the father of US deregulation, agreed and has commented that 'I said we should deregulate the airline industry. I didn't say we should abolish the antitrust laws' (Reno, 2000). The general attitude of the US Republican Party, which was in power during much of the 1980s, was to view most business-related legislation as an interference in the workings of the free market (Clarkson, Miller, Jentz, & Cross, 1992). This view was supported by the so-called Chicago School of anti-trust, whose members argued that while monopoly pricing hurt consumers, it had little effect on overall economic growth and productivity (Mandel, France, & Carney, 2000). However, these political and economic arguments do not entirely account for the level of consolidation permitted during the 1980s. In an effort to ensure competition, the Federal Aviation Administration and the Department of Transportation became caught in their own trap. When they allowed United Airlines to acquire the Pacific routes of the failing Pan Am, they created a carrier whose large domestic base and extensive, profitable international route system placed domestic rivals with smaller geographic reach at a major disadvantage. Thus, when Northwest petitioned the Department to purchase Republic, citing the need to expand their geographic reach in order to counter the United threat, the DOT agreed and so it went as other carriers pressed similar arguments.[2] In effect, the FAA created, somewhat reluctantly, a domestic market dominated by six or seven major carriers, each possessing an extensive continental network by the mid-1990s (Oum & Park, 1997; Gesell, 1993).

The airline crises following 9/11 and the Global Financial Crisis (GFC) have provided a backdrop for even further consolidation as the FAA and DOT continued to 'fall down the rabbit hole' trying to catch up to themselves and create a 'balanced' group of competitors. This time neither US political party seemed to see a merger that they did not like until US

Airways and the bankrupt American Airlines proposed to bring the number of major carriers down to three. In August 2013, the Department of Justice (DoJ) filed an anti-trust suit to block this proposed merger, citing reduced competition on over 1,000 connecting markets. Both carriers vowed to fight the DoJ, claiming that it not only fails to support its arguments that the merger is anticompetitive, but also that it holds this merger to a different standard than the Delta–Northwest, United–Continental, or Southwest–AirTran mergers. Of course, history offers little guide to the future of airline consolidation. American Airlines was permitted to go ahead with its acquisition of Reno Air based on the rationale that American had a very weak position in the California/West Coast market, where Reno Airlines was relatively strong, thus, competition was not likely to be harmed. When the DoJ filed suit against Northwest Airlines over plans to acquire a controlling stake in Continental, the acquisition was stopped but this did allow the two carriers to implement a number of their planned marketing activities (Carey & McCartney, 2000). UAL Corp, the parent company of United Airlines, once announced its own proposed $11.6 billion deal to purchase US Airways with great fanfare, but it ended its planned merger after consumer groups, fellow airlines, and local governments complained about the scope and nature of the acquisition, which would have created an airline with a combined market share of over 30 percent, making it twice as large as its nearest US competitor at the time (Hatch, 2000; Zellner, Carney, & Arndt, 2000). In the ever-larger mergers of America West and US Airways, Southwest and AirTran, United and Continental, and Delta and Northwest, the DoJ focused primarily on competition on nonstop service (Flottau, 2013). Unfortunately, on another level these mergers created situations such as the one at Baltimore-Washington International where, following the Southwest–AirTran merger, a single carrier-controlled 72 percent of the flights (Rohrer, 2013). In its defense, the DoJ is arguing that the dynamics of a three-airline oligopoly are very different from those of a four-airline oligopoly, but this may only be a matter of where you stand (which airport you fly out of, or which routes you fly most). As a consumer, the large market effects may matter less to you than the market share of the airlines at your local airport. This is what determines your fare, level of options, and also possibly the quality of service (Flottau & Shannon, 2013). According to Mazzeo (2003), flight delays are more frequent and longer in duration when only one airline provides direct service or dominates the market share of the airport in question.

It should be noted that a study conducted by Lehn and Kole on 18 airline mergers from 1979 to 1991 found that most of them resulted in negative long-run stock returns for the acquiring airline, including the US Air–Piedmont merger (Lehn, 2000). Short-run stock performance indicates that the market had a positive perception of AirTran and a negative one of Southwest following the merger announcement. Presumably, the market is concerned that Southwest will be able to further reduce costs (Manuela & Rhoades, 2013a). Short-run stock reaction to the announcement of the other mergers was mixed; however, the reaction to the completion of these mergers was positive (Manuela & Rhoades, 2013b). It is not yet clear how the market will view these mergers as they begin the often-painful process of merging operations. Still, American and US Airways argue that having allowed prior mega-mergers the DoJ should permit this latest one so that they will be able to compete and drive down prices. Delta and United have expressed official approval for the merger as it would help with continued capacity discipline and pricing power (Flottau & Shannon, 2013). If this latest merger did meet the expectations of Delta and United, then it might be 'good for the industry', but it remains to be seen if it will be in the long-term benefit of shareholders or consumers.

The existence of these large, overlapping network competitors explains in part the failure of US carriers to form the type of joint activity alliances common in Europe. Two cases explain the historic US governments' view that such joint activities are on balance anticompetitive. The first case, *In Re Passenger Computer Reservation System Anti-Trust Litigation CCH 21 AVI 17, 732*, was brought against US carriers' use of computer reservation systems in booking and marketing. It was charged that these systems, which were created by individual carriers, restricted competition by 1) displaying flight information in a biased manner, 2) imposing discriminatory fees on competing carriers, 3) using the data to identify travel agents who could be persuaded to divert business to the carrier owning the CRS, and 4) delaying the entry of competitor data. Since the development of computer reservation systems is expensive and beyond the reach of many carriers, such practices were considered an unfair use of market power and proprietary technology. In addition, the courts upheld the decision of the Civil Aviation Bureau in *Republic Airlines vs CAB 756 f.2d 1304 (1985)* to prohibit an exclusivity provision of joint operating agreements between carriers (Gesell, 1993).

Since deregulation took effect in the US, over 200 airlines have started up and failed, a number that is increasing by the week as we will discuss in later chapters (Rosen, 1995). Start-ups have also contended that major carriers unfairly use their market power advantages, specifically the ability to control price and capacity, in order to force them out of profitable markets. This is commonly known as predatory behavior. Unfortunately for regional carriers, the record of anti-trust cases in the US courts, particularly those involving charges of predatory behavior, has been very poor. In *Brookes Group Ltd v Brown & Williamson Tobacco Corp* (1993), the U.S. Supreme Court ruled that aggressive cost-cutting (even selling below costs) benefited consumers. Of the 37 cases to reach the Supreme Court since this decision, not one has prevailed (Carney & Zellner, 2000). The record for other cases of predatory behavior is equally poor (Walker, 1999). There was a renewed effort by the U.S. Department of Justice under the administration of President Clinton to enforce legislation relating to predatory behavior. As part of this new commitment, the US Department of Transportation issued the 'Proposed Statement on Enforcement Policy on Unfair Exclusionary Conduct by Airlines'. The statement outlined the following situations when the DOT was likely to act on predatory practice complaints: (1) a major airline adds seats and discounts fares reducing 'local revenue', or (2) a major airline carries more passengers at the new low fare than the new entrant has capacity, reducing the major's 'local revenue', or (3) a major airline carriers more at the new low fare than the new entrant carries, thereby reducing the major's local revenue. This issue had several implications for domestic alliances. First, many regional US carriers decided to avoid direct competition by entering into franchise agreements with major carriers acting as a feeder service to their hubs. Second, regional carriers themselves had begun to consolidate through either merger or alliance (AvStat, 1998). Most recently, successful regionals have avoided competition by pursuing an ultra-low-cost strategy like Spirit Airline and Allegiant (Saporito, 2013). The most recent merger under consideration in the US is JetBlue-Spirit. The US DOJ has said that approval of the merger would allow JetBlue to eliminate its largest low-cost rival; however, it remains to be seen if their argument will prevail in court. This proposed merger follows a rejection of a proposed American–JetBlue alliance because the court felt that the alliance did not serve consumers and was an unreasonable constraint on trade.

International airline issues. As discussed in Chapter 9, the deregulation of the US airline industry was accompanied by a renewed effort to liberalize international markets and anti-trust legislation had an important role to play in the US strategy, first as a means to attack the fare-setting power of IATA and then to encourage the spread of open skies bilateral agreements through the promise of anti-trust immunity for alliance partners from open skies countries. The first of the 'approved' alliances was Northwest and KLM. Four of the approved alliances are no longer in effect due to the failure (merger) of one or more of the carriers involved in the immunized alliance – American with Canadian International Airlines, Delta with Swiss Air, Sabena, and Austrian Airlines (formerly the Qualifyer group), Swissair with American, and Northwest and KLM (PR Newswire, 2000). The new EU–US Open Skies (2008) increased the pool of immunized alliances with AA–BA finally achieving immunized status.

The United States Department of Transportation released a report in 1999 on the benefits of Open Skies. According to this report, fares in Open Skies markets dropped 17.5% between 1996 and 1998. Non-Open Skies markets experienced only a drop of 3.5 percent (DOT, 1999). Thus, the United States rationale for waiving anti-trust provisions in approved alliances between Open Skies market partners is that the pro-competitive benefits to consumers of open skies outweighs the possible anti-competitive harm. A recent look at the effect of the EU–US Open Skies, a much-anticipated agreement, is less positive, but may be more a reflection of the 2008 Global Financial Crisis and continuing weakness in the EU since traffic growth on the North Atlantic for 2009 declined 6.2% and has remained relatively flat. This report noted that immunized alliances now control 83% of the market across the North Atlantic (CAPA, 2013).

Domestic issues in other sectors. Chapter 13 picks up the story of air cargo and notes that UPS struggled state by state with the Interstate Commerce Commission for the right to compete against the US Post Office in the delivery of parcels. UPS pointed out that the USPS was subsidized, paid no taxes, did not show a profit, and was often the subject of hearings and public outcry over mismanagement and incompetence. Their legal arguments centered on the value of competition, the lower rates of UPS, and the 'benefits to consumers'. They were ultimately successful in their struggles, but not without years of effort (Niemann, 2007). Obviously, when an entity is owned by the government, whether it is an airline or a postal system, there are incentives to protect it that create conflicts with the stated obligation of that government to protect competition for the benefit of consumers. In the case of the USPS, actions by the US Congress since 2006 have gone against this prevailing notion of government protection and appear determined to destroy the USPS by placing added conditions and restrictions on this entity without giving them any of the freedom a private entity would have to pursue innovate strategic options (Hicks, 2013).

As noted in the introduction to this book, aviation is often seen as a special case. One of the reasons for this is national defense. Therefore, it is unsurprising that there are a number of 'activities' that may be exempted from the application of competition rules, including any activity approved by the US president on the grounds of national defense (the Defense Production Act), activity involving research consortiums to develop new computer technology (the National Cooperative Research Act) or any activity of a regulated industry that is approved by the regulatory agency in that area (Clarkson, Miller, Jentz, & Cross, 1992). Further, there are 'special' circumstances that have led the US government, for reasons of national security, to approve mergers or acquisitions deemed to affect national security. The approval of the Boeing/McDonnell-Douglas merger and the Lockheed-Martin/Marietta merger are two relatively recent examples of aerospace firms (with military as well as civilian activities) that the US government felt merited exception.

International issues in other sectors. 'Fair Competition', of course, has been the stated reason behind the ongoing battles between Boeing and Airbus. Boeing has claimed that the initial launch aid provided to Airbus represented an 'illegal subsidy'. In 1992, the US and the EU had agreed that governments could provide money for no more that 33 percent of the development costs of a new aircraft. These development costs would be viewed as loans repayable if the plane were actually built, the first 25 percent at government rates and the remainder at commercial rates. Airbus has charged that the aid Boeing receives from the US military amounts to a sizeable 'indirect subsidy'. Neither side has ever been able to put a specific figure to the amounts of aid, but this has not stopped them from battling over the issue. The US would again revisit this issue at the urging of Boeing in 2004, after Airbus had surpassed Boeing in orders. Both sides eventually filed a complaint with the World Trade Organization. As Airbus went to EU governments for new launch aid, Boeing howled. As Boeing outsourced development costs to the Japanese heavies (supported by their government), Airbus cried foul. In 2008, the US Pentagon announced that it would award a military refueling tanker contract to a group of firms that included the parent company of Airbus, EADS. Boeing 'fought' this award, marshaling political pressure with presentations of job losses and gains in various political districts. One Washington State Congressman even worked to change the life-cycle cost calculations in the award process to assist in changing the cost dynamics of the bidding process (Giegerich, 2011). The battle continues.

The US engine manufacturers have also lodged complaints about subsidies against UK competitor, Rolls-Royce, who is reported to have received almost £450 million from the UK government, who also holds a 'golden share' in the company. Pratt & Whitney has noted that the CFM56 was partly funded by the French government in support of GE partner Snecma. The V2500, designed for the A-380, by Rolls-Royce and Pratt is another example of development aid in action. Once again, all sides of the debate can charge 'indirect subsidy' because of the engine manufacturers relationships with their respective government and defense spending (Newhouse, 2007).

Europe

While each individual European nation has its own legislation relating to competitive activity, we will address the development of anti-trust (or competitive policy as it is called in Europe) from the perspective of European integration.[3],[4] European competition policy is among the most extensive in the world and is generally stronger than the individual policies of member nations. It is also highly centralized. The period 1981–1991 represented a significant strengthening of these policies. One case in point is the Merger Regulation of 1989, which was used to block a proposed merger of ATR and De Havilland in 1991 and was an early sign that the EU was prepared to take a harder line of mergers than their US counterparts (Warlouzet, 2010). Although a common transport policy was one of the stated goals of the European Community, the Council of Ministers, under their authority to issue block exemptions, chose to exempt transportation from the enforcement of competition rules. In 1986 the Court of Justice ruled, in the *Nouvelles Frontières* case, that the air transport sector was subject to the general rules of the EEC Treaty. In the same year, the Commission began proceedings against ten Community airlines for the violation of various competition rules. The 'first package', adopted December 14, 1987, officially included an implementing regulation, giving the Commission the authority to investigate alleged violations of the competition rules and fine violators.

Domestic airline issues. The Commission's policy toward airline mergers has been shaped in large part by what they perceive as failures in US policy. According to European aviation experts, 'the experience of deregulation combined with the lack of antitrust enforcement, destroyed many of the benefits of that deregulation' in the United States (Soames, 1990, p. 82). Mario Monti, a former EC anti-trust commissioner, led a concerted effort to crack down on industries that attempted to set prices or divide markets. While there is a general feeling that cross-border ownership would benefit the EU system by reducing the tendency to favor 'local' firms and allow for greater economies of scale, the Commission has also been very cautious in approving mergers and acquisitions. The Commission's policy was questioned several years ago when Air France/UTA were allowed to merge; however, a series of Commission rulings, including one involving AirTours' planned takeover of First Choice, appeared to indicate that the Commission is prepared to take a tougher stance in aviation/aerospace mergers/acquisitions (Soames, 1990; Taverna, 1999). The EU has continued to reject proposals to merge between Ryanair and Aer Lingus on the grounds that the merger would create a monopoly at Ireland's Dublin Airport. Ryanair CEO, Michael O'Leary, has complained that the decision is at odds with the decision to allow Air France and KLM to merge, even though these two carriers would control about 60 percent of the aircraft movements at Charles De Gaulle Airport and Schiphol Airport, respectively (Media Limited, 2007). The EU also blocked the merger of Olympic and Aegean Airlines. Similarly, a previously suggested merger between British Airways and KLM raised questions over the fact that any merger would place a single airline in control of two of Europe's most important airports – Heathrow and Schiphol. The stated reason for ending the BA/KLM talks was 'intractable commercial and regulatory issues', but clearly there were also serious concerns over European Commission approval. The US was also concerned because The Netherlands was an Open Skies country while the UK still had not signed any such agreement (Field, 2000). In the case of the Air France–KLM merger, the Commission obliged the parties to agree to an unlimited period of slot divestment as a condition for approval. Further, slots surrendered initially would not be available for return to the parties even if the new entrant misused or underused it (Giannino, 2013).

While European officials have taken a hard line on the issue of mergers and acquisitions as a means of opening slots to new entrants, they were relatively quick to approve the American–US Airways merger with the provision that actions be taken to increase competition on the London–Philadelphia route (Business Spectator, 2013). The EU has also tended to have a more favorable view of cooperative agreements between carriers involving fleet rationalization and network efficiencies. While EC competition rules do not explicitly consider 'the public interest', they have often held that these types of agreements 'contribute to the promotion of economic progress and to the interests of consumers' (AEA, 1999). Some of the allowed practices include consultation on and coordination of tariffs, joint operations, interline agreements, route planning, coordination of schedules, and linked frequent flyer programs. Perhaps signaling the limits of its powers, the European Commission recently conducted a raid on the offices of Scandinavian Airlines and Maersk Air to determine whether Maersk Air stopped operating between Stockholm and Copenhagen 'in concert with SAS' following their recent cooperation pact (Dow Jones Newswire, 2000). US officials, on the other hand, have tended to view almost all actions relating to route planning, schedule coordination, and joint operations as violations of anti-trust law.

In an address at the 23rd Annual FAA Commercial Aviation Forecast Conference, Frederik Sorenson, then Head of the Air Transport Policy Unit Directorate General of Transport, European Commission, addressed the issue of competitive behavior by stating that the EU did not agree with the US 'free for all system depending on the good behavior of air carriers' (Sorensen, 1998, p. 125). The Commission has acted in several cases of alleged predatory behavior, ruling in favor of plaintive airlines (easyJet–KLM, easyJet–BA Go). BA's Go successfully lodged a complaint with the European Commission, charging that Deutsche Lufthansa AG was selling tickets at below cost (Independent, 2000). Given sufficient protection, many of these carriers may opt to remain independent, niche players rather than franchising feeders for the major airlines. The rapid growth of Ryanair, however, may give this carrier the market power to dampen the growth and development of the low-cost competition that the EU hoped to see from its deregulation and its Single Sky program.

One of the most vexing problems for the EU is government intervention to support airlines, first in Eastern Europe (Hungary's Malev Airlines in one of the most egregious examples) and, most recently, during COVID (Pantazi, 2023). EU law does allow state aid to compensate for damages caused by natural disaster or exceptional occurrences and guidance was issued on schemes likely to be approved.

International airline issues. While the US chose to tie alliance approval to Open Skies, European officials have tended to tie alliance approval to domestic market development. One key issue in alliance approvals has been the willingness of potential partners to relinquish slots at congested European airports (United–Lufthansa and BA–AA, for example). These slots were deemed necessary to the development of viable start-up competitors. Under the European Merger Control Regulation (EMCR), the Commission defines relevant markets on an origin and destination basis, considering slot and route dominance. The new generation slot remedies imposed on any merger seem to be solving this EU problem. The rejection of Ryanair–Aer Lingus and Olympic–Aegean was based on concerns over route dominance (Giannino, 2013). The European Commission argued for a multilateral approach to traffic rights negotiations on the basis of the 'one market' concept and launched a case against eight member states, arguing that the bilateral agreements that they signed with the US violated the EU external competence. The 2002 ruling by the European Court of Justice gave the EC the go ahead to 'demand' multilateral talks with the US (EurActiv, 2008). This effort finally resulted in the 2008 EU–US Open Skies agreement. In 1991, the EU and the US had agreed to notify and give weight to the competition policies of the other party in instances where their own enterprises were concerned. Most of the notifications involved proposed mergers. Unfortunately, the principle of positive comity has often merely served to highlight the differences between EU–US policy on competition policy. US authorities explicitly consider 'the public interest' when assessing the benefits of proposed action (AEA, 1999). Given that one part of the new multilateral agreement signed between the US and EU calls for regulatory convergence, it is not clear what criteria will be used for alliance approval in the future. It is unclear whether the divergence of opinion on American–US Airways reflects different overall approaches to competition analysis or the basic realities of different domestic markets.

Domestic issues in other sectors. In aerospace, the EU did block the proposed GE–Honeywell merger, claiming that it would reduce competition. GE and Honeywell had offered to unload some assets in the avionics area, but the European Commission asked that GE either spin off its aircraft leasing unit or sell shares (CNNMoney.com, 2001). In 1999, the EU rejected another aerospace merger between Honeywell and AlliedSignal on concerns over undue dominance in avionics. Complaints had been lodged several years earlier when the EC had approved French subsidies to Sextant and Smith Industries to build a flight management system for Airbus – a move that some saw as an attempt to reduce Airbus reliance on Honeywell (CNNMoney.com, 1999). It is unclear what the ruling of the EC would have been over the proposed BAE Systems and EADS merger since disagreements between the three governments involved – UK, France, and Germany – over ownership and industrial structure led to a collapse in the merger talks, but the merger would have created a military/aerospace company to rival Boeing (Scott & Clark, 2012).

International issues in other sectors. It is unsurprising, given the battles between Airbus and Boeing, that the EC waded into the debate about the Boeing–McDonnell merger, eventually approving the merger after Boeing agreed to give up an exclusive sales agreement with American, Delta, and Continental (Newhouse, 2007). The EC did agree, however, to the merger between Travelport and Worldspan. Travelport was the second-largest GDS in the EU while Worldspan, a subsidiary of the online travel provider Orbitz, ranked fourth in GDS systems. Amadeus and Sabre were the other main players in this area. The EU has stated that although the merged entity would have a very high market share in some of its member states, it did not feel that it would be able to increase prices due to high levels of competition with other providers (Michaels, 2008b).

Asia

There is no single legal framework for Asia, but most of its countries do have some kind of legislation dealing with monopoly and competition. The difficulty lies in understanding the degree to which these regulations are applied and/or enforced. In Japan, the Anti-Monopoly Act is intended 'to eliminate excessive concentrations of business power and to encourage fair and free competition' (Jetro, 1999). It prohibits holding companies and places restrictions on shareholding, interlocking directorates, mergers, and acquisitions. The Fair-Trade Commission is responsible for enforcing the anti-monopoly guidelines. The Korean Fair-Trade Commission is also charged with promulgating guidelines and enforcing the policies of their Monopoly Regulation and Fair-Trade Act. Like its Japanese counterpart, the Monopoly Regulation and Fair-Trade Act is intended to prohibit excessive concentration, abuse of market power, and unfair business practices. To the outside observer, the Japanese Keiretsus and the Korean Chaebols, forms of tightly linked industrial groupings, appear to violate much of this legislation. Critics have often complained that the legislation is primarily directed at limiting foreign access to domestic markets (Gibney, 1985; Prestowitz, 1988). The financial crisis in Asia put a great deal of pressure on these structures. In Korea, this crisis prompted some consideration of dismantling or weakening the chaebol structure to improve efficiency and transparency within their market.

Domestic airline issues. Efforts were underway in several Asian countries to deregulate aspects of their air transport sectors before the Asian crisis of the late 1990s. The events of 9/11 and the Global Financial Crisis were not as severe in Asia as in other parts of the globe. As noted in Chapter 10, two countries are taking significant actions to further liberalize their domestic aviation markets – India and Japan. The Indian government allowed private entry into the airline industry in the mid-1990s. Only one of the private carriers started at that time survives today. Four of the carriers founded in the last decade have also posted massive losses, including the once highly touted Kingfisher Airlines. The debate over possible intervention by the State Bank of India in favor of Kingfisher created a great deal of soul-searching in the 9th largest aviation market in the world over questions of market versus intervention. It has also prompted the government to open the market to more foreign investment (Choudhury, 2012). The Japanese government changed its policy in 1995 to make discounted fares easier and in 1996 it created a zone-fare system. On December 5, 1996, the Japanese Ministry of Trade announced an end to the supply–demand balance clauses that had effectively blocked new entry. A 1999 study of the changes, however, did not find a significant shift in market share or reduction in airfares (Yamauchi, 1999). Load factors for domestic routes have remained around 60 percent for the last two decades, prompting the government to encourage new LCC entry. In 2012, three such carriers were established – Peach, Jetstar, and AirAsia Japan (CAPA, 2013).

International airline alliances. As with aviation policy, there is no consistent 'Asian' strategy toward international alliances. Market access through code sharing has been the dominant form of alliance arrangement. The economic crisis that began in Thailand and spread throughout Asia affected all the region's air carriers. The hardest-hit were Thai Airlines, Philippines Airlines, Korean Airlines, Malaysian Airlines, and Garuda from Indonesia. High operating and financing costs combined with outbound and inbound traffic decreases to place severe stress on these and other Asian carriers (Li, 1999). There were talks of regional consolidation, but little action took place until the 9/11, SARS, and bird flu crises added further pressure to some of the Asia carriers. Many of these talks (and actions) included Singapore Airlines, which emerged as one of the strongest of the Asian carriers and has continued an aggressive campaign to improve its already impressive quality and position itself well in the mega-alliance world. Following the GFC, Asia has continued to be one of the strongest aviation regions of the world.

Stumbling Along

It should be clear from the above discussions that in the aviation/aerospace industry the line between politics and legal matters is very fine and frequently shifting. The industry is a highly visible, important employer with close ties to national security and defense; this places any matter affecting its profitability squarely into the political arena. In the all-important area of competition, the EU has been most consistent, maintaining a relatively hard line on mergers/acquisitions, predatory behavior, and slot allocation. The approval of the Air France–KLM merger certainly indicates that the EC is interested in selected cross-border merger activity. As noted above, the Commission has indicated on several occasions that it would like to see more consolidation in the relatively fragmented airline and aerospace industry, but this has not prevented them from denying several mergers for competition reasons (Sparaco, 1999). One of the key differences in merger activity between Europe and the US is the fact that the names of key national airlines continue to exist and air statistics continue to be reported separately (Financials do not).

As for predatory behavior, the EU provided start-up carriers greater protection than is typically afforded them in the US market. This protection could help ensure that deregulation increases competition at the route level within Europe; however, the start-up darling of Europe, Ryanair, has faced increasing charges that it has begun to practice the kind of market power tactics once used against it to compete against legacy and other start-ups (Creaton, 2005). The pool of start-ups in Europe has remained relatively small and many of the major European carriers did not feel the need to aggressively engage them. The events of 9/11 hit the major European carriers hard and regional European and LCC carriers began increasing their market share (Binggeli & Pompeo, 2002). The expansion of Ryanair alone has changed the dynamics of air travel in the EU. While a report in the late 1990s by the British Civil Aviation Authority found that no more than 7 percent of intra-European city pairs are served by three or more competitors, the expansion of easyJet and Ryanair have probably made air travel in the EU more accessible and price competitive than many US markets (Sparaco, 1998).

New Meaning

Recent events in Ukraine have brought renewed focus on the international frameworks in aviation, including the shoot down of ML 17 over eastern Ukraine in 2014 and now the invasion of Ukraine by Russia. As countries supporting Ukraine cut off overflight by Russian aircraft and Russia reciprocated, airlines are struggling to adapt networks. This is not the first time that entry to a nation's airspace has been cut off, but it is the most significant occasion and has been followed by other actions related to aviation, including restrictions of access to aircraft parts, maintenance and training restrictions, and the loss of leased aircraft to Russian nationalization. When the current crisis ends, there will be many legal issues to sort out in the aviation sector, but, as this book as noted before, aviation and politics have always been closely linked (IATA, 2022).

Questions

1 Discuss the following: The Warsaw Convention of 1929, The Hague Protocol of 1955, and the Montreal Conventions of 1971 and 1999.
2 What is anti-trust policy and what is the history of its enforcement in the US?
3 What are predatory behaviors? Is it a problem in the airline industry and what can be done about it?
4 How does the EU policy to anti-trust or competitive policy differ from the US?
5 What is the purpose of these types of policies, and have they been effective in protecting competition?
6 Compare and contrast the roles of the World Trade Organization (WTO) and the International Monetary Fund (IMF) in shaping global economic policies and regulations.
7 Analyze the evolution of intellectual property rights protection across different international treaties such as TRIPS (Trade-Related Aspects of Intellectual Property Rights) and WIPO (World Intellectual Property Organization).
8 Discuss the impact of free trade agreements (FTAs) on competition policy and market regulation, using examples from recent regional trade agreements like the Comprehensive and Progressive Agreement for Trans-Pacific Partnership (CPTPP) or the Regional Comprehensive Economic Partnership (RCEP).

Notes

1 Federal antitrust laws are enforced by the Department of Justice (DOJ) and the Federal Trade Commission (FTC). Violations of the Sherman Act fall under the jurisdiction of the DOJ and can be prosecuted as either a criminal or civil case. The Department can ask companies to divest certain holdings or dissolve a partnership. The FTC has the responsibility to enforce the Clayton Act through civil proceedings. In addition, private parties may sue for damages because of violation of the Sherman and Clayton Acts. Private parties may also seek an injunction to prevent antitrust violations. It should be noted that European law does not include possible criminal prosecution.
2 I am indebted to Paul V. Mifsud, Vice President, Government & Legal Affairs, US, for KLM Royal Dutch Airlines for his willingness to share his insight and experience.
3 Anti-trust legislation was first contained in Articles 4 and 65–67 of the European Coal and Steel Community treaty. It is incorporated in Articles 85–86, 90, and 92–94 of the Treaty of European Union. The European Commission (Directorate-General IV) is responsible for implementing competitiveness policy.

4 It should be noted that allowing cabotage in the US would require changes in US laws and would have to be approved by the US Congress. There is also some question as to whether the EC can negotiate a multilateral agreement with the US.

References

Abeyratne, R. I. R. (2002), *Frontiers of aerospace law*, Ashgate Publishing, Aldershot, UK.

AEA (1999), *Towards a transatlantic common aviation area*, Association of European Airlines, Brussels.

Aris, S. (2002), *Close to the Sun: How Airbus challenged America's domination of the skies*, Arum Press, London.

AvStat Associates Inc. (1998), '*Summary of passenger service by state*', AvStat Associates.

Binggeli, U. & Pompeo, L. (2002) Hypes hopes for Europe's low-cost airlines, *The McKinsey Quarterly* No. 4. Available at www.mckinseyquarterly.com

Business Spectator (2013) EU approves giant airline merger. Available at http://www.businessspectator. com.au/news/2013/8/6/aviation/eu-approves-giant-airline-merger

Carey, S. & McCartney, S. (2000), 'Antitrust trial pressures northwest airlines to cede controlling stake in continental', *Wall Street Journal*, November 7.

Carney, D & Zellner, W (2000), 'Caveat predator?' *Business Week*, May 22, pp. 116–118.

Centre for Aviation (CAPA) (2013) The North Atlantic: The state of the market five years on from EU-US open skies. Available at: http://centreforaviation.com/analysis/download/100315

Choudhury, G. (2012) SBI decides on 1,650-crone relief package for Kingfisher, *Hindustan Times*, February 22, p. 1.

Clarkson, K. W., Miller, R. R., Jentz, G. A. & Cross, F. B. (1992), *West's business law: Text, cases, legal and regulatory environment* (5th ed.). West Publishing Company, New York.

CNNMoney (1999) 'EC probes avionics merger', August 30, Available at: http://cnnmoney.com/pt/ cpt?action=cpt&title=EC+probes+AlliedSinanl

CNNMoney (2001) 'GE pessimistic on merger', June 14. Available at: http://cnnmoney.com/pt/cpt? action=cpt&title=GE%2C+Honeywell

Creaton, S. (2005), *Ryanair: How a small Irish airline conquered Europe*, Arum, London.

Daley, B. (2010), *Air transport and the environment*, Ashgate Publishing Ltd, Surrey, UK

Department of Transportation, (1999), '*International aviation developments: Global deregulation takes off*', DOT, Washington, D.C. ostpxweb.dot.gov/aviation

Dow Jones Newswire (2000), 'EU Raids Maersk, SAS In Connection with Cooperation Pact', June 21.

EurActiv (2008), 'EU-US 'Open Skies' Agreement' Available at: http://www.euractiv.com/en/transport

Field, P. (2000), 'BA, KLM ground merger plan. Airlines faced opposition from government which feared massive layoffs', *USA Today*, September 22, 1B.

Flottau, J. (2013) Court of contingency, *Aviation Week & Space Technology*, September 16, p. 37.

Flottau, J. & Shannon, D. (2013) Connecting fight, *Aviation Week & Space Technology*, August 19, pp. 24–27.

Gesell, L. E. (1993), '*Aviation and the law*' (2nd ed.). Coast Aire Publications, Chandler, AZ.

Giannino, M. (2013) The European Commission appraisal of airline mergers: The rise of a new generation of slot remedies, Available at: http://aerlinesmagazine.files.wordpress.com/2012/03/52_ giannino_eu_slot_remedies.pdf

Gibney, F. (1985), *The fragile super-power*, New American Library, New York.

Giegerich, S. (2011) Bumpy Road to Boeing tanker contract, St. Louis Post-Dispatch. Available at: http://www.stltoday.com/business/local/bumpy-road-to-boeing-tanker-contract/article_4b7e1993- c4f4-508a-89ee-1baf9e13ecd7.html

Hatch, M. (2000), 'Minnesota Attorney General letter to the DOJ re US-UA', June 5.

Hicks, J. (2013) Postal service financials improve, but big losses continue, The Washington Post. Available at http://articles.washingtonpost.com/2013-08-11/politics/41299747_1_u-s-postal- service-comprehensive-postal-reform-legislation-postmaster-general-patrick-donahoe

Independent (2000), '*BAs GO accuses Lufthansa of unfair competition*', London, February 28, p. 17

International Air Transport Association (2022), IATA Factsheet: The impact of the war in Ukraine on the aviation industry. Available at https://www.iata.org/en/iata-repository/publications/economic- reports/the-impact-of-the-conflict-between-russia-and-ukraine-on-aviation/

JETRO (1999), www.jetro.go.jp

Labrousse, F., DeVore, J. S. & Hayes, J. M. (2013) "European Union: Aviation and the EU ETS-What's Next" Jones Day. Available at http://www.mondaq.com/unitedstates/x/223598/Aviation/Aviation+and+the+EU+ETS+Whats+Next

Lehn, K. M. (2000), 'Why airline mergers are a disaster – Soaring labor costs may ground airline mergers', May 25.

Li, M. Z.F. (1999), 'Asia-Pacific Airlines amidst the Asian Economic Crisis', Presented at *the air transportation research group conference, Hong Kong, June 1999.*

Mandel, M. J., France, M. & Carney, D. (2000), 'The great antitrust debate', June 26, pp. 40–42.

Manuela, W. S. & Rhoades, D. L. (2013a) (Accepted) Merger activity and short-run financial performance in the US airline industry, *Journal of Air Transport Management*

Manuela, W. S. & Rhoades, D. L. (2013b) (Accepted) Southwest's acquisition of AirTran: An analysis of short-term stock performance, *World Review of Intermodal Transportation.*

Mazzeo, M. J. (2003) Competition and service quality in the US airline industry, *Review of Industrial Organization* 22, 275–296.

Media Limited (2007) 'EU steps in on Irish airline merger', June 27. Available at: http://www.airport-technology.com/news/news1701.html

Michaels, D. (2008b), 'Heathrow makeover to heat up airline wars', *The Wall Street Journal Online*, March 6.

Michaels, J. (2008a), 'Travelport completes acquisition of Worldspan' Aviation Daily. Available at: http://aviationnow.com/pt/cpt?action=cpt&title=Aviation+Week%3A

Newhouse, J. (2007), *Boeing versus Airbus: The inside story of the greatest international competition in business*, Alfred A. Knopf, New York.

Niemann, G. (2007) *Big Brown: The untold story of UPS*, John Wiley & Sons, San Francisco, CA.

Oum, T. H. & Park, J. (1997), 'Airline alliances: Current status, policy issues, and future directions', *Journal of Air Transport Management*, 3, pp. 133–144.

Pantazi, T. (2023) State aid to airlines in the context of COVID 19: Damages, disturbances, and equal treatment, *Journal of European Competition Law & Practice*, 13(4), 268–277.

Pender, K. (2013) Who will pay, collect claims arising from Asiana crash, SFGate. Available at: http://blog.sfgate.com/pender/2013/07/08/who-will-pay-collect-claims-arising-from-asiana-crash/

Prestowitz, C. V. (1988), *Trading places: How we are giving our future to Japan and how to reclaim it*, Basic Books, Inc, New York.

PRNewswire (2000), 'Northwest Airlines and Malaysia Airlines receive antitrust immunity; approval represents first immunized alliance between a US and Asian Carrier', November 21.

Reno, R. (2000), 'In several ways, United/US Airways merger might not fly', *STAR TRIBUNE*, June 1.

Rohrer, K (2013) Where was DoJ in Southwest-AirTran merger? The Baltimore Sun. Available at: http://www.baltimoresun.com/news/opinion/readersrespond/bs-ed-merger-letter-20130815,0,5846611

Rosen, S. D. (1995), 'Corporate restructuring: A labor perspective'. In *Airline labor relations in the global era: The new frontier*, P. Cappelli (Ed.). ILR Press, Ithaca, NY.

Saporito, B. (2013) Cabin pressure, *Time*, September 9, pp. 36–41.

Scott, M. & Clark, N. (2012) BAE and EADS merger talks disintegrate, *The New York Times*. Available at: http://dealbook.nytimes.com/2012/10/10/eads-and-bae-systems-abandon-merger-talks/?_r=0

Soames, T. (1990), 'Joint ventures and cooperation agreements in the air transport sector', in P. D. Dagtoglou and T Soames (Eds.), *Airline mergers and cooperation in the European community*, Kluwer Law and Taxation Publishers, Boston.

Sorensen, F. (1998), 'Open skies in Europe', in *FAA commercial aviation forecast conference proceedings*, US Department of Transportation, Washington, D.C., pp. 125–131.

Sparaco, P. (1998), 'European deregulation still lacks substance', *Aviation Week & Space Technology*, November 9, 53–57.

Sparaco, P. (1999), 'EC pushes quick aviation accord with US', *Aviation Week & Space Technology*, November 29, pp. 40–41.

Taverna, M. A. (1999), 'European rulings signal tougher antitrust stance', *Aviation Week & Space Technology*, October 4, pp. 42–43.

The impact of recent alliances, international agreements, DOT actions, and pending legislation on air fares, air service, and competition in the airline industry, 10x Cong., 2 Sess. (1999).

Walker, K. (1999), 'American justice', *Airline Business*, July, pp. 66–67.

Warlouzet, L. (2010) The rise of European competition policy, 1950-1991: A cross-disciplinary survey of a contested policy sphere, EUI Working Papers RSCAS 2010/80. Available at: http://cadmus.eui.eu/bitstream/handle/1814/14694/RSCAS_2010_80.pdf

Yamauchi, H. (1999), 'Air transport policy in Japan: Policy change and market competition', Paper presented at *the Air transportation research group conference, Hong Kong*, April 1999.

Zellner, W., Carney, D., & Arndt, M. (2000), 'How many airlines will stay aloft' *Business Week*, June 19.

13 The Quality Question

Learning Objectives

After reading this chapter, you should have a good understanding of:

LO1: the many definitions of quality and the selection of metrics to measure it
LO2: the metric and sources of quality data for the airline industry
LO3: the measurement of quality across alliances
LO4: ways to approach quality improvements

Key Terms, Concepts & People

Word-of-Mouth	Quality	Loyalty
Repurchase	Satisfaction	J.D. Powers
ATCR	AQR	SDI

Know It When You See It

Quality is a very elusive term. Consumers know (or think they know) it when they see it and firms have spent billions trying to get them to articulate their preferences or to convince them that what they get is what they want. A researcher will tell you that you cannot measure something until you define it. Unfortunately, the very act of defining and measuring a concept can change the concept itself, marketing's own 'Uncertainty Principle.' The term quality has been defined as excellence, value, conformance to specification, etc. The most commonly used definition comes to us from the total quality movement. It defines quality as 'meeting and/or exceeding customer expectations'. To comply with this definition of quality, companies must first know who their customers are and then continually strive to understand and meet their expectations (continuous improvement). While this sounds simple on paper, many companies find it difficult to put into practice. For airlines, revenue management systems that divided customers by their preferences on booking time, price, class, etc and frequent flyer surveys of services provided to these customers were often considered sufficient to comply with this quality definition. However, the movement to 'brand' airline and alliance service is focused new attention on issues of quality. This movement was fueled by the belief that 'a very real risk exists that the flight will be reduced to a commodity status, and that the individual choice of airlines will be factored out of the

DOI: 10.4324/9781003405306-15

buying process' (Fraser, 1996, p. 61). In short, consumer choice would be driven almost solely by price, a factor that drives down profits and forces airlines to continually strive for new cost-cutting measures whose revenue benefits would be transferred almost immediately to customers as lower prices. While this might sound great for customers, an airline that cannot make money cannot stay in business very long. The airline answer to the price/quality dilemma, as we discussed in Chapter 11, is to create products and services that send images and messages to the consumer that reassure them about quality, convenience, comfort... In short, the very name must separate one airline (one alliance) from another in terms of key consumer expectations whether they are 'global reach', 'superior service' or 'value for money'.

Measuring a Concept

For individual carriers, consumers have three basic sources of information on quality – personal experience (or word-of-mouth), third-party surveys or secondary reports. Personal experience or the so-called word-of-mouth (WOM) information that comes to us from friends and strangers alike is clearly a powerful force. This type of information has become even more powerful in the era of social media where consumers can post real-time reactions to the service they are experiencing and these reactions can go 'viral' in minutes, spreading exponentially before companies can even formulate a response. For many companies, this source calls to mind the old adage that a satisfied customer tells 5 other people about their experience while a dissatisfied customer tells at least 10 (or up to 1,000 in the age of social media). For most firms in the so-called service industries, satisfying customers is the first step toward creating loyal customers who will repurchase your product. Taking this concept one step further, marketing gurus such as Fred Reichheld (1996) have suggested that *The Ultimate Question* is 'Would you recommend us to a friend?' Reichheld believes that the best measure of a firm's success is the size of their net promoter score (or NPS) (promoters less detractors). Reichheld's promoters are the truly loyal customers. Loyal customers repurchase your products or services and recommend them to others. One of the advantages of the NPS is its simplicity when compared to other academic studies that rely on multiple factors to understand the process of quality, satisfaction, and loyalty.

The largest group of academic studies on quality have used the SERVQUAL or SERVPERF framework to approach the issues. The difference between these two methods is the role of prior expectations (SERVQUAL) in shaping a respondent's opinions on quality. The dictionary defines perception as the 'recognition and interpretation of sensory stimuli based chiefly on memory' (The American Heritage College Dictionary, 2000, p. 1014). Since individuals vary in terms of memory, sensory acuity, and cognitive ability, it is clearly possible that no two individuals will perceive a situation or event the same way. Parasuraman, Zeithaml, and Berry (1985) argued that service quality is the difference or gap between customer expectations of performance and customer perceptions of the 'actual' performance. They used this starting point to develop the SERVQUAL instrument. In the SERVQUAL instrument, quality is defined or operationalized in the form of five dimensions; tangibles, reliability, responsiveness, assurance, and empathy (Parasuraman et al. 1988). Cronin and Taylor (1992) took the argument one step further to suggest that all that really matters is real-time perception of performance; perception equals service quality. In a review of the service literature, Rhoades and Waguespack (2014) reported that these methods were very popular in exploring quality in international airline markets. These studies tended to find the expected relationships between quality and satisfaction;

however, there has been no longitudinal perceptual study on a given airline's service quality published in the academic realm, so these studies are only a 'snapshot-in-time' of quality for the airlines involved. This lack of follow-up study or an update of the work done is common in much of marketing research, not just airline service quality research. A further issue that deserves study is the relationship between perception and 'reality'. In other words: how does customer perception compare to some set of 'objective' measures of performance? One of the first attempts to address this question was Tiernan, Rhoades, and Waguespack (2008). They compared survey data asking for the respondents to identify the percentage of certain service failures – lost baggage, delayed flights, cancelled flights, etc. – to the available secondary data for the US and EU. They found that the perception of airline quality was, for the most part, far worse than the secondary metrics of performance would suggest. Even when secondary service metrics were reaching over 99%, respondents reported perceptions of increasingly poor service.

Publicly available surveys involving airlines are typically conducted by such organizations as J.D. Powers, Zagats, SkyTrax, or Conde Nast, who use information from frequent flyers to rank or award airlines on quality performance. Among the factors that have been used over the years to explore consumer satisfaction with airline quality include on-time performance, airport check-in, schedule/flight accommodations, seating comfort, gate location, aircraft interior, flight attendants, food service, post-flight services, frequent flyer programs (and qualification levels), availability of flight when desired, the helpfulness of reservations agents, ability to get seat preference, ability to get priority boarding, effective communication on flight delays/cancellations, carry-on luggage space, seating comfort, helpfulness of flight attendants, speedy baggage delivery, good connecting flight information, short check-in times, and good airport lounges (Glab, 1997). These surveys have several weaknesses from a research perspective. First, it is difficult to compare the surveys from different organizations because the factors included vary between them. Second, the cross-sectional nature (i.e. the respondents in 1996 are not the same as in 2008) and changing factors across years for the same organizations limit the ability to evaluate trends in the data. Third, they may not reflect the experience of occasional travelers. Finally, these surveys do not generally provide an overall ranking of all the airlines included but a category-by-category ranking of the top performers.

The final source of information on airline quality is reported secondary data. This information is gathered either routinely by airlines or is mandated by the regulatory authority in that country (region). This information may or may not be publicly available. If publicly available, it may be provided by the regulatory agency upon request, periodically published, or posted to a publicly accessible website. To illustrate the type, use, and limitation of such data, we will use the US example. The US Department of Transportation has published the *Air Travel Consumer Report* (ATCR) monthly since 1987. The ATCR contains data on basic areas of service quality of interest to consumers (complaints, denied boardings, mishandled baggage, etc.), but has changed somewhat over time as issues such as flight cancellation and animal handling in transport have become more important and problems of smoking on aircraft have declined in importance and occurrence. The data is provided in raw form with no effort made to adjust the data for the size of airline operations. Such adjustment is important for evaluating the performance between airlines and is usually based on either departures, miles, or hours flown. Two groups of US researchers have used the data in the ATCR to explore issues of airline service quality. In 1991, the Aviation Institute at the University of Nebraska published its first *Airline Quality Rating* (AQR) report on the ten major US carriers. The weighted AQR has been revised since its inception to disaggregate service, safety, and financial indicators. The second group of researchers began reporting on airline service in 1998, although they went back to the first publication of the ATCR in 1987 to begin their analysis of service quality (Rhoades, Waguespack, & Truedt, 1998; Rhoades & Waguespack, 2008). Service and safety quality were separated from inception to construct two different rankings of airline performance which could be compared for each carrier and the industry overall (Rhoades & Waguespack, 1999, 2004). Further, Rhoades and Waguespack (2000a) examined the service and safety quality of US national and regional carriers whose performance could be compared to the traditional legacy (major) carriers. Comparisons were also made between legacy and low-cost carriers (LCC) (Rhoades & Waguespack, 2001, 2005).

One of the advantages of the consistent application of secondary data is that it allows for trend analysis. For example, it is possible to say (based on the work of Rhoades and Waguespack) that the industry average service quality for the major carriers improved from 1987 to 1993 and then remained relatively stable at around 40 service problems per departure for 1994–1997 before it began to climb in 1998, reaching 47 service problems per departure in 2000. Service quality improved after 2001, but slowly began to climb to an industry high of 72 service problems per departure in 2007. Following the Global Financial Crisis in 2008, quality began to improve to a rate of 43 service problems per departure in 2012. In fact, by the 30th anniversary of the ACTR, US airline service quality was posting some of its best performances ever (Rhoades, Waguespack, & Ambrose, 2021). This quality performance coupled with a series of outstanding profit years for the airline industry prompted the trade group Airlines for America (A4A) to declare that air travelers were living in a 'golden age' of travel with online booking, electronic ticketing, mobile check-in and a wide array of choices for nonstop and 1-stop flights (A4A, 2019). Overall, there has been extensive research into airline quality that has generally supported the link between service quality and satisfaction as well as between loyalty and repurchase, but there is little evidence of a link between service quality and profitability, or at least there is little to show that high service quality itself leads to profitability (Economist, 2015). In fact, it could be argued that the years of profitability in the second decade of the twenty-first century allowed airlines to invest in the technology that helped them improve quality (improved airline apps, online check-in, bag tracking, etc.).

This same trend analysis can apply at the firm level to analyze how a given firm has changed over time where it is often easy to identify airlines in financial and/or labor trouble or those in the midst of merger reorganization. Delta is an interesting case in point. It was around the industry average between 1987 and 1991 but suffered a high disquality index in the period between 1992 and 1996 when it struggled to cut costs (Rhoades & Waguespack, 2008). They suffered another period of poor performance between 2002 and 2010 amid the events of 9/11, bankruptcy in 2005, and a merger with Northwest in 2007. Since this time, they have achieved a consistent improvement in service quality. They have improved across all the secondary measures (delays, denied boardings, cancellations, etc.). In contrast, United has maintained a consistently poor level of service quality with statistically worse service than the industry average in 22 out of 30 years (Rhoades, Waguespack & Ambrose, 2021).

Secondary data is easy and cheap to obtain and excellent for trend analysis, but there are also disadvantages. First, this secondary data does not specifically ask about many of the areas identified as important by the survey research – food service, legroom, aircraft interior. Critics have suggested that these amenities are important to understanding customer attitudes toward service quality. Second, it does not ask consumers to compare service across carriers. Third, it does not provide the sort of demographic information that is commonly collected in survey research. A final criticism has to do with the issue of perception. It is clearly possible that an airline will perform objectively well but be rated poorly by consumers.

There is irony in that fact that the global airline industry was in the midst of celebrating its golden age when the Global Pandemic struck. The industry has battled economic conditions and outbreaks of SARS and bird flu before, but COVID struck so quickly and created so much future uncertainty that they were left hanging by a thread. The world may have declared the pandemic over, but the effects are still being felt in the airline industry. The world appears to be set for another summer of chaos as staffing shortages at airlines, airports, and air traffic facilities are leading to cancellations and delays amid very high travel demand (Sweeney, Maile, & McMichael, 2023).

Over the years, airline service quality has often been at its highest when the industry is experiencing economic difficulty (recession, high fuel prices, etc.). During such times of crisis, airlines and customers retrench. Fewer planes fly, thereby reducing congestion in the airspace and on airport tarmacs. Less congestion means more on-time flights and less delay in take-off. Fewer passengers also means fewer bags to lose or mishandle. Some quality woes can be traced to the public meltdown of carriers such as JetBlue Airways where bad weather and lean operations resulted in the stranding of over 5,000 passengers during the Valentine's Day holiday and projected costs to JetBlue of US$14 million in refunds and overtime. Many other quality problems are chronic and long-standing such as the United problems in the summer of 2023 (Sloan & Ehrenfeld, 2007; Sweeney, Maile & McMichael, 2023). Despite all the research, a 2015 study by the International Air Transport Association captures the ongoing dilemma for airlines. In this survey, customers indicated that their first three key factors in quality were on-time performance, aircraft quality and interior, and customer interactions, yet the first three factors influencing ticket purchase were price, schedule and convenient times, and Frequent Flyer Program. Achieving high levels of quality alongside low prices continues to be the holy grail of the airline industry.

Achieving Airline Quality

Airlines are organized by function – flight operations, engineering and maintenance, marketing, and services. Under marketing, which composes approximately 50 percent of the workforce, there are units concerned with reservations and ticketing, cabin service, ground service, food service, etc. (Wells, 1994). The consumer view, however, is not segmented into functions. Consumers experience airline service as a series of processes. The order fulfillment process begins with check-in and proceeds to final destination and baggage retrieval (Ekdahl, Gustafsson, & Edvardsson, 1999). When a problem arises during the travel experience, consumers are not interested in fixing the blame on a particular function and they certainly do not wish to stand around while the airline attempts to do so. Consumers want the issue resolved to their satisfaction as quickly as possible by their first contact point. They do not wish to be shuffled from department to department or supervisor to supervisor looking for resolution. One of the greatest drawbacks to a functional structure is that consumers often 'feel they are forced into a system characterized by contradictions, redundant or insufficient information, misguided authority, and confusion' (Ekdahl, Gustafsson, & Edvardsson, 1999). In other words, the traditional functional structure often finds it difficult to provide a seamless service. Many companies claim that 'quality is everyone's businesses, but they fail to realize that quality must also be 'someone's responsibility'.

There are basically two ways to approach the process quality issue. The most obvious way is to restructure the organization on a process basis – order fulfillment, new product development, customer acquisition, etc. In a process-structured organization, coordination within the process eliminates the 'cracks' through which customers often fall. This coordination is usually achieved through the establishment of cross-functional teams that include at least one member from each functional areas involved in that process. All elements of the process become the responsibility of the process leader and his team. Their job is to 1) ensure that all elements of the process are addressed, and 2) act as liaison to the functional departments, providing input from and guidance to the process. According to SAS, three principles should govern the design of the process: (1) give passengers control, (2) make the process transparent, and (3) empower the staff (Ekdahl, Gustafsson, & Edvardsson, 1999). A related option would be to institute a matrix structure that would in fact overlay the functional structure with a process structure. This type of organizational restructuring was popular in the 1980s but met with resistance from employees who in effect now had two bosses – the function leader and the process leader.

There are many personal and organizational barriers to process restructuring. At the personal level, teamwork requires good interpersonal skills and demands more emphasis on cross-functional skill development. Since many companies tie some portion of an individual's compensation to team results, individuals may also feel a loss of control in this important area of organizational life. If team results are not compensated in any way, then firms run the risk that team activities will not receive the necessary level of individual attention. Organizationally, team make-up and training are critical. Firms must decide on functional skill requirements for membership, the number of representatives from each function, the level of functional representatives (customer service manager, vice-president of customer relations, etc.), the leadership of groups, etc. These decisions can become very politicized. Functional conflicts over resource allocation and differing goals or objectives require the establishment of some process or procedure for conflict resolution. There are clearly costs associated with such a massive change in structure. There is also likely to be resistance from within the organization.

Quality Function Deployment (QFD) is one way to retain a functional structure while 'systematically deploying operations and functions that make up the quality into step-by-step detail' (Akao, 1999). QFD requires companies to identify consumer desires, translate them into specific components, establish standards and procedures for delivery, and follow up on delivery. For example, consumers want reliability in several company-provided areas. One such area is food service. They expect food to be consistent in quality, to taste and look good, to provide a good portion, and to be hot or cold (depending on the type of food). Companies must translate these desires into specific parameters (i.e. temperature of food, size of portions, etc.). Then establish and enforce standards on the 'function' charged with delivering the item. Finally, there must be feedback and improvement (Barlow, 1999). While there is elaborate software to support the implementation of QFD, it is still a complex process that has yet to be fully embraced outside Japan. (See Akao (1990) for a fuller discussion of QFD.)

A Case Study in Quality – Baggage Handling

To illustrate some of the issues and problems encountered in airline service quality, an exploration into baggage handling is in order. According to SITA's (2013) ninth annual Baggage Report, baggage mishandling rates have dropped worldwide to 8.83 per 1,000 passengers, which is a 44.5 percent improvement on the previous year. Delayed baggage, the primary cause of mishandling, also dropped 2.4 percent over the same period. The SITA report outlined the primary causes of baggage delay as follows: Transfer mishandling (48%), failure to load (17%), ticketing error/bag switch/security/other (13%), loading error (7%), airport/customs/weather/space-weight restriction (7%), and tagging error (4%). Of course, these are global figures and will not necessarily reflect the exact numbers for any given airline or airport. The distinction is important for several reasons. First, airlines may have very different policies, procedures, and training related to this area. Second, the baggage handling system at one airport can be very different from that at another airport in speed, configuration, etc. Third, airlines may vary by location, that is airport, the nature of the baggage handling staff – airline employee, alliance partner employee, or third party outsource handlers. The SITA report outlines several different approaches that airports and airlines have taken to address baggage handling. On the airport side, the report notes that Iberia Airlines in Spain are trying to identify passenger baggage that requires priority handling (short connections, etc.) so that it can be diverted to higher speed belts. At Helsinki Airport, a transfer monitoring tool notifies staff of delayed flights so that special procedures can be implemented to insure that connecting bags make their next flight. On the airline side, airlines are investing in technology for self-printed bag tags, assisted self-baggage drop, software for bad tracking, including Radio Frequency Identification Device (RFID) tagging, smartphone apps for tracking, and portable scanning devices. Many of these efforts will allow airports and airlines to gain an even better understanding of the processes, resulting in loss and delay. Understanding the process and measuring and tracking the historical outcomes are the keys to quality improvement in any area.

Alliance Quality – Scale and Scope

To date, there have been few academic attempts to evaluate the quality of alliances, but many of the same issues cited for individual carrier quality would apply, such as whether the data comes from surveys or secondary sources. Unfortunately, there is no single entity that collects the type of secondary data available in the US and EU for individual carriers. Thus, it is impossible to take data from all the global members of an alliance, combine them, and compare across alliances. Tiernan, Rhoades, and Waguespack (2008) reported three areas of comparison available across the airline alliance groupings for US and EU carriers only based on reported data from both the US Department of Transportation (DOT) and the EU Association of European Airlines (AEA). Their findings indicate very few statistically significant differences across the main alliance groupings and the three indicators of service quality examined; on-time arrivals, baggage reports and flight cancellations. While there are some yearly differences between each of the alliance groupings it is the overall similarity which is of note.

There have been at least two other attempts to use secondary data to access alliance quality, mostly in terms of scale and scope (Chapter 11). Chapter 11 also outlined four basic reasons that carriers form alliances: 1) to gain market access, 2) to build global seamless networks, 3) to reduce costs, and 4) to maintain market presence. From a consumer perspective, airline cost reduction is only important if it allows the carrier or alliance to reduce consumer costs and/or improve other aspects of airline service valued by consumers. Reasons 1 and 4 relate to the scope and/or depth of the alliances' coverage and the area of schedule/flight accommodation identified above for customer satisfaction with an individual carrier. From an alliance perspective, the more destinations they serve and the more frequently they serve them should be a quality issue for consumers.

This issue of alliance coverage proved to be a key factor in the Merrill Lynch (1999) report on alliances. Merrill Lynch rated the mega-alliances in terms of geographical network, market size, network density, financial strength, and regulatory freedom. This study drew a distinction between geographic scope (number of destinations/departures) and network density (utilization of network or extent of duplication). In this regard, an alliance such as Wings (NW-KLM) outscored the other mega-alliances on network density but ranked lowest on geographic scope. From an alliance point of view, less duplication in the network lowers fears of anti-competitive outcomes and means a greater overall extension of geographic scope. From a consumer point of view, greater density means more frequency to desired destinations. Thus, the ideal alliance configuration would involve partners having extensive depth within their geographic scope but little network duplication of alliance partner networks. This has not been an easy combination to create. One of the major stumbling blocks to the proposed BA–AA alliance (part of Oneworld) was the extent of network overlap and the fear that such overlap would encourage the alliance partners to 'rationalize' their networks (i.e. dividing markets between partners in such a way that only one partner would effectively serve a particular route). Of course, the failure of the British to sign an Open Skies agreement with the US was another key factor in the US refusal to grant anti-trust immunity. With the 2008 multilateral Open Skies with the EU, this objection disappeared on the US side even if the overlap did not.

Anderson Consulting identified three integration platforms in strategic alliances based on the level of control (degree of carrier control over resources) and the degree of global coverage (Ott, 1999). According to Anderson, bilateral strings are essentially based on a series of international code shares between partners. These alliances string together a moderate number of international destinations. Andersen Consulting classified US Airways, Japan Airlines, and America West as string airlines. The Regional Cluster is the second type of integration platform. As the name implies, the backbone of this platform is several regional airlines. The geographic coverage is approximately equivalent to the bilateral string, but the level of control is greater. Swissair and the Qualifier alliance were examples of this type of platform. The final integration platform is the global skeleton which has greater coverage than the other two and slightly lower levels of control than the regional cluster. Based on their analysis, the four mega-alliances that existed at the time of their study were roughly equivalent in terms of global coverage while the ranking on control was as follows: Wings, Star, SkyTeam, and Oneworld. The informally named Wings alliance of KLM–Northwest was officially abandoned with the KLM–Air France merger and both are now part of SkyTeam now. Thus, there are officially now only three global alliances – Oneworld, SkyTeam, and Star. In any event, Andersen Consulting had envisioned all three platforms moving toward the Global Network with its maximum global coverage and balance between alliance control and member independence. According to Andersen, there were several areas of alliance development. The first area was route overlap or increasing 'unduplicated route miles/kilometers'. Several studies have shown that complementary (non-overlapping) alliance networks increase overall demand and passenger volumes (Park & Cho, 1997; US GAO, 1995) while parallel alliances decrease demand (Park & Cho, 1997). The problem for airlines and regulators lies with addressing pre-existing alliance overlap. Airlines clearly have some incentives to reduce overlap, especially if the overlap results in decreased demand and/or lower fares. The degree of intra-alliance competition could also damage efforts to build a cooperative alliance arrangement. Regulators are concerned with the degree of competition/cooperation and any action that decreases capacity and increase fares. The second area of development involved 'filling the gaps' in overall global coverage and in specific destination departure levels. Given the stated consumer preference for airlines with wide coverage and increased connections, the goal of a superior global alliance is to serve more destinations more frequently than their competitors. All the four old mega-alliance groups looked to fill major gaps in Asia, the Middle East, and Africa during the 1990s (Flint, 1999; Merrill Lynch, 1999; Taverna, 1999). Gap filling continued with the three mega-alliances. Oneworld stills trails the other two alliances in terms of total number of members as well as membership by region (Flottau, & Buyck 2013). In many ways, the alliance is still essentially a string-configured alliance that has yet fill its gaps and place more meat into its structure. In line with the notion of a superior global alliance is the third key area of alliance branding. In addition to the sort of advertising employed by the Star Alliance, alliances sought other areas of alliance integration and standardization such as joint facilities, alliance terminal grouping, harmonized (merged) distribution networks including CRS systems and joint internet booking sites, and common service standards such as seat pitch and reclining angle. The goal is to demonstrate that an alliance can do more than just extend networks; it needs to ease travel and deliver consistent services across the globe (Buyck, 2013). Cost reduction through such actions as facility sharing and maintenance and other ground personnel utilization is a fourth area for further development while a fifth area of development has been the creation of the secondary and tertiary tiers of national/regional carriers whose job it will be to increase feed to alliance hubs. From an alliance perspective, the more developed and exclusive these arrangements the better they will be able to extract benefits (Berardino & Frankel, 1998). However, such exclusivity raises anti-competitive fears in many countries as we have already discussed in the chapter on anti-trust law.

Coordinating Quality

While the Merrill Lynch Index does not provide a comprehensive overview of alliance quality, it is an important first step in the process of understanding alliance quality. From a consumer quality perspective, a more difficult area to address is the issue of 'global, seamless service'. 'Global' is a function of geographic reach, but 'seamless' suggests a great deal more. What does it mean to provide seamless service? How do independent airlines provide such service? This area continues to bedevil alliances. In fact, it has been suggested that seamless travel is often little more than a marketing gimmick. It is true that alliances can offer coordinated schedules, shared lounges, frequent flyer redemption, and coordinated baggage tracing, but there are still inconsistencies in product quality, communication, and service. Offering seamless quality service may be the key to revitalizing the alliance movement in the wake of recent shake-ups such as the Qantas departure from Oneworld (Buyck, 2013). To explore what it takes to get to seamless travel, let us start at the airline level.

As difficult as process quality can be for individual airlines, it is potentially nothing compared to the prospect of integrating the process across multiple carriers. As Deming and other have pointed out, no two processes are identical. Each process will invariably produce a certain amount of random variation (flaws or problems related to the nature of the system(s) in place). Special variations (flaws or problems related to a change in the system such as change in training procedures, receipt of a batch of faulty parts, etc.) also occur from time to time. Management must understand their process well enough to distinguish between random and special variation. Management must act to identify the source of special variation and remove its cause. Random variation, on the other hand, can only be reduced by changing the process itself.

When attempting to integrate the processes of two or more carriers, there are two primary areas of concern. First, are the processes compatible? A simple case from early integration efforts is the airline boarding pass. All carriers issue them and most require that they be run through an electronic devise before boarding. However, if the size of these boarding passes differs between carriers such that the boarding pass issued by one carrier will not pass through the system of the other (and customers are required to check-in again at the second airline for a new pass), then some of the seamlessness of the process is lost. The same question applies for many other standards and procedures, such as upgrade requirements, carry-on specifics, seating assignments, boarding procedures, etc. To the extent that these differences create snags in the seamless fabric of air travel for consumers, they will detract from perceived quality and can result in a loss of business to higher-quality alliances. We will discuss strategies for avoiding these snags later.

The second area of concern is potentially more serious and more difficult to resolve. It relates to differences in the quality level (or random variation) of alliance partners. Consumers who book a flight on one airline but find at least one leg of their journey flown by a carrier of lesser quality can develop a negative perception of the alliance as a whole. Obviously, the greater the difference in quality levels the more severe the problem becomes. In a truly seamless alliance, consumers should perceive no difference in quality levels. The most worrisome difficulty lies in equalizing the quality level of alliance partners. Again, there are no studies examining the overall quality levels of alliance partners or the effects of quality equalization, but a recent study suggests one possible scenario. Research on quality levels at major US carriers indicates that over the past ten years quality levels have begun to converge and now show little variation across the major US carriers (Rhoades & Waguespack, 2000b). In statistical research, the term 'regressing to the mean' refers to the tendency for extremes at both ends of a particular phenomenon to move over time toward the mean for that population. In the case of quality levels between alliance partners, there might be a similar tendency for quality levels to converge toward a mean. At the lower end, alliance partners quality will tend to rise. On the other hand, the alliance quality leaders could see declines in their quality toward the alliance mean. Singapore Airlines would likely find this prospect disturbing.

Of course, this is not the only possible scenario. However, an alliance seeking to brand itself as one of high quality must be aware of the fact that upward equalization of quality standards will not just happen. Higher quality standards will not just 'rub off' on alliance partners. This is where 'cross-alliance' teams become important in ensuring the quality of lateral/cross-airline processes. In the early years of their alliance, United and Lufthansa found it difficult to agree on something as seemingly simple as the joint purchase of airsick bags (Feldman, 1998). Imagine the potential for disagreement on an issue such as the operation of a key hub or yield management integration. At the very least, alliances are finding that coordination takes time and effort. Jurgen Weber, former Lufthansa CEO, had estimated that alliances consumed approximately one-third of his time (Feldman, 1998).

Improving Alliance Quality

There are two important steps in achieving and ensuring overall alliance quality. The first factor is conducting pre- and post-alliance audits of safety and service issues. These audits would establish a baseline quality level for each partner. Assuming that each alliance partner understands the needs and expectations of its customers, the next step is to reach some consensus among alliance partners on the level of desired quality and the priority of service quality goals. Finally, a plan must be created that outlines the goals, objectives, and tactics to be used by each carrier to achieve the necessary changes. The second step is to create a process that 'shows one face to the customer'. Alliances, like individual firms, are finding that it is essential 'to make it easy for the customer to access resources, products, and services across the horizontal spectrum' (Ashkenas et al., 1995, p. 128). When customers can enter the company or alliance through multiple doors (or portals as they are sometimes called), there are several problems that can arise that have the potential to adversely affect process quality. Without careful coordination, customers may find that the point-of-entry changes the final destination. For example, if alliance members are unfamiliar with the products and services offered by their partners, then a customer accessing the alliance through one partner may receive different scheduling, information, and service than another customer accessing the 'system' from a different partner. A related problem occurs when the parts of the system are unaware of the actions of each other and fail (or are unable) to take these differences into consideration when assisting customers.

In their book, *The Boundaryless Organization: Breaking the Chains of Organizational Structure*, Ashkenas, Ulrich, Jick, and Kerr (1995) outline five warning signs of dysfunctional horizontal boundaries: '(1) slow, sequential cycle times, (2) protected turf, (3) suboptimization of organizational goals, (4) the enemy-within syndrome, and (5) customers doing their own integration' (115). Slow, sequential cycle times occur whenever multiple divisions, departments, units, etc. must be consulted one by one to create new products or respond to customers' demands. Whenever protecting one's own resources or power interfere with customer service, quality suffers. The same thing is true when members of a process come into decision-making situations with different, often-conflicting goals, such as cost reduction versus higher service level or higher yield versus higher load factor. One of the most damaging problems related to horizontal boundaries occurs when members of a process come to see each other as enemies. Ashkenas, Ulrich, Jick, and Kerr (1995) give an example of an airline where baggage handling at a particular airport was the responsibility of two separate teams. One team handled check-in and ticketing while the other was responsible for loading, transferring, and off-loading. Teams were reluctant to help each other, to accept advice from 'them', and frequently argued over which team was responsible for baggage handling errors. Finally, horizontal boundaries can also create problems if it forces customers to do their own integration of products and services. In the airline industry, there are customers who would prefer to customize their own bundle of products and services to accommodate special needs in terms of price, scheduling, and destination. On the other hand, there are customer groups that want a one-stop-shopping experience. They do not either want to be handed from one airline to another because an airline cannot book to a code share partner directly or to be told that seats cannot be assigned through to final destination, etc.

Several problems can arise on the way to the upward equalization of quality. First, the traditional customers of alliance partners may not have similar expectations. After over twenty years of deregulation, the expectations of many US travelers in terms of seating comfort, food, etc. have declined below the expectations of many European and Asian travelers. This difference in expectations may make agreeing on a level of service more difficult. This is further complicated by airline cost, pricing structure, and available resources for quality improvements. Alliance partners may find it necessary to establish inter-alliance programs for training, cost sharing, and other quality improvements. Another stumbling block to success is the need to share more information between partners on service offerings, prices, and amenities. In short, partners may be called upon to share the revenue management information that has traditionally been treated as proprietary or share facilities that certain partners have spent years developing. Such attempts can create three problems for alliance members. The first problem is a legal one; without anti-trust immunity, this level of sharing would be deemed illegal in most regions of the world. The second problem relates to the technological difficulties of systems integration. The sheer size and cost of integrating information systems can be very daunting to alliance members. Finally, alliance members must perceive a benefit to such information sharing that is greater than the risk of 'giving up' the potentially valuable information on customers and operations. Alliances will need to find ways to track the costs and benefits of joint alliance activities and to maximize joint benefits (Berardino & Frankel, 1998).

Conclusion

Although it may seem to customers that airlines sometimes forget that they are a service industry, international competition, and the pursuit of profit in a tough industry, are forcing airlines to pay more attention to issues of quality, customer satisfaction, and customer loyalty. At both the carrier and the alliance level, airlines are trying to distinguish themselves from their competitors. At the carrier level, attention to basics is essential but branding requires memorable amenities. At the alliance level, seamless service requires intensive coordination to achieve high-quality, consistent service. To satisfy the desire for global coverage, alliances are taking two basic approaches – weave and throw a wider web or throw a finer web over a smaller area. While avoiding the legal stumbling block of anti-trust has been difficult for many alliance partners, it has not been as visible a failure to consumers as the hurtle of achieving seamless service. In large part, the alliance movement is about breaking down the barriers that separate companies from their suppliers, their customers, and, in many cases, their competitors. It is about creating linkages and networks. Alliances are 'about spinning a web to catch more customers' (Sparks, 1999, p. 106).

Questions

1 How do consumers perceive airline service quality, and what are the limitations of traditional functional structures in meeting their expectations?
2 What are the primary challenges associated with restructuring airlines on a process basis, and how do cross-functional teams address these challenges?
3 In the context of airline alliances, what are the key factors that contribute to quality, and how do alliance members navigate differences in service standards and processes to achieve seamless service for customers?

References

Akao, Y. (1990), *Introduction to quality function deployment*, JUSE Press.

Akao, Y. (1999), 'ISO 900 and 14000 systems supported by QFD', in S. K. M. Ho (Ed.), *Proceedings of the fourth international conference on ISO 900 and TQM*, pp. 325–331.

Ashkenas, R., Ulrich, D., Jick, T., & Kerr, S. (1995), *The Bounderyless Organization: Breaking the Chains of Organizational Structure*, Jossey-Bass Publishers, San Francisco, CA.

Barlow, G. L. (1999), 'QFD within the service sector – A case study on how the house of quality was used within service operations', in S. K. M. Ho (Ed.), *Proceedings of the fourth international conference on ISO 900 and TQM*, pp. 332–340.

Berardino, F. & Frankel, C. (1998), 'Keeping score', *Airline Business*, September, pp. 82–87.

Buyck, C. (2013) From scale to service: Alliances improve customer services in a move to keep the model relevant, *Aviation Week and Space Technology*, April, 29, 42–44.

Cronin, J. J. & Taylor, S. A. (1992) 'Measuring service quality: A reexamination and extension'. *Journal of Marketing*, 56(3), pp. 55–68.

Ekdahl, F., Gustafsson, A., & Edvardsson, B. (1999), 'Customer-oriented service development at SAS', *Managing Service Quality*, 9, pp. 403–410.

Feldman, J. M. (1998), 'Making alliances work', *Air Transport World*, June, pp. 27–35.

Flint, P. (1999), 'Alliance paradox', *Air Transport World*, April, pp. 33–36.

Flottau, J. & Buyck, C. (2013) Group dynamics: Once de regueur for legacy airlines, alliance membership is an evolving model, *Aviation Week and Space Technology*, April 29, 39–41.

Fraser, D. (1996), 'A personal approach', *Airline Business*, March, pp. 58–61.

Glab, J. (1997), 'The people's choice', *Frequent Flyer*, June, pp. 24–28.

Merrill Lynch, Pierce, Fenner & Smith, Inc. (1999), *Global airline alliances: Why alliances really matter from an investment perspective*, Merrill Lynch, Pierce, Fenner & Smith Inc., New York.

Ott, J. (1999), 'Alliances spawn a web of global networks', *Airline Business*, August 23, pp. 52–53.

Parasuraman, A., Zeithaml, V. A., & Berry, L.L. (1985) 'A conceptual model of service quality and its implications for future research,' *Journal of Marketing*, 49 (4), 41–50.

Parasuraman, A., Zeithaml, V. A., & Berry, L.L. (1988) 'SERVQUAL: A multiple-item scale for measuring customer perceptions of service quality', *Journal of Retailing*, 64 (1), 12–40.

Park, N. K. & Cho, D. (1997), 'The effect of strategic alliance on performance,' *Journal of Air Transport Management*, 3, pp. 155–164.

Reichheld, F. F. (1996). *The loyalty effect: The hidden force behind growth, profits, and lasting value.* Boston: Harvard Business School Press.

Rhoades, D. L. & Waguespack, B (1999), 'Better safe than service? The relationship between service and safety quality in the US airline industry', *Managing Service Quality* 9 (6), 396–400.

Rhoades, D. L. & Waguespack, B (2000a), 'Judging a book by its cover: The relationship between service and safety quality in US national and regional airlines', *Journal of Air Transport Management* 6, pp. 87–94

Rhoades, D. L. & Waguespack, B. (2000b), 'Service quality in the U.S. airline industry: Variations in performance within and between firms', *Journal of Air Transportation World Wide*, 5, pp. 60–77.

Rhoades, D. L. & Waguespack, B (2001), 'Airline quality: Present challenges, future strategies' in: Butler, G. F. & Keller, M. R. (Eds.) *Handbook of airline strategy: Public policy, regulatory issues, challenges and solutions*, McGraw-Hill, New York, 469–480.

Rhoades, D. L. & Waguespack, B. (2004), 'Service and safety quality in the US airlines: Pre- and post-September 11th', *Managing Service Quality* 14 (4), 307–316.

Rhoades, D. L. & Waguespack, B (2005), 'Strategic imperatives and the pursuit of quality in the US airline industry', *Managing Service Quality* 15 (4), 344–356.

Rhoades, D. L. & Waguespack, B (2008), 'Twenty year of service quality performance in the US airline industry', *Managing Service Quality. 18* (1), pp. 20–34.

Rhoades, D. L. & Waguespack, B (2014), Twenty five years of measuring airline service quality or why is airline service quality only good when times are bad.

Rhoades, D. L., Waguespack, B., & Ambrose, S. (2021) The best of times: 30 years of US airline service quality. *Services Marketing Quarterly*, 42 (3–4), pp. 180–193.

Rhoades, D. L., Waguespack, B, & Truedt, E. (1998) Service quality in the US airline industry: Progress and problems. *Managing Service Quality* 8 (5), 306–311.

SITA (2013) 2013 Air transport Industry Insights: The Baggage Report, STAT and Air Transport World.

Sloan, A. & Ehrenfeld, T. (2007) Lessons from JetBlue's meltdown, *Newsweek MSNBC*, www.msnbc. cim/id/17313450/site/newsweek

Sparks, D. (1999), 'Partners', *Business Week*, October 25, pp. 106–112.

Sweeney, S., Maile, A. & McMichael, C. (2023) As thousands of flights cancelled, feud between United CEO and FAA spills out into public again. ABC News. Available at https://abcnews.go.com/US/thousands-flights-canceled-united-ceo-partially-blames-faa/story?id=100417277

Taverna, M. A. (1999), 'Star Alliance approaches next phase of collaboration', *Airline Business*, August 23, pp. 58–60.

The American heritage College Dictionary (2000) 3rd ed. Houghton Mifflin Company, Boston.

The Economists 2015) The price of being nice: Treating flyers well is bad for airlines' business. Available at www.economist.com/blogs/gullive/2015/11/price-being-nice

Tiernan, S., Rhoades, D. L., & Waguespack, B. (2008) 'Airline service quality: An exploratory analysis of consumer perceptions and reported operational performance in the US and EU', *Managing Service Quality*, *18*(3), 212–224.

US General Accounting Office (USGAO) (1995), 'Airline alliances product benefits, but effect on competition is uncertain', *GAO/RCED-95*, April.

Wells, A. T. (1994), *Air transportation: A management perspective*, Wadsworth Publishing Company, Belmont.

14 The Need for Speed

Learning Objectives

After reading this chapter, you should have a good understanding of:

LO1: the aircraft needs of cargo operators
LO2: the elements of the logistics revolution
LO3: the development of the integrated cargo carriers
LO4: the role of belly cargo and freight forwarders

Key Terms, Concepts & People

Berlin Airlift	Perfect cargo plane	Logistics Revolution
Containerization	Air-Cargo Deregulation Act	Malcolm McLean
Fred Smith	Federal Express	Belly cargo
Hazmat		

Freight Comes of Age

If airmail was the driving force in aviation development in its first decade of life, then the decade of the 1940s and World War II were the time when other types of freight began to become a more prominent element in the air cargo story and to capture the interest of the aviation community. In 1938, freight accounted for only about 17 revenue ton kilometers (RTKs) of the total 53 RTKs of air activity. By 1951, freight RTKs had risen to 870, far outstripping the 230 RTKs for air mail in that year (Allaz, 2004). Military forces around the world would come to recognize the value of air freight in support of distant troops and far-flung activities. They would also begin to demand and order aircraft that could deliver these troops and supplies. The Berlin Airlift would prove its strategic geopolitical value as the British and Americans would be airlifting over 4,740 tons of cargo a day to Berlin within five months of the start of the blockade (Allaz, 2004).

Beginning in the 1970s, the deregulation of domestic industries and the liberalization of the rules of international trade began to spread throughout the world. Market forces would now lead many countries to reconsider the tight rules and standards that once protected firms and employees in their national markets. Firms would begin to look outside their home countries for lower-cost labor and the lower-cost manufacturing that came with

DOI: 10.4324/9781003405306-16

them. The concepts of outsourcing and just-in-time inventory would capture the imagination of the business community. These new concepts, however, created new dispersed supply chains that demanded a new system of logistics to support them. As computing power rose and information technology (IT) costs fell, the technology was ready for tracking and optimizing. The decline in transportation costs that came with deregulation, and, later, falling oil prices made it faster and cheaper to ship from distant locations. Further, consumers came to crave customized products delivered door-to-door. Faster, cheaper, and better was the new consumer mantra. This meant that businesses had to find ways to meet these new demands or risk falling victim to a host of new competitors.

These trends continued to pick up speed as the twentieth century approached its end. They also fostered tremendous growth in air cargo operations and operators. Airlines would offer cargo-only flights and order so-called combi-aircraft, half-passenger and half-cargo, to provide greater cargo capacity and additional revenue. New scheduled and charter cargo operators would come into the market offering to ship everything from letter-sized packages to massive oil-drilling equipment (Nelms, 2007). If the jet would make air cargo the transportation choice for speed, then FedEx would make overnight shipping a new business mindset. FedEx and UPS would lead the way for integrated shipping, that is, door-to-door delivery using multiple modes of transportation. However, before the commercial explosion of air cargo could take place, industry needed a plane suitable for its purposes. Once it had such an aircraft, it could begin to take advantage of the new rules and the changing nature of business.

The Perfect Plane

From a cargo perspective, the perfect cargo plane would have a fuselage that was rectangular rather than cylindrical. The floor would be sturdy and low-lying to accommodate heavy freight with a maximum vertical capacity. Large doors would be located at the sides and front (preferably) to make loading easy and quick. Using both would reduce loading time. The aircraft would be designed so that different types of cargo could be partitioned and anchored (Allaz, 2004). While cargo had, and would continue to be, flown in aircraft not specifically designed for cargo, there would often be a cost not only in terms of converting passenger aircraft to cargo use (reinforcing floors, adding, anchors, etc) but in terms of productivity. As in passenger service, cargo operators have to be concerned with load factors. Because operators have little control over the prices they charge, costs are critical and an aircraft that has a low capacity due to either shape or weight constraints represents a problem. Aircraft that require high levels of labor or expensive equipment to load create added costs.

Between 1960 and 1962, freight capacity doubled, in terms of both belly cargo, i.e. cargo carried in the belly of passenger aircraft, and cargo aircraft. Several factors account for this increase in capacity. First, the new jet aircraft coming on the market had a larger cargo capacity than previous vehicles. Second, as airlines switched to jet aircraft, there was a growing number of used propeller aircraft on the market and available for use by cargo operators. The first jet aircraft went into service in 1958 under the Pan Am colors, but others would quickly follow (Allaz, 2004). According to Allaz (2004), the Canadair CL-44D was the first modern jet cargo aircraft. It featured a swing tail, unit load devices, and a maximum payload of 28,000 kg. Packages were loaded onto pallets fitted with retention nets or into containers. In 1961, the famous Flying Tigers would be the first to take the CL-44D into service. With the arrival of the B707-320C and the DC-8F, costs would significantly decline while speed and capacity would dramatically improve.

Of course, the aircraft that would become most closely associated with air cargo would be the B747. The letter of intent signed with launch customer Pan Am specified a 400-passenger airline with a range of 5,000 miles, cruise altitude of 35,000 feet, and cargo nose loading. The latter requirement is telling; Juan Trippe, then CEO of Pan Am, saw the B-747 primarily as a freighter that could also carry passengers. Of course, the B-747 would become one of the most popular passenger aircraft in the world and a symbol of international aviation, but this was certainly not clear when the project began (Serling, 1992). In fact, the story of the 747 is a fascinating one. Production problems, redesigns, a launch in 1970 just as the economy began to slow, and the coming oil crisis would bring the Boeing Company almost to bankruptcy. The plane would not approach breakeven sales until 1978 (Lynn, 1998; Newhouse, 2007). Still, there is no doubt that it set new standards that few others could begin to meet. In the cargo area, the wide-bodied 747 could hold two standard pallets side-by-side on the main deck, with nine additional positions in the lower hold for either pallets or containers. Overall, the 747 could carry 90 tonnes of cargo, compared with 30 tonnes for the 707 and between 70 and 74 tonnes for the DC-10 (Allaz, 2004).

Play it Forward

Air freight had come a long way in the years just after the end of World War II, but in some ways it had changed very little from that early 1910 flight (Chapter 3) that carried the 200 pounds of silk and ribbon to Max Morehouse for his Home Dry Goods Store. In fact, several things were still true. First, small 'mom-and-pops' still made up a large portion of the air cargo operators. Like the early airlines themselves, cargo operators started flying small piston-powered aircraft from one point to the next on an unscheduled, as-needed basis. They were private firms and many continue to be privately rather than publicly held companies, making it difficult to assess their overall profitability. Second, the firms were essentially a specialized form of forwarder, that is, a carrier that transported freight by air under published freight tariffs. Shippers were responsible for seeing that the freight reached the operator and for arranging pick-up when it arrived at its destination. In some cases, shippers could add a step in the process and use a separate consolidator, someone who took their shipment and consolidated it with those of other shippers to form a 'larger' shipment eligible for lower rates. Third, most airlines would continue to see freight revenue as supplemental income. In the US, freight would continue to be a very small portion of the overall revenue. In Asia, freight tonnage would growth apace with the emerging economies of the region as the size and the scope of the shipments increased. As the volume increased and shippers began to ship to more markets around the world, pressure increased for industry consolidation. Both changes were driven in part by the logistics revolution that was sweeping the world.

Logistics Revolution

Logistics is defined as 'the process of planning, implementing, and controlling the efficient, effective flow and storage of raw materials, in-process inventories, finished goods, services, and relevant information from point of origin to the point of consumption' (Boske, 1998). In the capitalist system, the goal is to match supply to demand, but the system has often proven itself prone to overproduction. Producers are then forced to carry excess inventory or find some ways to increase sales – discounts, advertising, credit extension, etc. If the ideal is to carry only the inventory you need and produce only what consumers want, then the producers need accurate, readily available data to make their decisions. Point-of-sales (POS) data provides this type of information. Firms such as Wal-Mart began to use computers and scanning equipment to collect this information. This helped Wal-Mart to ensure that shelves were stocked with the goods consumers were demanding. As they linked up the system, their vendors were able to see in near real time what was and was not selling. This allowed them to adjust production accordingly, including controlling their own inventories. The ubiquitous bar codes are giving way in many areas to radio frequency identification devices (RFID). These devices collect and store (in many cases) lots of information that can be read and analyzed to improve the system. Unfortunately for the producers, there is a snake in the grass; this new system has shifted power to retailers such as Wal-Mart. As the Wal-Marts of the world grew, so did their requirements and demands – lower prices, more frequent deliveries, chargebacks (fines for failing to meet specifications like misplacing a bar code). For the consumers, the new fast, flexible production system and the close tracking of stock meant shelves with 'what I want when I want it' (Bonocich & Wilson, 2007; Castells, 1996; Fishman, 2006; Kumar, 1996).

All these advances would still not have been enough to create the logistics revolution; it needed two further ingredients – changing regulatory environments and falling transportation costs. Thomas L. Friedman, the popular press advocate of globalization and author of the bestselling books *The Lexus and the Olive Tree* (1999) and *The World is Flat* (2005), has argued that success in the global economy demands that nations put on a 'golden straitjacket'. This straitjacket is made from government and extra-governmental policies that promote 1) an expanding private sector, 2) low inflation and price stability, 3) shrinking government bureaucracy, 4) balanced governmental budgets, 5) low tariffs and the elimination of import quotas, 6) no restriction on foreign investment, and currency conversion and mobility, 7) privatization of state-owned enterprises, 8) deregulation of markets and industries, 9) no domestic sector protection, 10) increasing exports, and 11) labor mobility. Taken together, these policies laid the foundation for a global system in which production could take place wherever conditions favored it (cost of labor, environmental regulation, available resources, etc.), be shipped to wherever consumers demanded it, and be serviced (repair, 24/7 help lines) wherever it was most profitable for the company. Beyond the borders of individual nations, the global trading system advanced from the old Bretton Woods institutions of the World Bank and the International Monetary Fund to the later developments of the General Agreement on Tariffs and Trade (GATT) to the World Trade Organization (WTO). Global trading blocs would also emerge, such as the European Union (EU), the North American Free Trade Agreement (NAFTA), and MERCOSUR, the Latin American trade area. The goal of these blocks was to reduce (or remove) the impediments to trade and the flow of goods, services, and people between the member nations.

Transportation was one of the areas that witnessed a wave of deregulation beginning in the US in the late 1970s and early 1980s with a series of pieces of legislation: the Air-Cargo Deregulation Act of 1977, the Airline Deregulation Act of 1978, the Motor Carrier Act (that is, trucking) in 1980, the Staggers Rail Act in 1980, the Shipping Act in 1984, and the Freight Forwarder Deregulation Act in 1986. As noted in earlier chapters, transportation is considered in most countries to be an area of vital national interest and safety so there are still a great many areas of regulation remaining; however, the focus of transportation deregulation was to allow market forces to determine, to a much greater extent, the issues of pricing, capacity, networks, and service quality. In many nations, deregulation also opened greater opportunities for intermodal transportation. Intermodal transportation refers to the 'process of transporting passengers and freight by means of a system of interconnected networks, involving more than one transportation mode, in which all the component parts in the systems process are seamlessly linked and efficiently coordinated' (Boske, 1998). The technical innovations that helped make the supply chain of Wal-Mart successful – computers, scanning, RFID, etc – were utilized in intermodal transport systems to ensure that goods flowed with minimal delay through the system. Logistics leaders could use this technology to optimize their system based on specific needs – lowest cost, time-to-delivery.

There was one final piece of the puzzle that made the transportation and logistics revolution: the container. On April 26, 1956, the *Ideal X*, a converted tanker, became the first ship to have an aluminum truck body lifted onto the deck. The concept was the brainchild of Malcolm McLean, a trucker whose US firm had risen to become one of the 10 largest in the nation. He had observed that lots of trucks traveled between the seaports of the Gulf and the East Coast and figured that if he could find a way to reduce the time spent loading and unloading cargo he could gain an advantage on his competitors. Soon the aluminum container, now standardized to 8X8X20, would be decoupled from the wheel set and stacked onto specially designed vessels. Huge port cranes would load and unload containers from larger and larger vessels. These containers would be lifted from the deck of the ship directly onto either trailer trucks or railcars. Containerization made shipping cheap; the most expensive part of the process was the shifting of cargo from sea to land and the occasional need for drayage (transporting freight by truck, usually to link one mode of transport to another because it could not be done directly on the dock). Containerization thrives on volume and the reduction in cost and time of shifting cargo has meant that a doubling of the distance cargo is shipped now results in only around an 18 percent increase in shipping costs (Levinson, 2006).

Air cargo is often the choice for 'high value goods, perishable and emergency shipments, but also electronic equipment, apparel, shoes, printed material, [and] chemicals' (Muller, 1995, p. 73). It has benefited somewhat less than other modes from containerization because of the size of the standard container. While a B-747 air freighter could be loaded through the nose with an 8X8X40 container, it would only have inches to spare on the door. There is also the question of the container-to-fuselage fit; the typical rectangular box container leaves wasted space in the curve. There are specially designed air-surface 8X8X20 containers as well as containers for the lower decks on the B-747. A great deal of air cargo still travels on pallets (either 88in x 125in or 96in x 125in). There are also so-called pallet wings that attempt to utilize the full contour of the lower decks (Muller, 1995). One type of high-value good that has gained increasing popularity in the cargo world was the document and small package shipment. As the pace of global business increased, so too did the need and desire of global firms to stay connected.

Expressing It

In 1971, Frederick W. Smith founded Federal Express, based on a concept first developed in his Yale dissertation. The dissertation was not a big success, but the company, which began its operations in 1973, became the industry leader in the express mail industry. By the end of the twentieth century, FedEx revenues exceeded US$22 billion and its fleet of 600 aircraft and 200,000 employees would be delivering packages around the world (Birla, 2005). Unlike its competitor UPS, FedEx would start in the air and then move onto the ground. It would do this first through agreements with trucking and logistics companies, such as RPS, Inc., Viking, Roberts, and Caliber Logistics. RPS, Inc., specialized in the

Table 14.1 FedEx Growth 2017–2023

	2017	2018	2019	2020	2021	2022	2023
Revenues	60,319	65,450	69,693	69,217	83,959	93,512	90,155
Operating income	4,566	4,272	4,466	2,417	5,857	6,245	4,912
Net income	2,997	4,572	540	1,286	5,231	3,826	3,972

Source: Stock Analysis, https://stockanalysis.com/stocks/fdx/financials/
#Numbers in 000s.

ground delivery of small packages; Viking used the less-than-truckload model to ship 1- and 2-day packages; And Roberts specialized in surface-expedited shipping. Caliber Logistics joined the FedEx family in the late 1990s, incorporating its specialized contract logistics services (FedEx website; Aviation Week and Space Technology, 2007).

The FedEx model would be based on five key principles: hub-and-spoke operations, weight and size limitations on shipments, integrated door-to-door service, guaranteed time-definite delivery, and end-to-end traceability. Table 14.1 traces the growth of FedEx from 2006 to 2012. As the table illustrates, FedEx experienced a steady increase in revenues, fleet, employees, and the volume of shipping. Over the coming decades in 1971, the weight limits would go higher while the time-definite options and the delivery area would both increase. By 2006, the FedEx hub in Memphis would be the busiest in the world, shipping almost 3.6 million tonnes a year (Air Cargo World, 2005). The following decade would see continued growth heading into the COVID Pandemic, although 2019 witnessed falls in net income (Table 14.1).

Brown is Back

UPS, the company whose first venture into air cargo ended with the 1929 stock market crash would not return to the air for almost sixty years. When it did finally re-enter the air transport business in 1982 with new service from its hub in Louisville, Kentucky, it would do so under a very different set of circumstances than competitor FedEx. For one thing, UPS had acquired common carrier status with its early purchase of the Russell Peck Company in California. As a common carrier, it was regulated by the Interstate Commerce Commission (ICC) as well as various state commissions. By US law, common carriers were required to serve any shipper, carry any package regardless of size, and deliver to any destination in its region. It also could not commingle wholesale and retail packages. The ICC was the first regulatory agency in US history and expanded from its early mandate to protect against railroad malpractice to all areas of surface shipping. In effect, the ICC defined the rights of shippers and customers, engaging in rate making, regulation, and labor dispute resolution. UPS would fight the ICC for the right to expand its ground services and network to one city and one state at a time. While the ICC could become involved in labor disputes involving interstate transport, UPS was unionized relatively early in its history on a local and regional level; the UPS–Teamsters National Master Agreement was not signed until 1979. Its labor relationships were largely positive until the 1997 strike that lasted two weeks and cost the company $750 million.

The FAA would grant UPS authorization to operate its own aircraft in 1988 and over the next year, UPS would become the fastest-growing airline in FAA history, adding 110 aircraft by the end of 1989. These new employees would challenge some of the long-held ideas

Table 14.2 UPS Growth 2017–2022

	2017	2018	2019	2020	2021	2022
Revenues	66,585	71,861	74,094	84,628	97,287	100,338
Operating income	7,529	7,024	7,798	7,684	12,810	13,904
Net income	4,905	4,791	4,440	1,343	12,890	11,548

Source: Stock Analysis, https://stockanalysis.com/stocks/ups/financials/
#Numbers in 000s.

of the 'Brown' culture with its notion of working your way up the ladder from part-time to full-time, driver-to-top manager, but Big Brown would adjust (Niemann, 2007). By 1985, UPS Next Day Air was available in the lower 48 states. The Louisville hub, located on 550 acres at the Louisville International Airport, would become known as Worldport. The UPS facility would grow to 4 million square feet and explode with activity between 11 p.m. and 4 a.m., with over 5,000 employees engaged in sorting, routing, scanning, and loading/unloading. Like its competitor FedEx, package tracking and time-definite options would become an essential element to long-term success. The first two decades of the twenty-first century ended would see sustained growth for UPS as it headed into the Pandemic (Table 14.2).

Going Postal

A review of UPS' history reveals that its early beginnings were marked by an intense rivalry not with FedEx but with the US Postal Service (USPS). All countries have some form of postal service that is involved, by definition, in the delivery of parcels and small packages. To illustrate the involvement of these postal units in air cargo, a brief look at two companies will have to suffice. The first Postmaster of the United States was Benjamin Franklin, who was appointed in 1775. The Postal Reorganization Act of 1970 changed the status of the Postal Service to that of an independent unit of the Executive Branch of the US government, with a Board of Governors appointed by the President of the United States. Since it started as a unit of the US government, it had an obligation to serve all citizens wherever they were located. Further, it was not expected to make a profit from its operations. The German postal system officially began in 1490. In 1924 Deutsche Reichspost was founded as an independent agency. In 1995, the Posts and Telecommunications Act would reorganize the postal system into stock companies with the federal government holding all the initial shares but with private investment allowed. Deutsche Post would acquire Danzas Holding, a Swiss logistics company, in 1999 and go on to become the largest Initial Public Offering (IPO) in Germany in 2000, laying the groundwork for even greater changes in the coming century (www.dpwe.de). As we will see in Chapter 20, the fates of these two early systems begin to diverge in the twenty-first century with the USPS struggling to survive in an era of global cargo competitors and the Internet. It will also have to fight the lawmaking body of the US, the US Congress, to be allowed the freedom to respond to markets and competition. Deutsche Post, on the other hand, would throw off the shackles of a 500-year history to embrace change and globalization (see company websites).

Amazon

Little did anyone know when Jeff Bezos left his job at a Wall Street firm in 1994 to start a business in the emerging online retail sector what his company, Amazon, would mean for

Table 14.3 Amazon Growth 2017–2022

	2017	2018	2019	2020	2021	2022
Revenue	177,866	232,887	280,522	386,064	469,822	513,983
Operating income	4,106	12,421	14,541	22,899	24,879	12,248
Net income	3,033	10,073	11,588	21,331	33,364	−2,722

Source: Stock Analysis, https://stockanalysis.com/stocks/amzn/financials/

the retail sector or air cargo. Starting with books, but soon moving into an array of other products and services, in 2005 Amazon launched Amazon Prime whereby members could receive free shipping on products sold by the company in 48 hours or less (Ecomcrew, 2023). In 2015, Amazon would announce free same-day delivery to 14 cities. This service would spread across much of the US thanks to the assistance of an unlikely partner, the US Postal Service (Davies, 2016). It is likely no coincidence that Amazon Air also started in 2015. Initially, Amazon leased aircraft that other companies operated under their Air Operator's Certificates. Among these companies were Air Transport Services Group (ATSG), Atlas, and Kalitta Air. In 2017, Cincinnati/Northern Kentucky International Airport would become the main hub for Amazon Prime Air. Amazon would add more gateways and eventually start adding its own aircraft to its fleet, beginning in 2020. As of 2021, Amazon had an operational fleet of 67 aircraft with some projecting an increase to 200 aircraft by 2028. As we will discuss in Chapter 21, the Pandemic was very good for online shopping firms like Amazon and for the air cargo industry that supported it. As Table 14.3 shows, however, Amazon was already soaring.

How the Airlines Do It

In airlines, cargo began its life in the belly of the aircraft, the so-called belly cargo. The airline was simply one more air freight forwarder looking to fill space. For some carriers, cargo became a great deal more than additional revenue. A study into the productivity and cost competitiveness of world airlines found that while passenger revenue accounted for almost 90 percent of the revenue of most US major carriers, some international carriers derived between 20 and 40 percent of their revenue from cargo operations (Oum & Yu, 1998). Among the world's top international cargo carriers, three airlines have consistently appeared at or near the top – Korean Air, Lufthansa, and Singapore Airlines (Air Cargo World, 2005). After a rocky start, Korean Air Lines (KAL) was privatized in 1969 and began trans-Pacific cargo service to the US in 1971. KAL would continue to expand its cargo and passenger operations until a series of accidents in the 1990s would threaten their alliance membership and their future (Jeziorski, 1999). Fortunately, KAL would resolve these problems by the end of the decade and begin to post the kind of double-digit cargo growth that would propel them to the top of the cargo airline list in the early part of the new century (Air Cargo World, 2005). Lufthansa began operation in 1926 and carried over 258 tonnes of cargo in the first year of its operation. By 1966, they had converted a passenger B-707 to become their first dedicated freighter and would become the first airline to operate the B-747 Freighter in 1972. In 1977, Lufthansa created a cargo division, German Cargo Services (GCS), with a dedicated fleet of B-707-220F. A dedicated cargo center was completed at Frankfurt Main in 1982. Several events during the 1990s are indicative of the Lufthansa interest in cargo operations: 1) acquisition of an equity stake in DHL,

2) agreement with Deutsche Post for same-day service, 3) launch of Lufthansa Cargo as a wholly owned subsidiary, and 4) founding membership in the first cargo airline alliance WOW with SAS and Singapore Airlines (Lufthansa Cargo website; WOW website). Singapore Airlines was formed after the Singaporean and Malaysian governments decided to separate their joint airline in 1972. By 1978, Singapore was operating cargo service from Singapore to San Francisco. The Singapore cargo division was formed in 1992 using both dedicated and belly cargo options (Chan, 2000).

Catering to Cargo

Given the growth in air cargo operations during the last half of the twentieth century, it is unsurprising that airports would begin to seek this business out either to grow their overall revenue or to compensate for declining passenger traffic. Because cargo shippers often prefer night flights, airports could serve passengers during the day and cargo shippers during the usual nighttime lulls. While it is not surprising that the hub airport for the integrators (UPS, FedEx, DHL, etc) or the major cargo-carrying airlines post sizeable numbers of freight tonnage, other airports are attempting to attract cargo activity. In 2006, the 15 fastest-growing freight airports in Europe did not include the traditional big-name hubs; the top three were Leipzig/Halle, Oporto, and Liege. The growth of these smaller airports is attributed to their lower costs and improved service. It is not simply a matter of courting carriers and freight forwarders. Airports like Schiphol in Amsterdam are trying to draw businesses with interests in import/export near the airport itself (Conway, 2007). Of course, to attract cargo, the airport needs the necessary facilities – warehouse space, special services and facilities (refrigeration, Hazmat, customs), cargo handling equipment, and intermodal connections (the closer the better as drayage (short trucking) is one of the most expensive parts of the transportation equation (Muller, 1995). Given the explosive growth of the Asian export-oriented economies and the apparently insatiable appetite of the Western world for these cheap products, airports around the world are ready to play in the cargo game.

Flying High

The second half of the twentieth century witnessed the explosive growth of air cargo world as the logistics revolution and globalization pushed firms to seek out better, faster and cheaper means of shipping. However, the new century began to challenge air cargo as it had not been challenged since the early days of aviation. There will be rising fuel costs, 9/11 and new security rules, economic downturns, growing competition, and a global pandemic. This latter event would see massive disruptions in supply chains which had grown ever more complex and far flung. Some companies would begin to explore bringing activities back closer to home (Chapter 21). What this means for air cargo is yet unclear. Only time will tell.

Questions

1 Discuss the logistics revolution.
2 Define freight forwarder and integrated cargo carrier.
3 Outline the development of the US integrated carriers.
4 Discuss the airport infrastructure needs of cargo operators.

5 What role does belly cargo play in the air cargo industry?
6 How has Amazon changed retail and air cargo?

References

Air Cargo World (2005), *The world's top 50 cargo airlines*, September, pp. 22–28.

Allaz, C. (2004), *The history of air cargo and airmail from the 18th century*, Christopher Foyle Publishing, Paris.

Aviation Week and Space Technology (2007), 'Evolution of the air cargo industry: Road map', *Aviation Week and Space Technology*, 7 May, pp. 47–54.

Birla, M. (2005), *FedEx delivers: How the world's leading shipping company keeps innovating and out-performing the competition*, John Wiley & Sons, New York.

Bonocich, E. & Wilson, J. B. (2007), *Getting the goods: Ports, labor, and the logistics revolution*, Cornell University Press, Ithaca.

Boske, L. B. (1998), *Multimodal/intermodal transportation in the United States, Western Europe, and Latin America: Governmental policies, plans, and programs*, Lyndon B. Johnson Schools of Public Affairs, University of Texas, Austin.

Castells, M. (1996), *The rise of the network society*, Blackwell, Oxford.

Chan, D. (2000) The story of Singapore Airlines and the Singapore Girl, *Journal of Management Development*, 19, pp. 456–473.

Conway, P. (2007), 'Driven to the edge' *Air Cargo World*, October, pp. 21–27.

Davies, S. (2016) How same-day delivery wen from fantasy to reality. *Tech.co*. Available at https://tech.co/news/same-day-delivery-fantasy-to-reality-2016-01

Ecomcrew (2023) From A to Z: The complete history of Amazon. Available at https://www.ecomcrew.com/from-a-to-z-the-complete-history-of-amazon-com/

Fishman, C. (2006), *The Wal-Mart effect: How the world's most powerful company really works – And how it's transforming the America economy*, Penguin, New York.

Jeziorski, A. (1999), 'Humbled Korean air stages management upheavel', *Flight International*, 28 April.

Kumar, N. (1996), 'The power of trust in manufacturer-retailer relationships' in *Harvard business review on managing the value chain*, Harvard Business Press, Boston. pp. 91–126.

Levinson, M. (2006), *The box: How the shipping container made the world smaller and the world economy bigger*, Princeton University Press, Princeton.

Lynn, M. (1998), *Birds of prey: Boeing versus Airbus-the battle for the skies*, Four Walls Eight Windows, New York.

Muller, G. (1995), *Intermodal freight transportation*, 3rd ed., Eno Transportation Foundation, Lansdowne, Virginia.

Nelms, (2007), 'Oversized ambition', *Air Cargo World*, April, pp. 16–20.

Newhouse, J. (2007) *Boeing versus Airbus: The inside story of the greatest competition in business*, Alfred A. Knopf, New York.

Niemann, G. (2007), *Big Brown: The untold story of UPS*, John Wiley & Sons, San Francisco, CA.

Oum, T. H. & Yu, C. (1998) *Winning airlines: Productivity and cost competitiveness of the world's major airlines*, Kluwer Academic Publishers, Boston.

Serling, R. J. (1992) *Legend and legacy: The story of boeing and its people*, St. Martin Press, New York.

Websites

Deutsche Post World Net, https://www.dpwe.de
Lufthansa Cargo, https://www.lhcargo.com
WOW alliance, https://www.WOWtheworld.com

PART III

CRISIS TO CRISIS (2001–2022)

15 The Economies of Scale

Learning Objectives

After reading this chapter, you should have a good understanding of:

LO1:   the history of financial instability in the airline industry and the usual responses to crisis
LO2:   the key drivers of cost in airlines
LO3:   the changing labor patterns in airlines
LO4:   the range of new responses to crisis

Key Terms, Concepts & People

Economy of scale	Economy of scope	Diseconomies
Distribution system	SABRE	GDS

Old Joke

An old airline joke notes that the best way to become a millionaire in the airline industry is to start with a billion dollars. Like all jokes, this one is funny because it is so often true. Warren Buffet, the legendary investor who once quipped about shooting down the Wright brothers to save the money of thousands of investors, has admitted that despite all logic he is an 'aeroholic' who cannot seem to avoid investing here. Buffet first invested in the industry in 1989 with USAir. In 2016, Buffet spent US$7–8 billion to invest in Delta, United, American, and Southwest only to dump all the holdings in 2020 as prices continued to decline. It is believed that this sell-off contributed to massive losses for his company that year. Thus, the man who once used the airline industry as an example of gruesome enterprises, that is, an enterprise that pays inadequate interest rates and requires you to keep adding money to its disappointing returns, learned the same lesson again; airlines are a bad long-term investment and even the best investor is likely to lose money in an industry that hit a stock bottom in 2020 during the COVID Pandemic only to rise up 80–200 percent by the following year. Airlines investing is not for the faint of heart (Blikre, 2021).

Jokes aside, a look at airline performance in the twenty-first century tells the tale. The industry was already showing signs of weakness before 9/11 due to a recession-related slowdown. The terrorist attack made the industry's performance even worse. While some did

DOI: 10.4324/9781003405306-18

claim to have foreseen the Global Financial Crisis of 2008, these individuals were not in the airline industry and the scale and scope of the Global Pandemic which started in 2020 caught almost everyone off-guard. If the triggers were unique, then the industry responses were strikingly familiar because most of the basic issues remained the same: price-sensitive consumers, overexpansion and overcapacity, loss-making airlines flying in bankruptcy and keeping seat capacity high, high fixed and variable costs, contentious labor, and competition from low-cost and foreign carriers (Costa, Harned, & Lunquist, 2002; Derchin, 1995; Wolf, 1995).

In response to earlier crises, the US airline industry created the hub-and-spoke system as a means of funneling and managing traffic (remember from Chapter 10 that the European industry already had such a structure with a hub in the national capital), developed complex holding structures to manage debt, renegotiated labor contracts to manage wages and benefits, retired fleets and cut marginal routes to reduce capacity, merged and consolidated as weaker players faltered and stronger ones strived to position themselves for the next boom, created global alliance structures to expand the scale and scope of operations, and looked for marginal ways to reduce costs. With the next boom, the dominant logic of the industry reverted to expand and spend (Rosen, 1995). In the wake of 9/11, the industry did a better job of avoiding the 'temptation of capacity' that had plagued them since deregulation, even though new aircraft orders soared for 2005 and 2006 (IATA, 2007). Then the 2008 Global Financial Crisis (GFC) and record fuel prices became the next shock to the industry. Hedging fuel became a game that few were willing to play in such a volatile market. When Doug Parker, CEO of American Airlines, proclaimed in 2018 that his airline (and the industry) would never lose money again, he made a Buffet mistake because the COVID Pandemic made earlier losses seem mild (Kuehner-Hebert, 2018). In fact, it now appears that it may not be possible for an airline to muddle through unless they can count on government support from time to time.

This chapter will explore the historic struggle of the airline industry to remain profitable. We will begin with an overview of airline performance by region (Tables 15.1–15.4), looking at the years 2018, 2020, and 2022. Then, we will explore fundamental issues such as organizational scale (size) and scope, the battle between the traditional carriers and the low-cost carriers (LCCs), and three key areas of the airline industry – fuel, distribution, and labor. Finally, we will touch on one of the greatest unknowns in the industry – climate change.

Around the World

We will start with a look at selected North American carriers (Table 15.1). By 2018, most of these carriers had posted financial and nonfinancial performances that prompted J.D. Power to declare another 'golden age' of travel – newer planes, better ticket value, improved customer service, and higher overall customer satisfaction (Airlines for America, 2020).

Even better for the airlines in 2018, passenger revenue was solid and net margins were not only positive, but relatively healthy by industry standards. By 2020, pandemic losses reached new records as air travel ground to a halt in many areas. Emerging from the pandemic, the 2022 performance for all carriers was improved with almost half reporting positive margins. Table 15.2 looks at the performance of selected European carriers.

Again, we see the same basic pattern as North America. It should be noted that Aegean and Ryanair surpassed their 2018 performance in 2022. For Asian airlines, there are several

Table 15.1 North American Airline Performance 2018, 2020, and 2022

	2018	*2020*	*2022*
Air Canada			
Pax revenue	12,427	3,265	10,911
Net margin (%)	0.2	−79.7	−10.3
American Airlines			
Pax revenue	40,676	14,518	44,568
Net margin (%)	3.2	−51.3	−0.3
Delta			
Pax revenue	39,755	12,883	40,218
Net margin (%)	8.9	−72.5	2.6
JetBlue			
Pax revenue	7,381	2,733	8,586
Net margin (%)	2.5	−45.8	−4.0
Spirit			
Pax revenue	3,260	1,766	4,989
Net margin (%)	4.7	−23.7	−10.9
Southwest			
Pax revenue	20,455	7,665	21,408
Net margin (%)	11.2	−34	2.3
United			
Pax revenue	37.706	11,805	40,032
Net margin (%)	5.1	−46	1.6

Source: Cirium financial database.

Table 15.2 European Airline Performance 2018, 2020, 2022

	2018	*2020*	*2022*
Aegean			
Pax revenue	984	293	1,169
Net margin (%)	5.3	−57.3	9.1
British Airways			
Pax revenue	15,362	3,733	11,310
Net margin (%)	16.1	−87.5	0.0
EasyJet			
Pax revenue	6,311	2,956	4,838
Net margin (%)	6.1	−35.9	−2.9
Lufthansa			
Pax revenue	24,368	6,284	21,717
Net margin (%)	0.0	0.0	0.0
Ryanair			
Pax revenue	6,069	1,212	7,214
Net margin (%)	11.5	−62.1	12.2

Source: Cirium financial database.

differences in the pattern (Table 15.3). First, there were airlines already struggling in 2018 (Air India and Korean Air). Second, Chinese airlines were still locked into the pandemic in 2022, posting negative margins on lower passenger revenue. Finally, Table 15.4 shows the results for Latin American airlines, most of whom were struggling in 2018 and continue to struggle in 2022.

Table 15.3 Asian Airline Performance 2018, 2020, 2022

	2018	*2020*	*2022*
Air China			
Pax revenue	18,142	8,090	5,670
Net margin (%)	5.8	−55.1	−37.4
Air India			
Pax revenue	2,988	1,007	0
Net margin (%)	−33.6	−63.5	−36.3
China Southern			
Pax revenue	19,288	10,239	8.886
Net margin (%)	2.4	−12.8	−38.7
Emirates			
Pax revenue	21,510	3,057	23,086
Net margin (%)	1.1	−65.6	9.9
IndiGo			
Pax revenue	3,854	1,748	0
Net margin (%)	0.5	−37.2	−0.6
Korean Airlines			
Pax revenue	7,037	1,700	3,368
Net margin (%)	−0.9	−2.6	13.3
Japan Airlines			
Pax revenue	9,536	1,902	6,627
Net margin (%)	10.1	−59.8	2.5
Qantas			
Pax revenue	11,551	7,720	4,300
Net margin (%)	5.5	−13.6	−9.5
Qatar			
Pax revenue	9,346	2,189	13,616
Net margin (%)	0.0	0.0	0.0
Singapore			
Pax revenue	7,626	411	0
Net margin (%)	4.8	−98.0	13.4

Source: Cirium financial database.

Table 15.4 Latin American Airlines 2018, 2020, 2020

	2018	*2020*	*2022*
Aeromexico			
Pax revenue	3,350	1,065	1,954 (2021)
Net margin (%)	−2.7	−149.1	−41
Avianca			
Pax revenue	4,074	1,004	3,133
Net margin (%)	0.0	−63.90–8.0	
Azul			
Pax revenue	2,356	971	2,842
Net margin (%)	−4.5	−175.7	−8.7
COPA			
Pax revenue	2,587	761	2,825
Net margin (%)	3.3	−74.7	11.7

Source: Cirium financial database.

It should be noted that the pandemic has been credited with killing off 64 global airlines, including Flybe, Alitalia, and Flyr in Europe (Buckley, 2023). These failures occurred after over US$160 billion was provided to airlines, mostly in subsidies and loans as well as outright equity and cash injections (OECD, 2020).

Too Big to Fail

The Global Financial Crisis (GFC) led to a debate on the topic of 'too big to fail'. For the most part, the discussion centered on banks, but after 9/11, United made a similar argument for government assistance to their airline, claiming that it was too big to fail. Would the failure of a major national carrier in one of these regions or the largest national carrier in a country lead to major, even unthinkable, consequences for countries, consumers, and citizens? In Chapter 1, we discussed some of the major reasons why aviation is treated as a special case – defense, economic impact, and national pride. In the case of a country with a single, major flag carrier would the collapse of that carrier limit travel, reduce imports and exports, eliminate jobs that are not easily replaced, reduce the ability to attract investment into the country? These are precisely the arguments that were made in developed countries like Italy and developing countries like Kenya for saving airlines (Ngila, 2022).

Before asking if an airline is too big to fail, let's address the question of size. Does size really matter in the case of airlines? If so, is it the scale of the operations or the scope? Is size important for some factors of production but not others? What exactly does an airline produce? Is there such a thing as too big or do airlines need to get 'big enough' to finally make a profit? Where does an airline add value and how can this value be enhanced and captured? In the consolidations after the GFC, airlines argued that consolidation was good for industry and for consumers. Airlines benefited because it helped them maintain pricing power through a greater ability to control capacity. In defense of the American–US Airways merger, proponents suggested that the combination would create a competitor capable of providing truly 'competitive' prices and service to consumers forced to rely on United and Delta for their international travel (Flottau & Shannon, 2013). In a multi-carrier scenario, there are arguments that a smaller player is at a disadvantage in competition. It was this very consolidation, along with better logistics, and fee-based ancillary products, that led Doug Parker to declare the end of a loss-making American (Kuehner-Hebert, 2018). Size or economies of scale was one of the primary arguments presented in the debate over the 1978 deregulation of the US airline industry. If an airline is prevented from merging as often occurred prior to deregulation, then they would never achieve sufficient size to be profitable. Economies of scale occur when average costs decline as the production of a good or service increases. These economies can derive from several sources: technological, managerial, financial, marketing, commercial, and research and development. Technological economies may result when a larger firm is able to employ more expensive machinery and use it more intensively. Managerial economies arise when a firm is able to divide tasks and employ specialists. Financial economies result when a firm is able to borrow money at lower rates (primarily because size is usually associated with greater assets, age, credit record, etc). Marketing economies occur when firms are able to spread the high cost of advertising across a larger level of output. Commercial economies are gained from buying supplies in bulk and receiving larger discounts. R&D economies may appear when developing new or better products if basic research can give rise to multiple applications (Kenton, 2024). From this breakdown, it is obvious that a firm, industry, or strategic group within an industry may enjoy economies in one area and not in another. Technologically, the new generation of aircraft tended to be more economical and efficient; however, the hub-and-spoke system employed by the major carriers limited the utilization of aircraft that sat and waited for banks of smaller airplanes to feed passengers into the system. These small aircraft (50-seaters) were not economical for larger carriers to operate since higher wage scales made them less productive. High fuel prices made them uneconomical for even regional carriers, thus placing new pressure on the hub concept (Flottau, 2013).

Since economies of scale are concerned with unit costs, it is important to define the unit of production in airlines. In other words: what does an airline produce? Does it produce a seat, a trip from point A to point B (called a leg) or an end-to-end experience, i.e. many consumers connect from A to B to C as the final destination? The answer to this question may well matter since not all seats or trips are equal. The proverbial widget factory of business lore mass produces a product that is assumed to be the same – widgets. Economies of scale exist if the unit cost of the 10,000th widget is lower than that of the 1,000th. In the case of an airline, the seat on an aircraft from Atlanta to Boston is not necessarily the same as a seat from Atlanta to Denver or Atlanta to Dubai. Nor are the costs involved in producing these seats the same since they involve different lengths, flight crews, landing fees, aircraft types, passenger facilities charges, etc. Sophisticated systems can be employed to analyze costs by route, but this unit of analysis problem greatly complicates the economies argument for carriers. In part, this focus on unit costs is driven by the traditional approach to accounting which basically adds direct material costs, direct labor costs, and overhead (rent, utilities, insurance, etc.) then divides by the unit of output to determine per unit costs. Activity-based costing looks at costs from an activity standpoint. Business activities includes 'all of the processes that a company uses in order to conduct its business: order processing, procurement, engineering, production set-up, quality inspection, warehousing and material movement'. Under this approach, firms would determine the activities it performs and analyze them to determine the cost drivers within that activity. Costs to products are assigned based on how often they require inputs from that particular activity. The benefits of activity costing are found in the detailed cost information it provides and the focus on cost drivers within activities.

The notion of increasing scale leads to the question of whether a carrier can be too big to succeed. With size comes complexity – vertically, horizontally, and geographically. Large firms have more layers of management separating the top where 'decisions' get made from the bottom where 'decisions' and the actual work of the organization get carried out. These layers often mean that actions are delayed and communications are poor, leading to the misdiagnosis of problems or the misapplication of solutions. Horizontal complexity occurs when firms become increasingly divided into ever-finer units of specialized individuals who lose touch with the work (and importance) of other units as well as the overall goals of the organization. Geographic complexity occurs when firms spread across time zones and cultures, making collaboration difficult and product and managerial decisions culture-specific. A further complexity, external boundaries, is becoming more common as firms outsource functions and blur the lines between the firm and its external environment. In fact, each of these areas creates its own boundary within the firm. In many large (old) firms, these boundaries are clear and impermeable; what is inside stays inside and what is out cannot get in! Such organizations are slow to act, rigid in response, and poor in adaptation. Size becomes a disadvantage if the firm lives in a rapidly changing environment with younger, faster competitors (Ashkenas, Ulrich, Jick, & Kerr, 1995; Galbraith, 1995). Of course, one of the advantages of merger activity is that, in theory, firms can reduce redundancies, increase productivity, and spread costs. Larger firms can be said to have market power that could translate into a greater ability to control costs, capacity, or distribution which 'could' lead to lower prices for consumers. From a consumer perspective, the debate over the American and US Airways merger was a matter of answering two questions. First, would a three-firm oligopoly act differently than a four-firm oligopoly? In other words, would the remaining three carriers tacitly collude to maintain equilibrium, that is, would they accept a gentlemanly division of the market that allowed them to maintain pricing power and profits, or were there incentives to compete over routes and market share in a way that either lowered prices or improved service? To date, it is not clear if sheer size conveys over-all advantages to airlines, or if a carrier can indeed be too big. Several earlier studies did show a positive relationship between airline growth and profitability (Chin & Tay, 2001) while later studies have failed to find either a positive impact or any impact at all (Hazel, 2018; Maung, Douglas, & Tan, 2022). Even if the feared collusion with the American merger did not appear, there is still no reason to assume that competition in the imperfect airline market will not produce such an effect.

Economies of scope differ from those of scale in that they are not derived from increases in volume but occur as the result of circumstances that allow firms to achieve synergy in production, product development, and distribution. Economies of scope can occur in pro-duction when firms are able to lower the cost of producing one product by producing other, i.e. an airline flying both passengers and cargo. Economies of scope in product develop-ment arise when common knowledge or equipment is used to produce more than one prod-uct, i.e. laser technology can be used in many applications from surgery to metal cutting, an aircraft can be used for passengers during the day and cargo at night, a computer revenue management system can be used to manage airline seats, hotel room, rental cars, etc. This last example is a classic one, that is, an infrastructure system capable of distributing one type of product used to distribute others. An airline distribution system can also be viewed as a scope generator. The hub can be seen as a very large airport operation or 'a factory to combine itineraries' (Flottau, 2013). If consumers prefer more options to fewer, then an airline that can produce more combinations of services and routes would hold an advantage.

Of course, if size does create diseconomies of scale or scope, firms have several options in downsizing: retrenchment, downscaling, or downscoping (DeWitt, 1998). Retrenchment attempts to maintain scope and often even increases output by centralizing certain firm functions, changing supplier relationships, and realigning managerial functions. For exam-ple, firms may re-engineer processes to improve productivity or eliminate redundant facili-ties (Hammer & Champy, 1993). Downscaling operations entail the permanent reduction of human and physical resources to bring supply in line with demand (Harrigan, 1983, 1985; Mahoney, 1992). Downscoping involves efforts to actually shrink the boundaries of the firm by effecting permanent cuts in human and physical resources as well as simplifying the organization's structure by reducing vertical, horizontal, or product diversity (DeWitt, 1993). The path a firm takes to downsizing is a function of many factors, but one factor is clearly the barriers to exit and mobility. Exit barriers create an impediment to the removal of excess resources (Caves & Porter, 1976) while mobility barriers affect the ability of firms to move between segments in an industry (Caves & Porter, 1977). Firms make certain industry-specific investments that may make exit difficult or very costly. For example, labor contracts may lock a firm into maintaining certain levels of operation. Fleet acquisitions may mean that cutbacks will lead to underutilization in the short run, raising costs, and fleet sales may take time and not generate enough in certain market conditions to recoup costs. Cutting spokes out of the hub-and-spoke 'factory' can multiply in a network to eliminate a number of possible city pairs. Likewise, a high-cost labor force with rigid work rules may prohibit a firm from shifting to a lower-cost segment of the industry. The task ahead for airlines is figuring out how economies and value-adding activities can be used to shape a profitable airline. One of their first tasks will be deciding on a strategy.

What's Your Strategy?

Generically, there are three basic strategies for any industry – differentiation, low-cost, or hybrid – that is, a combination of the first two strategies that might have a firm following a differentiation strategy in one area but a cost reduction strategy in another. While the term low cost is self-evident, differentiation is not. Essentially, the idea is that a firm selects one or more dimensions on which it plans to differ from its competitors. These dimensions are chosen because the firm believes that consumers value the difference and will pay more money for it. In the airline industry, a full-service network carrier (FSNC) is based on the notion that consumers will pay a higher cost for a larger network of destinations and a selection of 'services' – lounges, frequent flier programs, bag tracking, etc. The traditional national flag carriers would all be classified as FSNC. Following deregulation in many countries, a new breed of airline arose – low-cost carriers (LCC).

One of the most famous LCCs is Southwest Airlines in the US. The LCC model traditionally had several key features: point-to-point service, secondary airport use, 'no frills' service, single fleet type, and outsourced maintenance. Southwest also included a host of employee-related/organizational culture features (employee ownership, teamwork, cross-training, etc). Their model has been the subject of several books including *Nuts: Southwest Airlines' Crazy Recipe for Business and Personal Success* (Freiberg & Freiberg, 1996). Following US deregulation, a number of new airlines attempted to implement this model, with varying degrees of success. In the four decades since Southwest, a host of variations on the LCC model have appeared. Ryanair in Europe is one of the most successful carriers to adopt the LCC model (even taking the cost-cutting no frills to new heights by removing the window shade, charging for carry-ons, requiring online booking, etc), but it did not adopt the cultural elements that Southwest believes added to employee productivity and airline success (Sparaco, 2011). The US carrier Spirit was growing at 20 percent a year after adopting the ultra-LCC model (like Ryanair) and took the concept of ancillary fees to new heights in the US (Saporito, 2013). This fare-and-fee approach has also been adopted to some extent by the traditional FSNC. Over the course of a decade, ancillary revenue for global airlines has risen from US\$42.6 billion in 2013 to US\$102 billion in 2022 (OAG, 2023). At the same time, some carriers, such as JetBlue in the US, EasyJet in the EU, and, of course, the Persian Gulf carriers (Emirates, Qatar Airways, and Etihad), went in the opposite direction in terms of frills, seeking to attract more business class passengers through the selected offering of additional services (Flottau, 2013; Sparaco, 2012). While nothing seems to be settled in the airline industry, recent research seems to suggest that FSNC are faced with a difficult trade-off between growth and operating profits while their LCC competitors can pursue both given the existence of the right regulatory policies (Maung, Douglas, & Tan, 2022).

The hybrid strategy remains a question mark in the industry with little evidence that it can create a sustainable airline. After 9/11, LCCs were the only airlines to expand, but in recent years even the anointed kings of the LCC model – Southwest Airlines and Ryanair – have experienced slowing growth. In some countries, LCCs have gained the majority of the traffic (Flottau, 2011). Evidence suggests that the presence of a well-developed LCC airline segment plays an important role in lowering airfares and increasing traffic, but the presence of government regulations limiting foreign ownership, investment, and leasing or regulations which prevent LCCs from charging ancillary fees (seat assignment, checked baggage, early boarding, etc.) seriously limit the effectiveness of this model (Curtis & Rhoades, 2023). More LCC competition and higher fuel prices changed the dynamics in many markets. Some LCCs tried to adopt a hybrid strategy to appeal to higher-yield passengers, but the results to date suggests that the operating margins for pure LCCs are better than those for hybrids such as Virgin Australia, Air Berlin, or Gol (Airline Leader, 2013). If the traditional carriers have had a hard time thinking like an LCC, then it is possible that the LCCs are also finding it difficult to think (and act) more high touch. There is no question that adding frills will increase costs; the question is whether the added costs (of service) raise more revenues. It may be too early to declare the hybrid dead, but it is struggling. While the merger of JetBlue and Spirit, known for its ultra-low-cost strategy, has been blocked, it would have been an interesting new experiment in merging two distinctive strategies in the airline industry (Raymond & Shepardson, 2024).

Searching for Profits

Don Carty, then CEO of American Airlines, told a Congressional panel after September 11th that American's main objective was to achieve permanent structural cost reductions (Fiorino, 2002). He singled out three factors for special attention – fuel, distribution, and labor (Zellner, 2002). The bankruptcy of American in 2011 illustrates the importance of these factors and the difficulties in reducing costs in these areas. One of the key features of the LCC model was to outsource maintenance. Over time, FSNCs also began to adopt this strategy, but American had lagged their competitors in this regard and had to catch up. By the time the J.D. Power 'golden age' of air travel arrived in 2018, airlines also had managed to greatly reduce distribution costs so that they only represented about 4 percent of operating costs. In part, this was due to the transition to direct marketing channels, but airlines have also reduced advertising budgets from 2 to 1 percent of operating expenses. Fees for Global Distribution Systems (GDS) represent only about US$4–6 per booking (Borko, 2018). Given the 'success' with distribution costs, the rest of the chapter will examine the other two factors.

Fuel

At the time of Carty's testimony to Congress, fuel prices represented roughly 10–15 percent of airlines' costs. According to Airlines for America (A4A), the US industry trade group, in 2013 fuel represented 28 percent of the operating costs, surpassing labor, which represented 23 percent (Airlines for America, 2013). In 2023, fuel accounted for 22 percent of operating expenses. In 2023, Jet A-1 fuel cost roughly US$43.86 per gallon, meaning that the per hour cost of operating an aircraft is between US$500 and US$2,000 per hour, depending on the type and size of the aircraft (Beers, 2023). There are several obvious things that airlines can do to reduce or stabilize fuel costs. First, newer, more fuel-efficient aircraft reduce fuel costs as well as overall maintenance costs. Many of the aircraft 'retired' after 9/11, the Global Financial Crisis (GFC), and the COVID Pandemic fell into the less efficient category. Unfortunately, financially troubled airlines often find fleet renewal difficult. Second, airlines can seek to hedge fuel costs, although this is not guaranteed to save costs since it depends on the financial and forecasting skill of the airline. Southwest Airlines has been viewed as one of the US carriers to have benefited from substantial fuel hedging, but even it has not always guessed right (USA Today, 2007). Hedging is difficult if 1) there is no clear sense of the future trend in fuel or 2) there are sudden changes in fuel price. Given very thin margins, 'guessing right' by even a few dollars could make a big difference. Third, there are a number of operational measures that can be employed. The first edition of IATA's 'Guidance Material on Best Practices for Fuel and Environmental Management' was issued in 2004. The manual goes through detailed information for weight management, pre-flight planning, engine start-up and taxing, reduced thrust take-off, etc. Fourth, airlines can simply shrink their operations, particularly their regional jet operations which may be flying at a loss because of the generally higher operating costs of smaller aircraft. In a piece of out-of-the-box thinking not common in the industry, Delta Air Lines even purchased its own oil refinery in 2012 to give them greater control over their costs. Still, it was unclear that they would be rewarded for this innovation. The refinery, operated by Delta subsidiary Monroe Energy LLC, made a profit in the third quarter of 2013 after posting losses in the previous two quarters and was losing US$114 million in the 'Golden Age' of aviation (Krauss & Chokshi, 2020; Reuters, 2013). Even if Delta is able to get the refinery to a sustainable profit, this does not appear to be a strategy that most other carriers can or would adopt in the battle to reduce fuel costs.

Labor

The second area of costs targeted for savings by American Airlines CEO Don Carty was labor (Fiorino, 2002). Prior to 9/11, labor was the single largest cost of major US carriers, at roughly 40 percent of total costs. Experts had suggested that labor costs needed to drop by 20 percent to return the airline industry to profitability. Unfortunately, in the absence of a major crisis there was little probability of gaining union agreement to these reductions. Bankruptcy is just such a crisis. Following September 11th, four major US carriers entered bankruptcy: United (2002), US Airways (2002, 2004), Delta and Northwest (2005). American Airlines avoided this round of bankruptcy by signing agreements with its three key unions to lower costs (Nelson & Francolla, 2008). This was not sufficient, however, to allow American to weather the 2008 Global Financial Crisis and $147 a barrel oil. Thus, in 2011, American joined the ranks of US airlines who have filed for bankruptcy. US carriers had reduced labor costs an industry average of 23 percent of operating costs by 2013 (A4A, 2013). By 2023, labor costs represented 31 percent of operating expenses (Beers, 2023).

As already noted, airlines have generally outsourced most maintenance operations, thus reducing employee to aircraft ratios, and improving productivity. Again, while none of the FSNC have reached the level of Southwest or Ryanair, they have shed employees and reduced the impact of labor on overall operating costs. With reductions in mechanics and other labor, pilots are the biggest single labor group in the airlines, followed by flight attendants. Unions have historically complicated airline mergers and acquisitions, as the pilot talks between groups from Delta and Northwest demonstrated (Weber, 2008). Following the Pandemic, pilots and flight attendants have been able to negotiate substantial raises (Faguy, 2023; Joseph, 2023). In the short term, labor costs are fixed and stable, unlike fuel. In fact, two-thirds of the cost of flying an aircraft are fixed in the short term, meaning that wild fluctuations in fuel costs have significant impacts on the quarterly financial performance of airlines.

Looking Ahead

The twenty-first century has been just as brutal for the airline industry as the last two decades of the twentieth century. 9/11, the GFC, and the Global Pandemic have demonstrated that a wise person would never suggest an end to losses in the industry. Still the demand for airline travel continues to rise. Aside from the general problems of profitability, global aviation has two other clouds over its future, namely global aviation liberalization (Chapter 18) and climate change (Chapter 20). Either of these issues could be the source of the next great industry downturn.

Questions

1 What are economies of scale and scope and how do they apply in the airline industry?
2 Discuss the three strategies open to airlines. What are their features?
3 Discuss the history of financial crisis and the responses taken by airlines.
4 Discuss some of the factors limiting the spread of the LCC model.
5 Discuss the key drivers of cost in airlines. What can be done to control these drivers?

References

Airline Leader (2013) Low-cost airlines, hybridization and the rocky path to profits. Available at https://www.airlineleader.com/this-months-highlights/low-cost-airlines-hybridisation-and-the-rocky-path-to-profits

Airlines for America (2013) A4A Quarterly Cost Index: US passenger airlines. Available at https://www.airlines.org/Pages/A4A-Quarterly-Cost-Index-U.S.-Passenger-Airlines.aspx

Airlines for America (2020) The state of the aviation industry: Examining the impact of the COVID-19 pandemic -Statement of Airlines for American before the United States Senate Commerce, Science, and Transportation committee. Available at: https://www.airlines.org/wp-content/uploads/2020/05/A4A-CST-Testimony-Final.pdf

Ashkenas, R. Ulrich, D., Jick, T., & Kerr, S. (1995), *The boundaryless organizations: Breaking the chains of organizational structure*, Jossey-Bass Publishers, San Francisco.

Beers, B. (2023) Which major expenses affect airline companies. Investopedia. Available at: https://www.investopedia.com/ask/answers/040715/what-are-major-expenses-affect-companies-airline-industry.asp#:~:text=The%20major%20expenses%20that%20affect,are%20labor%20and%20fuel%20costs

Blikre, J. (2021) How Warren Buffet's airline stocks have performed since Berkshore Hathaway sold them. Yahoo!finance. Available at: https://finance.yahoo.com/news/how-warren-buffetts-airline-stocks-have-performed-since-berkshire-hathaway-sold-them-134849843.html

Borko, S. (2018) Why airlines are finally seeing lower distribution costs: New Skift research. Skift. Available at: https://skift.com/2018/11/06/why-airlines-are-finally-seeing-lower-distribution-costs-new-skift-research/

Buckley, J. (2023) How the pandemic killed off 64 airlines. CNN Travel. Available at: https://www.cnn.com/travel/article/pandemic-airline-bankruptcies/index.html

Caves, R. E. & Porter, M. E. (1976), 'Barriers to exit,' in D. P. Qualls & R. T. Masson (Eds.), *Essays in industrial organization in honor of Joe S. Bain*, Ballinger, Cambridge, MA, pp. 39–69.

Caves, R. E. & Porter, M. E. (1977), 'From entry barriers to mobility barriers: Conjectural decisions and contrived deterrence to new competition,' *Quarterly Journal of Economics*, 91, pp. 241–261.

Chin, A. T. H., & Tay, J. H. (2001) Developments in air transport: Implications on investment decisions, profitability, and survival of Asian airlines. *Journal of Air Transport Management* 7 (5) 319–330.

Costa, P. R., Harned, D. S., & Lunquist, J. T. (2002), 'Rethinking the aviation industry,' *The McKinsey Quarterly*, Number 2: Risk and Resilience.

Curtis, T., & Rhoades, D. L. (2023) Overview of Low-cost carriers in Russia and post-Soviet states. Button, K (Ed.) *Airlines and developing countries* (Advances in airline Economics, vol. 10) Emerald Publishing Limited, Leeds, pp. 191–214.

Derchin, M. (1995), 'What went wrong?' in P. Cappelli (Ed.) *Airline labor relations in the global era: The new frontier*, ILR Press, Ithaca.

DeWitt, R. L. (1993), 'The structural consequences of downsizing,' *Organization Science*, 4, pp. 30–40.

DeWitt, R. L. (1998), 'Firm, industry, and strategy influences on choice of downsizing approach,' *Strategic Management Journal*, 19, pp. 59–79.

Faguy, A. (2023) United pilots win 40% raise as union ratifies new contract. Forbes. Available at: https://www.forbes.com/sites/anafaguy/2023/09/29/united-pilots-win-40-raise-as-union-ratifies-new-contract/?sh=31329951bd2d

Fiorino, F. (2002), 'Carty to analysts: AA aims to survive,' *Aviation Week and Space Technology*, September 20, pp. 47–48.

Flottau, J. (2011) "Hybrid hypothesis: Air Berline is trying to be everything to everybody – and may fail", *Aviation Week & Space Technology*, May 30, pp. 48–51.

Flottau, J. (2013) Evolving paradigm, *Aviation Week and Space Technology*, July 8, pp. 36–39.

Flottau, J. & Shannon, D. (2013) Connecting fight, *Aviation Week and Space Technology*, August 19, pp. 24–27.

Freiberg, K. & Freiberg, J. (1996) *Nuts: Southwest Airlines' crazy recipe for business and personal success*, Bard Press, Austin.

Galbraith, J. R. (1995), *Designing organizations: An executive briefing on strategy, structure, and process*, Jossey-Bass Publishers, San Francisco.

Hammer, M. & Champy, J. S. (1993), *Reengineering the corporation: A manifesto for business revolution*, Harper Business, New York.

Harrigan, K. R. (1983), *Strategies for vertical integration*, Lexington Books, Lexington, MA.

Harrigan, K. R. (1985), *Strategic flexibility*, Lexington Books, Lexington, MA.

Hazel, R. (2018) Airline capacity discipline in the US domestic Market. *Journal of Air Transport Management* 66: 76–86.

IATA (2007) 'IATA Economic Briefing: Passenger and Freight Forecasts 2007-2011', October. Available at: https://www.iata.org/economics

Joseph, L. (2023) Southwest flight attendants would get 36% pay raises in new contract. CNBC. Available at: https://www.cnbc.com/2023/11/01/southwest-flight-attendants-would-get-36percent-pay-raises-in-new-contract.html

Kenton, W. (2024) Economies of scale: What are they and how are they used. Available at: https://www.investopedia.com/terms/e/economiesofscale.asp

Krauss, C. & Chokshi, N. (2020) Delta Air Lines bought an oil refinery. It didn't go as planned. The New York Times. Available at: https://www.nytimes.com/2020/08/10/business/energy-environment/delta-oil-refinery-jet-fuel.html

Kuehner-Hebert, K. (2018) American Airlines will never lose money again, says CEO Doug Parker. Chief Executive. Available at: https://chiefexecutive.net/american-airlines-will-never-lose-money-says-ceo-doug-parker/

Mahoney, J. T. (1992), 'The choice of organizational form and vertical financial ownership versus other methods of vertical integration,' *Strategic Management Journal*, 13, pp. 559–584.

Maung, Y. S. Y., Douglas, I. & Tan, D. (2022) Identifying the drivers of profitable airline growth. *Transport Policy*, 115, 275–285.

Nelson, A. & Francolla, G. (2008) 'Airlines: A Tale of Mergers and Bankruptcy', CNBC.com, February 21. Available at: https://www.cnbc.com https://www.oecd.org/coronavirus/en/data-insights/government-support-to-aviation-industry-hits-new-highs-due-to-covid-19

Ngila, F. (2022) Kenya is looking for US investors to save its airline. Quartz. Available at: https://qz.com/ruto-hopes-delta-air-lines-will-save-kenya-airways-1849902363

OAG (2023) Shaping airline retail: The unstoppable rise of ancillaries. Future of Travel. Available at: https://www.oag.com/blog/shaping-airline-retail-unstoppable-rise-ancillaries#:~:text=Comprehensive%20research%20conducted%20by%20IdeaWorks,%24102%20billion%20USD%20in%202022

OECD (2020) Government support to aviation industry hits new high due to COVOD-19. Available at: https://www.oecd.org/coronavirus/en/data-insights/government-support-to-aviation-industry-hits-new-highs-due-to-covid-19

Raymond, N. & Shepardson, D. (2024) US court to hear JetBlue, Spirit appeal over blocked merger in June. Reuters. Available at: https://www.reuters.com/business/aerospace-defense/us-court-sets-expedited-schedule-jetblue-spirit-merger-rejection-appeal-2024-02-02/

Reuters (2013) Delta's refinery turns small profit for first time. Available at: https://www.reuters.com/article/2013/10/22/delta-refinery-idUSL1N0IC11W20131022

Rosen, S. D. (1995), 'Corporate restructuring: A labor perspective,' in P. Cappelli (Ed.) *Airline labor relations in the global era: The new frontier*, ILR Press, Ithaca.

Saporito, B. (2013) Cabin pressure, *Time*, September 9, pp. 36–41.

Sparaco, P. (2011) "The crazy recipe" *Aviation Week and Space Technology*, May 18, p. 48.

Sparaco, P. (2012) 'OLeary vs McCall', *Aviation Week and Space Technology*, May 7, p. 18.

USA Today (2007), 'Southwest Airlines' fuel hedging pushes profits' USA Today Online. Available at: https://www.usatodat.com/pt/cpt?action=cpt&title=Southwest+Airlines%27

Weber, H. R. (2008) 'Delta Pilots Say No Deal With Northwest' WTOPnews.com, March 18. Available at: https://www.wtopnews.com/?nid=111&sid=1347940

Wolf, S. M. (1995), 'Where do we go from here: A management perspective,' in Peter Cappelli (Ed.) *Airline labor relations in the global era: The new frontier*, ILR Press, Cornell, pp. 18–23.

Zellner, W. (2002), 'What's weighing down the big carriers,' *Business Week*, April 29, p. 91.

16　Seeking Liberal Markets

Learning Objectives

After reading this chapter, you should have a good understanding of:

LO1:　the evolution of the open skies concept
LO2:　the issues dividing the US and EU on liberalization
LO3:　the potential winners and losers in liberalization
LO4:　the prospects for continuing liberalization around the world

Key Terms and Concepts

ECA	TCAA (CAA)	Right of Establishment
AEA	Wet lease	Winners & Losers
Single Sky	Open Skies	Cabotage

Truly Open Skies

Europeans complained for many years that open skies was an 'American term' that did not in fact truly involve open markets, but represented an extension of what bilateral air service agreements had always been about, namely negotiating to achieve maximum national benefit (Lobbenberg, 1994; Sorenson, 1998). In other words, they did not believe the rhetoric of open skies; they charged that open skies bilateral agreements were simply another attempt by the US to dominate their aviation systems without allowing them an equal opportunity to compete (Wallerstein, 1991). In the aftermath of World War II, the inequality was largely due to external factors relating to the destruction of commercial aircraft and aviation infrastructure. The inequalities that existed after European infrastructure were replaced and its economy had recovered were created by a bilateral system that initially granted US carriers greater access to European markets than European airlines received into the US. Indeed, US carriers often had better access than European carriers into their own markets. This trend continued with the US push for Open Skies since the US defined open skies to include unlimited fifth freedom rights. The bilateral system with individual open skies European countries prevented European companies from taking full advantage of the European market, but it did allow US carriers to string together the fifth freedom (beyond) rights to fly all over the European market in a more profitable way (European Cockpit Association, 2000).

DOI: 10.4324/9781003405306-19

Given these perceived disparities in access, it was unsurprising that many of the European nations that had been opposed to the establishment of an open sky system in Chicago (1944) began to call for more liberal markets in aviation as the European Single Sky approached. Further, they wanted issues of ownership and domestic market access addressed to eliminate the remaining barriers within the aviation marketplace. When aviation barriers dropped in the EU with the 1997 establishment of the Single Sky, they proclaimed the US exercise of fifth freedom rights 'cabotage' and wanted the same privileges in the US (Sorenson, 1998). The European vision to extend the single aviation market created by the 15-nation EU across the Atlantic was embodied in the so-called Transatlantic Common Aviation Area (TCAA) proposal. At the time that the TCAA was first proposed, the rhetoric of liberalization was certainly in the 'best interests' of European carriers. The question was whether it would benefit US and Canadian carriers, individual consumers, and local communities on both sides of the Atlantic. The events of September 11th took this trans-Atlantic fight off the table for a time, but the stakes were too high to leave it off for long and the US would eventually find a need for its EU allies.

December 21, 2001, marked the signing of the Multilateral Agreement on the Liberalization of International Air Transportation (MALIAT). Multilateral treaties included all the basic principles of open skies to a group of countries with the addition of seventh freedom cargo services. For its part, the EU favored the concept of multilateralism. They had insisted for some time that European integration also placed the right to negotiate treaties with third party countries squarely on the 'European' community level rather than with individual countries. Bilateral agreements violated this principle, but the US had refused to consider a treaty between the US and combined countries of the EU because this eliminated the US ability to play one country off against another for more favorable rights (which was one of the complaints raised by the EU). Negotiations began between the EU and US in 2003 on such a treaty, with a final agreement completed in 2007. Even with the March 30, 2008, the start of the new multilateral EU–US Open Skies agreement was seen by the Europeans as only one step in a process toward an 'Open Aviation Area'. Ironically, the effects of the 2008 Global Financial Crisis (GFC) made it very difficult to determine if this agreement, decades in the making, had achieved its purpose, but talks continued, with second stage discussions beginning in 2010. Unfortunately, the 'Holy Grail" of cabotage in the US has yet to be achieved. Still, it is worth following this long journey to understand the issues and concerns in international liberalization before we explore the recent trends that reverse the road to liberalization and free aviation markets unhindered by politics and national interest.

The Long Road

In a 1995 policy paper on EU external aviation relations, the Association of European Airlines (AEA) put forth a proposal for a new regulatory framework between Europe and the US. The following year the Council of Ministers for the European Union issued a mandate to the Commission's work toward establishing a 'Common Aviation Area'. This Common Aviation Area proposed that air carriers from both sides of the Atlantic be allowed to provide their services within a common commercial framework that ensured competition on a fair and equal basis within an equivalent regulatory regime (AEA, 1999). Under a TCAA, the US and Europe were expected to 'harmonize' the following key areas: (1) rules governing market entry, access, and pricing, (2) rules governing airline ownership and the right of establishment, (3) rules governing competitive behavior and policies, and (4) rules governing leased aircraft.

Entry, Access, and Pricing

The basic objective of a TCAA (or the Common Aviation Area, as it was commonly called) was to insure unrestricted commercial opportunities allowing carriers (and market forces) to determine routes, markets, capacity, and pricing without discrimination anywhere within the countries party to a TCAA agreement. Under the proposal, a distinction would be made between TCAA countries as a group and third parties with whom the traditional bilateral air service agreements would still apply. In other words, the two parties to the bilateral would be the TCAA (as a single unit) and the third party. This was one of the general principles behind economic integration. One of the problems of a free trade area (the first step in economic integration) is that although members of the FTA have eliminated internal barriers to the movement of goods, the external tariff barriers to third party goods remain in place and may vary in such a way that third parties can benefit by selectively entering the FTA country with the most favorable tariff conditions and then gaining access from there to other member states (Hill, 2001). The AEA suggested a phased approach to establishing this new single aviation area that was like the EU liberalization that took place through a series of three packages (Chapter 10). The envisioned approach would have allowed EU countries the flexibility to negotiate with the US subject to achieving some minimum standards set by the overall parties (AEA, 1999).

Ownership and Right of Establishment

The right of establishment is a legal term relating to the national control of companies. In other words, TCAA proposed granting firms that are 1) majority-owned or controlled by nationals of any of the TCAA parties or their governments or 2) incorporated and have their principal place of business within the territory of a TCAA country equal rights and recognition. With the right of establishment comes the end of 'foreign national' restrictions on cross-border mergers, acquisitions, and entry. Under the second definition, airlines from third party countries could begin operations in a TCAA country and then gain the right to operate throughout TCAA airspace. It would, of course, be possible under option one for a country to apply for membership into the TCAA, thereby opening up their aviation system to all TCAA members in the process.

Competition Policy

In Chapter 12, the issue of anti-trust or competitiveness policy was discussed as it related to airlines and strategic alliances. From that discussion, it should be clear that although the basic concepts underlying both the US and EU policies are similar, the application of these policies differed in several significant ways. The Association of European Airlines (1999) suggested that common standards be developed in the following areas:

a   Basic criteria for granting exemptions, and in particular means of reconciling the relevant criteria of the EC competition rules and the US concept of the 'public interest';
b   The definition of the 'relevant market';
c   The concept of 'market power' as distinct from 'market share';
d   The notion of 'predatory behavior';
e   The question what 'essential facilities' airlines would have to share with each other;
f   The treatment of airline co-operative arrangements;
g   The nature of remedies and sanctions to be applied (AEA, 1999)

The AEA argued in their proposal that strategic alliances whose objective were to create TCAA airlines that were competitive in world markets should be considered by both EU and US standards to contribute to economic progress, the interests of consumers, and the interest of the public at large (AEA, 1999). Further, they believed that code sharing, blocked space, franchising, and other co-operative agreements, including activities involving tariff (fare) consultation for interline purposes, should be considered indispensable to the operation of strategic networks.

Leasing Aircraft

There were differences between the US and Europe over the question of wet leasing aircraft. The US prevented US airlines from wet leasing non-US-registered aircraft from other airlines and required that non-US leasers have route authority for the operation concerned. EU rules required registration in a member state but permitted this to be waived for short-term lease arrangements or other exceptional circumstances. The Association recommended that the US–EU rules be modified to allow any TCAA carrier to lease from or to any other TCAA carrier and that if third party leasing were permitted, a maximum percentage of fleet standard be set. These rules would be contingent upon all parties complying with established safety standards.

Raising Objections

The European Cockpit Association, which represented over 2,600 pilots from EU countries, endorsed TCAA with several reservations. First, they were concerned that relaxing ownership and leasing rules might create 'Flags of Convenience' in aviation similar to those developed in the maritime industry. In the United States, for example, the Jones Act requires that ships carrying cargo from one domestic port to another be built, maintained, and operated (and flagged) in the US, but the act does not have any such requirement for ships coming from a foreign port. This same act also applies to aviation in the US and is also related to the leasing issue. There are a number of foreign countries that allow open registries whereby ships owned by individuals or corporations in other countries may be flagged in their country rather than the country of the ship's owner. Critics have charged that the practice of open registries allowed owners to avoid the fees, taxes, safety requirements, and manning rules of their home country and posed a risk to crews, the marine environment, and the ports into which they enter (Morris, 1996; Ryan, 1996). The ECA was concerned that if TCAA included countries with safety and social standards below EU/US standards, there would be a cost incentive to flag aircraft in that country, leading to lowered safety standards for airline operations as well as the shifting of operations to common aviation areas offering lower taxes, wages, benefits, etc. This would obviously affect employment opportunities, local tax bases, and merchants in affected areas. The ECA also expressed concern at that time that liberalized ownership would result in the conversion or merging of alliances into mega-airlines dominated by US carriers with route structures and associated carriers being manipulated for cost-cutting purposes (ECA, 2000).

TCAA did not provoke a significant reaction from US aviation groups. Labor delegates at a 1999 aviation summit in the US cautioned against rapid change and any liberalization that failed 'to maintain the integrity of companies and to protect jobs' (Ott, 1999, p. 45). Their reasoning and concerns were very similar to the position stated by the ECA, although they did not even offer a conditional endorsement of TCAA. By and large, US airlines ignored the proposal. The US government was lukewarm to TCAA, although Rodney Slater, the then US Secretary of Transportation, committed the US to examining the proposal. This US reaction of 'committing to study the issues' was repeated when the President and CEO of Air Canada, Robert Milton, proposed a single aviation market for North America, stating that he 'urged the two governments to build on the success story of the 1995 Canada–US Open Skies Agreement by progressively removing all restrictions in order to arrive at a fully integrated, common air transport market with the United States' (Melnbardis, 2001, p. 1). Reacting to the Canadian proposal, American Airlines and United Airlines indicated that they supported the principle of liberalized air policy, but needed time to study the specifics (Chase & McAuthur, 2001).

The whole matter of Atlantic liberalization fell by the wayside the first time with the events of September 11th. Not only did the US feel that it had more important issues to consider, but security considerations suddenly loomed much larger on everyone's agenda, as did the crisis in international aviation. The fact that US airlines were particularly hard hit by these events did not encourage US airlines or the government that represented them to consider any efforts to open the US market. Further. the US Congress became increasingly concerned about issues of foreign ownership and control of important US industries and assets. US carriers would struggle back to profitability by 2006 only to be hit with rising fuel prices and the GFC which again sidelined the idea of a Common Aviation Area (CAA).

Balancing Acts

Before looking at the possible effects of a CAA and potential winners and losers in open aviation markets, it might be instructive to examine why it might make sense for the US to consider it (aside from the political pressure of EU allies). To start, the TCAA/CAA is the first time that the United States has been officially asked (or considered) trading roughly equivalent domestic markets. A quick look back at Table 9.2 shows that the Open Skies Agreements of the past essentially involved countries with significantly smaller domestic markets. Ideology aside, it never made 'economic sense' for the United States to trade access to its large domestic market for the domestic markets of Singapore, The Netherlands, or even Germany. Given some of the differences between US and EU transportation markets noted in Chapter 10, namely more developed EU intermodal competition and charter market and the higher domestic departures of the US (Sinha, 2001), these markets appear to be roughly similar in size, particularly if we add in the estimated population of Canada.

This 'equivalent markets' argument raised a question about the proposed single North American market proposed by Air Canada. While the two countries have roughly equal land masses (9,976,140 square kilometers for Canada and 9,629,091 for the US), there is a major difference in terms of the two countries' population sizes (CIA Factbook, 2023). Much of the Canadian land mass is in the far north where the Canadian government has declared many communities in need of essential services, particularly in the winter months, when air service is a vital link to the outside world. US carriers had little interest in gaining access to these markets and under open skies had already gained access to the southern Canadian markets. Air Canada, on the other hand, had a great deal to gain from single markets. The Air Transport Association of Canada, which represents a number of Canadian carriers, supported the idea of 'modified sixth-freedom rights' between the US and Canada, but this wording appeared to be only a limited endorsement of the single market concept and probably reflected the view of 'other Canadian' carriers, not Air

Canada. The chairman of WestJet Airlines was on record as opposing the concept of a single market, arguing that it would do nothing to lessen the grip of Air Canada on the domestic market and would put Canadian carriers at a disadvantage since they paid much more for fuel than their US counterparts (Chase & McAuthur, 2001). In short, it did not appear that any North American carrier had anything to gain except Air Canada. While the Canadian government considered a single market approach as a way of deflecting consumer complaints over the decision to allow Air Canada to become a monopoly, the US government was always likely to receive a great deal of pressure from the US airline industry to oppose a deal.

A second issue that argued in favor of CAA was that the safety and security levels of European carriers were equal, if not higher, than those of their US counterparts. European airports had a longer history of incorporated security designs and policies that limited access in gate areas to ticketed passengers, encouraged bag matching, and other sophisticated screening techniques. In a post-9/11 environment, this was an important consideration, and a CAA could facilitate closer cooperation on improving these areas. Finally, the European Commission was committed to implementing a multilateral aviation approach for the EU to end the current system of bilateral air service agreements. In 1998 the Commission launched a case against eight member states with US Open Skies agreements claiming that these agreements breached single market rules because they disadvantaged other member nations. Further, they charged that the bilateral agreements infringed on the EU external competence in foreign affairs. In January 2002, the European Court of Justice ruled that these countries had broken EU laws in signing such bilaterals. The key issue is the nationality requirements (contained in Article 52) and Article 307 of the EC treaty that requires states to make every effort to amend international agreements that violate EC law. In effect, the EU had declared themselves a single market for external purposes and repeated their belief that extensive fifth freedom rights exercised by US carriers were cabotage. The Commission demanded reciprocal access to the US for their carriers, as well as ownership privileges. A 2005 compromise was opposed by the US Congress, throwing the matter back to the respective governments, but the EU was clearly determined to keep the pressure on the US concerning liberalization.

Winners and Losers

Calculations were made on both sides of the Atlantic about the costs and benefits of single markets. These calculations included consumer groups, airlines, employee organizations, local communities, and national governments. In this section, the issues relating to these group-specific calculations are discussed. The next section will discuss any evidence of effects on various groups as a result of the EU–US Open Skies.

Consumers

General economic theory suggests that consumers benefit from having more choices of products, services, and firms. Single aviation markets do promise to broaden the choices of consumers. However, the same problems may arise in this next phase of liberalization that have occurred in earlier deregulation efforts. First, the heightened competition of earlier periods could be jeopardized by failures to enforce laws regarding predatory behavior and merger/acquisition, leading to high failures rates of 'new entrants' and mergers that result in the concentration of the market in a few select carriers. Second, consumers in some markets may lose service as US–EU carriers redeploy their fleets to new, more lucrative markets. Given the cost structure of the entering international carriers, they would likely concentrate on higher yield markets, with the all-important business travelers. Markets vacated by these carriers in Europe would be open for low-cost carrier entry. In fact, given the changes in Europe caused by the expansion of Ryanair, EU carriers might relish competition in the US. In any event, neither the North Americans nor Europeans were likely to drop their right to ensure that essential services are provided to local communities. The difficulty lies in harmonizing the implementation of the rules and policies that define relevant markets, frequency requirements, carrier types, etc. in the determination of essential services.

Airlines

Sorting out the potential winners and losers among the airlines is in large part a function of two factors – relative costs and relative service levels. One major study has examined the cost competitiveness of international airlines at the end of the twentieth century (Oum & Yu, 1998). They examined the cost of airline inputs (labor, fuel, aircraft, capital, and materials) and the revenue of airlines (outputs) from passengers, freight, and mail to determine the efficiency of carriers and their cost competitiveness. As mentioned briefly in Chapter 9, almost thirty years of deregulation in US markets had created carriers with much lower costs and higher levels of productivity and cost competitiveness. In the Oum and Yu (1998) study, only British Airways and KLM were close to achieving a level of cost competitiveness comparable to that of their US counterparts. Of course, if many of the European carriers did begin to operate in the US, they would likely be able to reduce many of these costs, at least in US operations, since fuel prices, the benefits component of labor costs, and many related fees all tend to be lower in the US. Oum and Yu's (1998) study did not consider the low-cost European carriers such as Ryanair and EasyJet, who may well have had costs structures more comparable to those of Southwest in the US. From a firm point of view, single markets increases strategic flexibility by allowing firms to move assets as well as perform work where it makes the most sense to do so from a cost and logistical standpoint. This flexibility was precisely the concern of labor groups, as we will see in a minute. The fact that European airlines recovered more quickly from September 11, and that they were able to post profits well in advance of their US counterparts, probably alleviated the old concern about US carrier dominance in alliances, possible mergers, etc., but 2008 and the slow recovery in Europe again gave US carriers a slight upper hand in performance.

The second issue is relative service levels between US and European carriers. At least some of the cost differences between US–EU carriers were the result of the generally higher levels of service provided by EU carriers. In an environment where carriers are free to operate anywhere within the single market, there are some carriers that may clearly be disadvantaged by high cost structures and poor quality. At the margin, consumers will decide the issue of price and service level. In general, the trend in the US has been toward viewing air transportation as a basic commodity that is cheap and relatively indistinguishable from one provider to another and shifting toward a model of basic fares plus ancillary fees. European markets are also increasingly moving in this direction, given the success of their own low-cost carriers such as Ryanair. Nationality issues aside, single markets increase the competition on international routes where service-level issues are considered more important and would tend to favor the European carriers.

Labor Groups

Single markets open up the very real possibility that firms will shift operations from one region to another or utilize labor from one area over another as a means of reducing costs. This shift has occurred in other liberalizing industries and is very likely to occur in aviation. Pilots, who account for more labor costs than do mechanics and flight attendants, would be at a higher risk of replacement by lower-wage colleagues. It should be noted that the cost of labor is not the only issue that managers would consider; the productivity of labor can balance this cost in the long run. Oum and Yu (1998) found that while Thai Airways had input costs that were 52.1 percent lower than American Airlines (22.4 percent of which were attributable to labor), in terms of overall efficiency (outputs to inputs) Thai was 42.9 percent less efficient. A higher-cost, but more efficient labor force can still be cost-competitive. In many western countries, productivity gains have been achieved through the adoption of improved information systems, but productivity can also be improved through more flexible work rules, attention to work flows, cross-functional team implementation, and other redesign options. Bankruptcy allowed most of the major US carriers to reduce their labor (and pension) costs even further in the first decade of the twenty-first century. US network carriers had removed 13 million seats of capacity in 2012 alone. US consolidation had also created redundancy that directly eliminated jobs (Saporito, 2013).

Local Communities

If we define local communities broadly as nations, then there are clearly risks involved in single markets. High-cost, low-productivity, and low-service carriers will probably not survive without government assistance. The EU had to deal with this issue as part of its integration and was forced to consider under what conditions national carriers could receive government assistance. The EU faced this issue early in its existence with Sabena in Belgium, then with flag carriers in Eastern Europe, and, most recently, with COVID Pandemic aid. More narrowly defined, there will be some cities and city-pair markets that will see reduced service as carriers adjust their route structure toward higher-margin routes. Many of these markets could continue to receive service from low-cost carriers, but the quality and frequency of service is likely to change.

National Governments

There is a saying that 'all politics is local.' Given the historic attachment of localities to their airlines and the strategic flexibility that single markets give to airlines, there will be pressure on governments to intervene in the process to influence local outcomes. Economists talk in terms of long-run equilibriums and structural adjustments; politicians are concerned about the next election. Predicting the outcome of this political wrangling is far more difficult, particularly when questions of local, national, and supranational jurisdiction, responsibilities, and calculations come into play.

Evidence to Date

In 2013, the Centre for Aviation (CAPA) released a report on the EU–US Open skies market five years after the agreement went into effect. Traffic growth had been modest to flat after a 6.2 percent drop in 2009, although North Atlantic traffic growth was close to world rates for 2008. For airlines, load factors and yields had improved. While CAPA credited these modest improvements to the Open Skies, it argued that the Global Financial Crisis (GFC) dampened the effect on expected results. What appeared to be clear was that the mega-alliances dominated traffic across the North Atlantic, controlling 83 percent of the capacity. The American Enterprise Institute review of 2010 was even harsher in tone. It noted that EU consumers could find far cheaper airfares there than consumers in many US markets. The reason for this disparity, according to the report, was US opposition to cabotage and foreign ownership (Milke, 2010). IATA (2006) examined the results of air service liberalization and found 12–35 percent traffic growth with associated growth in aviation system employment, but none of these studies truly spoke to the benefits that many proponents promised – more choices, lower fares, better secondary outcomes (employment, community growth). Clearly, US carriers have never been convinced that anything beyond traditional open skies serves their best interest. With no clear sign of consumer benefits and some dire predictions of labor and small communities' losses, there is no political will to move beyond the talk of free markets to test the possibilities of single market extension.

Reversing Trends

Brexit, the UK's departure from the EU, was an unprecedented reversal of liberalization. While most of the world's attention was focused on the broader implications of Brexit, there were major concerns within the industry about its impact on aviation, some of which have not yet been resolved. Third and fourth freedoms were reserved for both parties with no limits on capacity, frequency, or aircraft, but cabotage was removed. Airlines that took advantage of these rights before Brexit, the LCCs, established subsidiaries to preserve their networks. Brexit eliminated fifth freedom for passenger rights, but not for cargo if the UK and the individual EU nation agree. EU carriers with high percentages of non-EU ownership have reduced this ownership. Until the end of the transition period, the UK is still a party to 17 air service agreements between the EU and outside countries. The UK and the US signed a new bilateral in November 2020 (Centre for Aviation, 2021). For UK airlines, Brexit has required new operating licenses to operate across the EU. In fact, they must obtain a license for each individual country into which they wish to operate. UK airlines are subject to the same regulations as non-EU airlines, meaning that they must obtain visa and travel documents for passengers. There is some evidence that Brexit has changed UK consumer travel with a shift in demand to on-EU destination, although this might also be due to the decline of the pound (Varley, 2023). It remains unclear what Brexit might mean for domestic travel as this was largely provided by LCCs who might decide to redeploy assets to European markets where there is more flexibility.

If Brexit sent a shockwave through the aviation world, then Ukraine sent the system into shock. Before we begin to discuss this issue, remember that the first freedom addresses the right to overfly a country WITH PERMISSION. No country accepts the notion that foreign aircraft may enter their airspace without prior approval. Unauthorized aircraft may be intercepted and escorted out of airspace. The Soviet Union shot down Korean Air Lines 007 when it strayed into their airspace and did not respond (Tikkanen, 2023). There are several reasons why countries might close their airspace or parts of their airspace. The US grounded all aircraft and closed its airspace in the wake of 9/11 (Liles, 2023). Airspace may be closed temporarily in some areas for special events, air shows, fireworks. Airspace may be closed to commercial traffic over military bases and government buildings. Airspace may be closed due to system issues – outages, crowding, etc. Airspace may be closed to all or some traffic in areas of military conflict. The War in Ukraine has seen this latter kind of closure happen on a much grander scale as the UK and EU banned Russian aircraft from flying over or entering their airspace at the start of the conflict and were soon followed by the US. Russia reciprocated (Collins, Liptak, & Sullivan, 2022). Even if airlines were not concerned with the risk of flying through 'enemy airspace', they were ill-prepared for the added travel time and cost of flying around this much-closed airspace. This is but the biggest example of airspace closure in conflict. The OPSGroup (2023) website also lists the following active conflict closures: Iran/Iraq, North Korea, China/Taiwan, Turkey. Other closures include Algeria/Morocco, Azerbaijan/Armenian, and Sudan/South Sudan (Alcock, 2023; SafeAirspace, 2023; Sharp, 2023). In other words, global airspace may be more closed than at any time since World War II. Consumers and airlines are facing changes in routes (particularly into Asia) that mean longer flying times, higher costs, and higher fares. Countries such as Russia face the loss of substantial revenue previously paid to traverse their airspace. What all of this means for a post-war world is unclear, but it has raised issues that consumers, airlines, and countries will have to consider going forward.

Moving Ahead

After years of negotiations and setbacks, the EU and US finally reached a multilateral agreement to open the trans-Atlantic in 2008, just in time for the GFC. The agreement did remove restrictions on the number of carriers allowed to fly trans-Atlantic routes and allowed carriers to fly from any EU city to any American city and onward to a third destination. From the US perspective, it achieved one of its major goals in opening up Heathrow Airport, but not until the long awaited Terminal 5 was opened. The Europeans did not get the right of cabotage in the US, but many of the restrictions of the Fly America Act, which required all federal government travel to occur on US carriers, were lifted in 2007 (US General Services Administration, 2023). Ownership and cabotage remained critical issues for debate between the EU and US in the second stage. While government officials on both sides suggested that the new deal would create 80,000 jobs and generate 12 billion euros in economic benefits, the evidence remained unclear and unconvincing (Center for Aviation, 2013; EurActiv, 2007). Of course, some industry watchers never expected much beyond a few introductory low fares and new flights targeted to the already well-trafficked, high-yield markets (Wilen, 2008).

In short, there was no 'Big Bang' approach to trans-Atlantic liberalization or 'Big Bang' benefits to moving the liberalization forward. While the Europeans would have preferred an agreement that went farther than the current one, most EU groups were satisfied with greater initial access. The US never seriously considered cabotage and it is unclear if there are any conditions that might cause serious consideration. It is also true that whenever the world gets close to considering more liberal changes, a crisis arises that threatens the world's airlines and halts or reverses any progress. At some point in the future, industry will have to grapple with what might be its greatest challenge – climate change. If, as some claim, the world cannot afford aviation, then restriction, not liberalization will be the order of the day. We will deal more with this issue in Chapters 19 and 20. For now, the industry is considering a world after the Russian–Ukrainian war. Which way will the liberalization pendulum swing?

Questions

1 What does open skies mean to the US? To the EU?
2 Explain the issue of right of establishment.

3 What was the TCAA proposal? Discuss its history and progress.
4 What role does competition policy play in liberalization?
5 Who stands to gain from open aviation markets? Who is likely to oppose them, and why?
6 What evidence is there that the EU–US Open Skies agreement has produced positive benefits?
7 What does Brexit mean for aviation liberalization?
8 How has the Russian–Ukrainian war affected liberalization?

References

Alcock, C. (2023) Azerbaijan shuts Armenian Airspace as conflict escalates. AIN. Available at: https://www.ainonline.com/aviation-news/air-transport/2023-09-19/azerbaijan-shuts-armenian-airspace-conflict-escalates

Association of European Airlines (1999), *Towards a transatlantic common aviation area: AEA policy statement*, September.

Centre for Aviation (2013) The North Atlantic: The state of the market five years on from EU–US Open Skies. Available at: https://centreforaviation/analysis/the-north-atlantic-the-state-of-the-market-five-years-on-fromeu-us-open-skies-100315

Centre for Aviation (2021) Brexit and aviation: All's well that ends. Well, almost... Available at centreforaviation.com/analysis/Brexit-and-aviation-alls-well-that-ends

Chase, S. & McAuthur, K. (2001), 'US warm to proposed increased air competition,' *Global Interactive*, December 8.

CIA Factbook (2023), www.odci.goc/cia/publications/factbook

Collins, K., Liptak, K., & Sullivan, K. (2022) Biden announces ban on Russian aircraft from US airspace. CNN. Available at: https://www.cnn.com/2022/03/01/politics/russian-aircraft-to-be-banned-us-airspace/index.html

EurActiv (EU News, Policy Positions) (2007), 'EU–US Open Skies agreement' Available at: https://www.euractiv.com/en/transport/eu-us-open-skies

European Cockpit Association (2000), *From EASA to TCAA: The flight crews view on a new regulatory framework in aviation*, ECA, Brussels.

European Commission (2013) International aviation: United States. Available at: https://ec.europa.eu/transport/modes/air/international_aviation/country_index/united_states_en.htm

Hill, C.W. (2001), *Global business*, 2nd ed., Irwin-McGraw Hill, Boston.

IATA (2006) The economic impact of air service liberalization, Available at: https://www.iata.org/en/iata-repository/publications/economic-reports/the-economic-impacts-of-air-service-liberalization---intervistas/

Liles, J. (2023) Was 2023 the first time since 9/11 that the FAA grounded all US flights. Snopes. Available at: https://www.snopes.com/fact-check/faa-orders-flights-grounded-first-time-since-911/

Lobbenberg, A. (1994), 'Government relations on the North Atlantic: A case study of five Europe–USA relationships,' *Journal of Air Transport Management*, 1, pp. 47–62.

Melnbardis, R. (2001), 'Air Canada wants open US–Canada air market,' *Reuters Newswire*, December 6.

Milke, M. (2010) Economics: Regulation outlook. Available at: https://www.aei.org/article/economics/open-skies/

Morris, J. (1996), '*Flags of convenience give owners a paper refuge*,' Houston Chronicle online edition, www.chron.com

OPSGroup (2023) Active conflict zones. Available at: https://ops.group/blog/airspace-risk-conflict-zones-and-security-in-2023/

Ott, J. (1999), 'Aviation summit yields EU plan for open market,' *Aviation Week and Space Technology*, December 13, pp. 43–45.

Oum, T. H. & Yu, C. (1998), *Winning airlines: Productivity and cost competitiveness of the world's major airlines*, Kluwer Academic Publishers, Boston.

Ryan, G. J. (1996), 'Testimony by George J. Ryan, President-Lake Carriers' Association', *Presented before the House Subcommittee on Coast Guard and Maritime Transportation*, June 12, Washington, D.C.

SafeAirspace (2023) Sudan. Available at: https://safeairspace.net/sudan/#:~:text=Following%20a%20military%20coup%20in,at%20the%20end%20of%20April

Saporito, B. (2013) Cabin pressure, *Time Magazine*, September 9, pp. 36–41.

Sharp, A. (2023) Algeria cracks open diplomatic ties to assist Morocco. FP World Brief. Available at: https://foreignpolicy.com/2023/09/11/morocco-earthquake-algeria-reopens-airspace-humanitarian-aid/

Sinha, D. (2001), *Deregulation and Liberalization of the Airline Industry: Asia, Europe, North America, and Oceania*, Ashgate Publishing, Aldershot, UK.

Sorenson, F. (1998), 'Open Skies in Europe,' *FAA commercial aviation forecast conference proceedings: Overcoming barriers to world competition and growth, March 12-13, Washington, DC*, pp. 125–131.

Tikkanen, A. (2023) Korean Air Lines Flight 007, Britannica. Available at: https://www.britannica.com/event/Korean-Air-Lines-flight-007

US General Services Administration (2023) Fly America Act. Available at: https://www.gsa.gov/policy-regulations/policy/travel-management-policy-overview/fly-america-act

Varley, L. (2023) How has Brexit affected UK airlines and air travel. AviationSource. Available at: https://aviationsourcenews.com/analysis/how-has-brexit-affected-uk-airlines-and-air-travel/#:~:text=UK%20airlines%20are%20now%20subject,and%20additional%20costs%20for%20airlines

Wallerstein, I. (1991), *Geopolitics and geoculture: Essays on the changing world-system*, Cambridge University Press, Cambridge.

Wilen, J. (2008), 'Open Skies: More flights, same fares', Available at: https://biz.yahoo.com/ap/080326/open_skies.html

17 Spreading the Promise

Learning Objectives

After reading this chapter, you should have a good understanding of:

LO1: the issues that have hindered aviation development in Africa, Latin America, and other developing regions
LO2: how the regional/country issues have been addressed
LO3: what the international community might do to help
LO4: how these actions would change the historic nature of the international aviation industry

Key Terms, Concepts & People

Flight Safety Foundation	Yamoussoukro Declaration	ECA
Asymmetric Liberalization	GATS	Open Skies
Waiver of Nationality		

Problems and Promises

Aviation and globalization promised to transform domestic and global economies by linking distant communities in an ever-shrinking, complex web of interaction. Along these links flowed a vast variety of goods, services, and people. As the flow increased, income, standards of living, and the general welfare of the people were expected to increase too. This was the promise of globalization and aviation, but reality has not always lived up to the promise, and some regions around the world have yet to benefit. While the Middle East 3 (ME3) have changed how we look at that region, Latin America and Africa did not have such visible successes. (The ME3 carriers refer to the three Middle East airlines which use a hub and spoke model: Qatar Airways, Emirates, and Etihad Airways.) Latin American airlines had high costs and limited global reach which North American airlines exploited to their benefit, but rapid growth in low-cost carriers (LCCs) has changed this picture. LCCs began the process of restructuring to reduce costs and the Global Pandemic accelerated the process through bankruptcy and consolidation. Consolidation has now created four large airlines, who are each part of a global alliance. Combine these changes with

DOI: 10.4324/9781003405306-20

rising standards of living and the region has become one of the fastest-growing areas of the aviation world, with projected annual growth of 5 percent (Baldanza, 2022). While there are still some issues of access and connectivity in the Caribbean, where IATA estimates that the air travel industry provides US$36 illion in GDP annually, air travel in June 2023 increased by 31 percent from the same time last year. US carriers are adding routes from a growing number of US cities. Even better news for this region is the expansion of intra-Caribbean service (Garbuno, 2021; Mahor, 2023).

This leaves the African continent still seeking the promise, but even here there are signs of hope. The purpose of this chapter is to explore the last major region of the world seeking to create a sustainable civil aviation industry. It will identify the issues and problems holding back progress as well as ways that the world community and national governments can work to spread the promise.

Africa – Understanding the Problems

Africa is the second-largest continent in the world and possesses the population base and the geographically challenging terrain to make it ideal for air transportation. Africa accounts for 18 percent of the global population, but it only accounts for 2.1 percent of the world's air transport activities. The International Air Transport Association (IATA) has recently announced a new initiative, Focus Africa, to address the issues holding the region back. It has highlighted six factors that need to be addressed: infrastructure constraints, high costs, lack of connectivity, regulatory impediments, the slow adoption of global standards, and skills shortages. IATA hopes to create partnerships between public and private stakeholders to address six critical areas: safety, connectivity, infrastructure, finance and distribution, sustainability, and future skills (IATA, 2023a).

Before exploring these aviation constraints, it is important to explore the single greatest macro constraint – African poverty. Before the start of the Global Pandemic, economic growth in Africa had reached 4.6 percent a year, a rate some thought impossible two decades ago. By 2022, the growth rate had dropped to 3.6 percent, largely because of the impact of COVID. According to recent statistics, there are 546 million people in Africa living in poverty, which is around half of the continent's population. While the Economic Commission for Africa (ECA, 2023) is predicting a 2023 growth rate of 3.9 percent, the region is particularly vulnerable to global headwinds such as rising fuel prices, interest rates, and recession (ECA, 2023). Table 17.1 looks briefly at each country in terms of land area, population, GDP in 2012 and GDP in 2021. Overall, poverty is concentrated in the sub-Saharan region, with Central Africa posting the highest rate of extreme poverty (54.8 percent) followed by Southern Africa (45.1 percent). Western and Eastern Africa fare better with rates of 36.8 percent and 33.8 percent, respectively. Looking country by country, there are marked differences as well. South Sudan had a poverty rate above 80 percent in 2019 while that in countries like Morocco, Algeria, Libya, and Egypt was at or below 3 percent. Unfortunately, high fertility rates have tended to mean that economic growth rates translate into smaller improvements in per capita income (Aikins & McLachlan, 2022). Still, some countries did post gains. Kenya's estimated population in 2021 was 44 million and the GDP per capita was US$1,800. The population was estimated at 57 million in 2023 and the GDP per capita was US$2,500. Despite a population growth of 13 million, this country managed to more than double its GDP per capita. This is no small feat, but there is still much to accomplish.

Table 17.1 Information on African Countries (A through Z)

Country	Area*	Population**	GDP (2012)***	GDP (2021)****
Algeria	2,381,741	44,758,398	7,300	11,000
Angola	1,246,700	35,981,281	6,100	5,900
Benin	112,622	14,219,908	1,600	3.300
Botswana	581,730	2,417,596	15,700	14,800
Burkina Faso	274,200	22,489,126	1,400	2,200
Burundi	27,830	13,162,952	600	700
Cameroon	475,440	30,135,752	2,300	3,700
Cabo Verde	4,033	603,901	4,400	6,100
Central African Republic	622,984	5,552,228	900	800
Chad	1,284,000	18,523,165	2,500	1,400
Comoros	2,235	888,378	1,300	3,200
Congo, Democratic Republic of the	2,344,858	111,859,928	400	1,100
Congo, Republic of the	342,000	5,677.493	4,600	3,200
Côte d'Ivoire	322,463	29,344,847	1,700	5,300
Djibouti	23,200	976,143	2,600	4,900
Egypt	1,001,450	109,546,720	6,500	11,600
Equatorial Guinea	28,051	704,001	7 (6)	26,500
Eritrea	117,600	6,274,796	700	1,600
Ethiopia	1,104,300	116,462,712	1,300	2,300
Gabon	267,667	2,397,368	18,100	13,800
Gambia, The	11,295	2,468,569	1,900	2,100
Ghana	238,533	33,846,114	3,300	5,400
Guinea	245,857	13,607,249	1,100	2,600
Guinea-Bissau	36,125	2,078.820	1,200	1,800
Kenya	580,367	57,052,004	1,800	4,700
Lesotho	30,355	2,210,646	2,100	2,300
Liberia	111,369	5,506,280	700	1,400
Libya	1,759,540	7,252,573	11,900	22,000
Madagascar	587,041	28,812,195	900	1,500
Malawi	118,484	21,279,597	1,100	1,500
Mali	1,240,192	21,359,722	1,100	2,100
Mauritania	1,030,700	4,244,878	2,100	5,300
Mauritius	2,040	1,309,448	15,400	21,000
Morocco	446,550	37,067,420	5,200	8,100
Mozambique	799,380	32,513,805	1,200	1,200
Namibia	824,292	2,777,232	7,800	9,100
Niger	1,267,000	25,396,840	800	1,200
Nigeria	923,768	230,842,743	2,700	4,900
Rwanda	26,338	13,400,541	1,400	2,200
Saint Helena, Ascension, and Tristan da Cunha	308	7,935	7,800	7,800
São Tomé and Príncipe	964	220,372	2,100	4,100
Senegal	196,722	18,384,660	2,000	3,500
Seychelles	455	97,617	25,000	28,800
Sierra Leone	71,740	8.908,040	1,300	1,600
Somalia	637,657	12,693,796	600	1,100
South Africa	1,219,090	58,048,332	11,300	13,300
South Sudan	644,329	12,118,379	1,100	1,600
Sudan	1,861,484	49,197,555	2,500	3,700
Tanzania	947,300	65,642,682	1,600	2,600

(*Continued*)

Table 17.1 (Continued)

Country	Area*	Population**	GDP (2012)***	GDP (2021)****
Togo	56,785	8,703,961	1,100	2,100
Tunisia	163,610	11,976,182	9,700	10,400
Uganda	241,038	47,729,952	1,400	2,200
Zambia	752,618	20,216,029	1,700	3,200
Zimbabwe	390,757	15,418,774	600	2,100

Source: CIA Factbook as of October 2, 2023; https://www.oag.com/blog/african-aviation-another-crossroads
   * Square Km
  ** Estimated October 2023 figures
 *** Estimated 2012
**** Estimated 2023

Aviation Issues

Safety was the first issue highlighted by Focus Africa. In 2002, the Flight Safety Foundation reported that Africa had the highest level of accidents per departure of any region in the world, at nearly 9.8 accidents per 1 million departures, compared to a world average of 1.2 accidents per 1 million departures. This rate of accidents is attributed to poor training for pilots, controllers, and regulatory officials, poor-to-non-existent radar coverage, high numbers of non-precision approaches, and non-enforced or non-existent legislation (Phillips, 2002). A decade later, IATA (2013) reported the accident rate at 10.85 accidents per million flight hours, compared to a world average of 2. In other words, there had still been little or no progress in the safety areas. IATA, working with the International Civil Aviation Organization (ICAO), developed the African Strategic Safety Improvement Plan 2012–2015 as well as the Operational Safety Audit System (IOSA) to help improve airline safety (ETN, 2013). In 2019 the accident rate stood at 10.34 per million departures, but this did not experience a significant drop to 3.64 in 2020, helped by the events of the Global Pandemic (ICAO, 2021). IATA's Operational Safety Audit (IOSA) reported that there was no jet hull loss in Africa in 2020 and 2021, although there were increases in turboprop hull losses in both years (IATA, 2022). While it is too early to predict the post-Pandemic safety outlook, there are signs of progress.

Connectivity is another issue to be addressed. Traffic patterns in the region tended to reflect Africa's colonial past running north to south, placing African airlines at the wrong end of the route, i.e. principal flows originate in the northern, wealthy nations of Europe where passengers tend to fly on European national carriers (Graham, 1995). The ME3 began to shift these patterns, pulling African passengers bound to Europe or Asia to Dubai, Doha, or Abu Dhabi. This still placed African airlines in competition with bigger, better-funded carriers. For African carriers to compete effectively, they must provide equal or superior service in a number of areas, including flight punctuality, in-flight service, superior aircraft, comfortable seats, clean cabins, seats, and washrooms, good food, efficient reservation systems, competitive pricing, good check-in, attractive frequent flyer programs, and superior first and business class accommodations at a price reasonably close to that of their competitors. At least seven of these areas are heavily dependent on the quality of the aircraft. Unfortunately, the aircraft of many African airlines were aging and investment in new aircraft was often non-existent. These ageing aircraft also did not meet the noise restrictions imposed by many countries and are, therefore, not eligible to land at many international airports. Aircraft leasing was not well developed in Africa at the end of the last century, making the acquisition of new aircraft difficult for many carriers who might have found this a preferred way to modernize their fleets (Abeyratne, 1998). Still, there is some cause for hope. There are increasing signs that demand is growing for domestic and regional flights in Africa (Skyllence, 2023). There are now more scheduled airlines operating in Africa and 45 percent of these carriers are African-domiciled. Unfortunately, only eight of these carriers are LCCs and their penetration and growth rates are very low (Grant, 2023).

In 2019, ICAO undertook a gap analysis of the aviation infrastructure in Africa. Overall, the survey concluded that there remains very little connectivity in the African continent, with most flights falling in the direct, no stop category. Only 30 percent of African international passengers traveled through connecting flights. Twelve states had no international flights served by African carriers. Thirty-five countries had less than 20 international flights per day. Forty states had less than two million international passengers a year. Seven states accounted for over 90 percent of the total aircraft fleet and the average load factors for African airlines was below 70 percent (ICAO, 2019). All these factors have implications for the next critical area for African aviation.

As the ICAO noted above, the face of African aviation is very complex, but there are some consistent themes. First, the cost of operating an airline in Africa is much higher than in other regions of the world. Jet fuel is almost 12 percent higher while the cost of maintenance exceeds global averages. Financial distribution has also become a major issue, with a 10 percent increase in blocked funds just at the beginning of 2023. It is estimated that 66 percent of the blocked funds worldwide are in Africa (Karuwa, 2023). These funds are the proceeds of ticket sales made in local currency that cannot be recouped due to the nonavailability of foreign exchange. Nigeria alone was blocking US$812 illion, causing Emirates Airlines to suspend flights in November 2022 (Casey, 2023). While every country has a somewhat different reason for blocking these funds, it threatens the distribution system that most of the world's airlines have come to count on and risks other international airlines cutting off service.

In at least one area – sustainability – Africa can claim to be on par with the rest of the world's airlines. IATA has committed to Net Zero by 2050 as their initiative to combat climate change and carbon. While many of the leading international airlines have conducted demonstration flights with some percentage of renewable fuels, as we discuss in Chapter 20, none have made any significant progress toward this goal (Harris, 2023).

IATA has projected that Africa will need over 50,000 aviation professionals over the next 20 years. This includes 15,000 pilots, 17,000 technicians, and 23,000 cabin crew. While Africa is not alone in facing pilot shortages, it does face several challenges not found in other regions. One of the most significant is the lack of training infrastructure and the high cost of the training that does exist. Ethiopian Airlines is addressing this issue by upgrading its own flight training center into a comprehensive university with the support of aircraft manufacturers (Karuwa, 2023). Developing high-quality, domestically trained aviation professionals would be a significant step toward creating a more successful industry in Africa.

Addressing the Issues

Given the historic lack of domestic demand, the need to compete globally with larger, better-established carriers, and the limited funding for aviation development, African nations have attempted to join together. In 1961, ten African nations signed the Treaty on Air Transport in Africa, popularly known as the Yaounde Treaty. Under Articles 77 and 79 of the Chicago Convention, which provide for joint or international operating organizations, these nations established Air Afrique to operate international services between contracting states and other nations and also to provide domestic service within the territories of contracting states. The second major event in African aviation was the Yamoussoukro Declaration on a New African Air Transport Policy (1988). The Yamoussoukro Declaration (YD) committed African states to achieving the total integration of their airlines through the liberal exchange of air traffic rights, the use of an unbiased computer reservations system, and other joint aviation infrastructure developments. The first phase of the Declaration was expected to last two years and result in recommendations for integrating African airlines with the rest of the world. Phase two was to be a three-year effort dedicated to the commercial aspects of aviation, including the integration of CRS, the joint purchasing of spare parts, maintenance, and overhaul equipment, the training of personnel, etc. In Phase three, African carriers were to be integrated into a consortium of competitive entities that would bring about sustained progress in air transport in Africa (Abeyratne, 1998, p. 34). Originally, the Declaration was to be implemented in two years, but this was extended to 2006. Progress has been made in a few areas, including the establishment of the Air Tariff Coordination Forum of Africa to assist airlines in adapting to international air tariff policies, the opening up of South Africa to intra-African aviation, increased fifth freedom rights, and more cross-border activity, but more challenges remain (Abeyratne, 1998; Kajange, 2009). As of 2019, only 28 of the 44 nations were implementing the YD. There was no independent dispute oversight, unified competition rules, harmonized taxation, airport charges regime, or consumer rights protections (Bryan, Cave, Leighton, & Paisner, 2019).

Given the slow progress toward liberalization, several suggestions have been advanced. One suggestion is to focus on relaxing ownership rules to help create more connections and coordinate direct investment (Bryan, Cave, Leighton, & Paisner, 2019). Unfortunately, relaxing ownership rules and encouraging consolidation, particularly across borders, has not seemed to deliver promised results even when attempted. Another possibility is to pursue an African airline alliance around the concept of commercial benefits (networks, connectivity, etc.). As global alliances have discovered, ownership is not necessary, but cooperation and the willingness to engage in long term partnership are (Grant, 2023).

As IATA continues with 'Focus Africa', they have reported that the first quarter of 2023 saw an 87.1 percent year-on-year growth in revenue passenger miles for African airlines with northern and eastern Africa experiencing the most significant growth (IATA, 2023b). Further, they are projecting passenger traffic to double to 260 million passengers by 2035 (Campbell, 2023). This projection, and the new focus by IATA and other aviation organizations, public and private, is certainly good news, but many experts have argued that the developed nations could do more, but have not.

Helping the Developing World

It has been suggested that developed nations could do more than offer funding and technical advice. They could consider adopting a number of the recommendations by international agencies and scholars. ICAO addressed these issues in a 1996 report on preferential treatment for member states who are at a competitive disadvantage in international markets. The following is a list of their recommendations for preferential treatment:

1 The asymmetric liberalization of market access in bilaterals with developed countries, including access to more cities and greater fifth freedom rights.
2 More flexibility for air carriers in changing capacity and gauge between routes in bilaterals.

3 Trial periods for carriers of developing nations to operate under liberal arrangements for an agreed period.
4 Gradual introduction of more liberal market access over longer periods of time for developing country carriers.
5 Use of liberalized arrangements.
6 Waiver of nationality requirements for ownership.
7 Special allowances for developing nation carriers to use more modern, leased aircraft.
8 Preferential treatment for the purpose of slot allocation.
9 More liberal policies for ground handling, conversion of currency, and employment of foreign personnel (ICAO, 1996).

Several scholars have made some additional recommendations. Abeyratne (1998), for example, has suggested that developed nations consider allowing an air carrier from one country to exercise the air traffic rights on behalf of another carrier in the event that no carrier from that country were able to launch a service on that route for economic reasons. Other recommendations by aviation scholars in Findlay, Sein, and Singh's (1997) book on policy reforms in Asian markets include opening freight and charter markets between countries in a region, relaxing code sharing and ownership rules, liberalizing markets before airline privatization, and expanding multilateral agreements with regional neighbors. Over the longer term, these expanded multilateral agreements could become regional open skies and general trade agreements, even inclusion in GATS (these ideas summarize the recommendations of Oum, Forsyth, and Trethaway in Findlay et al., 1997).

Conclusion

To date, the policy recommendations of aviation experts have not received serious consideration, but there is hope in the new focus of IATA and the aviation industry. Africa is the last great region of the world, waiting on the fulfillment of the promise of aviation. While the past might lead some to doubt the future, it is always possible that humanity can take a different path. In the next chapter, we will look at one of the most significant movements in aviation development – liberalization. If the YD were to lead to greater liberalization between African countries, then the growth, connectivity, and pricing issues would help fuel the growth that experts continue to predict. Of course, the path to liberalization is an uncertain and bumpy road.

Questions

1 What are the problems facing aviation development in Africa and Latin America? How has each region approached them?
2 Can the developing nations afford a national airline? What are the advantages? And the disadvantages?
3 What are some actions that national, international, and governmental organizations can take to improve safety?
4 Discuss aviation development in the Middle East. How has it differed from that in the other two regions?
5 What are some of the actions that developed nations can take to help aviation development? Why have they not been offered or accepted?

References

Abeyratne, R. I. R. (1998), 'The future of African Civil Aviation,' *Journal of Transportation World Wide*, 3, pp. 30–48.

Aikins, E. R. and McLachlan, J. D. (2022). *Africa is losing the battle against extreme poverty*. Institute for Security Studies. Available at: https://issafrica.org/iss-today/africa-is-losing-the-battle-against-extreme-poverty

Baldanza, B. (2022) The quickly changing landscape of Latin American aviation. Forbes. Available at: https://www.forbes.com/sites/benbaldanza/2022/06/13/the-quickly-changing-landscape-of-latin-american-aviation/?sh=5368c4c2523e

Bryan, Cave, Leighton & Paisner (2019) Understanding African skies – the liberalization of civil aviation in Africa. Available at: https://www.bclplaw.com/en-US/events-insights-news/under-african-skies-the-liberalisation-of-civil-aviation-in.html

Campbell, R. (2023) IATA forecast very positive outlook for African airlines over the next 12 years. Creamer Media Engineering News. Available at: https://www.engineeringnews.co.za/article/iata-forecasts-very-positive-outlook-for-african-airlines-over-next-12-years-2023-04-04

Casey. D. (2023) Connectivity continues to be threatened by blocked funds. Aviation Week. Available at: https://aviationweek.com/air-transport/location/connectivity-continues-be-threatened-blocked-funds

CIA Factbook (2023) www.odci.gov/cia/publications/factbook

ECA (2023) Africa needs to curb poverty and social inequality to meet development goals. Available at: https://www.uneca.org/eca-events/stories/africa-needs-curb-poverty-and-social-inequality-meet-development-goals#:~:text=%E2%80%9CIn%20Africa%2C%20growth%20dwindled%20from,poor%20at%2054.8%20per%20cent

ETN (2013) IATA: High airline accident rate in Africa still a concern. Available at: https://www.eturbonews.com/35290/iata-high-airline-accident-rate-africa-still-concern

Findlay, C., Sein , C. L., & Singh, K. (Eds.), (1997), *Asian Pacific Air Transport: Challenges and policy reform*. Institute of Southeast Asian Studies, Singapore.

Garbuno, B. (2021) The Caribbean urgently needs air travel: How can it be restored. Simple Flying. Available at: https://simpleflying.com/carribean-urgently-needs-air-travel/

Graham, B. (1995), *Geography and air transport*, John Wiley and Sons, New York.

Grant, J. (2023) African Aviation – Another set of crossroads. OAG. Available at: https://www.oag.com/blog/african-aviation-another-crossroads

Harris, J. (2023) Airlines can eliminate up to 70% of emissions by 2050, but many will miss their net zero goals if air traffic continues to grow faster than GDP. Bain & Company. Available at: https://www.bain.com/about/media-center/press-releases/2023/airlines-can-eliminate-up-to-70-of-emissions-by-2050-but-many-will-miss-their-net-zero-goals-if-air-traffic-continues-to-grow-faster-than-gdp/

IATA (2013) 'Strong passenger growth trend continues'. Available at: https://www.iata.org/pressroom/pr/Pages/2013-07-03-01.aspx

IATA (2022) No jet hull loss accidents in Africa for 2020 and 2021. Available at: https://airspace-africa.com/2022/03/02/no-jet-hull-loss-accidents-in-africa-for-2020-and-2021-safety-report/

IATA (2023a) IATA's "Focus Africa" to strengthen aviation's contribution to African development. Press Release No. 11. Available at: https://www.iata.org/en/pressroom/2023-releases/2023-04-03-01/

IATA (2023b) *IATA: Air passenger traffic in Africa shows strong recovery with room to grow*

ICAO (1996), *Study on preferential measures for developing countries*, ICAO Doc AT-WP/1789, August 22.

ICAO (2019) Aviation infrastructure for African gap analysis – 2019. ICAO Uniting Aviation. Available at: https://www.icao.int/ESAF/Documents/meetings/2019/Aviation%20Infrastructure%20For%20Africa%20GAP%20Analysis%202019/GAP_%20Airlines.pdf

ICAO (2021) RASG-AFI Annual Safety Report 2020. ICAO. Available at: https://www.icao.int/WACAF/Documents/RASG%20AFI/ASRT-7/7th%20Edition%20of%20RASG-AFI%20ASR%20-%20FINAL.pdf

Kajange, D. (2009) Air Transport Market Liberalization in Africa: The Yamoussoukro Decision Process. Available at: https://ec.europa.eu/transport/modes/air/events/doc/eu_africa/session_1_air_transport_market_liberalisation_in_africa.pdf

Karuwa, T. (2023) IATA acknowledges a need for 50,000 more aviation professionals in Africa. Simple Flying. Available at: https://simpleflying.com/iata-focus-africa-skills-shortage/

Mahor, B. (2023) Caribbean visitor boom drives expanding flight schedules TravelPulse. Available at: https://www.travelpulse.com/news/destinations/caribbean-visitor-boom-drives-expanding-flight-schedules

Phillips, E. H. (2002), 'Africa leads in hull losses: FSF cites challenges to flying,' *Aviation Week and Space Technology*, April 22, pp. 44–45.

Skyllence (2023) Navigating the skies: The rise, fall, and revival of African Aviation. Available at: https://skyllence.aero/navigating-the-skies-the-rise-fall-and-revival-of-african-aviation/#:~:text=Challenges%20Faced%20by%20African%20Aviation,profitability%20of%20African%20aviation%20players

United Nations Economic Commission for Africa (1988) Declaration of Yamoussoukro on a new African Air Transport Policy. Available at: https://respository.uneca.org/handle/10855/13773

18   Diverging Visions – Changing Times

Learning Objectives

After reading this chapter, you should have a good understanding of:

LO1:   the cases made by Boeing and Airbus for a very large jet.
LO2:   the comparison between the A380 and the B787
LO3:   the aircraft market outlook for large commercial aircraft (LCA)
LO4:   the competitive outlook for aircraft manufacturers

Key Terms, Concepts & People

LCA	AVIC	OEM
Aftermarket services	Honda	Mitsubishi
Turboprops	ATR	

Getting from Here to There

A strange thing happened in the closing years of the twentieth century – the vision of the two remaining large commercial aircraft (LCA) makers – Boeing and Airbus – began to diverge in ways that suggested that they could not both be right. For its part, Boeing saw a world in which passengers seek to skip the overcrowded hub with its security lines and airline transfers. Passengers, they believed, would choose to fly point-to-point to their destination in an airplane with the range to reach distant shores without stopovers. In short, the market of the future involved fragmenting, rather than concentrating passengers. In such a world, airlines would need an aircraft that could fly internationally to roughly 8,000 nautical miles at an economical cost. The Boeing solution was the B-787, a mid-sized, twin-engine widebody aircraft that would use 20 percent less fuel than a comparably-sized aircraft. The twin-engine B-777 had proven to be a very popular twin-aisle aircraft for many international carriers. On the other hand, Airbus saw a world where continuing population growth in major hub cities, time-zone differences, and pressures on airport capacity would necessitate a more intense, efficient use of the hub-and-spoke system. To achieve this efficiency, they believed that airlines would need larger aircraft to land more passengers with fewer flights. The Airbus solution was the A-380. The story of how these two giants of the aerospace world came to their visions depends on who is telling the tale, but the story

DOI: 10.4324/9781003405306-21

is instructive in many ways as it highlights the interconnection between the manufacturers and airlines that began in the early days of aviation, both groups gazing forward and trying to predict future needs and conditions. What will happen to fuel prices? Where is the next big destination and can it be served by the existing fleet? How many aircraft will the industry demand in the future?

If the point-to-point versus hub argument started with a high-level vision of the future, then the 'development' of the B737 MAX itself started with a phone call from American Airlines, a long-time Boeing customer, suggesting that they were close to a deal with Airbus for the new A320NEO (new engine option). What followed became a tragedy for 346 people and their families, a nightmare for international regulators, a black mark on the reputation of the company's reputation, and a wake-up call for Boeing and their US regulator, the Federal Aviation Administration (FAA). It is a story that continues to unfold as 'new' issues of quality and safety continue to arise for Boeing and this troubled aircraft. It is also a story that needs to be told in the hope that financial considerations never trump engineering considerations in an industry long admired for its achievements in flight (Slotnick, 2020).

First, we will look at the vision of the future of aviation. Where did it start, and why? What was the result? Then, we explore the tragedy that was the MAX. How did it come about? What were the critical decision points? Where were the failures? Second, we will review the order book for these two companies to help understand the state of play this intense competition. Then we will examine the future of aerospace manufacturing with a look at the 20-year forecasts of Boeing and Airbus. Finally, we will explore some of the new technologies that promise to reshape the industry and the future of flight.

Downturns and New Visions

The early years of the 1990s were not good for the airlines, or for the people who supplied them with aircraft. As the economy slowed, airline losses mounted. Airlines engaged in all the usual responses to crisis cited in Chapter 16. It seemed to both aircraft makers as though the answer to the cost pressures on world airlines was a bigger plane, with the lower seat mile costs that size would bring. By this time, Airbus had a family of aircraft that could compete with their Boeing rival in every class except the top one, where the B-747 dominated. Airbus was convinced that it was at this end of the market that Boeing was making its biggest profits. In fact, Aris (2002) calculated that Boeing was making US$30 million per B-747, although Newhouse (2007) disputed this notion and claimed that Boeing's most profitable aircraft was the extended-range B-767. Whatever the truth of the matter, Airbus believed these profits allowed Boeing to undersell Airbus on competing models. Further, Airbus felt that they could not achieve their stated goal of 50 percent market share without having an aircraft to compete with the B-747. Bearing these considerations in mind, Airbus was determined to enter the market with what they first called ultra-high-capacity aircraft. They knew that the cost of development would be high and had considered various partnerships; however, it was not until Boeing CEO Phil Condit mentioned in an interview one month before the Farnborough Air Show that they were exploring 'larger aircraft' that Airbus decided to put their planning into high gear and contact Boeing about a possible joint project to study the concept (Aris, 2002).

The results of this joint study would be the subject of much debate, while the motives of the two players would result in endless speculation. Both players calculated the cost of development at between US$14.5–15.5 billion, but they did not agree on the market size. Airbus forecasted a market for 500–600 aircraft over a ten-year period. Boeing, by contrast, saw a much smaller market, of between 300 and 350. This difference was significant because it determined the all-important breakeven number that is a key factor in deciding whether or not to proceed with an aircraft project. To Boeing, the analysis meant that 'for some unknown period of time these airplanes, if built, would be sold for much less than it had cost to develop them because the various factories building them would not yet have come down the learning curve' or not be operating at full capacity (Newhouse, 2007, pp. 149–150). It is difficult to determine at this stage whether the Boeing reluctance to proceed with the project was because they truly did not see a market for the very large aircraft, or because the rising costs of the B-777 and the need to modernize the B-737 made the company averse to assuming the risk of this new endeavor. Some inside Boeing even claimed that their initial interest was simply a way to trap Airbus in a losing proposition (Newhouse, 2007).

Meanwhile Boeing's behavior during this period seemed to indicate to many observers that the company did not have a strategy for moving forward. It explored a series of new B-747 versions with prospective customers before announcing their intention to proceed with the so-called Sonic Cruiser, an aircraft capable of flying just below Mach 1 over extended ranges. Unfortunately, this aircraft met with even less interest than the slight modifications proposed to the B-747 because trans-sonic flight would save little time and would use far too much fuel. Ultimately, Boeing would decide to produce the B-747-800, an aircraft with a new wing and several advanced features, including lighter construction materials and higher-performance engines that would make it a much bigger leap in design than the earlier proposed derivations, and a totally new aircraft, the B-787. For their part, Airbus would push on alone with the A-3XX, as it came to be called. As the 1990s slump turned into a booming new economy, Boeing attempted to ramp up its production and bury Airbus only to be caught in a production nightmare of their own. This disarray and the confusion of its earlier efforts to come up with a strategy certainly helped Airbus in their marketing efforts, their attempt to get launch aid from various European governments, and their reorganization of the Airbus structure itself. The starting gun for the great aircraft order race was fired in April 2000 with the Emirates Airline order for 10 A-3XX aircraft, soon to be given the name A-380 (Aris, 2002).

Comparing Cases, Comparing Planes

The Airbus case for a very large jet was made on several grounds. First, the 747 was nearing the natural end of its life. The design had been conceived in the 1950s and developed in the 1960s. The oldest were now approaching 25 years of age. These aging aircraft would have to be replaced by the world's airlines with a craft of equal or larger size that utilized the newest in aviation technology. Second, Airbus looked to the rapidly growing regions of Asia, with their large mega-cities and eight of the world's ten top airports in terms of passenger numbers. This area seemed to be an ideal market for the A-380. The vast time differences also meant that an airline catering to passenger preferences for arrival would bunch flights around these preferences, making fewer, larger planes a matter of capacity for airports. Third, Airbus reasoned that the operating costs of the A-380 would be 15–17 percent better; the plane would have almost 50 percent more space in the cabin but would require only 12–15 percent more to lift this weight into the air; thus, the cost per seat mile would be less (Aris, 2002). Fourth, Airbus believed that the A-380 would help to protect the A-340 which was not faring well against the B-777. The A-340 was a longer-range mini-jumbo with four engines while the B-777 could fly a similar range with two fewer engines, making it more economical to operate. Airbus hoped that fleet commonality would encourage 'Airbus customers' to choose the A-340 despite this operating cost issue. Fifth, Airbus countered critics concerned with the size (and potential engineering challenges associated

Table 18.1 Comparison of B-787 and A-380

	B-787	A-380
Seating	290–330	525–853
Range	2,500–3,000 nautical miles	8,200 nautical miles
Wing span	170 feet	261.8 feet
Length	186 feet	239.3 feet
Cruising speed	Mach 0.85	Mach 0.89
Maximum takeoff weight	364,000 pounds	1,235,000 pounds
Cargo volume	4,400 cubic feet	650 cubic feet
Fuel savings	20 % < per comparable plane	12 % < per passenger
Orders to date	979	259

Source: Boeing website www.boeing.com. Airbus website www.airbus.com

with size) with the argument that the A-380 was only 35 percent bigger than the B-747 (Newhouse, 2007).

In addition to their concerns about market size resulting from fragmentation of the market itself, Boeing believed that the A-380, with its 550 seats, would be too large for many markets, making the B-747-800 with 450-plus seats a better option. Further, they believed the freighter version of this aircraft would prove a better cargo carrier than the A-380 and that it would cost much less. In effect, they believed that the A-380 would be squeezed at the top of the market, further stretching out its time to profitability. Publicly, Boeing remains convinced that they had 'guessed right' and that their line-up of the B-747-800, B-777, and the new B-787 will outperform the A-380 (Newhouse, 2007). Table 18.1 compares the vital statistics on the A-380 and the B-787.

And the Winner Is…

The A-380 entered service in 2002. The launch customer was Singapore Airlines, who made their first flight in October 2007 (Walker, 2023). Airbus would announce the end of production in 2021, having built just 252 aircraft. While the aircraft was sold to 14 different airlines, most would be bought by Emirates Airlines in Dubai. During the COVID Pandemic, many airlines would retire the aircraft, although it has made something of a comeback with the post-Pandemic increase in traffic (Goldstein, 2023; Walker, 2023). While passengers loved the roomy aircraft, the A-380 never came close to the Airbus ten-year forecast of sales (500–600). In fact, it never even reached the much lower Boeing forecast (Reed, 2019). If there were those at Boeing celebrating the misfortune at Airbus, then they did so quietly or at least not in public. This was a wise decision because Boeing was about to enter one of its darkest periods since the development of the B-747. The financial crisis surrounding the development of the 747 at least had a happy ending. The saga of the 737MAX has not yet written any happy endings. In fact, it continues to stretch out in a long, slow drip of problems that point to poor design, bad manufacturing, and weak oversight.

Tale of Two Boeings

Boeing spent almost four years (2006–2010) debating its strategy with regard to the 737. The 737-100 first flew in 1967. The 737-200 was a slightly longer version of the first. The next three versions (-300, -400, -500) would be called 'The Classic Series.' These aircraft were released in the early 1980s and 1990s and would be some of the most popular aircraft ever released, with more than 10,000 delivered worldwide. By the beginning of the new century, there were concerns that Boeing had pushed the 737 as far as it would go so the debate became a question of designing a whole new single-aisle aircraft or pushing for one more modification. In this case, a new, more efficient engine was the main consideration. When the call came in from American Airlines in 2011, the time ran out on this debate. There was no time to design a new aircraft and get it through the extensive certification process required for a new aircraft if they wanted to have a plane to compete with the new A320. Here is where the trouble began.

The new engines were larger than those on previous 737s and thus had to be mounted further forward and higher on the wing. Unfortunately, this changed the weight/balance of the aircraft; the nose of the aircraft 'wanted' to pitch upward in some situations, namely low speed, and high angle. This could cause the aircraft to stall, so something needed to be done to correct the problem. To argue with regulators that the aircraft was still a part of the common 737 family, Boeing decided to correct the problem using a software system, the Maneuvering Control Augmentation System (MCAS). This system would only activate when the plane was hand-flown, a situation that usually took place on take-off (flying relatively slow and with a high angle profile). A single sensor was designed to alert the MCAS to the appropriate conditions. Because Boeing did not want to alert regulators to any significant changes, pilots were only asked to do a short, virtual training session on the program (Slotnick, 2020).

On October 29, 2018, Lion Air flight 610 crashed into the sea on take-off from Soekarno–Hatta International Airport, Tangerang. As regulators began to investigate this crash an Airworthiness Directive (AD) was issued by the FAA regarding trim stabilizers. On March 10, 2019, a second aircraft, Ethiopian Airlines 302, also crashed on take-off. The reaction from world regulators was swift. China grounded the plane on March 11, with also all other global regulators following suit by the following day. The last authority to ground the plane, on March 13, was the FAA. The plane would fly again in late 2020 after changes were made to the MCAS and Boeing would reach a settlement with the US Justice Department for US$2.5 billion, but the reputation of Boeing and its home country regulator, the FAA, would be severely damaged by the stories and investigations that took place. The aircraft that one Boeing pilot describes as 'designed by clowns, who in turn are supervised by monkeys' would have serious ramifications for Boeing, internally and externally.

Sadly, the tale of the saga is not yet over. On January 5, 2024, a panel on an Alaskan Air MAX 9 blew out midflight, grounding the MAX 9 and leading to safety investigations. These investigations have revealed loose bolts, improperly drilled holes, and a quality control system in chaos (Costello & Wile, 2024). The CEO of one of the major international carriers, Emirates Airlines, has said that he has witnessed a progressive decline in Boeing performance and hinted that in future his airline would send its own engineers to monitor Boeing production lines (Hoskins, 2024).

While the bad press, congressional hearings, and increased oversight have done considerable damage to Boeing's image, the loss of sales has been even harder on their financial performance. Table 18.2 shows the gross aircraft orders for both companies from 2011 to 2021. There are several things to note from this table. First, Airbus has been able to achieve its goal of 50 percent market share in terms of overall aircraft orders; however, Boeing has a much longer history of sales into the global market, and it will take time to overcome the in-service lead of Boeing. Second, the impact of the MAX on orders can be seen here as well as the that of the Pandemic effect on both manufacturers. One area that this table does not highlight is the sales of both companies into China. China is one of the largest aviation

Table 18.2 Boeing-Airbus Gross Aircraft Orders (2011–2021)

	Boeing	Airbus
2021	909	771
2020	184	383
2019	246	1,131
2018	1,090	831
2017	1,053	1,229
2016	848	949
2015	878	1,190
2014	1,550	1,796
2013	1,531	1,619
2012	1,339	914
2011	921	1,608

Source: Statista, Number of gross orders for airbus and Boeing aircraft between 2006 and 2021. Available at: https://www.statista.com/statistics/264492/aircraft-orders-from-airbus-and-boeing/

markets and any 20-year forecast of sales will be heavily weighted toward sales here. Looking at the 'Commercial Aircraft Deliveries' pages of both manufacturers indicates that over the past five years (2019–2023), Boeing has delivered 79 aircraft to Airbus' 858, a remarkable imbalance in a critical region of the world (Company websites). While some of this imbalance may reflect political tensions between the US and China, there are other issues that Boeing will need to address going forward.

Forecasting the Future

Table 18.3 presents the market outlook issued by these two companies for 2022–2042. Both forecasts agree that the bulk of the market continues to be in single-aisle aircraft. Boeing has a slightly larger forecast for the overall market (42,600) with Airbus predicting more demand for wide-body aircraft, 8,200 versus 7,440. Once again, both see the most significant demand over this timeframe coming from growth in Asian markets. Both roughly see about 50 percent of the aircraft demand coming from replacement.

Table 18.3 Boeing/Airbus – Twenty-Year Demand (2022–2042)

Aircraft Size	Boeing	Airbus
Widebody	7,440	8,200
Freighter	925	820
Regional jet	1,810	
Single-aisle	32,420	32,600
Total	42, 60	40,850

Source: Walker, K. (2023) Boeing a little rosier than Airbus in 20-year outlook for new airliners. Aviation Week. Available at: https://aviation week.com/air-transport/location/boeing-little-rosier-airbus-20-year-outlook-new-airliners

A Second Life

For Bombardier, a Canadian aircraft manufacturing company, the year 2003 was the peak of their deliveries for the CRJ 100/200 (50-seater) and CRJ 700/900 (70–90-seat) aircraft. Between 2003 and 2006, deliveries for the 50-seat CRJs declined an average of 70 percent a year. For Embraer, the 50-seat decline in deliveries was not as sharp (at 37 percent), but the trend has been clear for both manufacturers; the demand was now for larger jets (Kownatzki, Hoyland, & Watterson, 2009). At Bombardier, it was to be the new CSeries with a 110-seat configuration. This aircraft would have fly-by-wire technology, composite wings, and new turbofan engines (Warwick, 2013). For Embraer, deliveries of their E 170/175/190/195 (70–122 seats) overtook the 50-seat aircraft in 2005 and accounted for almost all their deliveries by 2006 (Kownatzki, Hoyland, & Watterson, 2009). As the industry has always known, the development of a new aircraft is expensive and uncertain. For Bombardier, this would eventually lead them into the arms of Airbus who would rebrand the aircraft as the A220, and would also work to increase the production rate and drive down costs (Memon, 2023).

Even more startling to some observers was the revival of the turboprop aircraft. ATR and Bombardier had been joined by the Chinese firm Avic, Indian firm RTA, and the South Korean firm DRA in proposing the development of 90-seat turboprop aircraft. Both ATR and Bombardier were already active in the turboprop market with ATR's 72-seat option straining to meet demand and Bombardier's Q400 also selling well. None of the bigger turboprops are scheduled to launch before 2018 and not all of them will eventually become products on the market. It is also possible that even larger versions may be considered (Perrett, 2013). While oil prices had been driving the revival of the turboprop aircraft, there remains a perception that propeller aircraft are accident-prone and 'old technology'. This perception is regional and could be subject to change with new technologies on the horizon (The Economist, 2012). In other words, there appears to be serious competition on several fronts for single-aisle aircraft and these manufacturers have their sights set on seating in the 90–100-plus range, placing them in more direct competition with the big two Large Commercial Aircraft (LCA) manufacturers.

The Asia Airbus

The expectation of the emergence of an Asian competitor in the LCA market has been around for years. While Airbus does its share of outsourcing, typical of aerospace manufacturing, Boeing has relied heavily on Asian companies for manufacturing and, increasingly, also design work. The Japanese 'heavies' helped to design the fuselage for the B-767 in 1978. By the time it came to designing the B-777, Japanese companies were working side by side with Boeing engineers for critical component design. The electronic, paperless design of the B-777 saved time and money, but it also facilitated the free flow of design information that would previously have been unthinkable. To many people in Boeing, the real value-added skill is systems integration, the broad systems understanding of how things work. If Boeing retained this position, they believed the competitive risks of information sharing were minimal; however, this close collaboration has periodically raised concerns from others inside Boeing, who fear that the company is training a future competitor and losing vital knowledge and skills in its push to outsource more of its operations. Ultimately, many in Boeing believed that the Japanese are too risk-averse to strike out on their own and would be content with the roles they were allowed to play (Newhouse, 2007). This belief may have been an error. Honda, Mitsubishi, and Toyota have all announced plans to enter the market, and Honda and GE have announced a joint effort to produce a jet engine for a new generation of small, low-cost business jets (Woodyard, 2008). Mitsubishi Heavy Industries is not only entering the regional jet market in the 70–90-passenger range but has also announced that All Nippon Airways will be their launch customer (Reuters Limited, 2008). Toyota has agreed to invest 10 billion yen in the Mitsubishi project (Watanabe, 2008). It appears that Boeing (and now Airbus) may have underestimated the potential for competition from Japan. The final assembly of the first MRJ aircraft got underway in October 2013 with delivery in 2017 expected. To date, there have been 325 orders for the plane, which was expected to be delivered in 2015 (Narabe & Kimura, 2013).

The same cannot be said for the Chinese, who have shown themselves capable of moving rapidly into high tech manufacturing and design. The Chinese are now manufacturing the complete wing for the A-320 as well as landing gear. AVIC International was born out of the restructured China National Aero-Technology Import & Export Corporation (CATIC) in 2008 and now has 70,000 employees in more than 180 countries, making it China's largest aerospace company. On the civilian front, the ARJ21 is its first product offering. The ARJ21, developed by the Commercial Aircraft Corporation of China (COMAC), had its first commercial delivery to Chengdu Airlines in 2016, not 2014 as initially planned. The first flight took place on June 28, 2016, marking a significant milestone in China's regional jet production (Aviation Nepal 2023). While these aircraft currently compete against the regional jets of Embraer and Bombardier, there is no reason to believe that the Chinese are not interested in expanding their line of aircraft. An Asian Airbus would be well positioned to take market share in one of the most rapidly growing aviation regions of the world and there is only one buyer of aircraft, the Chinese government. As noted throughout this book, the link between aviation, economics, and politics is always close. If China is successful in re-establishing its ancient hegemony over the Asian region, then the aircraft it produces are certain to benefit, directly and indirectly, inside and outside of China.

At the present time, the Asian efforts are targeted at the lower end of the commercial market and not a direct threat to the LCA manufacturers; however, this end of the market appears to be getting very crowded. If the trend toward small aircraft, point-to-point operations continues, then there may be room for all these new players. On the other hand, two other possibilities are clearly possible. The most immediate threat may come from the prospect that Embraer will be successful in moving up the food chain to produce aircraft to compete with the successor to the B-737/A-320. Given their expertise and existing facilities it would seem to be a less difficult move than for either the new Japanese or Chinese competitors. Further down the road is the potential for competition from the Asia players who, like Airbus before them, may not be content with the lower end of the market. China has the ability inside its nation to force carriers to purchase its own aircraft and could use political pressure in the region to 'encourage' other nations to do the same. In any event, neither Boeing nor Airbus can afford to underestimate their potential competition, as Boeing learned in the case of Airbus. A firm backed by the resources and will of its government is not to be taken lightly.

Real Men Sell Big Engines

There is an old joke in the aviation industry that men sell engines, but real men sell big engines (the same, of course, can be said of planes). It is certainly true that the twenty-first century would see the big three LCA engine makers producing engines for big planes. All three have a version for the biggest commercial plane ever produced, the A-380 (Table 18.3), but in some ways the times are changing. The old way of doing business in the aerospace industry was driven by an engineering mentality that said that if you built it to some engineering ideal of performance and standard then they (the airlines) would buy it; real men would sell it in the great game of high-stakes/high-politics aerospace. Increasingly, engine manufacturers are finding that customer service is the driving factor in sales. For the men selling these engines, this is a profound change. The job no longer centers on dazzling 'them' with specifications and performance data; it is all about finding out what the customer wants, listening to their concerns, addressing their needs. In short, customer service, not engineering specifications, win the day. Further, the money is not made from the engine sale itself but in the aftermarket services. As an example, GE offers OnPoint Solutions, a comprehensive program to meet operational, financial, and technical needs. The program will collect historical data, establish baselines for use and performance, identify upcoming changes in demand, and forecast future need costs. The program offers lower, predictable, guaranteed pricing, asset management, leasing, engine swaps, and spare parts control (GE website). Given the critical nature of the aircraft engine, airlines find that outsourcing the maintenance to the Original Equipment Manufacturer (OEM) only makes sense. The engine makers find that over the life of the engine itself they make far more money in the afterlife service.

Flying Forward

In what Newhouse in a previous book called the sporty game, the future still looks like a high-stakes competition to make big sales. Each side will announce the total sales after each airshow as proof that they are winning, closing the gap, meeting customer needs, etc. If the past holds true in the future, both Airbus and Boeing will be 'surprised' when a new competitor challenges them for a share of the market. The B-787 and A-380, while touted as 'changing the experience of flying', will likely end up packing the seats in so that airlines can get the most out of their assets. Presidents and prime ministers will still go out around the world privately pitching 'their' aerospace company. However, sometimes things really do change. The industry faces several challenges in this new century – carbon emissions limits (Chapter 20), new technology and capacity demands (Chapter 22), rising costs, particularly for fuel (Chapter 16), and liberalizing markets (Chapter 18). If it can keep its eyes on the skies and not on the current sales numbers, then the future may be bright.

Table 18.4 Large Commercial Aircraft Engines

Manufacturer	Engine	In-service date	Aircraft example
Pratt & Whitney	GP7000	2008	A-380
	PW6000	2007	A-318
General Electric	GP7000	2007	A-380
	GEnx	2019	B-787
Rolls-Royce	Trent 900	2007	A-380
	Trent 1000	2014	B-787
	Trent XBW	TBD	A-350

Source: Various company websites.

Questions

1 Discuss the differing vision of the future airline market that divided Boeing and Airbus.
2 Why might Airbus have felt that they needed s ultra-high-capacity aircraft in their 'family'?
3 How do the A380 and the B-787 compare? What does the current order book say about airline needs?
4 What is the market outlook for aircraft?
5 Discuss the comeback of the turboprop aircraft and the future of the regional jet.
6 Discuss changing sales concepts at the engine manufacturers.

References

Aris, S. (2002), *Close to the Sun: How Airbus challenged America's domination of the skies*, Arum Press, London.
Aviation Nepal. (2023) Meet Comac ARJ21: China's First Jet-Propelled Regional Airliner. *Aviation Nepal*, 2023. Available at: Aviation Nepal
Costello, T. & Wile, R. (2024) Alaska Airlines CEO: We found 'many' loose bolts on our MAX 9 planes following near disaster, NBC News. Available at: https://www.nbcnews.com/business/business-news/alaska-airlines-found-more-loose-bolts-boeing-737-max-9-ceo-says-rcna135316
Goldstein, M (2023) The Airbus A380 makes an improbable comeback. *Forbes*. Available at: https://www.forbes.com/sites/michaelgoldstein/2023/08/02/the-airbus-a380-makes-an-improbable-comeback/?sh=29059c2f7995
Hoskins, P. (2024) Boeing in 'last chance saloon,' warns Emirates boss. BBC News. Available at: https://www.bbc.com/news/business-68201371
Kownatzki, M., Hoyland, T. & Watterson, A. (2009) *The 50 seat jet: A plane with no future. Thnk again*. Oliver Wyman Aviation, Aerospace and Defense Practice, Oliver Wyman, New York.
Memon, O. (2023) How the Bombardier C-Series program transitioned to the Airbus A220 family. Simple Flying. Available at: https://simpleflying.com/bombardier-c-series-airbus-a220-transition-story/
Narabe, T. & Kimura, H. (2013). Mitsubishi aircraft delays delivery of 1st passenger jet to 2017. Available at: https://ajw.asahi.com/article/economy/business/AJ201308230064
Newhouse, J. (2007) *Boeing versus Airbus: The inside story of the greatest competition in business*, Alfred A. Knopf, New York.
Perrett, B. (2013) Field of five, *Aviation Week & Space Technology*, August 5, pp. 38–40.
Reed, D. (2019) The plane that never should have been built: The A380 was designed for failure. Forbes. Available at: https://www.forbes.com/sites/danielreed/2019/02/15/the-plane-that-never-should-have-been-built-the-a380-was-designed-for-marketplace-failure/?sh=c0080403c59d
Reuters Limited (2008), 'ANA weighs buying 30 Mitsubishi regional jets, report says,' *USA Today* online edition. Available at https://www.usatoday.com/pt/cpt?action=cpt&title=ANA+weighs+buying
Slotnick, D. (2020) The first Boeing 737 MAX crash was two years ago today. Here's the complete history of the plane that has been grounded since two crashes killed 346 people 5 months apart. Business Insider. Available at: https://www.businessinsider.com/boeing-737-max-timeline-history-full-details-2019-9
The Economist (2012) Turbo aversion, turbo reversion. Available at: https://www.economist.com/blogs/gulliver/2012/02/air-travel-and-turboprop-revival
Walker, S. 2023 The Airbus A380: 5 little-known facts about the world's largest passenger aircraft. Simple Flying. Available at: https://simpleflying.com/airbus-a380-little-known-facts/#the-a380-is-as-wide-as-32-double-decker-buses
Warwick, G. (2013) Bombardier CSeries conducts second flight. Available at: https://atwonline.com/airframes/bombardier-cseries-conducts-second-flight
Watanabe, C. (2008), 'Toyota asked to invest in jet project,' *USAToday* online edition. Available at: http://www.usatoday.com/pt/cpt?action=cpt&title=Toyota+asked+...
Woodyard, C. (2008), 'Honda, GE build new jet engine,' *USAToday* online edition. Available at: http://www.usatoday.com/pt/cpt?action=cpt&title=Honda+GE+build+...

Websites

GE Aerospace https://www.geaerospace.com/propulsion/commercial
Pratt & Whitney https://www.prattwhitney.com/en/products/commercial-engines
Rolls Royce https://www.rolls-royce.com/products-and-services.aspx

19 Carbon Emission and Sustainability

Learning Objectives

After reading this chapter, you should have a good understanding of:

LO1:   the issue of carbon emissions and climate change
LO2:   the role of aviation in emissions
LO3:   the actions of different segments of the industry to address carbon
LO4:   the future of carbon policy and the impact on the aviation industry

Key Terms, Concepts & People

ETS	Corsia	Greenhouse Gases
ATAG	ACI	Jet-A
Biodiesel	Avgas	CDA

In the Spotlight

The December 19, 2006 cover story for *USA Today* proclaimed that 'Concern grows over pollution from jets: Aviation emissions will take off along with worldwide air travel'. The article pointed out that each passenger on a commercial jet from New York City to Denver would generate between 840 and 1,600 pounds of carbon dioxide, roughly the same amount of carbon as a Sports Utility Vehicle (SUV) driven over the period of a month (Stoller, 2006). With US air travel projected to climb to one billion passengers per year by 2024, US environmentalists certainly felt they had reason for concern (FAA, 2012). The European Commission, responding to the concerns of its citizens, had already included emissions from civil aviation into the European Union (EU) Emissions Trading Scheme (ETS) for all internal EU flights and intended to include all flights to and from EU airports in 2012, but the ETS ran into several problems. First, the price of carbon was falling, which created a problem in the carbon trading scheme because 'rational' firms would elect to purchase cheap permits to emit carbon rather than investing in means to reduce carbon pollution. To bolster the price of carbon, the EU decided to reduce the number of free permits distributed to members (Reuters News Agency, 2013). Second, the global backlash against the inclusion of international carriers in the ETS included threats of legal action and retaliation. These threats caused the EU to back down on enforcement. The fight in the European

DOI: 10.4324/9781003405306-22

Parliament to limit the ETS also proved to be difficult and contentious. To save face, the EU insisted that it acted because it feared that the International Civil Aviation Organization (ICAO) would be unable to act. In a global compromise, all sides in the debate agreed to a plan to allow ICAO to craft a global solution (Keating, 2013). The resulting plan, Carbon Offsetting and Reduction Scheme for International Aviation, or CORSIA for short, reflected all the strengths and weaknesses of that organization, as we discussed in Chapter 6. We will discuss these issues and the state of CORSIA later in the chapter.

At the time of the *USA Today* story, the issue of carbon emission and climate change was not on the agenda of the US government under the George W. Bush Administration, who barely acknowledged that any issue existed. Under President Obama, climate change seemed set to take center stage until the healthcare debate dragged on and the Democratic Party lost seats in the 2010 midterm elections, creating a Republican House of Representatives. There would be little national legislative action on the issue until the Biden administration and the Inflation Reduction Act, which was billed as the largest climate-focused investment in US history (Ward, 2023). Still, the Obama Administration did attempt to take administrative action with limited success and defended earlier efforts to use stimulus money directed to 'Green' projects in the wake of scandals such as Solyndra (Stephens & Leonnig, 2011). (The Solyndra scandal involved the Obama administration's 2009 decision to grant a $535 million loan guarantee to the solar panel company, which went bankrupt in 2011, raising concerns about the administration's due diligence in funding green energy projects. Critics pointed to the company's failure as evidence of flawed oversight, while the administration defended its broader green energy initiatives, despite the controversy.) Progress in Great Britain was no smoother than the in US as the British Parliament 'considered' measures to limit the growth rate of aviation to the rate at which the industry improved its fuel efficiency and local citizens rejected planned increases in aviation activity, such as new airport runways or additional flights due to concerns over the environment and global warming (Stoller, 2006). Still, complaints did not stop expansion efforts at Heathrow Airport in London, where a fifth terminal was finally added (Michaels, 2008).

Groups such as Sustainable Aviation continued to work on plans to ensure that aviation becomes part of the solution to the problem of greenhouse gases (GHG) and various airlines conducted biofuel demonstration flights (Sustainable Aviation, 2006). At the 77th Annual General Meeting of IATA, a resolution was passed committing member airlines to achieving net-zero carbon emissions from their operations by 2050 (IATA, 2021).

If political infighting at the start of the twenty-first century kept carbon off the table, then the spike in fuel prices to US$147 in 2008 seemed to provide the US and the aviation industry with a reason to consider alternative fuels. The 2008 recession resulted in US consumption of roughly 8.74 million barrels of oil a day in 2011, almost 6 percent less than the 2007 peak (US Energy Information Administration, 2013). Still. transportation continued to account for almost two-thirds of the total oil consumed with gasoline accounting for 47 percent of all petroleum consumption. Aviation emissions were not included in the Kyoto Protocol as they were believed to be a minor contributor to climate change when the agreement was first negotiated. It was the projected growth in aviation that changed the debate (Stoller, 2006). The US Energy Information Administration (2023) recently reported that US petroleum consumption remained relatively flat in 2022, but it predicted that global demand would make the US a net exporter of petroleum through 2050. In short, while the US would not use more petroleum, it would not discourage others from buying its products.

The airline industry, which had struggled to post a profit after September 11th only to see the Global Financial Crisis (GFC) of 2008 destroy any brief gains, was reluctant to address carbon emissions. It is even less pleased with the predictions of some geologists and environmentalists such as Colin Campbell, author of *Oil Crisis* and a chief proponent of an early peak for oil production. Campbell suggested that the 'airline business will go into near extinction as fuel costs soar. Very few people actually need to travel by air. Modern communications makes most business travel unnecessary' (2005, p. 298). Lester R. Brown, president of the Earth Policy Institute, offered a less dire prediction for the aviation industry, but he still suggested that cheap airfares, fresh fruit transported by aircraft to out-of-season consumers, and citizens willing to 'subsidize this high-cost mode of transportation for their more affluent compatriots' would soon be a thing of the past (Brown, 2006, p. 234). Under pressure to address the issue of carbon and fuel, one of its three biggest expenses, airlines continue to search for answers (Grose, 2013).

Subject to Debate

The debate about the reality of climate change, and its causes, has largely been settled in much of the world, but it has remained a 'hot' political topic in the US where there is more talk of hoax than change (Gopal, 2023; Kaplan, 2013; Kluger, 2007). On the other hand, the EU instituted plans to cut energy use 20 percent by 2020 and to increase the share of renewable energy to 12 percent by 2010. According to the European Environment Agency (EEA), they achieved their three main goals – 'reducing GHG emissions by 20%, increasing renewable energy use by 20%, and energy efficiency by 20%'. In fact, the EEA reported that GHG emissions were 31 percent below 1990 levels. For 2030, the goal is a 55 percent net reduction as an intermediate target toward net neutrality by 2050 (EEA, 2023). Meanwhile, the US government has continued to have no comprehensive plan to address the issue of energy use, carbon emissions or renewable energy in the first two decades of the twenty-first century, relying on markets to drive change (Brown, 2006; McKinnon & Meckler, 2006). Quietly, it was counting on the US military to invest for strategic, security reasons and to use their massive market power to drive down the costs of alternative fuel for everyone. New estimates of self-sufficiency created political backlash to military projects for alternative fuel that forced a reduction in these programs (Bruno & Warwick, 2013). The alternative fuels debate in the US has tended to focus on automobile use, with ethanol production from corn and soybeans its key feature (Grunwald, 2008). The newest trend has been on electric vehicles and charging stations with EV sales climbing over 7 percent for the first time in 2023 (Johnson, 2023). As we will discuss later, alternative fuels in aviation are a known, possible solution, but there are serious issues regarding the scale of production. Early hopes for solutions focused on technological improvements and air traffic modernization efforts (Pilling & Thompson, 2007).

Growing Impact

The Federal Aviation Administration (FAA) had predicted that the US will continue to see 2–3 percent growth over the next 20 years, with some 1.2 billion passengers flying in 2032 (FAA, 2012). Despite the interruption of the Pandemic, the FAA has extended and revised its growth estimate to 2.7 percent annual growth through 2043 (FAA, 2023). Transportation accounts for roughly 29 percent of US GHG emissions, increasing more in absolute terms between 1990 and 2021 than any other sector. Air transport accounts for 12 percent of this total (Environmental Protection Agency, 2023; Ott, 2007). The jet engine is the chief source of carbon emissions. A jet engine emits more carbon dioxide than the actual weight of the fuel that creates combustion within it (Bond, 2007). According to Environmental Defense, burning a gallon of jet fuel will produce 21.1 pounds of carbon dioxide (or about half a pound per passenger per domestic mile or one pound per passenger per international mile). The average domestic US fuel efficiency of a jet engine now averages 0.54 aircraft-miles per gallon, a 40 percent increase in efficiency since 2000. For international flights, the average fuel efficiency is only 0.27 aircraft miles per gallon. Multiply this fuel efficiency level by the length of a typical airline flight and the amount of fuel consumed (and carbon emitted) is staggering (Grose, 2013). Further complicating the issue is the fact that these emissions tend to take place at high altitude, which may represent a greater problem for global warming than those that occur at sea level (Environmental Defense, 2007; Stoller, 2006). Some sources suggest that non-carbon dioxide greenhouse gas emissions (GHG) may be even more significant. These include nitrogen oxide, sulfur oxide, soot, and water vapor (Stoller, 2006).

The aviation industry can roughly be divided into six segments: airlines, manufacturers, airports, general aviation, airspace, and air cargo. These segments exist, to some extent, throughout the world, although there are some important structural differences. US airlines and air cargo operators are privately owned. Almost all are publicly traded stock companies and subject to financial as well as operational reporting. Airports in the US, on the other hand, are owned by the city or county in which they are located except for some small general aviation airports and military airfields. All but a small number of airports are open to general aviation traffic. The airspace in the US is tightly regulated with an air traffic system managed by the US Federal Aviation Administration. Controllers are public employees who, while unionized, have limited ability to engage in work actions. For the rest of the world, full or partial government ownership of airlines is common. Airports, on the other hand, are increasingly being privatized or the management of the airport outsourced. General aviation is much less common, and many airports are closed to this type of traffic. Airspace is less restricted, and in some cases such as Africa radar coverage is limited (Rhoades, 2003). These differences may not be the primary factor in driving sector contribution to carbon emissions, but they may affect future support for carbon constraint. Currently, each segment contributes to carbon emissions in a multitude of ways, and each is approaching (or not approaching) the issue of emissions at their own pace and in their own way.

Flying Green

US carriers consume roughly 14 billion gallons of jet fuel in 2021, down from 18 billion in 2019 prior to the start of the Pandemic (Statista, 2023). With regard to emissions, an aircraft engine emits carbon dioxide and nitrogen oxide on the ground and while in flight. On the ground, fuel may be burned when the aircraft backs from the gate under power, taxis to the runway, or is repositioned on the airport, either to a new gate or to a maintenance hangar on airport property. Fuel burned on the ground has tended to raise concerns about local air and noise pollution rather than carbon emission and has been the subject of complaints from citizens surrounding busy commercial airports. It is the in-flight, upper atmosphere emissions and the creation of contrails (condensed water vapor formed in the wake of an aircraft which are believed to contribute to cloud cover) that has raised the greatest concern from scientists and environmentalists. These aspects are also the most difficult to address (McKinnon & Meckler, 2006).

Greening the Neighborhood

Airports continue to be a focal point for residents and environmental groups concerned about environmental impacts arising from noise and air pollution. In addition to the activity of the aircraft themselves, airports utilize powered vehicles for baggage transfer, aircraft maintenance, emergency response, terminal-to-terminal transportation, terminal-to-parking transportation, etc. In the US, most airports are accessed through private automobiles, which adds to the local pollution levels. Since parking fees represent a substantial source of revenue, airports are often reluctant to tamper with this aspect of their operations. Although airport master planning in the US requires that intermodal transportation issues be addressed through the design of parking facilities, rental cars, and public transportation access, the reality is that only 14 airports in the US are linked to rail systems, one of the least-polluting forms of transportation, leaving the rest to rely on other forms of surface transportation. (ACI-ATAG, 1998).

Airspace is restricted to a certain extent in all countries due to noise, security, safety, and radar coverage. Examples of restrictions include military facilities, residential neighborhoods, and key public buildings. In the US, airspace is more tightly controlled than in many other regions and is the responsibility of a single entity, the FAA. In regions such as the European Union (EU), multiple air traffic control systems increase the inefficiency of the airspace. Another source of global inefficiency are country limitations on the entry of foreign aircraft, either by closing entrance to foreign aircraft or by charging fees for entry or overflight, thereby encouraging aircraft operators to fly around restrictions, in turn adding to flight times and fuel consumption. The current system of air traffic management also utilizes step-down approaches that require progressive altitude changes and thrust applications in descent to landing, adding to fuel burn (Hughes, 2007).

Freight Green

World air freight growth is closely linked to the overall growth in world GDP. Air freight is one of the most sensitive areas of the economy and it is also one of the first segments to decline in the face of economic slowdowns. It recovered slowly after 2001 and was deeply affected by the downturn in the wake of the Global Financial Crisis (IATA, 2013). The impact of the Pandemic was mixed since the commercial airline capacity was greatly reduced while there was a growing demand in the medical and online markets. In 2022, the air freight market size was US$200 billion, with a projected 5 percent growth over the next 20 years (Global Market Insights, 2023). As noted above. air freight can be carried either as belly cargo on commercial airlines or on dedicated freighter aircraft, some of whom are operated by the airlines themselves. Many all-cargo operators act as air freight forwarders, handling the air segment of a shipping operation. This includes operators handling oversized cargo, such as Volga-Dnepr. Oversized carriers use some of the largest aircraft in the world, the C-17 and the AN 124, to ship large industrial equipment. These services have been attractive to firms in industries such as oil and gas, where the time saved by shipping equipment by air rather than using slower modes of transportation may prove an ideal trade-off to get operations up and running quickly or to keep them in operation (Nelms, 2007).

The best-known global shippers are the so-called integrated carriers such as UPS, FedEx, and DHL. While air forwarders such as airlines and all cargo operators are responsible for only the air portion of travel and require shippers to make their own arrangements to get freight to and from the airport, the 'integrated' carriers combine all modes of transportation to provide seamless, door-to-door shipping. FedEx started life as an overnight air freight delivery company, while UPS was a ground delivery company that expanded into air freight later in life. This has not stopped either company from amassing an air fleet that would now rank them among the largest airlines in the world (Neimann, 2007).

And the Answer Is...

The aerospace industry is pursuing several actions to reduce GHG emissions. The primary hope for significant reduction lies in new technologies. This is certainly true in the US, where faith in the free-market system means that government 'interference' in the system is controversial. Aircraft engines have continued to increase the efficiency of their fuel burn, doubling fuel efficiency over the past 40 years, and manufacturers are committed to a further improvement of almost 50 percent (Sustainable Aviation, 2006). These technologies would also reduce carbon dioxide emissions, but are estimated to increase nitrogen oxide emissions by about 40 percent over the same period (Dailey, 2010; McKinnon & Meckler, 2006). In terms of engine advances, there are several innovations that could represent game-changing technology. Manufacturers are currently working on open rotor engines. In an open rotor design, the rotors (propellers) normally encased inside the engine housing are mounted outside. The propeller diameter can be increased, and the heavy, drag-inducing nacelle removed. Two common configurations are the puller, with the propeller mounted at the front of the engine, and the pusher, with the propellers mounted behind the turbine (SBAC, 2013). The main drawbacks of the open rotor are increased noise and market acceptance of this unusual design. Pratt & Whitney announced breakthroughs in engine designs that 'add a gear' to the turbofan engine and promise potential fuel reduction of 16 percent, 20 percent reductions in operating costs, lower noise levels, and reduced emissions; however, the new engine has a larger fan and cannot be retrofitted beneath the wings of existing aircraft, limiting its use to new aircraft (Grose, 2013). Even the 'design classic' turboprop engine, the PT6 from Pratt & Whitney, has made remarkable improvements in technology, with four times more power and 20 percent better fuel efficiency (Norris, 2013). In a new breakthrough, Rolls-Royce announced the first run of an aero engine on hydrogen. This was only a ground-based test, however, and there will be years of future testing before the engine sees any time in the air (Rolls-Royce, 2022).

In addition to new engine designs, there are new design options for the fuselage, including the following: the double bubble, a design that merges two fuselages together, thereby allowing some of the lift to come from here not just the wings; blended wing designs that fall just short of the flying wing design; a new split winglet; new composite and ceramic designs that reduce weight; various space plane designs; and several new supersonic designs, including the ninja, which that flies like a normal aircraft until it rotates to present a narrower profile (Grose, 2013; NASA, 2012; Warwick, 2013). Aircraft and their engines are long-lived assets. The replacement of existing fleets with newer more fuel-efficient aircraft is a slow process given the cost to aircraft operators. Currently, modifications to existing aircraft yield only modest improvements in efficiency (Bond, 2007).

Another option for airlines is the use of alternative fuels. At present, the turbine engine of a large commercial jet uses a high-octane form of diesel fuel, commonly called Jet A. Jet A must perform under extreme temperature conditions, particularly the cold of high altitude. By contrast, smaller general aviation aircraft use Avgas. As the name implies, Avgas is more closely related to gasoline than diesel (US Department of Energy, 2005). The list of airlines that have announced biofuel demonstration flights continues to grow and includes such well-known names as Virgin Atlantic, Delta, China Eastern, Alaska Airlines, United, and KLM (Biofuels Digest, 2013; Carey, 2013; United Press International, 2008). Synthetic jet fuel can be manufactured through a conversion process from natural gas or coal that produces 1.8 times the carbon dioxide of conventional jet fuel production. Other alternative fuel technologies will require engine modification. There are many different feedstocks for alternative fuels – waste oil and fats, municipal waste, food, and non-food crops. The use of some of these feedstocks is not viable in aviation as they freeze at the normal cruising temperatures of large commercial aircraft (Daggett, Henricks, Walther, & Corporan, 2007). The Renewable Aviation Fuels Development Center (RAFDC) at Baylor University has run a series of experiments using alternative fuels for aviation. RAFDC tests examined biodiesel blends of 5, 10, 15, 20, and 25 percent, with the best results being obtained for the 20 percent blend. Beyond this level of blend, major changes in engine configuration would be required and significant clouding at cold temperatures is likely. The recent biodiesel test run by Virgin Atlantic used a 20 percent blend. Airbus has also conducted a trial run of the A-380 from Filton, UK to Toulouse, France. The A-380 was using a Rolls-Royce Trent 900 engine and also a 20 percent blend (Next Energy News, 2008; United Press International, 2008). Boeing is currently exploring the use of cryogenic hydrogen and liquid methane (Daggett, Henricks, Walther, & Corporan, 2007). Despite these pledges and high-profile demonstration flights, Sustainable Aviation Fuel (SAF) currently represents less than 0.1 percent of the fuel needed to achieve the net zero goal of the airline industry. While some would suggest the whole idea is a public relations stunt, others point to signs of increased production. The reality is that the industry would need production to rise from 9 million gallons (300 million liters) at present to 117 billion gallons (450 billion liters) by 2050 (Foster, 2023). If this seems like an overwhelming challenge for airlines, it is at least one with a future that can be planned and mapped out (even if not implemented). All other 'solutions' rely on technology, which is largely out of the hands of the airlines themselves. Fuel itself is not the only problem facing the industry. The efficiency of airlines' operations is currently improving at 3 percent a year while passenger demand is growing at 5 percent. Reducing CO_2 emissions still does not address the other GHGs that are produced and might even make them worse. Roughly 15 percent of flyers (Frequent Flyers) account for 70 percent of all flights, but 'taxing' this high-income part of the population is politically challenging. The proposed policy solution of Corsia was still in its 'establishing a baseline phase' when the Pandemic hit and is struggling to establish long-term goals. Middle-income nations are now 'discovering' air travel and are adding to global growth in demand. Finally, the aviation industry is again flirting with supersonic travel, which has much higher fuel demands (Timperley, 2021). In short, on its current path, the airlines will not come close to their target goals.

General aviation includes all non-commercial, non-military aviation. Most of this segment relies on piston-powered, propeller engines. These craft use Avgas rather than Jet-A fuel. Avgas is more closely related to ethanol. There are over 320,000 general aviation aircraft, including helicopters, single, piston engine craft, and turboprops. In the US, general aviation aircraft fly over 27 million hours annually (General Aviation Manufacturers Association, 2006). RAFDC has tested ethanol and Eythyl Teriary Butyl Ether (ETBE) against Avgas in the piston engines commonly used in general aviation propeller aircraft. While some engine modification is required, tests showed that engine efficiencies were higher for ethanol than Avgas. These improved even more with increased compression, although the mileage per gallon of ethanol was lower. Tests indicated that at 80 percent power, ethanol consumed 11 percent more fuel than Avgas. Ethanol and ETBE were shown to produce lower emissions of carbon monoxide and unburned hydrocarbons, but to increase the emission of carbon dioxide and nitrogen oxide because of lower energy conversion rates, a fact which is reflected in the level of fuel consumed (Shauck & Zanin, 2001). A modified piston aircraft was flown without significant problems across the Atlantic using ethanol (Shauck & Zanin, 1990). During the trans-Atlantic flight no fuel-related problems were encountered. The overall cost of the ethanol for the crossing was US$160 compared to US$230 for Avgas, even including the reduced mileage (Shauck & Zanin, 2001). The results also indicate that ethanol burns more completely and cleanly than gasoline. The observed reduction in range (mileage) was between 10 and 15 percent Unlike commercial aviation, which faces many challenges in electric powered flight, GA is an excellent candidate and Rolls-Royce announced in 2021 that its all-electric 'Spirit of Innovation' aircraft set three new world records during its debut flight (Rolls-Royce, 2021). This technology could be a game changer in the general aviation world.

On the airport front, there are several technologies that can be, and have been, implemented to improve airport arrival and departure procedures (see Chapter 21 for more information). The Next Generation Air Transportation System (NGATS) is looking at technologies such as 4D Trajectory Management. This technology would involve runway-to-runway planning with auto negotiation equipment in the aircraft that would allow flight crews to adjust the flight plan as necessary to accommodate weather, aircraft separation, airport delays, etc. ATM technologies combined with Global Positioning Satellites (GPS) and Automatic Dependent Surveillance-Broadcast (ADS-B) to implement proper spacing could be used to replace the step-down descents with Continuous Descent Arrivals (CDAs). It is estimated that CDAs could save 100–300 pounds of fuel (Hughes, 2007). The US Air Transport Association, a trade organization representing US airlines, and the FAA support an airspace management initiative called Secure America's Future Energy (SAFE). SAFE would link a satellite-based air traffic system to ground-based technologies in order to reduce delays and shorten travel. SAFE has estimated that the implementation of these actions could save 400,000 barrels of oil daily by 2030 and reduce carbon emissions by 57.5 million metric tonnes per year (Air Transport Association, 2007). The European equivalent of this program is the Single European Sky ATM Research Programme (SESAR) and the Advisory Council for Aerospace Research in Europe (ACARE).

While there are several technological solutions being studied, changing processes can also have an impact on carbon emissions. Airlines have taken several actions that reduce fuel burn and emissions on the ground, primarily out of concern with rising fuel costs. These actions include the elimination of power backing (backing the airplane from the gate using its engines) in favor of small tugs that push the aircraft back from the gate and 'supertugs' that can be used to tow aircraft around the airport itself (repositioning it to another gate or a maintenance hangar). Lufthansa is experimenting with a semi-robotic tug, controlled by the pilot that would take the aircraft from the ramp to the runway, using 7–15 gallons of fuel rather than the 126 gallons that would be used by the aircraft engines. There are also options for taxiing on electricity with an auxiliary power unit (Warwick, 2013). EU airlines are addressing government and customer concerns by developing explicit plans to manage and report on a range of environmental issues. For example, British Airways has a section on their website that reports on their environmental actions around noise, air quality, waste and biodiversity. There is also a way to calculate and offset your carbon dioxide emissions.

Unlike their airline counterparts, airports have been more aggressive in their approach to environmental issues. Three examples highlight the types of actions that airports are employing. Dallas-Fort Worth Airport (DFW) is the world's third busiest airport with 1,900 flights per day. DFW has taken a very proactive approach to environmental issues and was recently recognized by the US Environmental Protection Agency as part of their National Environmental Performance Tracking program. Over the past five years, DFW has reduced its air emissions by 95 percent and converted 100 percent of its light-to-medium vehicles on airfield fleet as well as bus and shuttle operations to alternative fuels (DFW New Release, 2007). The Port of Seattle, which includes the Sea-Tac airport as well as the seaport in Seattle, is another example of a committed and proactive local entity. The Port has a staff of 22 individuals responsible for environmental issues and compliance and has converted most of their on-airport vehicles to natural gas. In addition, they have redesigned field operations to reduce the number of tanker trucks needed on the airfield (Port of Seattle, 2006). Finally, the Airport Carbon Management Group (ACMG), based in the UK, was created to explore ways to reduce carbon emissions, primarily through improved energy use. To date, the efforts of this group have reduced carbon emissions by 13,000 tons per year (Sustainable Aviation, 2006). Unlike the US, there are also over 40 airports in Europe with air-rail links and an additional 49 links are planned. It has been estimated that Heathrow Express removes over 3,000 cars a day from London roads (ACI-ATAG, 1998).

The integrated freight carriers are making some of the greatest efforts to address environmental issues, including carbon emissions. DHL has launched its GoGreen program, which allows shippers to select low-carbon emission modes of shipping. This option was provided to delegates attending the World Economic Forum in Davos as part of the Forum's carbon-neutral goal for the 2007 conference. DHL has entered a joint venture with Lufthansa Cargo called AeroLogic. AeroLogic will utilize the more fuel-efficient B-777, primarily to Asia. DHL has explored the use of biogas, hybrid, and fuel cell vehicles for ground shipping and packaging options that reduce GHG emissions (DHL, 2024; Turney, 2008). FedEx is also exploring alternative fuels for its ground vehicles and has recently launched 18 Optifleet E700 hybrid vehicles to its fleet. On the aviation side, FedEx has retired its remaining B727 aircraft and hush-kitted older aircraft, both of which reduce the overall fleet emissions and noise levels. Beginning in 2009, FedEx will begin acquiring B-777 freighters which provide 18 percent greater fuel efficiency. The FedEx Oakland, California facility has one of the largest industrial solar operations in the US (FedEx, 2023; Moorman, 2008). UPS was the launch customer in the mid-1990s for the low-emission version of the GE CF6-80C2 engine and is installing ADS-B in all its aircraft. It expects to save a million gallons of jet fuel a year and to reduce noise and nitrous oxide emissions (Moorman, 2008). UPS has also taken several actions to reduce fuel consumption and emissions from its ground fleet, including trailering trucks onto railcars and optimizing driving routes. In addition, they deployed 50 new hybrid vehicles to their fleet in 2006. These hybrids join a fleet of 12,000 low-emission vehicles already in operation (Neimann, 2007). UPS has established Key Performance Indicators (KPI) for environmental performance that include ground and aviation emissions targets. These are reported on their website (UPS, 2022).

Aviation in Green

Except for airlines, other sectors of the aviation industry are taking major steps to address GHG and climate change. While it would be incorrect to say that the airline industry has taken no actions to reduce energy use, switch to renewable fuels, or reduce emissions, these actions in the twenty-first century were driven largely by higher fuel prices rather than other concerns. In fairness, this segment of the industry has also struggled over time to post a consistent profit and the first decades of the twenty-first century have been particularly hard on it with 9/11, the Global Financial Crisis of 2008, and the Global Pandemic. Many of the 'solutions' to the issue are technological and thus out of their hands, as well as being unpredictable. Some of the solutions that they can 'control' are particularly unpalatable, such as raising prices to reduce demand or any scheme that would impact 'frequent flyers'. In fact, it is estimated that US$5 trillion in capital investment would be needed to deliver on the Net Zero promise and the idea of passing along these costs to consumers is something that the industry will avoid, if at all possible, unless government policy demands it (Whitley, 2023).

Questions

1 How does aviation contribute to carbon pollution?
2 How much carbon is produced by burning a gallon of fuel?
3 What impact might carbon restrictions have on the industry?
4 What are the various sectors of industry doing to address carbon emissions?
5 Discuss the new technologies for reducing carbon and/or fuel burn.
6 What issues are preventing the airline industry from reaching Net Zero 2050

References

Air Transport Association (2007), 'ATA and 'safe' agree that modernized ATC will significantly reduce fuel consumption and US oil dependence', *ATA News Release*. Available at: www.airlines. or/government/issuesbrief/alt+fuels,htm

Airport Council International (ACI) and Air Transport Action Group (ATAG) (1998), *Air rail links: Guide to best practice*, Geneva: ACI-ATAG Press.

Biofuels Digest (2013) China Eastern Airlines to run 100% biofuel flights after successful test run. Available at: https://www.biofuelsdigest.com/bdigest/2013/04/29/china-eastern-airlines-to-run-100-biofuel-flights-after-successful-test-run/

Bond, D. (2007), 'Green is for go', *Aviation Week and Space Technology*. August 19: 52–55.

Brown, L. R.(2006), *Plan B 2.0*. London: W.W. Norton & Company.

Bruno, M & Warwick, G (2013) Energy equation, *Aviation Week & Space technology*, July 29: 40–41.

Campbell, C. J. (2005), *Oil crisis*. Essex, UK: Multi-Science Publishing Company, LTD.

Carey, B. (2013) KLM begins biofuel flights between New York, Amsterdam, Available at https://www.ainonline.com/aviation-news/2013-03-08/klm-begins-biofuel-flights-between-new-york-amsterdam

Daggett, D. L., Henricks, R. C., Walther, R., & Corporan, E.(2007) '*Alternative fuels for use in commercial aircraft*', Boeing Company, Seattle.

Dailey, B. (2010) *Air transport and the environment*. Ashgate Publishing Ltd: Aldershot, UK.

DFW New Release (2007), 'DFW International Airport's Environmental Success Lands EPA Recognition –Earns Participation in National Environmental Performance Track Program', Available at: www.dfwairport.com

Environmental Defense (2007), 'How your pollution is calculated', Available At: https://www.fightglobalwarming.com/content.cfm?contentid=5043

Environmental Protection Agency (2023) Carbon pollution from transportation. Available at: https://www.epa.gov/transportation-air-pollution-and-climate-change/carbon-pollution-transportation#:~:text=Transportation%20and%20Climate%20Change,-Burning%20fossil%20fuels&text=%E2%80%8BGreenhouse%20gas%20(GHG)%20emissions,contributor%20of%20U.S.%20GHG%20emissions

European Environment Agency (2023) EU achieves 20-20-20 climate targets, 55% emissions cut by 2030 reachable with more efforts and policies. Available at: https://www.eea.europa.eu/highlights/eu-achieves-20-20-20

FAA (2012) FAA Aerospace Forecast Fiscal Years 2012-2032. Available at https://www.faa.gov/about/office_org/headquarters_offices/apl/aviation_forecasts/aerospace_forecasts/2012-2032/media/2012%20FAA%20Aerospace%20Forecast.pdf

FAA (2023) FAA Aerospace Forecast: Fiscal years 2023-2043. Available at https://www.faa.gov/sites/faa.gov/files/FY%202023-2043%20Full%20Forecast%20Document%20and%20Tables_0.pdf

Foster, T. (2023) Qatar Airways CEO says aviation industry will miss 2050 net zero target. CNN Business. Available at : https://www.cnn.com/2023/06/05/business/qatar-airways-net-zero-aviation

General Aviation Manufacturers Association (2006), 'Industry Facts', Available at: www.gama.aero/aboutGAMA/industryFacts.php

Global Market Insights (2023) Air Cargo Industry Analysis. Available at: https://www.gminsights.com/industry-analysis/air-cargo-market

Gopal, K. (2023) Mike Huckabee is now peddling climate disinformation to children. Mother Jones. Available at: https://www.motherjones.com/politics/2023/08/mike-huckabee-kids-guide-climate-misinformation-denialism/

Grose, T. K. (2013) Reshaping flight for fuel efficiency: Five technologies on the runway. Available at: https://news.nationalgeographic.com/news/energy/2013/04/130423-reshaping-flight-for-fuel-efficiency/

Grunwald, M. (2008), 'The clean energy scam', *Time*, 7 April, pp. 39–45.

Hughes, D. (2007), 'ATM is no silver bullet', *Aviation Week and Space Technology*. August 19: 66–68.

International Air Transport Association (2013) Fact Sheet: Industry Statistics. Available at https://www.iata.org/pressroom/facts_figures/fact_sheets/Documents/industry-facts.pdf

International Air Transport Association (2021) Resolution on the industry's commitment to reach net zero carbon emissions by 2050. Available at https://www.iata.org/contentassets/d13875e9ed784f75bac90f000760e998/iata-agm-resolution-on-net-zero-carbon-emissions.pdf

Johnson, P. (2023) Car wars report says Ford, GM, and Stellates will gain the most US EV market share. Electrek. Available at: https://electrek.co/2023/06/23/car-wars-ford-gm-stellantis-gain-most-us-ev-market-share/

Kaplan, J. (2013) Warming whoops: Scientists debate the failing rate of rising temperatures, Fox News. Available at : https://www.foxnews.com/science/2013/09/17/is-global-warming-actually-far-lower-than-scientists-predicted/

Keating, D. (2013) EU offers retreat on aviation emissions. Available at https://www.europeanvoice.com/article/imported/eu-offers-retreat-on-aviation-emissions/78094.aspx

Kluger, J. (2007), 'What now?' *Time*, April: 50–60.

McKinnon, J. D. & Meckler, L. (2006), 'Bush eschews harsh medicine in treating US oil 'addiction''. *The Wall Street Journal*, August 9, pp. A1, A9.

Michaels, D. (2008), 'Heathrow makeover to heat up airline wars', *The Wall Street Journal* Online, March 6.

Moorman, R. W. (2008), 'Greening the fleet', *Air Cargo World*, January, pp. 21–27.

NASA (2012) NASA shells out award from ninja star supersonic plan design. Available at: https://rt.com/news/nasa-grant-supersonic-plane-254/

Neimann, G. (2007), *Big Brown: The untold story of UPS*. San Francisco: John Wiley and Sons.

Nelms, D. (2007), 'Oversized ambitions: The outsized air cargo market is growing rapidly'. *Air Cargo World*, April: 16–20.

Next Energy News (2008), 'Airbus A-380 becomes first commercial jet to use biofuel'. Available at: https://www.nextenergynews.com/news1/next-energy-news2.4d.html. https://www.biofuelsdigest.com/bdigest/2013/04/29/china-eastern-airlines-to-run-100-biofuel-flights-after-successful-test-run/

Norris, G. (2013), 'Timeless turbine', *Aviation Week and Space Technology*. July 22: 40–43.

Ott, J. (2007), 'Clearing the AIR', *Aviation Week and Space Technology*. August 19: 54–55.

Pilling, M. & Thompson, J. (2007), 'Carbon storm', *Airline Business*, February, pp. 54–56.

Port of Seattle (2006), 'Environmental Programs'. www.portseattle.org/community/environment

Reuters News Agency (2013) EU ETS wins lifeline after tight EU parliament vote. Available at: https://www.businessspectator.com.au/news/2013/7/4/carbon-markets/eu-ets-wins-lifeline-after-tight-eu-parliament-vote

Rhoades, D. L. (2003), *Evolution of international aviation: Phoenix rising*. Aldershot, UK: Ashgate Publishing.

Rolls-Royce (2021) 'Spirit of Innovation' stakes claim to be the world's fastest all-electric vehicle. Available at https://www.rolls-royce.com/media/press-releases/2021/19-11-2021-spirit-of-innovation-stakes-claim-to-be-the-worlds-fastest-all-electric-vehicle.aspx

Rolls-Royce (2022) Rolls-Royce and EasyJet set new world record. Available at: https://www.rolls-royce.com/media/press-releases/2022/28-11-2022-rr-and-easyjet-set-new-aviation-world-first-with-successful-hydrogen-engine-run.aspx

SBAC (2013, SBAC Aviation and environment briefing papers: Open rotor engines. Available at: https://www.sustainableaviation.co.uk/wp-content/uploads/open-rotor-engine-briefing-paper.pdf

Shauck, M. E. & Zanin, M. G. (1990), *The first transatlantic flight on ethanol fuel*. Renewable Aviation Fuel Development Center. Baylor University. www3.baylor.edu/bias/publications/trasnatlantic flight.pdf. Accessed February 3, 2007.

Shauck, M. E. & Zanin, M. G. (2001), *The present and future potential of biomass fuels in aviation*. Renewable Aviation Fuel Development Center, Baylor University. www3.baylor.edu/bias/publications/bomassfuels.pdf

Statista (2023) Total fuel consumption of US airlines from 2004 to 2021. Available at: https://www.statista.com/statistics/197690/us-airline-fuel-consumption-since-2004/

Stephens, J. & Leonnig, C. D. (2011) 'Documents show politics infused Obama 'green' programs', Washington Post. Available at https://www.washingtonpost.com/politics/specialreports/solyndra-scandal

Stoller, G. (2006), 'Concern grows over pollution from jets: Aviation emissions will take off along with worldwide air travel', *USA Today*, December 19, pp. 1A–2A.

Sustainable Aviation (2006) *Sustainable Aviation Progress Report 2006*. www.sustainableaviation.co.uk. Accessed April 30, 2007.

Timperley, J. (2021) The six problems aviation must fix to hit net zero. The Guardian. Available at: https://www.theguardian.com/environment/2021/sep/05/the-six-problems-aviation-must-fix-to-hit-net-zero

Turney, R. (2008), 'Virtual air, Air Cargo World', March, pp. 1314.

United Press International (2008) Virgin Atlantic to test jet biofuel. Available at: https://www.upi.com/NewsTrack/Top_News/2008/02/06/virgin_atlantic

US Department of Energy 2005. *Biofuels encyclopedia*. USDOE, Washington, D.C.

US Energy Information Administration (2013), Frequently asked questions. Available at: https://www.eia.gov/tools/faqs/faq.cfm?id=23&t=10

US Energy Information Administration (2023), Annual Energy outlook 2023. Available at https://www.eia.gov/outlooks/aeo/narrative/index.php#TheElectricityMixinth

Ward, M. (2023) Biden faces calls to declare climate emergency as he heads to Maui, Available at: https://www.politico.com/news/2023/08/20/biden-climate-emergency-hawaii-00111973

Warwick, G. (2013) Energy-savings technologies to watch, *Aviation Week & Space Technology*, July 29: 44–45.

Whitley, A. (2023) Airline passengers will be forced to pay for $5 trillion carbon cleanup. Bloomberg, Available at https://www.bloomberg.com/news/features/2023-08-10/airline-travelers-will-pay-trillions-to-clean-up-carbon-footprint-of-flying#xj4y7vzkg

Websites

DHL (2024), https://www.dhl.com/global-en/delivered/sustainability/future-of-alternative-fuels.html

FedEx (2023), https://newsroom.fedex.com/fedex-express-begins-the-trial-of-renewable-diesel-to-reduce-well-to-wheel-carbon-emissions-in-uk-linehaul-truck-network

UPS (2022), https://about.ups.com/us/en/our-impact/sustainability.html

PART IV

FUTURE CHALLENGES (2023–)

20 After the Revolution

Learning Objectives

After reading this chapter, you should have a good understanding of:

LO1: the impact of 9/11 security concerns on the cargo industry
LO2: the role of fuel prices in air cargo
LO3: the role of 3PL and 4PL in the cargo industry
LO4: the growth of the integrated carriers

Key Terms, Concepts & People

TSA	FIATA	RFID
3PL	4PL	Diversification
9/11 Commission		

Trading Time for Money

If the closing decades of the twentieth century saw the creation of a tightly linked, liberal, global trading economy, then the opening decades of the twenty-first century put that system to the test in a succession of ways. Starting with the events of September 11, 2001, the new century was not kind to most sectors of the aviation/aerospace industry. The airline and air cargo world were rocked by the events of 9/11 and it took much of the first decade of the new century to work through issues related to security and technology. Chapter 15 addressed the technological side of the equation. This chapter will consider the global and national policy side. While companies struggled to deal with these issues, the industry entered a period of fuel price volatility as it headed unknowingly into the next big crisis – the Global Financial Crisis (GFC) of 2008. The GFC saw economies around the world falter and contract. If the airline industry is cyclical, that is, sensitive to the business cycle, then air cargo is the 'canary in the coal mine' that signals when the business cycle is starting to turn down. Unlike the proverbial canary, which dies in the presence of toxic gas in the mine, air cargo does not die, but sharp drops in air cargo volumes signal that firms are cutting costs in their supply chain by moving to lower-cost transportation options or closer suppliers. In effect, they are trading longer shipping times for lower costs or moving suppliers closer to reduce shipping costs at the expense of somewhat higher manufacturing or supply costs.

DOI: 10.4324/9781003405306-24

Table 20.1 Price of Fuel and Air Travel

Year	Crude oil ($)*
2000	27.39
2001	23.00
2002	22.81
2003	27.69
2004	37.66
2005	50.04
2006	58.30
2007	64.20
2008	91.48
2009	53.48
2010	71.21
2011	87.04
2012	86.46
2013	91.17
2014	85.60
2015	41.85
2016	36.34
2017	43.97
2018	57.77
2019	50.01
2020	32.25
2021	60.84
2022	87.40

* Annual average domestic crude oil prices.
Source: Mahon, Historical crude prices. Available at: https://inflationdata.com/articles/inflation-adjusted-prices/historical-crude-oil-prices-table/

Combine the GFC with a dramatic jump in fuel prices in 2008 (Table 20.1) and the industry began talking about the 'depressed levels' of air cargo. While air cargo volume rebounded 18.5 percent at the start of the second decade of the twenty-first century (2010), there was another slowdown in 2011 and 2012. Since 2001, annual air cargo growth has only averaged 3.7 percent a year. Evidence from freighter conversion orders, particularly for widebody conversions, seemed to support the idea that air cargo operators would continue to see a challenging and uneven landscape in the second decade of the new century (Boeing, 2012; McCurry, 2013). In the December 2013 issue of *Air Cargo World*, the lead editorial was entitled 'How to reflect on a year best to forget.' The article lamented the troubles at key all-cargo operators such as Air Cargo Germany, CargoLux, the cargo alliance of Air France–KLM, etc. before ending with the hope that the new year would provide some sign of recovery in air freight (Air Cargo World, 2013).

Air freight was the only major mode of transportation whose average length of haul rose during the 1990s (Bureau of Transportation Statistics, 2005). If falling transportation costs helped to create the logistics revolution, then the rising cost of fuel and security combined to slow its progress. Of course, rising costs also prompted a classic, economic response – consolidation, which helped industries try to lower their costs by creating economies of scale. As we saw in Chapter 16, the bleak beginning of the second decade of the twenty-first century would herald an amazing turnaround in aviation as the decade neared its end. Of course, the history of the industry has always been one of boom and bust, so we should not be surprised when the 'golden ages' turn bleak. The Global Pandemic, which can be dated precisely to the World Health Organization declaration of a Public Health Emergency of International Concern on January 30, 2020, managed to combine a bit of both for the air cargo sector of the industry (WHO, 2020). In this chapter, we will consider what this latest crisis meant for the air cargo industry as the global system considers the lessons of a tightly linked, complex supply chain.

While other industries were undergoing their twentieth-century transformation in logistics and supply chains, the aviation/aerospace manufacturers underwent a revolution of their own. In the case of Boeing, the percentages of outsourcing by model were as follows: 30 percent for the B-767, 50 percent for the B-777, and 70 percent for the B-787 (Scott & Kelly, 2013). While the major manufacturers are outsourcing more and more of the aircraft, they are also trying to reduce the overall number of suppliers to reduce the transaction costs of monitoring. While outsourcing was intended by Boeing to reduce the development time of the B-787 from six years to four years, quality and monitoring issues pushed the project back three years and also added billions to the budget. Technical problems forced Boeing to send out hundreds of engineers to suppliers and restructure their entire sub-assembly process (Denning, 2013). The Global Pandemic would also disrupt aerospace supply chains, but the nightmare struggle of the global airline industry would overshadow these problems.

Taking the new century crisis by crisis, we will start by examining the policy changes that grew out of the 9/11 attacks, then look at the issue of fuel costs before we grapple with the ramifications of the Global Pandemic and the current and, possible, future of air cargo. Finally, we will look at our integrators (FedEx and UPS), the postal system, and the new player in air cargo, Amazon.

Securing the Goods

In the US, the 9/11 Commission made several recommendations for securing cargo entering the United States, including a requirement for 100 percent physical inspection of all cargo. Of most concern was the cargo carried on passenger aircraft. Only in 2012 did the Transportation Security Administration (TSA) finally set a December 2012 deadline for 100 percent screening for explosives on international inbound passenger carriers. However, the 9/11 Commission envisioned the requirement applying to all types and forms of cargo, surface, and air. While the concept received wide support when it was first released, it faced several obstacles on the road to implementation. Legislation in the US House of Representatives called for a three-year phase-in to 100 percent screening in 2009, although the Bush White House argued that the technology did not yet exist to handle the level of cargo entering the US without substantially impeding the flows of trade. A debate even developed over the wording between the House and US Senate versions: that is, how does 100 percent inspection differ from 100 percent screening? After all, screening could involve a system for evaluating risk, gathering intelligence, and assessing documentation rather than physically inspecting/scanning cargo. Air cargo operators argued that they already screened all their freight shipments in one fashion or another. Further complicating the matter, auditors for the US Congress suggested that full physical inspection of all cargo on passenger aircraft alone would cost approximately US$3.6 billion over 10 years (Moorman, 2007a). The October 2010 terrorist bomb, which involved supposed printer cartridges coming from Yemen to the US, was another major blow to the TSA program of 100 percent physical screening. Although the plot was thwarted, it prompted US and EU officials to rethink their policies in many ways, including mandating security controls at the point of origin (Solomon, 2013).

One major change to cargo shipping was the 24-hour rule. As the name implies, shippers to the US were required to submit advance electronic transmissions of information pertaining to cargo bound for the US. This detail information on shippers and the items to be shipped (bill of lading) was to be approved before the cargo could be loaded on any vessel bound for the US (Customs and Border Protection, 2004). As one means of facilitating clearance, Customs and Border Patrol stationed personnel at several foreign locations to prescreen freight. While this move was initially controversial in a few countries, it has largely been accepted as the price of doing business with the US. Approximately 80 percent of maritime shipments are not prescreened before reaching the US port of entry (US Customs Clearance, 2019).

Early efforts of the TSA to improve cargo security were severely criticized in a report by the US Department of Homeland Security's Office of Inspector General who cited the TSA as having too few cargo inspectors, vague regulations, and an ineffective database for tracking violators (Moorman, 2007b). One response by the TSA to these issues was to create a cargo version of the Known Traveler program, now called the Certified Cargo Screening Program (CCSP). Under the program, the TSA certified cargo screening facilities to screen cargo provided to airlines for shipment on passenger flights. Beyond these achievements in 100 percent screening for passenger flights, the 100 percent physical inspection mandate gave way to the more realistic approach of risk-based assessment. The TSA signed agreements with several trading partners, simply acknowledging that they accepted the cargo security programs of these nations as being commensurate with those of the US. Thus, the US 'found a way' to declare 100 percent screening without the inspection (Hienz, 2012). This outcome pleased the International Air Transport Association (IATA) and the International Federation of Freight Forwarders (FIATA), whose 2007 Global Air Cargo Security Industry Task Force recommended the harmonization of security regimes across countries and expressed concern that some of the national laws being proposed, particularly in the US, were 'not proportionate to the threat'. John Edwards, then-IATA head of cargo security, suggested that governments avoid comparing security for passengers to air cargo because most air cargo travels on pallets or in containers that have been packed under secure conditions. Like much of the air cargo industry itself, the Task Force argued that the security focus should be shifted to the point of origin rather than the point of departure (airport) and that mandating costly, unproven equipment would be prohibitively expensive and damaging to world trade and economies (Doyle, 2007).

Future of Fuel

Airlines reported an overall rise of 90 percent in their costs between 2000 and 2008, with fuel costs surpassing labor costs in total operations expenses (26 percent to 23 percent) (Associated Press, 2008). This was before the oil spike of 2008. Table 20.1 shows the annual average domestic (US) crude oil prices from 2000 to 2022. The new century started with crude oil prices below US$30.00. Prices hit US$91.48 in 2008 before dropping back to US$71.21 in 2010. In the second decade prices fluctuated between US$91.17 and US$41.85. The first year of the Global Pandemic crude oil prices dropped to US$32.25, but have begun to climb back toward US$90.00 a barrel. As noted in Chapter 16, fuel prices are one of the many costs over which air carriers have little leverage. Aside from hedging strategies, fleet renewal, weight reduction, and operational flight changes, there is little that carriers themselves can do to affect fuel costs.

Before the scope of the Global Financial Crisis was fully understood, the Air Cargo Management Group had forecast a 5–8 percent decline in global air freight traffic on an average monthly jet fuel cost of US$2.769 a gallon. This was predicted to result in some increases in fuel surcharges. Surcharges rose from 50 cents in early 2007 to 80–85 cents by January 2008 (Air Cargo World, 2008). In 2009, air cargo plummeted from 15.5 billion Freight Ton Kilometers (FTKs) per month to roughly 10 FTKs per month. At this time, the cost of air freight was roughly 14 times that of sea transport. Shippers began to rethink their supply chains and restricted air freight to perishable, high-value cargo. Some even began moving high-value cargo such as LCDs and integrated circuits from air to sea (Pearce, 2011). Air freight growth for 2013 continued at a weaker pace than the 3.7 percent that it had averaged since 2001, with only the Middle East and Latin America seeing robust growth year-over-year (IATA, 2013). Despite dire predictions, air cargo freight tonne kilometres grew 9 percent in 2017, the best rate since 2010 (IATA, 2017). Things appeared to be looking up. Then came the Global Pandemic.

Global Pandemic

Chapter 16 dealt extensively with the impact of the Global Pandemic on airlines, including their efforts to increase revenue through an emphasis on cargo. Here we will examine the impact on the non-passenger airline segment of the industry. The Pandemic was a boom for freight forwarders and air cargo who posted profits of 4 percent and 9 percent, respectively, in 2020. Initially, demand was driven by the need for protective personal equipment and medication, but challenges in the ocean shipping sector and strong growth in e-commerce sales continued to benefit this sector. Air cargo yields rose 40 percent in 2020 and 15 percent in 2021. Load factors in 2021 were 10 percentage points higher than 2019 (Bouwer, Krishnan, Saxon, & Tufft, 2022). Boeing predicted a 4 percent growth for the air cargo industry through 2021, slightly above the historic 3.7 percent rate; however, the usual threats to aviation – war and recession – continued to loom large (Weeks, Henderson, & Galvez, 2023).

Two more factors should be considered in predicting the future of air cargo demand. The first is the changing nature of supply chains. As the Pandemic clearly demonstrated, the more complex a system becomes, the less resilience it demonstrates. The 'breakdown' in supply chains was one of the big stories of the Pandemic. A *Wall Street Journal* article in 2021 attempted to explain the problems using the Utah manufacturer of Bullfrog Spas. In a typical day, 60,000 components arrived by plane, train, and air from multiple manufacturers in multiple countries. If some of these components were delayed because the factory was closed for COVID, transportation backed up or snarled at ports, or open factories could not get the parts they needed from their suppliers, then assembly lines were shut down, with partially completed products on the line waiting (Hufford, Kim, & Levinson, 2021). The Pandemic 'may' be over, but companies are reconsidering supply chains and KPMG (2023) has reported seven trends that may reshape things: nations are skeptical about cooperation; cybercrime is ramping up; material access is in turmoil; manufacturing footprints are changing shape; retail and distribution supply chains are morphing; technology investment is accelerating; and Scope 3 emissions are scrutinized. The exact nature of the changes remains unknown, as does the speed with which companies will move to create more resilient supply chains, but change does appear to be coming.

The last trend highlights an issue that neither airlines nor air cargo have addressed – emissions and sustainability. If either segment of the industry attempted, or were forced, to implement actions to address their emissions, then the future would be radically changed. In the US, these efforts have also become so politicized that the fight itself will have major repercussions on the industry.

Hard Times and New Friends

As the new century opened, the venerable US Postal Service (USPS) announced that it would record a $300 million loss for the fiscal year. Reasons given for the loss included a decline in first class cards and letters, increased gasoline prices, and additional labor costs (Robinson, 2000). Although the loss proved to be only US$199 million, the USPS was clearly struggling under the weight of growing competition and changing times. Some of the challenges facing the USPS are well known to older, established firms such as growing fixed expenses for pension plans, workers' compensation, health benefits, and the interest expense of debt. Further adding to these challenges were concerns that postal volumes would continue to decline due to competition from other express and parcel companies as well as new electronic alternatives. Unfortunately, the USPS has a limited ability to deal with these issues. Even postal rate changes must be approved by the Postal Rate Commission, who often hear arguments from 'interested parties' for lower rates. The USPS attempted to address these basic problems through several classic business tactics: restructuring, layoffs, asset sales, accounting adjustments, and outsourcing (Ho, 2001; Robinson, 2000). It is ironic that one outcome of these struggles was a June 2006 announcement that the USPS had signed a US$100 million deal with UPS to carry US mail on its jets. The three-year contract made UPS responsible for delivering mail to 96 US cities. After years of battling the USPS for the right to deliver packages across the US, UPS had now made a 'pact with the devil' in a sign of the changing world of airmail and small packages (Niemann, 2007). Also in the same year, the Postal Accountability Enhancement Act was passed separating the USPS services into market-dominant and competitive products. Under this legislation, the USPS was able to make and retain profits on competitive product offerings but prohibited from cross-subsidizing between the two categories. The USPS could cut some of its cost in international markets, if it were allowed to include foreign carriers in the bidding process; at the present time, however, they are prohibited from doing so unless the services of US carriers are deemed 'inadequate.' Sadly, 2006 also witnessed the imposition of new rules mandated by the US Congress; these rules required the USPS to make annual payments of US$1.4 billion to a healthcare fund for future retirees. While the USPS reported that operating revenues for the third quarter of 2013 were up 3.6 percent in part due to increased parcel shipping from online purchases, this still equated to a loss of US$740 million for the quarter. Given losses of US$16 billion for the prior year, the USPS has asked to do away with Saturday delivery and the re-payment to the healthcare fund, but action by the US Congress appears unlikely (Nagaguna, 2013).

After years of fighting in the US Congress over the fate of the USPS, in 2022 Congress passed the Postal Service Reform Act. Among other things, this act ended the requirement for the USPS to pre-fund retirement benefits, forgave $57 billion in scheduled payments to retiree health benefits funds, mandated future retiree enrollment in Medicare, committed to a six-day mail service, and encouraged the USPS to work with local, state, and tribal governments on non-postal services. The end of the mandate alone will save the USPS over US$50 billion (National Labor News, 2022). This bill was a victory for the USPS and the many rural areas that rely mostly on them for service.

Meanwhile, in sharp contrast to its American cousin (USPS), January 1, 1990, marked the beginning of a new era for a company that traced its roots to a time 500 years ago; legislation enabled the privatization of public postal and telecommunication services and Deutsche Post would seize their opportunities. They turned around old losses to break even by the mid-1990s and went public in 2000. They acquired Danzas Holding, a Swiss logistics company, Air Express International, and the remaining shares of DHL and Excel. These acquisitions were simply the largest in a series of acquisitions noted in a 2007 feature in *Aviation Week & Space Technology* entitled 'Evolution of the Air Cargo Industry'. In the center foldout, the article traced the history of the key players among the integrators, forwarders, and airlines since the 1980s. It visually displayed the name, size, and region where each player was acquiring companies and assets. In the middle of all this activity was a very busy Deutsche Post (CRA International, 2007). Although DHL would withdraw from the US, Deutsche Post DHL would become the world's leading mail and logistics company with a presence in 220 countries (World Economic Forum, 2012). Deutsche Post DHL announced in 2013 that it would begin a German-wide grocery delivery service by 2015 (Postal News, 2013). Deutsche Post DHL is now considered to be one of the most diversified transport and logistics companies and is looking for to a 'soft landing' after the Pandemic highs in cargo (Solomon, 2023).

Logistics in Brown

While the deal with the USPS was a sweet one for UPS, they also began a series of acquisitions in 2000 that would strengthen their ground and logistics operations (CRA International, 2007). During the period, 2002–2006, UPS completed 11 such acquisitions. Some of these acquisitions were designed to strengthen their operations in key regions such as China, Japan, and Europe. Others were undertaken to broaden their capabilities in freight-forwarding, heavy freight, and less-than-truckload services. The 2001 acquisition of Mail Boxes Etc, at the time the largest franchisers of retail shipping and postal services, would set the stage for The UPS Store. Overall, UPS grew during this period at a compound rate of 4 percent a year. Domestic package delivery accounted for 64 percent of their 2006 revenue, with international package delivery accounting for another 19 percent. The remaining 17 percent of their revenue came from their supply chain and freight division (UPS Annual Report, 2006).

In 1999, their logistics/supply chain services became known as UPS Logistics Technologies. This set the stage for UPS Solutions and the ad campaign to rebrand on their love of logistics. As part of this journey, the company's transportation, and logistics software, ROADNET, would help firms like Frito-Lay, Costco, and SYSCO optimize routes, plan territories, dispatch vehicles, and track deliveries. UPS would help manufacturing companies with their supply chains, redesigning Ford Motor Company's system for getting cars from the assembly plant to showroom floors, helping Harley-Davidson Motor Company track and inventory inbound parts and accessories, and improving the logistics of the service center of European medical supplier, Royal Philips Electronics (Niemann, 2007). The integration of several acquired units in 2006 – the Motor Cargo unit of Overnite and Menlo Worldwide Forwarding – led to some disappointing revenue results for that year, but overall revenues for the freight and supply chain unit were up 33 percent from the prior year (UPS Annual Report, 2006). By 2012, total revenue would stand at US$54.1 billion. Package operations would account for US$45 billion while supply chain and freight solutions would represent US$9.1 billion of the total (UPS website, 2013).

Table 20.2 provides an overall snapshot of the operational results for UPS, a company that still defines itself by its primary business of time-definite delivery even as it expands into the broader area of logistics and supply chains. The Global Pandemic saw UPS posting record revenues at the same time as they took pension losses and an impairment chair for the sale of UPS Freight (Yamanouchi, 2021). The sale of UPS Freight, a troubled unit dealing in less-than-truckload shipping, is part of an effort to improve return on invested capital and focus on its core parcel delivery business (Solomon, 2021).

Table 20.2 UPS Growth 2004–2022

Year	Revenue*	Net income*	Assets*
2004	36,582	3,333	33,088
2005	42,581	3,870	35,222
2006	47,547	4,202	33,210
2007	49,692	382	39,042
2008	51,486	3,003	31,879
2009	45,297	2,152	31,883
2010	49,545	3,338	33,597
2011	53,105	3,804	34,701
2012	54,127	807	38,863
2013	55,438	4,372	36,212
2014	58,232	3,032	35,440
2015	58,363	4,844	38,311
2016	62,610	3,422	40,377
2017	66,585	4,905	45,574
2018	71,861	4,791	50,016
2019	74,094	4,440	57,857
2020	84,628	1,343	62,408
2021	97,287	12,890	69,405
2022	100,338	11,548	71,124

* $ (In millions).
Source: UPS website. Data available at:
https://www.investors.ups.com/phoenix.zhtml?c=62900&p=irol-reportsannual
Macrotrends: https://www.macrotrends.net/stocks/charts/UPS/ups/total-assets

Related Diversifications?

The year 2000 marked a new evolution at Federal Express, whose corporate identity changed in 1994 to simply FedEx and which has now established a separate unit called FedEx Express to oversee development in its express-specific service offerings. Ground operations, which began in 1985 with Roadway Package System, a division of Roadway and later Caliber System, became FedEx Ground in 2000 with the acquisition of Caliber. FedEx acquired American Freightways in 2001, adding to earlier acquisitions of Viking Freight (part of Caliber). In 2006, FedEx acquired Watkins Motor Lines, a ground, freight-forwarding company. These units created FedEx Freight, which became a leading provider of next- and second day less-than-truckload freight services. By 2013, FedEx would segment itself into four basic units: FedEx Express, FedEx Ground, FedEx Freight, and FedEx Services. Total annual revenues for 2013 topped US$44 billion (FedEx website, 2013).

Table 20.3 shows the growth at FedEx from 2004 to 2022. FedEx has not witnessed the kind of growth in express package volumes that UPS has experienced. In fact, the number of packages fluctuated over this period and remains relatively static. With the various acquisitions, there has been an overall rise in the number of employees, although FedEx has yet to reach the levels of UPS.

Amazon – Changing Roles

The Pandemic might have decreased the passenger traffic at Cincinnati/Northern Kentucky International Airport (CVG), but with the 798,000-square-foot sorting center and the 3-million-square-foot air cargo hub of Amazon, things are booming. Amazon Air has arrived with a different strategy for routes and facilities. Its cargo consists of goods sold in

Table 20.3 FedEx Growth 2004–2022

Year	Revenue*	Net income*	Assets*
2004	24.7	838	19,134
2005	29.4	1,449	20,404
2006	32.3	1,806	22,690
2007	35.2	2,016	24,000
2008	38.0	1,125	25,633
2009	35.5	98	24,244
2010	34.7	1,184	24,902
2011	39.3	1,452	27,385
2012	42.7	2,032	29,903
2013	44.3	2,716	33,567
2014	45.6	2,324	33,070
2015	47.5	1.050	36,531
2016	50.4	1,820	45,959
2017	60.3	2,997	48,552
2018	65.5	4,572	52,330
2019	69.7	540	54,403
2020	69.2	1,286	73,537
2021	84.0	5,231	82,777
2022	93.5	3,826	85,994

* $ (In millions).

Sources: FedEx website:
https://investors.fedex.com/phoenix.zhtml?c=73289&p=irol-reportsannual
Zippia: https://www.zippia.com/fedex-careers-4259/revenue/#annual-revenue
Macrotrends: https://www.macrotrends.net/stocks/charts/FDX/fedex/total-assets

its own online market and its airport facilities are located near its own fulfillment centers (Schneider, 2021). Increasingly, Amazon Air is becoming a hub-focused carrier, but CVG is still much smaller than the hubs of either FedEx or UPS. It is not considered a truly integrated carrier because it offers only one-way delivery (no package pick-up or B2B delivery). Amazon is increasing flight activity three regional hubs – Fort Worth Alliance Airport in Texas, San Bernadino International Airport in California, and Lakeland in Florida. While Amazon's fleet growth since 2020 has exceeded 200 percent, it is still well behind rivals such as FedEx and UPS in many respects, including cubic volume of available cargo space, number of aircraft, number of flights, and aircraft utilization (Kulisch, 2023). Still, Amazon is making its presence known in the air cargo industry like never before.

Millions of Parts Flying Together

There was probably no better illustration of the complexity possible in a logistics supply chain than the aviation/aerospace industry. An aircraft such as the B-747 had as many as 6 million parts (Chamberlin, 2012). Similarly, the Airbus A-360 had 4 million individual parts produced by 1,500 companies in 30 countries. The aerospace supply chain consists of three main tiers (some might include a fourth) that sit below the Aircraft and Engine Original Equipment Manufacturers, commonly called OEMs. Tier 1 companies supply aircraft systems and major aerostructures as well as engage in aircraft design. Tier 2 companies are responsible for components and sub-assemblies. Tier 3 companies produce components and software. These companies are machine shops, many make-to-print operations, makers of fasteners, pins, etc.. Finally, some would include a Tier 4 that represents the materials firms as well as specialty process companies. The latter may include companies engaged in forging or casting parts. There has been a good deal of consolidation in the supply chain, particularly at the Tier 4 level, which has some combining Tiers 3 & 4. Several factors are driving the consolidation. First, there is vertical consolidation that allows raw material firms to capture the scrap produced in machining at Tier 3. There are estimates that up to $8 billion could be lost to scrap in machining, and recapturing and re-using can be quite beneficial. A second reason for consolidation is the desire to move up the supply chain since profit margins tend to rise as you move from raw materials to finished products. The same logic of moving up the chain would also apply to Tiers 1–3 (Michaels, 2013). There are concerns with the aerospace supply chain since roughly 70 percent of the chain for all aerospace manufacturers consists of the same companies. So, if there are only a few companies making composite material or the fasteners used for airframe construction, then there is concern that surging demand might result in a shortage that raises prices and may slow production. The reverse problem has also plagued the industry, that is, slumps in demand place great financial pressure on these lower-tier firms. A general slump in air-craft demand, such as the one the industry experienced after 2008 or the Global Pandemic, means that firms must operate below capacity. The farther down the supply chain a firm resides, the more likely it is to be forced to 'submit' to cancellations and/or delays in orders that are built into contracts. Contracting power normally resides higher in the supply chain, OEM and Tier 1. In any case, these firms dictate terms and conditions to the rest of the supply chain. In fact, many small firms have been forced out of business or into consolidation because of stringent requirement to meet rates of production, quality standards, conduct specific testing, bear the cost of tooling or logistics software, etc. (Canaday, 2013).

The B-787 illustrates some of the issues that challenge complex supply chains. Table 20.4 gives a brief overview of the parts breakdown by country and company. Some of the major problems encountered include an industry-wide shortage of fasteners (June 2007) as well as

Table 20.4 Boeing 787 Parts Breakdown

Part	Country	Company
Wingtips	Korea	KAA
Fixed and moveable leading edges (wings)	US	Spirit
Wing	Japan	Mitsubishi
Centre fuselage	Italy	Alenia
Forward fuselage	US	Spirit
	Japan	Kawasaki
Centre wing box	Japan	Fuji
Landing gear structure forward	France	Messier-Dowty
Lithium-ion batteries	Japan	GS Yuasa
Rear fuselage	US	Boeing
Wing-to-body fairing	US	Boeing
Engine nacelles	US	Goodrich
Engines	US	General Electric
	UK	Rolls-Royce
Horizontal stabilizer	Italy	Alenia
Tail fin	US	Boeing
Passenger entry door	France	Latecoere
Main landing gear	Japan	Kawasaki
Fixed trailing edge (wings)	Japan	Kawasaki
Cargo access doors	Sweden	Saab

Source: Ro, S. (2013) Boeing's 787 Dreamliner is made of parts from all over the world.

the discovery of a misalignment of the cockpit section with the fuselage at the same time (September 2008)), the installation of improper fasteners and a union strike (June 2009), the discovery of a need for reinforcements in the wing-to-fuselage section and microscopic wrinkles in the fuselage (August 2009). Boeing had approximately 50 Tier 1 suppliers around the world for the B-787 and while they did have open applications logistics software that was supposed to help coordinate multi-tier supply chains, this cannot guarantee there are no communication problems with different languages, cultures, or time zones. Further, Boeing mandated that its Tier 1 suppliers coordinate with those in Tiers 2 and 3 to relieve pressure on themselves and thus they relied on these suppliers to monitor quality. Its own relationship with the Tier 1 firms was strained by a company mandate that suppliers had to design and build all tooling for their part of the aircraft without any compensation from Boeing. While outsourcing was not new to Boeing, the level of outsourcing, and the fact that the top tier suppliers were in complete control of the design and lower-tier suppliers, were both unprecedented (Collins, 2010; Gates, 2013).

The Pandemic marked the end of almost 15 years of uninterrupted growth for the aerospace industry. There are three likely changes on the horizon. First, aircraft and aeroengine OEM and Tier 1 will likely begin to shed noncore and underperforming assets. Second, there will likely be widespread failures and consolidation in Tier 3. Third, there will be deleveraging at the Tier 4 level, and the same acquisitions mentioned above between Tier 3 and 4 are likely to unravel. In short, there will be fewer Tier 3s and more Tier 2s as Tier 1 and the OEMs spin off units (Michaels, 2020). As is usually the case, those at the top make the rules and change the system while those at the bottom adapt or die.

Conclusion

Now, the logistics revolution appears to be reversing itself, but the jury is still out as to how far and fast the movement will go. Like most things in life (and business), the pendulum tends to swing between extremes before settling on a temporary 'new-normal'. If supply chains move toward less outsourcing, more inventory, and more simplified supply chains for now, then only time will tell how long the system will remain stable. As the Pandemic revealed, the costs of coordinating and monitoring a highly complex task can be daunting and complexity in created systems decreases resilience. Without further shocks, the system will stabilize. If this book has succeeded in communicating the industry reality, however, then readers will know by now that stability is not a defining feature of the aviation/aerospace industry.

Questions

1 How did 9/11 change the cargo industry?
2 What role might technology play in security and logistics?
3 What effect do rising fuel prices have on the air cargo industry?
4 Discuss the changes at the integrated carriers.
5 What was the impact of the Global Pandemic on cargo carriers?
6 What is the future of the logistics revolution?

References

Air Cargo World (2008) 'Freight's on-off peak', January, p. 4.
Air Cargo World (2013) How best to reflect on a year best to forget, *Air Cargo World*, December, pp. 6–8.

Associated Press (2008) 'Airlines' costs rose in 3Q led by fuel-price jump; Soars 91 percent above 2000 levels'. Available at: https://biz.yahoo.com/ap/080129/airleins_costs_index.htnl

Boeing Corporation (2012) World Air cargo Forecast 2012–13, retrieved at https://www.boeing.com/boeing/commercial/cargo/

Bouwer, J., Krishnan, V., Saxon, S., & Tufft, C. (2022) *Taking stock of the pandemic's impact on global aiation*. McKinset & Company. Available at: https://www.mckinsey.com/industries/travel-logistics-and-infrastructure/our-insights/taking-stock-of-the-pandemics-impact-on-global-aviation

Bureau of Transportation Statistics (2005) 'National transportation statistics 2004'. Available at: www.bts.gov

Canaday, H. (2013) Volume is not the issue, *Aviation Week & Space Technology*, October 28, pp. 46–48.

Chamberlin, C. (2012) *Trends in aerospace industry*, Boeing Shared Services Group Supplier Management. Available at: https://washingtonports.org/wp-content/uploads/2013/02/annual12-chamberlinboeing.pdf

Collins, M. (2010) The Boeing supply chain model. Available at https://www.manufacturing.net/news/2010/07/the-boeing-supply-chain-model

CRA International (2007) 'Evolution of the air cargo industry' *Aviation Week & Space Technology* May 7–14, pp. 48–53.

Customs and Border Protection (2004) 19 CFR Parts 4, 103, 113, 122, 123, 178 and 192. Available at https://www.cbp.gov/bulletins/37genno52.pdf

Denning, S. (2013) What went wrong at Boeing?, Forbes Magazine, January 21. Available at: https://www.forbes.com/sites/stevedenning/2013/01/21/what-went-wrong-at-boeing/

Doyle, J. M. (2007) 'Intervention prevention' *Aviation Week & Space Technology*, May 7–14, pp. 63–64.

Gates, D. (2013) Boeing 787's problems blamed on outsourcing, lack of oversight, The Seattle Times, February 2. Available at: https://seattletimes.com/html/businesstechnology/2020275838_boeing outsourcingxml.html

Hienz, J. (2012) 100 percent air cargo screening exists without fanfare. Available at: https://www.defensemedianetwork.com/stories/100-percent-air-cargo-screening-exits-without-fanfare/

Ho, D. (2001) 'Post office may stop Saturday mail delivery' Associated Press, April 3. Available at: https://www.apwu73.com/bulletin/Post%20may%20stop%20Saturday%

Hufford, A., Kim, K., and Levinson, A. (2021) Why is the supply chain still so snarled? We explain, with a hot tub. *Wall Street Journal*, August 21. Available at: https://www.wsj.com/articles/why-is-the-supply-chain-still-so-snarled-we-explain-with-a-hot-tub-11629987531

IATA (2013) Air freight volumes show signs of life in June. Available at: https://www.iata.org/pressroom/pr/pages/2013-07-30-01.aspx

IATA (2017) Air freight market analysis. Available at: https://www.iata.org/en/iata-repository/publications/economic-reports/air-freight-monthly-analysis---dec-2017/

KPMG (2023) The supply chain trends shaking up 2023. Available at: https://kpmg.com/xx/en/home/insights/2022/12/the-supply-chain-trends-shaking-up-2023.html#:~:text=At%20KPMG%2C%20from%20within%20our,and%20distribution%20supply%20chains%20are

Kulisch, E. (2023) Amazon Air's new reliance on hub airports increases efficiency. FreightWaves. Available at: https://www.freightwaves.com/news/amazon-airs-new-reliance-on-hub-airports-increases-efficiency

McCurry, J. W. (2013) Narrow-bodies pace conversion market, *Air Cargo World*, August, pp. 24–27.

Michaels, K. (2013) Revolution from below, *Aviation Week & Space Technology*, September 9, p. 18.

Michaels, K. (2020) Three predictions for the Post-COVID Aerospace supply chain. Available at: https://www.linkedin.com/pulse/three-predictions-post-covid-aerospace-supply-chain-kevin-michaels

Moorman, R. (2007a) 'Drawing new security lines', *Air Cargo World*, March, pp. 20–24.

Moorman, R. (2007b) 'Secure funding' *Air Cargo World*, October, pp. 10–11.

Nagaguna, E (2013) US postal Service loss narrows on cost cutting. Available at: https://www.reuters.com/article/2013/08/09/us-usa-postal-idUSBRE9780VC20130809

National Labor News (2022) Senate passes bill to save Post Office, St Louis/Southern Illinois Labor Tribune. Available at: https://labortribune.com/senate-passes-bill-to-save-post-office/

Niemann, G. (2007) *Big Brown: The Untold Story of UPS*, Jossey-Bass, San Francisco, CA.

Pearce, B. (2011) Understanding air cargo markets and their importance. Available at: https://www.aci.aero/aci/aci/file/2011%20Events/WAGA2011/presentations/Brian_Pearce_IATA.pdf

Postal News (2013) Deutsche Post to launch online groceries service. Available at: https://postalnews.com/postalnewsblog/2013/08/07/deutsche-post-to-launch-online-groceries-service/

Ro, S. (2013) Boeing's 787 Dreamliner is made of parts from all over the world, Business Insider. Available at: https://www.businessinsider.com/boeing-787-dreamliner-structure-suppliers-2013-10

Robinson, A. M. (2000) 'USPS finances: Are we on the road from universal to invisible?' Available at: https://www.aircargoworld.com/features/0208_1.htm

Schneider, K (2021) Air cargo construction is booming, thanks to Amazon. The New York Times. Available at: https://www.nytimes.com/2021/01/12/business/air-cargo-airports-amazon.html

Scott, A. & Kelly, T. (2013) Analysis: Boeing's JAL loss may bring work back to the US. Available at: https://www.reuters.com/article/2013/10/11/us-boeing-suppliers-analysis-idUSBRE99A0Y4 20131011

Solomon, A. (2013) A new day for global air cargo security, Air Cargo World. Available at: https://www.aircargoworld.com/Air-Cargo-News/2013/03/a-new-day-for-global-air-cargo-security/0812813

Solomon, M. (2021) UPS closes curtain on tough 15 year old LTL run. FreightWaves. Available at: https://www.freightwaves.com/news/ups-to-sell-ups-freight-after-a-tough-15-year-run

Solomon, M. (2023) Deutsche Post DHL reports strong 2022 results, moderating Q4 performance. FreightWaves. Available at: https://www.freightwaves.com/news/deutsche-post-dhl-reports-strong-2022-results-moderating-q4-performance

UPS Annual Report (2006) 2006 Annual Report. Available at: https://www.ups.com

US Customs Clearance (2019) How to clear US customs with cargo, AFC International. Available at https://usacustomsclearance.com/process/how-to-clear-u-s-customs-with-cargo/

Weeks, J., Henderson, F., & Galvez, J. (2023) Emerging from COVID-19: Transformations in the air cargo market. AviationPros. Available at: https://www.aviationpros.com/ground-handling/article/53028343/emerging-from-covid19-transformations-in-the-air-cargo-market

WHO (2020) COVID-19 Public Health Emergency of International Concern (PHEIC) global research and innovation forum. Available at: https://www.who.int/publications/m/item/covid-19-public-health-emergency-of-international-concern-(pheic)-global-research-and-innovation-forum

World Economic Forum (2012) Deutsche Post DHL. Available at: https://www.weforum.org/strategic-partners/deutsche-post-dhl

Yamanouchi, K. (2021) UPS reports record reb=venue as pandemic fuels online orders, shipping. The Daily Item. Available at: https://www.dailyitem.com/business/ups-reports-record-revenue-as-pandemic-fuels-online-orders-shipping/article_4f3a90b6-5d72-5ff1-babe-ae26350be470.html

Websites

Deutsche Post DHL, https://www.dp-dhl.de

FedEx (2013), https://www.fedex.com

UPS (2013), https://www.ups.com

21 A Twenty-First-Century Air Space

Learning Objectives

After reading this chapter, you should have a good understanding of:

LO1:   the projected growth in air travel
LO2:   the advantages of using technology to expand airspace over infrastructure expansion
LO3:   the key elements of NextGen/SESAR systems
LO4:   the stumbling blocks to NextGen deployment

Key Terms, Concepts & People

NextGen	SESAR	ADS-B
SWIM	DataComm	user fee
FMS	ERAM	NATCA

Crowded Skies

In their Vision 2050 report, the International Air Transport Association (IATA) predicted that there would be continued growth in passenger traffic, with 16 billion passengers world-wide by 2050 (IATA, 2011). While the Global Pandemic was not on anyone's radar when this report came out, once travel restrictions were lifted, demand for air travel surged past airline expectations and appears to be back on track for continued growth. In fact, Airports Council International (ACI) World Airport Traffic Forecasts 2022–2041 are predicting 19.3 billion passengers by 2041, an increase over the earlier IATA prediction (ACI, 2023). While much of this growth is still expected in the developing world, the United States and China will continue to be the leading markets, with 23 and 16 percent, respectively, of the world's aircraft movements in 2041. As air travel entered the twenty-first century, the air traffic systems of developed nations were already straining to meet growth rates (IATA, 2011). Given the size of the existing base in the US, even a small annual increase can add up quickly. The Federal Aviation Administration (FAA) had predicted that traffic levels would reach one billion passengers per year by 2024 (FAA, 2012). In fact, the US reached this figure in 2018 and rose to 1.1 billion for 2019 (Bureau of Transportation Statistics, 2020).

DOI: 10.4324/9781003405306-25

Meanwhile, the European Union also predicted significant growth and posted their own record of 2.43 billion passengers in 2019 (ACI-Europe, 2023).

It was clear in the final years of the twentieth century that accommodating these levels of air traffic would require nations to make some very significant investments in aviation infrastructure; otherwise the capacity shortfalls would threaten both growth and safety. In developing nations, the emphasis was on building the basic infrastructure of an aviation system – airports (runways, terminals), radar stations, and supporting infrastructure (access roads, warehouses, intermodal links, maintenance facilities). These regions also needed to address the need for trained personnel to man the system. While some of these nations have made rapid strides, others have continued to struggle, usually because of a lack of money. Specific regional issues have already been covered in earlier chapters. Here it is important to note that the nations that can invest, and are doing so, could take advantage of technological advances in air space management without facing the difficult and sometimes abrupt transitions that more developed regions are facing. In some ways, the situation is like the industrial rebuilding that took place in Europe and Asia after World War II. A new steel mill would incorporate the new closed-hearth rather than the less efficient open-hearth technology. In a similar way, developing nations can leapfrog to a satellite-based system rather than the old ground-based radar of the post-World War II era.

For the early pioneers in aviation (mostly those in United States and Europe), the problems are different – maintaining an aging infrastructure while transitioning to a new system of organization. James C. May of the Air Transport Association has noted that Charles Lindbergh, who made history in 1927 with his solo trans-Atlantic flight, would have been surprised to discover that 80 years later 'we still rely on old technology that forces aircraft to fly inefficient, less direct routes, with unnecessarily inefficient separation requirements' (May, 2006). In fact, the current ground radar and voice communication system dates from the period just after World War II. The system had been modernized over the decades, but was essentially still based on the same general technology and framework. Key indicators that the aviation systems of North America and Europe were struggling with capacity issues included slot controls at airports, flight delays, flight cancellations, and air traffic system outages. Although North America had the space to construct more basic infrastructure, i.e. airports and runways, doing so raised environmental concerns as well as the more general 'not-in-my-backyard' (NIMBY) reaction. The closing of several US military bases had raised the hope that some of these facilities could be converted to civilian use, but in many cases local opposition blocked these plans (FAA, 2008). Europe, unlike the US, did not have the land or inclination to consider building new airports and runways as a possible solution. Both regions began exploring technical solutions to their problems.

In this chapter, we will explore the technologies that are expected to shape the air space and aviation system of the twenty-first century in the context of the developed systems of North America and Europe. While some of the conditions and constraints vary, both regions are facing the difficult task of changing the tires on a rapidly moving vehicle. Further, each region has been dealing with a set of political and economic problems that have threatened to derail timely deployment.

Creating the Future

In the US, the Next Generation Air Transportation System (NGATS), commonly referred to as NextGen, was the air transportation solution for the twenty-first century that began to take shape in the closing decades of the previous century. The System Integrated Plan was created in 2004. In Europe, roughly equivalent concepts fall into a program called the Single European Sky ATM Research (SESAR) program. One key difference between the developments in the two regions is that European efforts are also attempting to integrate the airspace and air traffic systems of multiple countries in the EU in accordance with the Single Sky concept. The definition phase (2005–2008) of SESAR was jointly funded by EUROCONTROL and the European Commission. It was tasked with delivering a European ATM Master Plan based on future aviation requirements as defined by key stakeholders in the system. This plan was adopted in October 2012.

SESAR and NextGen envision a totally new architecture that will allow information integration, combining new technologies on the ground and in the sky to create a more efficient system. They are expected to 'create' new capacity by allowing air traffic to utilize the existing airspace more efficiently. The proposed new systems will also help to address many of the economic and environmental concerns facing industry and the public. More efficient, direct descents and ascents that eliminate the need to vector around the airport waiting for a landing slot use less fuel, thus contributing less carbon and other greenhouse gases to the environment and reducing the national dependence on petroleum. The improved utilization of existing airspace relieves some of the need for more airport construction with the environmental impacts that such construction almost always entails. Both US and European efforts began at roughly the same time and were planned for full implementation sometime around 2020–2025.

As with all things in the aviation, the discussion is filled with acronyms. To avoid confusion, the technological discussion that follows will try to broadly identify the systems and concepts. As envisioned. the NextGen system required the development and implementation of eight capabilities: network-enabled information access, performance-based services, aircraft trajectory-based operations, weather assimilation into decision loops, broad-area precision navigation, equivalent visual operations, super density operations, and layered adaptive security (FAA, 2007). There were at least four key technologies:

Automatic Dependent Surveillance-Broadcast (ADS-B) is a satellite-based system that allows aircraft to broadcast their position to others. ADS-B *out* will replace many ground radars with ground-based transceivers. ADS-B *in* would allow aircraft to receive signals from the ground-based transceivers as well as from ADS-B equipment onboard other aircraft.

Performance-Based Navigation is the use of satellite-enabled routes and procedures that provide a high level of positioning accuracy.

System-wide Information Management (SWIM) is a new system architecture that would allow airspace users to access a wide array of data on the National Air Space (NAS) and weather. SWIM is a net-centric link between air traffic management, customers, and the departments of Homeland Security and Defense which would provide full automation and data convergence/synchronization across all authorized users on a common display format.

DataComm is the data communication system that will link airport towers, airline operations centers, and aircraft. It is the satellite, internet-based communication platform of the twenty-first century that will replace much of the old voice communication system. The Data Comm service was completed to 55 airports in December 2015 (FAA, 2020).

While it was originally intended simply as a replacement for an earlier air traffic control system and predates NextGen, the En Route Automation Modernization (ERAM) system has come to be viewed as another critical foundation for NextGen capabilities. ERAM is the high-altitude traffic platform used to control en route aircraft in the US. After a five-year delay, ERAM was declared operational in 2015 (Schofield, 2013). Still, as the General Accounting Office feared, this delay flowed downstream, causing delays in the NextGen system that they expected to extend for years (FAA, 2013; Perera, 2012). Further, there were issues synchronizing ERAM with other systems used on board aircraft and in the airport area to provide the common situational awareness that is viewed as critical to proper, optimized airspace management (Schofield, 2013). For example, since ERAM was designed to manage high-altitude, en route traffic, it did not have the detailed airport information (runway configurations, arrival fixes, etc.) that was contained in modern on board Flight Management Systems (FMS).

The driving vision of modernization has been to replace the old system of ground-based radar and positive voice control with an 'intelligent' aircraft capable of using satellite technology to find its own position, calculate its best flight path, communicate, and coordinate its position with other craft in the airspace and with ground traffic control, and integrate multiple streams of information. Working within this overall system, specific tools such as broad-area precision navigation would allow for optimized descent profiles while 4D trajectory flight management would allow for time-based arrival/departure planning; the aircraft would arrive at the airport just in time to join the line of landing aircraft and avoid the need to vector around in the airport area until a landing slot was available. The system would create the kind of precision necessary to allow for reduced aircraft separation and the simultaneous use of closely spaced parallel runways. In addition, new groundside technologies would detect runway and intruder incursions, improve taxiway, and ramp management, and permit improved all-weather operations (FAA, 2007b). These new Surface Management Systems would generate moving maps of the airport surface, provide data-linked taxi instructions, and allow flight planning feedback and negotiation.

The US and NextGen

In the US, the last major airport constructed was Denver International Airport (DIA), which opened in 1995. While DIA was the largest piece of real estate dedicated to commercial aviation in the world, it could not make up for capacity shortfalls at other key airports (Dempsey, Goetz, & Szyliowicz, 1995). The FAA (2007) report *Capacity Needs in the National Airspace System, 2007–2025* reviewed 291 commercial service airports in the US, including 35 large hubs. The first report (FACT 1) was published in 2004 and identified capacity constraints at many of the hub airports reviewed. Following FACT 1, six new runways were opened, and runway improvements and extensions were targeted for other key airports. The FACT 2 (2007) report found that two of the airports – Atlanta and Philadelphia – had seen improvements in capacity; however, the report projected that by 2015 the following airports would need additional capacity even after already planned improvements: Charlotte Douglas International, Fort Lauderdale-Hollywood International, George Bush Intercontinental, John F. Kennedy International, John Wayne-Orange County, LaGuardia, Long Beach-Daugherty Field, McCarran International, Metropolitan Oakland International, Midway Airport, Newark Liberty International, O'Hare International, Palm Beach International, Philadelphia International, Phoenix Sky Harbor International, T.F. Green, Tuscon International, and William P. Hobby.

Although new airport construction helped the situation, it alone was not expected to be sufficient to solve the current (and predicted) capacity crunch. Another area requiring major investment was the air traffic management system and related ground-based systems on the nation's airports. In the highly complex New York/New Jersey area which hosts three large, international airports, John F. Kennedy (JFK), Newark, and La Guardia, the FAA was forced to cap flights into JFK in order to reduce delays at peak times (Schofield, 2008). Further, the Port Authority of New York and New Jersey assumed the operation of Stewart International Airport, 55 miles north of New York City, to use it and some redesign of the airspace to reduce delays (FAA, 2007).

According to the NextGen Implementation Plan (FAA, 2013), NextGen improvements were estimated to reduce delays by 41 percent and result in fuel savings of $38 billion by 2020, but this assumed that funding hurtles would not intervene to throw the program into disarray (Bruno & Schofield, 2013). Sadly, this funding assumption and a series of technical challenges would indeed arise. The most visible issue would be funding.

Funding NextGen

There has been almost universal agreement that the 'FAA's funding structure is obsolete and unpredictable'. In fact, special commissions, such as the so-called Mineta Commission, called for reform for over 20 years (May, 2006; Oster & Strong, 2006)). However, beyond this recognition, there was no agreement on a new means of funding the FAA or NextGen. While some FAA funding comes from the General Fund, most of their funding comes from the Airports and Airways Trust Fund, whose revenues are generated through excise taxes. Roughly 70 percent of the 2004 revenues came from the passenger ticket tax, flight segment tax, rural airport tax, and frequent flyer tax (Oster & Strong, 2006). The trend in the US has been for low-cost carriers (LCCs) to drive down average fares and this has certainly impacted the Trust Fund's revenues (Cordle & Poole, 2005). The balance in the Trust Fund is also subject to economic and external events that curb demand for air travel. The unbundling of ancillary fees from airfares has also adversely affected the fund (Tang & Elias, 2017). As of 2023, the Congressional Budget Office is projecting that the fund will cover all outlays and end the year with solid balance. While outlays are expected to continue rising, so are revenues, assuming no unforeseen events (CBO, 2023).

The FAA had originally

estimated that ATC modernization efforts would cost $12 billion and be completed over 10 years. Two decades and $35 billion later, the FAA estimated another $16 billion would be needed through 2007 to complete key projects, for a total of $51 billion.

(GAO, 2004)

In a 2012 GAO report, 15 of 30 programs were facing delays that averaged four years or more, and the total project was once again over budget by some US$4.2 billion. The FAA 2007 Reauthorization bill proposed moving from the excise taxes system to a cost-based user fee system in which the aircraft operator would pay for the air traffic services they used. The Reauthorization legislation ran into early trouble over contract talks with the air traffic controllers' union (NATCA). NATCA, angered over the FAA-imposed contract in 2006, also charged that the FAA had neglected facilities maintenance, thereby creating unsafe conditions, and wasting money in ATO reorganization and modernization efforts (NATCA, 2008a, 2008b, 2008c). Further opposition to reauthorization came from the general aviation community because the proposed charge would be levied whether the aircraft carried 2 or 200 people. The general aviation (GA) community argued that many GA flights

operated in uncongested airspace under visual flight rules and hence did not make significant use of air traffic services. Several studies disputed this fact and estimated that the GA
share of ATC costs was between 10 and 25 percent, well above their 3 percent contribution
to the Trust Fund (Oster & Strong, 2006). The 2014 FAA reauthorization bill attempted to
reintroduce the user fee concept, calling for a US$100 per flight surcharge for the use of
federal air traffic services. The Experimental Aircraft Association and the General Aviation
Caucus, which included the General Aviation Manufacturers Association (GAMA), again
opposed the user fee (Aero News Network, 2013).

Unfortunately, the FAA has historically been unable or unwilling to deal with the issue
of cost of service. The FAA can account for its inputs – labor, facilities, equipment, and
supplies – and it can provide a broad list of outputs from its activities, such as aircraft
movements and departures, but it has not clearly connected the cost of inputs to the cost
of specific outputs. The FAA's (1996) report, "A Cost Allocation Study of FAA's 1995
Costs (CAS)", assigned costs to various services, but these appear to be based more on the
ability to pay than on the actual cost of the services provided. This inability to clearly identify the usage and cost of service hampered the FAA's ability to make an argument for user
fee charges. Broadly speaking, the FAA has five key services that it provides to external
customers: air traffic control, regulation and certification, civil aviation security, airport
development, and commercial space. Air traffic control accounted for almost two-thirds of
the total FAA budget while airport development was roughly 18 percent at the end of the
last century (FAA, 1996). In 2005, the FAA outsourced the Automated Flight Service
Station (AFSS), formerly a part of their air traffic services program, to Lockheed-Martin.
The AFSS provided weather briefings, flight plan filing services, and other assistance to
private pilots. This contract was expected to save the FAA $2.2 billion over the next 10
years (Cordle & Poole, 2005). Several years later, the FAA announced the closing of 149
small contract towers and plans to limit 72 others to daytime operation. There were also
plans to eliminate/furlough of some controllers and control shifts, but these did not materialize (Lowy, 2013).

If funding has been difficult to obtain and even more difficult to predict, then the development and deployment of the NextGen system has been equally frustrating to the aviation industry because it involves multiple systems created by multiple vendors, which must
ultimately be able to 'talk' with each other. Thus, system integration has been a critical
element of success.

Deploying NextGen

The air traffic control function was reorganized in 2004 into the Air Traffic Organization
(ATO) with a newly appointed chief operating officer. The new ATO was billed as a
'performance-based organization' that breaks the existing 'stovepipes' within FAA, bringing together the key units responsible for management and modernization. While this reorganization changed the reporting lines of ATS-related branches within the FAA, the ATO
remained an agency within the FAA subject to the annual budget appropriations process of
Congress. In 2005, the ATO was reorganized from 9 to 3 service areas and staff support
services for En Route, Terminal and Technical Operations were placed in shared service
centers in the three service areas. Both this reorganization and the original one was con-
trary to the recommendations of the FAA-hired consultant Booz Allen Hamilton, which
called for ATO headquarter consolidation into five service and two staff units, and for
greater cuts in managerial staff (NATCA, 2008b).

In addition to the structural issues that complicated deployment, the FAA contended with its own poor performance record on previous projects. Specifically, they were cited for '(1) promising more capability than they ultimately deliver, (2) being completed later than promised, and (3) costing far more by the time they are completed than the initial cost estimates' (Oster & Strong, 2006). A 2005 report by the USDOT inspector general noted 'that cost growth, schedule delays, and performance shortfalls with major acquisitions continue to stall air traffic modernization.' Eleven of the 16 projects cited in the 2005 report were experiencing total cost growth while more than half were experiencing schedule slips, ranging from 2 to 12 years. One of the examples noted was the development and implementation of the Wide Area Augmentation System (WAAS). WAAS was projected in 1994 to cost $509 million. In 2004, the Inspector General testified to Congress that the projected cost of the yet-to-be implemented program was over $2.9 billion. This represents a 227 percent increase in the cost of a program whose implementation has been extended by 13 years (NATCA, 2008c). The 2012 GAO report has noted that delays in ERAM deployment will cause additional delays in the DataComm and SWIM programs, which could extend for years (Perera, 2012). Still, the FAA NextGen Implementation Plan notes that ADS-B will be deployed at about 700 ground stations by 2014 and equipage incentives will speed the way to a critical mass needed to demonstrate system benefits (FAA, 2013).

The FAA announced in their 2020 update that the initial implementation of 'all major planned systems' would be completed by 2025 but have given no date for the full integration of the systems. This report estimated the savings to date to be US$7 billion, including 17 percent fuel savings, 21 percent other operating savings, and 57 percent passenger travel time. Optimized descent alone was estimated to save almost 115 million gallons of fuel. The FAA is predicting that an additional US$115 billion will be saved between 2020 and 2030 (FAA, 2020).

Europe and SESAR

In Europe, the physical expansion of infrastructure – new airports and new runways – is expected to be very difficult because of space, environmental and social constraints. As in the US, the European answer is to unlock the latent capacity in the system through the application of new technologies to air and groundside operation. In other words, Europe too must create and deploy their answer to a twenty-first-century airspace system. The key elements of SESAR are traffic synchronization, airport integration and throughput, 4D trajectory management, network collaboration and capacity balancing, and conflict management and automation. SESAR program set a series of performance goals for 2020: 1) a 27 percent increase in Europe's airspace, 2) a 40 percent reduction in accident risk per flight, 3) a 2.8 percent reduction per flight in environmental impact, and 4) a 6 percent reduction in cost per flight. They expected the new technologies to shorten flights by 9 minutes and result in 50 percent fewer cancellations and delays (SESAR, 2012a). As noted above, the SESAR concept embodies not only the European answer to the aviation system of the future, but the first-ever European effort to involve all the aviation stakeholders (civil and military, legislators, industry, operators, users, ground and airborne) in the process of defining, committing to and implementing a pan-European program consistent with the Single European Sky legislation. In 2011, SESAR launched a Release program which involved validating research and development projects in operational environments. In 2012, Release 2 involved 30 exercises conducted over 18 EU destinations (SESAR, 2012a). As of 2019, the first wave of SESAR 2020 industrial research projects was completed in Release 9 (SESAR Joint Undertaking, 2020).

Funding SESAR

To develop the system, a legal entity was created under EC law, the SESAR Joint Undertaking JU). The SESAR JU has been tasked with: 1) securing the appropriate funding and concentrating the necessary research and development resources into SESAR, 2) defining and updating the work program, including allocating tasks and organizing calls for tender, 3) ensuring technical progress, and 4) reporting on the development phase. The first phase of tender contracts closed on February 29, 2008 (EUROCONTROL, 2008). It was estimated that funding for all three steps in the Master Plan would be between 23 and 32 billion euros over the period 2014–2030 (SESAR, 2012b). This estimate assumed that SESAR, unlike NextGen, could stay on target with its implementation program. Like the US, SESAR has lagged in meeting some of its performance targets. In fact, Eurocontrol noted in May 2011 that ATM performance was getting worse in some areas such as delays and en route extensions that increased miles flown. There were also serious issues of funding for planned projects, as well as questions about the best way to encourage early equipage (CAPA, 2011). As in the US, efforts to change the air traffic control system received backlash from controllers who believe that it is a direct assault on working conditions and a threat to aviation safety. Strikes and threatened strikes by controller unions continue to plague the EU and further slow the program for a European Single Sky and SESAR (Keating, 2013).

To date, SESAR JU has validated 63 ATM solutions and has another 79 others in the pipeline. Solutions have been deployed to over 300 locations; however, there are still issues related to national ATM systems that are creating interoperability and maintenance issues. As in the US, the key is the ability to integrate multiple systems to create a seamless, high-functioning whole (Bolic & Ravenhill, 2021). For SESAR like NextGen, this is a compelling work-in-progress.

Conclusion

As both the US and EU have discovered, it is one thing to have a notional idea of the capabilities that you need to reshape the air traffic system, but developing, testing, and integrating the various technologies while still operating the existing system is an entirely different proposition. Add in budget constraints and a free-market system that mandates only the final date for equipage for operators whose incentive may be to wait as long as possible before making the investment and the future of the twenty-first century airspace can seem very cloudy. The issue of incentives has been very thorny. In effect, if an operator does not invest in equipment while others do, then they could gain some benefit without the cost, but the true benefits of NextGen and SESAR do not begin to truly materialize until a critical mass of operators participate. Without this critical mass, the argument for others to equip become weaker, the benefits are smaller, and the costs rise. In the end, the success of both projects requires political will and public support to implement these systems BEFORE the twenty-second century arrives or before it becomes what US Rep. Rick Larsen calls LastGen (Bruno & Schofield, 2013). A solution would seem to be in the best interest of all parties, but in the highly contentious aviation industry it is often difficult to get 'agreement' on issues, even when the parties do agree.

Questions

1 What is NextGen and what does it hope to accomplish?
2 What are the key components of the NextGen system?

3 How is air traffic service funded in the US?
4 What are the differences between NextGen and Sesar?
5 Debate air traffic management privatization.
6 Debate airspace automation.

References

Aero News Network (2013) EAA opposes user fees proposed in President's budget. Available at: https://www.aero-news.net/index.cfm?do=main.textpost&id=d154f01e-031d-42df-9664-49434a6f06f8

Airports Council International (2023) What to expect: Latest air travel outlook reveals short- and long-term demand. Available at: https://aci.aero/2023/02/22/what-to-expect-latest-air-travel-outlook-reveals-short-and-long-term-demand/#:~:text=ACI%20World%20Airport%20Traffic%20Forecasts%202022%E2%80%932041&text=Passenger%20traffic%20worldwide%20is%20expected,tonnes%20of%20air%20cargo%20worldwide

Bolic, T & Ravenhill, P. (2021) SESAR: The past, present, and future of European air traffic management research. *Engineering* 7 (4), 448–451.

Bruno, M. & Schofield, A. (2013) Dark skies, *Aviation Week & Space Technology*, July 29, pp. 16–17.

Bureau of Transportation Statistics (2020) Passenger and Freight. Available at: https://www.rita.dot.gov/bts/data_and_statistics/by_mode/airline_and_airports/airlines_and_airports_passengers_and_freight

CAPA (2011) Europe faces up to question of funding for Single European Sky. Available at: https://centreforaviation.com/analysis/europe-faces-up-to-question-of-funding-for-single-european-sky-54971

Congressional Budget Office (2023) Airport and Airways Trust Fund: Baseline Projections. Available at: https://www.cbo.gov/system/files/2023-05/59126-2023-05-aatf.pdf

Cordle, V. & Poole, R. C. (2005), *Resolving the crisis in air traffic finding*, Reason Foundation, Washington, D.C. Available at: www.rppi.org/ps332.pdf

Dempsey, P. S., Goetz, A. R., & Szyliowicz, J. S. (1995) *Denver international airport: Lessons learned*, McGraw-Hill Publishers, New York.

EUROCONTROL (2008) Available at: https://www.eurocontrol.int/sesar/public/subsite_homepage/homepage.html

FAA (1996), '*A cost allocation study of FAA's 1995 costs*', UD Department of Transportation, Washington, D.C.

FAA (2007) Capacity Needs in the National Airspace System,. Available at: https://www.faa.gov/airports/resources/publications/reports/media/fact_2.pdf

FAA (2007b) National Plan of Integrated Airport Systems. Available at https://www.docstoc.com/docs/840312/National-Plan-of-Integrated-Airport-Systems-(NPIAS)-March-2007

FAA (2008), 'Capacity: Annual Service Volume'. Available at: www.faa.gov/about/plans_reports/portfolio_2008/media/annaul%20service%20volume.pdf

FAA (2012) FAA Aerospace Forecast Fiscal Years 2012-2032. Available at https://www.faa.gov/about/office_org/headquarters_offices/apl/aviation_forecasts/aerospace_forecasts/2012-2032/media/2012%20FAA%20Aerospace%20Forecast.pdf

FAA (2013) NextGen Implementation Plan. Available at: https://www.faa.gov/nextgen

FAA (2020) NextGen Annual Report : A report on the history, current status, and future of nNational airspace system modernization. Available at: https://www.faa.gov/sites/faa.gov/files/2022-06/NextGenAnnualReport-FiscalYear2020.pdf

GAO (2004). '*Air traffic control, FAA's modernization efforts—Past, present, and future, statement of Gerald L. Dillingham, Director, Physical Infrastructure Issues*', GAO-04-227T.

IATA (2011) Vision 2050. Available at: https://www.iata.org/contentassets/bccae1c5a24e43759607a5fd8f44770b/vision-2050.pdf

Keating, D. (2013) Air traffic strike set for 10 October. Available at: https://www.europeanvoice.com/article/2013/september/air-traffic-strike-set-for-10-october/78091.aspx

Lowy, J. (2013) FAA to staff 72 airport control towers at night. Available at: https://bigstory.ap.org/article/faa-staff-72-airport-control-towers-night

May, J. C. (2006), '*Speech by James C. May: Smart – and fair – skies: Blueprint for the future*', International Aviation Club, Washington, DC. Available at: www.airlines.org/news/speeches/speech_4-18-06.htm

National Air Traffic Controllers Association (2008a), 'NATCA opposes the nomination of Bobby Sturgell for FAA administrator', Press release. Available at www.natca.org/mediacenter/press-release-detail.aspx?id=460

National Air Traffic Controllers Association (2008b), 'ATO service area restructuring: When change may not guarantee progress', Available at: www.natca.org/legislationcenter/ATOService.msp

National Air Traffic Controllers Association (2008c), 'Modernization: Still doing today's work with yesterday's tools', Available at: www.natca.org/legislationcenter/Modernization.msp

Oster, C. V. & Strong, J. S. (2006), *Reforming the federal aviation administration: Lessons from Canada and the United Kingdom*, IBM Center for the Business of Government, Virginia.

Perera, D. (2012) ERAM lateness having secondary NextGen effects, says, GAO. Available at: https://www.fiercegovernmentit.com/story/eram-lateness-having-secondary-nextgen-effects-says-gao/2012-02-20

Schofield, A. (2008), 'Debate over JFK delays sparks talk of congestion pricing', *Aviation Daily*.

Schofield, A. (2013) Gaining ground, *Aviation Week & Space Technology*, July 29, pp. 17–19.

SESAR (2012a) Annual Report 2012. Available at https://www.sesarju.eu/news-press/documents/2012-annual-report

SESAR (2012b) European ATM Master Plan: The roadmap for sustainable air traffic management – Executive summary-Air navigation service providers. Available at: https://www.atmmasterplan.eu/

SESAR Joint Undertaking (2020) Delivering the Digital European Sky. Available at: https://www.sesarju.eu/

Tang, R. & Elias, B. (2017) The Airport and Airways Trust Fund (AATF): An overview. Congressional Research Service 7-5700. Available at: https://sgp.fas.org/crs/misc/R44749.pdf

22 Selling Space

Learning Objectives

After reading this chapter, you should have a good understanding of:

LO1:   the current issues surrounding the space programs of the US and Russia
LO2:   the direction of the EU, India, and China in space exploration
LO3:   the issues driving the commercialization of space
LO4:   the new players, ships, technologies, and spaceports participating in the commercial space race

Key Terms and Concepts

Mars Direct	Spaceport	Dragon X
Space X	Blue Origin	Bigelow Aerospace
XCOR	Sierra Nevada	Virgin Galactic

The Next Step to Where?

Chapter 7 ended with the great spacefaring pioneers, the US and Russia, apparently in two very different places. President Putin of Russia had announced an increase in the budget for Roscosmos to 'catch up to NASA' and was pouring money into an over-budget new spaceport at Vostochny to replace Baikonur, now in the independent nation of Kazakhstan (Steadman, 2013; Zak, 2013). In theory, catching up with NASA should have been easy in budgetary terms since the NASA budget shrank from its moon landing peak to less than one half of one percent of the US budget (Wikipedia 2013). Budgetary issues aside, the accepted long-term goal of space exploration had been to send humans to Mars. Unfortunately, there was no clear, accepted path from here to there. Aside from conceptual drawing of bases on the Moon and/or Mars or largely conceptual work on launch systems and crew capsules, little actual actions and no long-term budgetary commitment was available to support these missions. Meanwhile, China, shut out of US–EU efforts, set a course to recreate the accomplishments of bygone days with their own space station and manned launches to support it. Where did all of this leave the space aspirations of mankind? Were we destined to watch science fiction but never participate in space fact? Had governments and their citizens lost their appetite for space spending? What would the future of space exploration be?

DOI: 10.4324/9781003405306-26

In the first part of this chapter, we explore the halting, uncertain steps taken by the US in the first decade of the twenty-first century and the eventual 'consensus' on the Artemis program. We will examine the lack of Russian missions beyond Low Earth Orbit (LEO) and the failure of its vaunted return to the Moon. Next, we will examine the space programs of the Europeans, India, Japan, and China. These nations joined the space club and have already played an important part in the future of mankind in space.

The remainder of the chapter examines the new element in the space race – commercial space operators. Communication companies have been involved in space before (Chapter 7) to build satellites and fund their launch, but now a host of new companies have emerged with a wide range of goals for space involvement. This new development is partly the result of US policy. In May 2012, the US Congress passed the Commercial Space Launch Activities Act. The purpose of this act was to align government and private space activities. Specifically, it required private entities to receive approval for launch and re-entry and to have insurance in the event of death, injury, or property loss. It also opened the door for NASA to contract with these entities to supply the International Space Station (US Congress, 2012). Many of these new operators are truly new private firms seeking to find profit in space, entrepreneurs like Richard Branson, whose Virgin Galactic is aiming for the space tourist in all of us, or Elon Musk of SpaceX, which became the first private company to provide cargo delivery to the ISS but who has also announced plans to go to Mars, or Jeff Bezos of Blue Origin, who is privately funding efforts to further human space exploration. Other ventures are public–private partnerships or the traditional government contracting that has existed since the beginning of space activities. To explore this new frontier in space, this chapter will look at the space companies, space vehicles, and spaceports that hope to participate in the new commercial space frontier.

Getting from Here to There

If 'we' all agreed that Mars was the goal of manned exploration for the coming century, then why was it so difficult to agree on what it would take to get there, and what interim steps needed to be established. This was one of many questions asked by the US House Science, Space, and Technology Committee in a May 21, 2013, meeting (Morring, 2013a). A report by the National Research Council, commissioned by NASA at the behest of Congress, concluded that the space agency was under increasing stress from more expensive missions, an aging infrastructure, and a lack of national consensus over a long-term vision for human space flight. While the report concluded that the problems NASA faced were not primarily their fault, it did suggest that their response (and strategic plan) could have included a clearer set of priorities and a more transparent budget. In fact, NASA's 2011 strategic plan and accompanying vision and mission was called 'generic', vague on detail, and of little value in helping them to set a clear direction (National Research Council, 2012). The fault, as Shakespeare would say, is in ourselves. Without a clear national (and political) consensus on the goals of exploration, then NASA would 1) attempt to be 'all things to all people' or 2) blow with the political wind, aiming for one target as it was moving elsewhere.

When it came to Mars, Robert Zubrin and others had proposed The Mars Direct plan, arguing that the US had the capability – with the Saturn rockets – to pursue manned missions to Mars. Their plan would first launch an Earth Return Vehicle (ERV) to Mars (rather than carry the vehicle with the mission as was done for the Moon landing). This unmanned unit would land on Mars and begin making the fuel necessary for a return trip to Earth, eliminating the need for the manned missions to transport their own return fuel, thus reducing the launch weight. While the ERV made the necessary fuel, robotic units would explore the area. Once the ERV had produced the necessary fuel, a manned mission would be launched to land near the ERV sight with their habitat (Zubrin & Wagner, 1996).

As we know, this vision did not occur. President George H.W. Bush proclaimed, on July 20, 1989, that the ten-year plan for US space exploration was to be a space station (ISS), then a return to the Moon, with the 'journey of tomorrow', a manned mission to Mars, pushed into some indefinite future. The path was laid out, for now. It pleased the contractors already working on the ISS who wanted to get the money for their first step on the journey and it would please the contractors for the Space Shuttle that was to serve the station. It left Zubrin unimpressed and had little for those interested in the science of deep space. In response to the call, NASA produced 'The 90-Day Report' which sets out a 30-year plan for space infrastructure build-up (Zubrin & Wagner, 1996). Once this train left the station, there would be no Mars Direct. The immediate focus of US space efforts would remain the ISS and the Space Shuttle that would serve it.

As former astronaut, Vance Brand, pointed out, in a 2012 editorial in *Aviation Week & Space Technology*, that it had been 40 years since the Apollo 17 mission to the Moon. The capabilities in manned exploration that had been built up since the 1950s were on the verge of withering and dying (Brand, 2012). Again, much of the fault lay not with NASA. A Mars mission would require a ten-year program with some assurances of funding. Instead, NASA was left struggling with the Space Shuttle (Chapter 7), attempting to cobble together constituencies (with influence on funding) to get the necessary resources. As the cost of the Shuttle program soared, the political will dwindled. As first *Challenger* (1986) and then *Columbia* (2003) crashed, it became clear that not only was the vehicle never destined to meet its performance goals, but the Shuttle was also the most dangerous space vehicle in history (based on the number of deaths). The vehicular failure rate was 40% and the flight failure rate was 1.5% (Pinchefsky, 2012). All these factors combined to produce a series of political shifts on the path for NASA as one US president killed the approach of the last (Constellation for the Space Launch System, a Moon orbit in 2017, an asteroid capture by 2025). According to the National Research Council, even NASA personnel themselves were divided regarding direction. The options under consideration were: 1) flight around the Moon with eventual landing, 2) a space station at a Lagrange point near the Moon, 3) asteroid landing and/or capture with possible placement near the Moon, and 4) manned orbital mission to Mars with eventual landing (Brand, 2012; Wilson, 2013). Of course, if this menu of options looked simple, then consider that there was no agreement about whether they (or some combination of them) were a necessary stepping stone to Mars. Brand, like Zubrin before him, argued that space stations, Moon landings, etc. were not necessary steps to Mars, certainly not the shortest path. Brand even argued that mission dissimilarity made these goals inconsistent (Brand, 2012). The National Research Council (2012) report did not weigh into details of vision and steps, but it did lay out four options to avoid the cost overruns that had plagued NASA and that would keep the projects in their existing portfolio of operations on track: 1) restructure the agency, 2) commit more to cost-sharing partnerships with the private sector and other countries, 3) grow NASA's budget, or 4) reduce the size and scope of its mission portfolio (National Research Council, 2012).

After more than a decade of vacillation on direction, NASA settled on Artemis. This is a complex mission with multiple components, including the Space Launch System (SLS), a super-heavy-lift launch vehicle originally powered by four RS-25 engines (Russian), but with plans for Blue Origin replacement, the Orion space capsule, new space suits, Gateway, a space station orbiting the Moon (vehicles will fly from the Earth to the Station before taking the Human Landing System (HLS) docked there to the Moon), the HLS, and new ground space exploration systems. The SLS involved a group of companies, including Boeing, Northrop Grumman, Aerojet Rocketdyne, and Teledyne Brown. Orion, the partially reusable crewed capsule developed by Lockheed Martin, was launched as part of Artemis 1 on 2022 (Boeing, 2023). SpaceX and a host of other companies are working on Gateway and various private consortiums are working to design spacesuits, including one that includes the fashion icon Prada (Axiom Space, 2023). Of course, the logistics/supply chain system of aerospace means that the above companies are just the tip of an iceberg with dozens of subcontracting firms beneath them. As of now, the plan includes the Artemis I launch (November 16, 2022), an unmanned trip around the Moon, Artemis II, a 10-day crewed mission around the Moon, and Artemis III, flying to the Gateway station for a landing on the Moon (NASA, 2020). Artemis I was a successful mission. Artemis II is currently planned for late 2025, but the mission date has been slipping. In an unsurprising admission, NASA has said that at current costs the SLS is unaffordable and unsustainable. A General Accounting Office (GAO) report stated that NASA lacks the tools to measure production costs accurately, has not accounted for the costs of delays to the program, and appears to lack a plan to correct these problems. Replacing the Russian engines with Blue Origin or SpaceX engines would help, but there is still a long way to go (Berger, 2023a). Remember (Chapter 7) that the Space Shuttle suffered from similar issues that were never resolved. After NASA acknowledged that the potential price tag for the spacesuit that they were designing was US$1 billion per suit, a proposal was sent out asking for private firms to design a suit (Nadel, 2023). In other words, the path has been set, but the obstacles to success are many.

Lost in Space

Meanwhile, in Russia, they also had their 'NASA' moment with a host of proposed projects, insufficient funding, and little agreement on the way forward. Sadly, the lack of transparency in Russia makes it difficult to follow the twists and turns in a space program that has been plagued by corruption, delays, quality issues, and ever-decreasing budgets. In fact, a 2021 law in Russia threatened independent media outlets for efforts to report on Russian space activity (McKay, 2021). What we do know is that the new cosmodrome, Vostochny, came into service in 2016 and that it has hosted almost a dozen launches, but it cost billions to complete (Roth, 2023). Russia announced plans for a new space station (having notified NASA of their intent to withdraw from the ISS) and also initiated a partnership with China for lunar exploration (Skibba, 2023). There has even been talk of a nuclear-powered deep space transport vehicle. However, these plans face a major challenge, namely further budget cuts. After years of ever-grander plans for space, Roscosmos, the Russian Space Agency, has virtually nothing to show for progress and a great many public failures (Berger, 2023b).

Like NASA, Roscosmos has suffered its share of public failures, including a series of Mars probes, leaks on ISS components, and, most recently, the loss of Luna-25, an attempt by Russia to land on the Moon 50 years after its last landing. Now, Russia faces a host of sanctions for the invasion of Ukraine that will further hamper their efforts and add to the substandard component issues that doomed their Mars probes (Associated Press, 2023). After NASA 'retired' the Space Shuttle following the *Columbia* accident, NASA was forced to use Russia and the Soyuz rocket to service the ISS. In fact, from 2006 to 2020, NASA paid an average of US$56 million per seat for rides to the ISS (Chang & Troianovski, 2022). With SpaceX already providing regular services and Boeing's Starliner expected to join after final approvals, alongside other companies like Northrop Grumman, Sierra Space, and Blue Origin securing contracts, NASA is reducing its reliance on Russian spaceflight capabilities. Even if the Ukrainian war ends, Roscosmos will face even greater budgetary losses (Skibba, 2023). Sadly, the struggles of Russian space make the progress of NASA look amazing.

A European Vision

The European Space Agency (ESA) and its 22 member states have established four pillars for its activities in space: science and exploration, space safety, applications, and enabling and support. Despite its late entry into space exploration and research, ESA's budget now comprises approximately 16 percent of global space funding (EU Funding Overview, 2023). ESA has had some impressive accomplishments, as Table 22.1 makes clear. Of note is the Huygens probe landing on Titan, the first ever landing of a human craft in the outer solar system. ESA is currently working on Voyage 2050, a new updated vision for ESA. Potential themes for inclusion range from detecting life beyond our solar system to establishing the habitability of space. One ESA effort has been halted between ESA and Russia. The European ExoMars rover was being designed to search for life on Mars, but the Ukrainian War led to the end of this relationship and no new partnership has been announced (Ramage, 2022). Most recently, the European Space Agency has announced plans to follow NASA in fostering a commercial cargo capability (Jones, 2023).

The Latest Entrants

If ESA has sought collaboration more than competition, then perhaps the competition that once spurred the Great Space Race will come from two new entrants – China and India. China has announced plans to expand its current space station to six modules from

Table 22.1 European (ESA) Space Accomplishments

Year	Accomplishment
1980	Arianespace formed to produce, operate, and market the Ariane 5 rocket
1983	First ESA astronaut to fly on the Space Shuttle
1986	Giotto: First deep-space mission to study comets
1990s	Cooperation with NASA on Ulysses and Hubble Telescopes and Cassini-Huygen
2003	Mars Express orbiter
2005	Huygens probe lands on Titan, Saturn's largest moon
2008	Columbus Laboratory for ISS
2009	ESA astronauts to the ISS
2010	Node-3 and Cupola installed on ISS to study ice cover
2013	ESA astronaut to the ISS
2017	ESA astronaut on ISS completes spacewalk
2018	Copernicus Sentinel 3B launched as part of ESA environmental monitoring program
2019	First exoplanet exploration vehicle, Cheops, launched

Source: https://www.esa.int/ESA

its current three and offer other nations an 'alternative' to the ISS. China launched their first satellite in 1970, but the manned space program did not begin until 2003. The pace of their activity has increased dramatically since 2010. The Tiangong space station has only been fully operational since 2022 and is currently only about 40 percent of the size of the ISS. However, the ISS is planned for decommission in 2030, just as China has announced its plan to be a major space power (Reuters, 2023). China notched a first in space in 2016 with a landing on the dark side of the Moon. This came only three years after a Chinese landing in 2013, which made them only the third country in the world to land successfully on Earth's satellite (Pruitt, 2016). China is currently planning two launches by 2030 to become the second nation to land a man on the lunar surface (Wall, 2023).

Meanwhile India has announced plans to send astronauts to the Moon by 2040, following the first-ever successful robotic landing near the south pole of the planet. The Indian space program began in the 1970s with a satellite program. Their first interplanetary effort was in 2013 with the Mars Orbiter Mission (MOM), making them only the fourth nation to successfully orbit Mars. In preparation for 2040, India plans to send three astronauts into LEO in 2025. By mid-2030, India is planning to have its own space station in orbit, a Venus orbiter, and a second Mars orbiter (Kuthunur, 2023). Like the original spacefaring nations, these nations are reaching for space not only to generate new technologies but also to demonstrate to themselves and the world that they can participate in the challenge and excitement of space exploration.

Japan became the fifth nation to successfully land on the Moon in January 2024, shortly before the US company Astrobotic Technology failed due to a fuel leak (Klug, 2024). The Moon could become a crowded place soon as both South Korea and the United Arab Emirates have also announced plans for missions there (Pickrell, 2022). The recent activity has made several things very clear. First, there are likely to be as many failures as successes. Second, private companies are no longer content to participate simply as contractors to government efforts.

Opportunities in Space

While governments have struggled to find their way in space amid the challenges of funding and political disagreement, the new pioneers are looking for money in space. It is almost impossible to cover every company seeking to get their own piece of the space pie as activity in this area has been accelerating rapidly. In fact, 2022 set a record for the most space launches with 180, mostly from private companies such as SpaceX (Witze, 2023). This section will explore some of the space companies, vehicles, and spaceports searching for their place in the new frontier.

Companies and vehicles. Table 22.2 provides a list of some of the companies active in space. Many of the names are familiar to anyone interested in aviation or aerospace. Arianespace, created in 1980, is most associated with its family of Ariane and Vega rockets. Other well-known names include Boeing, Northrop Grumman, and Pratt & Whitney, three large US companies who are all involved in aviation/aerospace. Boeing is currently developing the Orion seven-person commercial crew vehicle that would be powered by four P&W Rocketdyne Bantam abort engines (Morring, 2011). Boeing is also on a path to deliver crew to the ISS with its Starliner vehicle. The last name in the table, SpaceX, has become a household word, serving the ISS and driving the growing space launch segment of the industry. It has been very active, launching 31 missions in 2021 and 61 in 2022, and hoping to have a launch rate of 12 per month in 2024 (Slashdot, 2023). If the SLS is

Table 22.2 Leading Space Companies

Name/location	Ownership	Mission	Technologies
Arianespace	Ariane Group	Space transportation, satellite systems and service	Ariane & Vega, satellite design
Astra Rocket Co., TX	Public–Private	Development of plasma rocket launch propulsion	VASIMIR, propulsion technology
Blue Origin, WA	Private	Reliable, cost-effective human access to space	Suborbital and orbital craft BE engines
Boeing	Private	Commercial launch provider	Heavy lift rockets (SLS) Orion space capsule, Starliner
China Aerospace International Holdings	Private	Launch vehicle manufacturer	Spacecraft, carrier rockets, satellites
China Aerospace Science & Technology Corp	Public	Development of space technologies and products	Rockets
Dubai Aerospace Enterprise, UAE	Public		
National Aerospace Laboratories, India	Private	Aerospace Laboratory	Trainer and transport aircraft
Northrop Grumman/ Orbital Science	Private	LEO launch	Cygnus, Pegasus, Taurus, Antares
Pratt & Whitney Space Propulsion	Private	Design and manufacture liquid propellant rockets	Rocket engines
Rocket Labs	Private	Small Satellite launch	Electron Launch vehicle
Space Explorations Technologies (SpaceX)	Private	Develop rocket systems and provide Launch	Falcon 9, Falcon heavy

Source: Various company websites.

unsustainable, then SpaceX is demonstrating the power of reusability and the relationship of increasing volume and decreasing price.

Many of the new companies in Table 22.2 are associated with the development of their own systems, as Table 22.3 shows. There are currently three broad areas of focus for these private companies: cargo operations (currently to the ISS, but possibly expanding in the future to Gateway, the Moon, Mars), space tourism, and launch operations, mostly of satellites. The cargo delivery area has already been discussed. It posted its first success with the SpaceX delivery. Richard Branson and his Virgin group, through the company Virgin Galactic, are booking flights on SpaceShipTwo. With over 500 prospective astronauts, Branson is hoping to make the Galactic name a reality (www.virongalactic.com).

Bigelow Aerospace is currently the only company in the private space habitats/facilities area. Billed as the' next generation space station', its patented, inflatable design is based on work by NASA which was licensed to the company in 1999 (Vastag, 2013). In 2015, Bigelow launched (SpaceX) a new module for the ISS. The goal has been to test the use of inflatable modules as laboratories and living space. Two prototypes were launched in 2006–7 and are considered a successful preliminary test of the system (www.bigelowaerospace.com). Robert Bigelow envisions not only a series of research facilities in space, but also a space hotel for the up-and-coming space tourist industry (McGarry & Miller, 2013). Some of

Table 22.3 Space Vehicles

Vehicle	Company	Technology	Mission
Armadillo's Vertical Tourship	Space Adventures	Vertical launch	Suborbital Flight
Cygnus/Taurus 2	Orbital Sciences	Antares Launch vehicle with two stages powered by Aerojet AJ26-62	Cargo delivery to ISS
Dragon/Falcon 9	SpaceX	Falcon 9 launch vehicle with 6 Merlin engines-first stage & one Merlin engine-second stage	Cargo delivery to ISS
Dream Chaser	Sierra Nevada Corp	Atlas V launch vehicle with conventional landing	Cargo delivery to ISS
Lynx	XCOR	Horizontal takeOff and landing powered by four kerosene/liquid oxygen XR-5K18 rocket engines	Suborbital vehicle
New Shepard	Blue Origin	Reusable Propulsion Module	Suborbital Launch
Silver Dart	PlanetSpace	Under development	Suborbital rapid point-to-point delivery of cargo/passengers
Space Launch System	Boeing (Prime)	Vertical, heavy payload rockets	Artemis
Space Ride	Excaliber Almaz Ltd	4 Reusable Reentry Vehicles and Salyut-class spacecraft	Refurbish/reuse Russian spacecraft
SpaceShip/ WhiteKnight Two	Virgin Galactic & Scaled Composites	Launch vehicle to LEO	LEO Space tourism; micro-gravity
Starliner	Boeing		Suborbital vehicle/ISS
Sundancer	Bigelow Aerospace	Inflatable space Habitats	

Source: Space.com, https://www.space.com/2-top-10-fantasy-spaceships-headed-reality.html

these companies could also participate in microgravity activity which requires limited weightless flight for crystal growth, pharmaceutical development, etc. While China and Russia are already talking about space stations to replace the ISS once it reaches the end of life, the US is counting on private entities for space station development and research (Morring, 2013b).

Spaceports. Of course, all this space activity requires a port to launch and return and there are a growing number of facilities offering a solution to this problem. The first question to answer is what a facility needs to be a spaceport, aside from governmental recognition. To answer this question, it is first necessary to understand the different types of orbits possible. There are essentially three types: geostationary, polar, and molniya. A geostationary orbit is a circular orbit at 22, 236 miles (35, 786 kilometers) above the Earth. An object in this type of orbit has an orbital period equal to the Earth, and thus it maintains a fixed position in the sky. This type of orbit is ideal for most communications and weather satellites. A polar orbit is one in which an object passes above both poles each revolution. This type of orbit is most often used by earth-mapping, observation, and reconnaissance satellites. The third type of orbit, a molniya orbit, is highly elliptical with an inclination of 63.4 degrees North and will spend most of its time over the northern hemisphere. Rockets launched at or near the equator in an easterly direction can utilize the Earth's rotational speed to attain orbit more easily. This type of launch profile is best for achieving a geostationary orbit. More northerly launches can be utilized for the other types of launches. Other important features for a spaceport would include distance from population centers and/or launch over water, launch facilities (runways for horizontal launch vehicles and launch pads for vertical launch), and facilities for mission control.

Table 22.4 shows the 14 licensed US spaceports and three exclusive-use sites. Table 22.5 highlights the international options. Spaceport America houses the first purpose-designed launch facility for space tourism and is the base for Virgin Galactic. It is adjacent to the White Sands Missile range and has already hosted vertical launches using the nearby restricted airspace. Compare this to the first spaceport in the Table, Cecil Field, which officially became the 8th designated spaceport in the US in August 2012 (www.cecilfieldspaceport. com). Cecil Field started life in 1941 as a Naval Air Station, but it was closed in the 1993 Base Realignment and Closure (BRAC) decision. This former home of the Atlantic Fleet is now a joint civil–military airport and spaceport authorized for horizontal operations. Of special note in this list is Sea Launch, which is headquartered in Bern, Switzerland. Sea Launch has two specialized sea vessels – Odyssey and Sea Launch Commander – based on Long Beach, California which transport the contracted payload to a platform located on the equator. While the January 2013 launch of Intelsat 27 failed, Sea Launch claimed several successes (https://www.sea-launch.com/about.aspx). Kennedy Space Center in Florida may be one of the most recognizable names in space activity, but Florida now has three federally recognized spaceports – Cape Canaveral Space Force Station, Cecil Spaceport, and Titusville-Cocoa Space Coast Regional (FDOT, 2024).

Table 22.4 US Spaceports

Name/location	Ownership/license	Facilities	Operations
Blue Origin Launch Site One, TX	Private/Exclusive		
Cape Canaveral Space Force, FL	FAA	4 paved runways	Horizontal
Cecil Spaceport, FL			
Colorado Air & Space, CO	FAA		Horizontal
Houston Spaceport, TX	FAA		Horizontal
Mid-Atlantic Regional , Wallops, VA	Virginia Commercial Space Flight Authority	2 active launch pads	Vertical
Midland Intl Air & Space, TX	FAA		Horizontal
Mojave Air and Space port, CA	FAA		Horizontal launches of reusable craft
Oklahoma Spaceport	FAA		Horizontal
Pacific Spaceport Complex, AS	FAA		Horizontal
SpaceX Launch-McGregor, TX	Private/Exclusive		
SpaceX Launch Boca Chica, TX	Private/Exclusive		
Space Coast Regional Airport, FL	FAA		
Space Florida Launch Complex 46, FL			
Space Florida Launch, FL			
Spaceport America, NM	State of New Mexico	1 paved runway	Suborbital
Vandenburg Space Force Base, CA	Federal		Operations

Source: Medium. Available at: https://medium.com/faa/spaceports-are-where-the-spaceships-go-f3f07d219ac2#:~: text=The%20U.S.%20has%2014%20licensed,a%20license%20from%20the%20FAA.FAA Spaceports by state. Available at: https://www.faa.gov/space/spaceports_by_state

Table 22.5 International Spaceports

Name/location	Ownership	Facilities	Operations
Baikonur, Kazakhstan	Public	1 launch pad	Manned launches
Guiana Space Centre, Guiana	Public		Satellite Launch; equatorial launch
Jiuquan Launch Center, China	Public	Launch pads, control & command center	Satellites
Plesetsk, Russia	Public	Launch pads	Unmanned LEO; polar orbit; satellites
Ras Al Khaimah, UAE	Prodea and Space Adventures	Under construction	Suborbital Tourism
Satish Dhawan, India	Indian Space Research Agency	3 launch pads	Satellite Launch
Spaceport Curacao, Netherland Antilles	Public		Suborbital Operations
Vostochny, Russia	Government	7 launch pads	

Table 22.5 starts with the original Russian spaceport or cosmodrome (Baikonur) and ends with the planned replacement for this cosmodrome (Vostochny). In between, we have Jiuquan, the current site of the Chinese manned program, Satish Dhawan, the primary satellite launch site of India, and Guiana Space Centre, the European Space Agency (ESA) site for launches of the Ariane 5.

Questions with no Answers

There are several questions raised by the last forty years of space exploration. The first question is whether the US and Russia can recapture their dedication to space and map out a path forward that will receive the funding and national support necessary to succeed. The second question concerns the US approach to privatizing space. In Chapter 4, we discussed the different international approaches to supporting the development of the air transport system. The Europeans and many others opted for a direct governmental approach that involved governments assuming all or partial ownership as well as direct governmental action to forge consolidation in the aviation industry. The US used an indirect approach, choosing instead to 'support' the airlines through payments for the carriage of airmail. In a sense, this is the same approach that the US government is trying now with space. They have contracted with private companies to deliver supplies and people to the ISS and are hoping that private space stations will fill the void once the ISS is no more. Will this approach work? Is it enough? Remember that the Postmaster General also resorted to illegal means to force the consolidation of airlines as a prerequisite for airmail contracts. If the ISS comes to rely on private firms for delivery to the ISS, then financial troubles could destabilize some firms and might 'force' some governmental intervention. It is too early to tell if a viable private space industry can be fostered with the current approach, but it will be an interesting exercise to watch. The private sector has a great deal that it could bring to the table, but it all comes down to profit. Is there money to be made in space? Once someone demonstrates a viable business case for some space proposition, then there will be others willing to take the risks. Of course, this leads to the last set of questions. Can a private company own a piece of the Moon? Can it then mine it for minerals? Can it buy its own asteroid? Can a private developer establish their own gated community on Mars?

These are not trivial questions. If you remember the discussion from the early days of aviation, then you remember the debates about 'freedom of the skies'. A similar debate took place over the 'freedom of the seas'. As we know, many nations raced to declare ownership and control of the air above their nation. Similarly, nations declared ownership and control of the sea adjacent to their country – 3, 10, 200 miles. This still left the open ocean (and air) to be 'regulated' and fought over. The open seas debate is particularly applicable since many of the arguments centered on questions over the 'riches of the sea' – who owned them and who could harvest them. A similar situation can certainly arise regarding space. The United Nations 1967 Outer Space Treaty opened by declaring outer space to be the 'province of all mankind' and forbidding any state from making territorial claims of sovereignty (United Nations, 2002). Non-governmental entities require authorization and supervision by the State Party to the Treaty; however, treaties are only as good as the willingness of the parties to it to agree to abide by them and/or the other members' preparation to enforce them. Dr. David Livingston, a respected commercial space consultant, has raised the notion of a 'Code of Ethics for Off-Earth Commerce'. This code of ethics would provide a framework for a modified free-market economy within outer space. It could also help to facilitate private company involvement by clearly defining the requirements, obligations, and responsibilities of private parties. (Livingston, 2002). Of course, this code is no different than a treaty in that it is only as good as the enforcement behind it. How far can privatization extend? This is a final question to be answered. Currently NASA is seeking to raise interest in a private commercial lunar probe (Morring, 2013c). If private companies begin to take on more of the risks of space, then they are likely to demand more of the rewards and shape space activity to suit their profit motive.

What Next?

This coming decade should provide key clues to the future of space exploration. If national governments are unwilling or unable to increase funding for space efforts, then it is likely that governmental plans for manned exploration and colonization will be deferred to the latter half of the century – if they occur at all. The FY 2024 budget for NASA is US$17.9 billion or 0.2 percent of the US total budget (NASA, 2023). It is unclear what Russian and Chinese governmental funding will be going forward. If governments continue to withdraw from space funding, then increased private sector involvement is likely. In this case, the key issue may well be a global debate on who owns space and who has the right to profit from it.

Questions

1 Discuss the issues and challenges facing the US and Russian space programs. What can be done to overcome them?
2 What is the Artemis program? What are the issues and concerns facing it?
3 What are the goals of the newest entrants into space? Why have they chosen to participate in space activity?
4 What is driving the commercialization of space?
5 What are the key segments in the commercial space industry? Who are the key players in each segment?
6 Analyze the developing commercial space industry and discuss the possible winners and losers.

References

Associated Press (2023) Russia's lunar mission failure raises questions about state of space program. Public Broadcasting System. Available at: https://www.pbs.org/newshour/world/russias-lunar-mission-failure-raises-questions-about-state-of-space-program

Axiom Space (2023) Axoim Space and Prada join forces on tech, design for NASA's Next-Gen lunar spacesuits. Available at: https://www.axiomspace.com/news/prada-axiom-suit

Berger, E. (2023a) NASA finally admits what everyone already knows: SLS is unaffordable. ARSTechnica. Available at: https://arstechnica.com/space/2023/09/nasa-finally-admits-what-everyone-already-knows-sls-is-unaffordable/

Berger, E. (2023b) Russia talks a big future in space while its overall budget is quietly cut. ARSTechnica. Available at: https://arstechnica.com/space/2023/10/russia-talks-a-big-future-in-space-while-its-overall-budget-is-quietly-cut/

Boeing (2023) The Rocket. Available at: https://www.boeing.com/space/space-launch-system/launch/rocket.html

Brand, V. (2012) US human space exploration in Peril, *Aviation Week & Space Technology*, October 8, p. 58.

Chang, K. & Troianovski, S. (2022) In space, US-Russian cooperation finds a way forward, *The New York Times*. Available at: https://www.nytimes.com/2022/07/15/science/nasa-russia-astronauts-space.html#:~:text=From%202006%20to%202020%2C%20NASA,spacecraft%20became%20operational%20in%202020

EU Funding Overview (2023) The European Space Agency Available at: https://eufundingoverview.be/funding/the-european-space-agency-esa#:~:text=ESA's%20budget%20for%202023%20is,equivalent%20to%20each%20country's%20contribution

FDOT (2024) Welcome to the spaceport office. Available at: https://www.fdot.gov/spaceport#:~:text=Florida's%20three%20Federal%20Aviation%20Administration,Coast%20Regional%20Airport%20and%20Spaceport

Jones, A. (2023) Europe wants a private cargo spacecraft by 2028. Space.com. Available at: https://www.space.com/european-space-agency-private-cargo-spacecraft-2028#:~:text=And%20the%20freighter%20must%20be,supplies%20safely%20down%20to%20Earth.&text=The%20European%20Space%20Agency%20is,return%20capability%20within%20five%20years

Klug, F. (2024) Japan attempts moon landing. Associated Press. Available at: https://apnews.com/article/japan-moon-lunar-landing-pinpoint-b10cd4217199ff513dc744bf785d6b89

Kuthunur, S. (2023) India wants to land astronauts on the Moon in 2040. Space.com. Available at: https://www.space.com/india-land-astronauts-moon-2040

Livingston, D. M. (2002). *A code of ethics for off-earth commerce*. Manuscript submitted for publication, American Institute of Aeronautics and Astronautics, Inc.

McKay, T. (2021) New Russian law threatens space journalists with foreign agent designation. Gizmodo. Available at: https://gizmodo.com/new-russian-law-threatens-space-journalists-with-foreig-1847812740

McGarry, B & Miller, K. (2013) NASA goes IKEA to test inflatable annex for state station, retrieved July 17 at https://www.bloomberg.com/news/2013-01-16/nasa-goes-ikea-to-test-inflatable-annex-for-space-station.html

Morring, F. (2011). Tunnel tests, *Aviation Week & Space Technology*, October 24, p. 26.

Morring, F. (2013a) Stepping stones, *Aviation Week & Space Technology*, June 3, p. 22.

Morring, F. (2013b) What's next: After ISS, a mix of human outposts, *Aviation Week & Space Technology*, September.

Morring, F. (2013c) Getting down, *Aviation Week & Space Technology*, July 15, p. 18.

NASA (2023) National Aeronautics and Space Administration – Overview. USASpening.gov. Available at: https://www.usaspending.gov/agency/national-aeronautics-and-space-administration?fy=2024

NASA (2020) Artemis Plan: NASA's lunar exploration program overview. Available at: https://www.nasa.gov/wp-content/uploads/2020/12/artemis_plan-20200921.pdf

National Research Council (2012) NASAs Strategic Direction and the Need for National Consensus, retrieved from The National Academies Press at https://www.nap.edu/openbook.php?record_id=18248&page=2

Nadel, D. (2023) How much does a NASA spacesuit cost?. SpaceStore. Available at: https://thespacestore.com/blogs/blog/how-much-does-a-nasa-spacesuit-cost#:~:text=The%20Cost%20of%20a%20NASA%20Spacesuit&text=At%20the%20moment%2C%20NASA%20is,to%20a%20lack%20of%20funding

Pickrell, J. (2022) These six countries are about to go to the Moon – here's why. Nature. Available at: https://www.nature.com/articles/d41586-022-01252-7

Pinchefsky, C. (2012) 5 horrifying facts you didn't know about the space shuttle. Forbes. Available at: https://www.forbes.com/sites/carolpinchefsky/2012/04/18/5-horrifying-facts-you-didnt-know-about-the-space-shuttle/?sh=3b1827a6f9d4

Pruitt, S. (2016) China makes historic landing on 'Dark Side' of the Moon. History. Available at: https://www.history.com/news/china-plans-historic-landing-on-dark-side-of-the-moon

Ramage, J. (2022) European space agency wnds cooperation with Russia over Mars rover mission. Euronews. Available at: https://www.euronews.com/next/2022/07/13/european-space-agency-ends-cooperation-with-russia-over-mars-rover-exomars-mission#:~:text=The%20European%20Space%20Agency%20(ESA,over%20the%20war%20in%20Ukraine

Reuters (2023) China to double the size of its space station as it offers an alternative to NASA-led ISS. Available at: https://www.cnn.com/2023/10/06/china/china-space-station-double-size-intl-hnk-scn/index.html

Roth, A. (2023) Vostochny cosmodrome: the remote Russia spaceport hosting Kim and Putin. The Guardian. Available at: https://www.theguardian.com/world/2023/sep/13/vostochny-cosmodrome-the-remote-russian-spaceport-hosting-kim-and-putin

Skibba, R. (2023) Russia's space program is in big trouble. Wired. Available at: https://www.wired.com/story/russias-space-program-is-in-big-trouble/

Slashdot (2023). Next year, spaceX aims to average one launch every 2.5 days. Available at: https://science.slashdot.org/story/23/10/20/2337211/next-year-spacex-aims-to-average-one-launch-every-25-days

Steadman, I (2013). Vladimir Putin announces big new budget for Russian space agency, retrieved June 16, 2013 at https://www.wired.co.uk/news/archive/2013-04/12/russian-space-budget

United Nations. Office for Outer Space Affairs, (2002). *United Nations treaties and principles on outer space* (ST/SPACE/11 No. E.02.I.20). Retrieved from United Nations website: https://www.unoosa.org/pdf/publications/STSPACE11E.pdf

US Congress, (2012). *Commercial space launch activities* (51 USC Chapter 509). Retrieved from Congress Printing Press website: https://uscode.house.gov/download/pls/51C509.txt

Vastag, B. (2013). International Space Stations to receive inflatable module, The Washington Post, retrieved July 16 at https://www.washingtonpost.com/national/health-science/international-space-station-to-receive-inflatable-module/2013/01/16/8a102712-5ffc-11e2-9940-6fc488f3fecd_story.html

Wall, M. (2023) How China will land astronauts on the Moon by 2030. Space.com. Available at: https://www.space.com/china-astronauts-moon-landing-2030-plan

Wikipedia (2013) Budget of NASA. Available at: https://www.ask.com/wiki/Budget_of_NASA?o=2800&qsrc=999&ad=doubleDown&an=apn&ap=ask.com

Wilson, P. (2013) NASA's rocket to nowhere, *Aviation Week & Space Technology*, April 1, p. 66.

Witze, A. (2023) 2022 was a record year for space launches. Nature. Available at: https://www.nature.com/articles/d41586-023-00048-7

Zak, A. (2013) Vostochny (formerly Svobodny) Cosmodrome, retrieved April 10, 2013 from https://www.russianspaceweb.com/svobodny.html

Zubrin, R. & Wagner, R. (1996) *The case for Mars: The plan to settle the Red Planet and why we must*, Touchstone, New York, NY.

23 Wave of the Future

Learning Objectives

After reading this chapter, you should have a good understanding of:

LO1: the consolidation and profitability of the airline industry.
LO2: the issues facing Boeing and the manufacturing sector.
LO3: the prospects for commercial space

Key Terms, Concepts, & People

Consolidation	Merger	LCC
PSOD	Ryanair	re-regulation
Single Sky	GFC	

Waves of Change

In *The Third Wave*, Alvin Toffler, the noted futurist, talked about wave-front analysis, by which he meant the examination of history as a succession of waves of change that represent the discontinuities or breakpoints in the pattern. The goal of the futurist or forecaster is, of course, to identify the wavefront, the leading edge of the approaching wave; the goal of the firm is to position itself to ride the 'wave of the future.' Unfortunately, the present sometimes resides between two waves of change or, worse still, the trailing wave has begun to overtake the earlier wave, creating a clash of currents that makes it difficult to see the wavefront, much less to catch it. In the 1960s, an observant watcher of aviation might have detected the rolling motion that would eventually become the breaking wave of change as the bottom began to shallow. On this wave, among other things, rode the principle of deregulation. Even as this wave washed back from the shore in the early 1990s, another wave was gathering momentum that carried with it another change to the way we see aviation, international liberalization. The international airline industry was already swimming hard to catch the trailing wave of liberalization before 9/11, trying to prepare its national carriers for global competition. For a moment, September 11th seemed to freeze this scene, but after catching a long, slow breath the wave began moving again. The US finally came to the table with the EU over a multilateral treaty that recognized the Single Sky but never considered extending that sky to North America (or any variation that involves foreign carriers

DOI: 10.4324/9781003405306-27

flying between two points within the US). The Russian–Ukrainian War now threatens this wave of liberalization. The wave that is climate change has not yet appeared on the horizon, but it could sweep away aviation as we know it.

For the manufacturing sector of the industry, a decade has made a world of difference. The placid duopoly of Boeing and Airbus has been shattered by the 737 Max. Boeing may have crowded when the end of the A-380 appeared to vindicate their view of a market headed toward smaller, point-to-point service, but their triumph did not last long. The tragedy that is the 737 Max appears to be a long, slowly unfolding tale of finance over engineering. It could well take another decade to turn this take around. Meanwhile, Airbus and a host of potential players will try to surf the waves.

As you recall, the first wave of space exploration began in 1957 with Sputnik, but it now appears that the latest wave of commercial space will move much more quickly and eclipse this first wave. Barely a day has gone by over the past few years without news of a new launch, a new company, or a new plan for space. Few would have suggested ten years ago that a commercial space company would become one of the most valued firms in the world, while an electric vehicle company would struggle. Such are the surprises in the aviation/aerospace industry.

Before the ink was dry on the first edition of this book, United Air Lines became the second US carrier to file for bankruptcy in the wake of 9/11. Before the post-9/11 bankruptcy wave was over, US Airways would file twice, emerge from bankruptcy, and then merge with America West in 2005. Delta and Northwest would enter bankruptcy in 2006 and emerge from it the following year (Nelson & Francolla, 2008). US Airways would pursue a merger with Delta, but be strongly rebuffed by that carrier whose employees could be seen wearing buttons saying 'Keep Delta My Delta' (Steffy, 2007). By April 2008, Delta and Northwest would work out the details on a merger plan that would (temporarily) create the world's largest carrier (Grantham & Tharpe, 2008). As the ink was drying on the second edition, the Global Financial Crisis (GFC) was beginning to emerge but was not yet clearly understood. Certainly, few knew the range, scope, or depth of the looming crisis. Few would have predicted in 2014, when the third edition was released, that by 2018 the airline industry would be hailing a 'golden age' of profits and quality or that the Global Pandemic would hit the industry like a tidal wave. It is almost inevitable that sometime between the submission of this manuscript and the time the first copy hits the bookshelves something will happen to change the face of the aviation/aerospace industry. This seems to be the nature of the industry itself. This is what makes it such an exciting and risky business. Forecasting is also a risky (and thankless) business; however, the purpose of this final chapter is to summarize what 'we think we know' about what is happening in the aviation industry and where 'we think it is going'. There are no certainties, and miraculous turnarounds do occasionally happen, but the odds-makers in Las Vegas and the practitioners of hindsight in industry and academia will have to deal with these issues when the future becomes the past and 'prediction' becomes easy.

Not Dead Yet!

It certainly appeared that the legacy mega-carrier concept in North America was dead (or at least dying) when the first issue of this book went to press in 2003. The mega-carrier concept, as articulated by Taneja (1988) and pursued by the large US carriers, demanded the creation of large domestic and international route networks linked at key hubs to a low-cost feeder system of regional airlines that many of the majors would eventually acquire.

The system was managed by a system of mainframe legacy computers with some add-on 'new' hardware. Software (often designed in-house using the extensive historical data of these carriers) sought to maximize revenues (yields), manage capacity, match aircraft to routes, and aircraft to flight crew according to 'established work rules', and recover the schedule as quickly as possible when disruptions occurred. Carriers consolidated their hold on their strategic hubs, utilizing large aircraft that waited at the gates for banks of smaller feeder aircraft to arrive with passengers to fill the available seats. These large aircraft allowed carriers to spread their higher-cost worker salaries over more passengers, giving them a somewhat better productivity per worker. On the other hand, these crews waited at the gates, often for extended periods, for the arriving bank of passengers. The revenue system which 'managed' these passengers often had as many as 10 different fare classes with attached rules and restrictions. The system was run frequently to determine if the pre-assigned number of seats in each class were fulfilling expectations. If not, adjustments were made in fares to achieve maximum yield. These two factors created conflicting demands on the mega-carrier. First, the pressure of low-cost price competition necessitated cuts in airline spending, many in the visible area of service quality, fare restrictions, meal quality, etc. Second, the revenue system placed consumers in the same cabin who were receiving the same service but at very different fare levels. This gave rise to the ultimate airline shopper, the individual whose mission in life was to shop until they had achieved the lowest fare possible and 'beaten the system'. (They were usually sitting next to you so that they could tell you all about their great deal just to make sure you knew that your shopping skills were subpar.) In the past, these 'shoppers' were primarily leisure travelers who could, and did, arrange their travel around deals. Business passengers had continued to pay higher fares in exchange for the ability to book with little notice and travel at specific times of the day or week.

The events of 9/11 did not create the problems that the industry faced in its aftermath, but it did accelerate many of the trends; two trailing waves seemed to endanger the mega-carrier concept. The first change was the growth of low-cost carriers (LCCs), who had increased their expansion rates in North America and Europe. In fact, post-9/11 these carriers were the only parts of the industry to be expanding. As major carriers around the world pulled out of marginal markets to improve profitability, low-cost carriers moved in to fill the gaps. These carriers offered simplified fare structures, few restrictions, and, in many cases, reliable, consistent basic service. In Europe, 'doing a Ryanair' became a catch-phrase for buying a cheap ticket to some out-of-the-way location for a weekend jaunt (Creaton, 2005). Communities across the US that had lost service in the early years of deregulation or struggled along with high fares from one or two legacy carriers intent on flying them miles out of their way to the closest hub before putting them on a bigger plane to their final destination actively courted the LCCs with some success (Grossman, 2007). The second change was the flight of the traditional business traveler away from the high-fare–high-restriction traditional carriers and toward either less travel overall, LCCs, or one of the new boutique international carriers offering single, business class cabins and better service. Domestically, the per-seat-on-demand (PSOD), air taxi concept of firms like DayJet tried to lure the domestic business passenger away with promises of more convenience and less hassle. These business travelers had subsidized the cost-minded, post-deregulation leisure traveler for years and accumulated more frequent flyer miles than they could ever use. They had sat in lounges around the world drinking little bottles of wine while reading the financial publications of a dozen nations. They did not need any more gifts from the 'frequent flyer' magazine or little salt-and-pepper shakers with their meals. If the business traveler of bygone days was truly gone in sizeable numbers, then the high-cost legacy carrier sensed that they were in serious trouble.

It now clear that the death of the mega-carrier was greatly exaggerated, as was shown by the new merger wave in the mid-2000s. Following the Global Financial Crisis (GFC), this merger wave continued, creating even larger carriers. Some carriers disappeared, falling victim to more efficient, low-cost carriers or to their own mistakes – overexpansion of routes, industry-high labor costs, uncompetitive route structures, etc. It can be argued that some carriers fell victim to 'bad timing', that is, starting up in a capital-intensive business just as fuel prices were rising. Fuel prices were the primary reason cited for four US bankruptcies in 2008 – Aloha Airlines, ATA, Skybus, and Frontier (Associated Press, 2008). Even more damning for the airlines may be the harsh realities of the industry itself. Robert Crandall, the former CEO of American Airlines, has said that

> [i]f some of the steps that have been proposed to restore the industry's health are implemented, such as reducing labor costs and rationalizing fleets, US carriers would stop hemorrhaging cash. But that's different from saying [the industry] can be economically and financially successful – which is to say, earn its cost of capital.
>
> (Crandall's Rx for Airlines, 2002)

Robert Crandall's own American Airlines had resisted bankruptcy and maintenance outsourcing through ruthless cost control until finally the pressure became too great. Now it has joined the mega-merger list with US Airways (Flottau, Ray, & Shannon, 2013). Bankruptcy allowed the legacy carriers to reduce labor costs, rationalize fleets, and recapitalize. Following the crisis in 2008, the industry has also shown an unusual ability to resist adding capacity. New attention to service for business travelers has returned many to their legacy home.

Riding the Waves in the Airline Industry

In a report to the US Congress, the General Accounting Office (GAO) called the airline industry inherently unstable because of the structure of the industry and its economics (GAO, 2005). While the airlines have been the most visible victims of change over the last few decades, they have not been alone; air cargo operators, manufacturers, and related suppliers have also felt the tension and experienced many a sleepless night. However, it seems inconceivable that the overall industry can thrive without a more stable airline industry. Airline deregulation has been praised for the dramatic lowering of fares and faulted for creating the destructive price competition that has been a part of the financial crisis experienced by the industry over each of the last three decades. International liberalization has faced similar charges. The truth is that the industry is not regulation-free. The question is: what do you regulate and whose interests do these regulations serve? The airline industry will never achieve the ideal of perfect competition extolled by economists. This will not prevent consumers from demanding more protections or governments from trying to save their national carriers if they can. One issue that will surely test the resolve of consumers, governments, and airlines will be climate change. Can the industry make the necessary changes on its own? Who will bear the cost of these efforts – consumers, airlines, taxpayers? Will the changes be voluntary or regulatory?

The Pandemic helped to highlight the link between the commercial airlines and the broader air cargo industry; when passenger planes weren't flying with cargo in their belly, the system was not at its peak. It remains to be seen if this segment of the industry will see the kind of supply chain changes that were discussed during the Pandemic. The long, complex supply chains created by globalization were blamed for the supply chain problems of the Pandemic. Even if companies decide to change their supply chains to create more resilience, these efforts will take time and money. Many firms will be tempted to fall back into old habits or make minor contingency plans. Few will be motivated to totally redesign their supply chains to move production closer to assembly or create redundancies. Air cargo will wait for the next downturn or disruption and adjust on the fly.

Waves in Manufacturing

The breaking wave in manufacturing contains smaller more fuel-efficient aircraft. If Boeing is down for now, it is not out. While Airbus can ramp up their production rate to meet extra demand, adding substantial new capacity would be very expensive and would likely come online just as the industry hits the next downturn. The trouble at Boeing does give other potential rivals an opportunity to enter and build market share while it attempts to address its many production and quality problems, but this window will not last long. The manufacturers are known for their 20-year forecasts, and they need to be thinking and planning now for the aircraft of 2050 if they hope to catch the wave. The work facing Boeing will be hard and painful, as all organizational culture change tends to be. The US FAA does not have the funding, employees, or technical expertise at the present time to resolve these issues with new regulations, oversight, or enforcement.

The Wave in Space

The commercial wave of space is gaining speed rapidly as new records are being set for space launch all the time. The number of countries and private firms interested in space continues to grow. The commercial segment will quickly outpace and overshadow the old governmentally driven sector. There are several questions to be answered as the wave moves forward. Who will determine the goals? Who will pay for the progress? What rules will govern the new space? The first space race was dominated by two great governmental players intent on using the race to pursue national goals and validate national systems. The costs were paid by the citizens of these nations. The players 'generally accepted' the great space agreements negotiated at the United Nations. As more governments and private players become involved in space exploration, it is unclear what the future holds. Will we see private firms leading the charge in space mining? Will the Earth be orbited by a host of private space stations and hotels? Will private companies seek to establish their own manned colonies on Mars and elsewhere? Science fiction has explored a few different options. In one strain of fiction, the Earth has united behind a global vision of space to benefit all mankind. In another strain, humanity has simply recreated all the problems, struggles, and strife of Earth on other planets. In some visions of the future, great corporations dominate space, owning the means of transport and even whole planets. While these visions seem far off, it is not too early to think about what we hope to achieve and who it will benefit.

A Buffet Ending?

It is difficult to imagine a future without some form of commercial air transportation since this sector has been vital to the growth and prosperity of the world economy. This is good news for those who have loved this industry for so long, but this does not mean that there will not be significant changes and challenges ahead. The telegraph has been described as the Victorian internet, and it did link people around the world in a network of communication that was unimaginable to earlier generations. Will the airline industry be seen as the quaint travel mode of the twentieth century? Is it possible that Delta, United and the other airlines will be the Western Unions of the twenty-second century. In 1880, Western Union controlled 80 percent of the telegraph traffic in the US and while there were at the time 30,000 of those new telephones, it was certainly unclear that the one of the most profitable businesses of its day was in danger. While Western Union still helps the world move money, it is in a very different place now (Standage, 1998). In the twenty-second century, SpaceX or Blue Origin may be the household names and the dominant forces in transportation. It is even possible that one of the 'dinosaurs of the twentieth century' will reinvent itself and survive to surprise a new generation of business students unfamiliar with its beginnings. Shaping this new world of transport is a challenge worthy of the next generation. It is my hope that the students of today will take up this challenge, not forgetting the past but not bound to its old ways and conventional wisdom.

Questions

1 Discuss the waves of change that have swept the segments of aviation/aerospace.
2 Which segment faces the greatest challenge?
3 What changes can/should be made at Boeing and its regulator?
4 What do you see as the major challenges facing the aviation/aerospace industry for the remainder of the twenty-first century?

References

Associated Press (2008), 'Frontier Airlines Files for Bankruptcy', 11 April, Available at: http://www.cnbs.com/id/24060605

Crandall's Rx for Airlines (2002), *Aviation Week and Space Technology*, November 18, pp. 54.

Creaton, S. (2005), *Ryanair: How a small Irish Airline conquered Europe*, Arum Press, London.

Flottau, J., Ray, S.& Shannon, D. (2013) Scale tale, *Aviation Week & Space Technology*, November 25, pp. 35–36.

GAO (2005), 'Structural Costs Continue to Challenge Legacy Airlines Financial Performance' GAO-05-834T, Washington, D.C.

Grantham, R. and Tharpe, J. (2008), "NWA Merger Agreement Keeps Delta in Atlanta', *The Atlanta Journal-Constitution*, Available at: http://www.ajc.com/pt/cpt?action=cpt&title=NWA+merger+agreement

Grossman, D. (2007), 'Bringing a low-cost airline to town', USAToday.com. Available at: www.usatoday.com/pt/cpt?action=cpt&title=Bringing

Nelson, A. and Francolla, G. (2008), 'Airlines: Tale of merger and bankruptcy' CNBC.com, 21 February. Available at: www.cnbc.com/id/23260075

Standage, T. (1998) *The Victorian Internet: The remarkable story of the telegraph and the nineteenth century's on-line pioneers*, Berkley Books, New York.

Steffy, L. (2007), 'Airline mergers usually don't fly', Houston Chronicle, Available at: http://www.chron.com/disp/story.mpl/business/steffy/5309876.html

Taneja, N. K. (1988), *The international airline industry: Trends, issues & challenges*, Lexington Books, Lexington, MA.

Index

Printed in the United States
by Baker & Taylor Publisher Services